Roger Churchill

Jane
widow of
Nicholas Meggs

Matthew Churchill

Alice
daughter of
James Gould

Jasper Churchill

Elizabeth Chaplet
daughter of
Sir Henry Winston

John Churchill
d. 1685

Sarah Winston

r Winston Churchill
1620-1688

Elizabeth Drake
daughter of
Sir John Drake of Ashe

John Churchill
st Duke of Marlborough
1650-1722

Sarah Jennings
daughter of Robert Jennings
1660-1744

Henrietta
Duchess of Marlborough
1681-1733

Francis
2nd Earl of Godolphin

Coat of Arms of Sir
Winston Churchill

Lord Randolph
Churchill
1849-1895

Jennie Jerome
1854-1921

Winston Churchill
1874-1965

Clementine Hozier
1885-

Diana
1909-1963

Randolph
1911-1968

Sarah
1914-

Marigold
1918-1921

Mary
1922-

THE GREAT MAN
WINSTON CHURCHILL
ROBERT PAYNE

illustrated with photographs

IN THE GREAT MAN, Robert Payne turns his impressive talents to a probing biography of one of the most complex, charismatic, and misunderstood giants of the twentieth century. Payne presents a well-rounded and honest portrait of a man who was intimately and equally familiar with glory and despair. Everything Churchill did, whether in triumph or defeat, was done on a massive scale, and the legacy he left presents a challenge to the biographer who attempts, as Payne does here, to confront the reality behind the image of "the man with the lion's roar and the indomitable spirit, fixed forever in the attitude of defiance."

The author sees Churchill as a consummately ambitious man whose haunting preoccupation with "greatness"—as a modern-day conqueror and as the chronicler of his own flamboyant legend—caused him to take risks that played with the destiny of the world.

We witness all the well-known facts of Churchill's life: the history of his illustrious family, a lonely childhood lived at frustrating distance from his

(Continued on back flap)

7404

The Great Man

A PORTRAIT OF
WINSTON CHURCHILL

By Robert Payne

The
Great Man

A PORTRAIT OF
WINSTON CHURCHILL

Robert Payne

Coward, McCann & Geoghegan, Inc.
New York

SBN: 698-10562-1

Library of Congress Catalog Card Number: 73-78766

PRINTED IN THE UNITED STATES OF AMERICA

For permission to quote from copyrighted material, the author acknowledges the
following: Dodd, Mead, Inc., for an excerpt from *Pillars of Society* by A. G. Gardiner,
used by permission of the publisher; Dodd, Mead, Inc., and the Canadian publisher,
McClelland and Stewart, Ltd., Toronto, for excerpts from Volume II (*The New World*)
and Volume IV (*The Great Democracies*) of *The History of the English-Speaking Peoples*
by Winston S. Churchill, reprinted by permission of the American and Canadian
publishers; the Hamlyn Publishing Group, Ltd., for excerpts from *Great Contemporaries* by Winston S. Churchill, and excerpts from *Savrola: A Tale of the Revolution
of Laurania* by Winston S. Churchill, reproduced by permission of The Hamlyn
Publishing Group, Ltd.; Holt, Rinehart and Winston, Inc., and The Society of Authors
(London) as literary representatives of the Estate of A. E. Housman for an excerpt from
"A Shropshire Lad," taken from the Authorized Edition of *The Collected Poems of A. E.
Housman,* copyright 1939, 1940, © 1965 by Holt, Rinehart and Winston, Inc.,
copyright © 1967, 1968 by Robert E. Symons, reprinted by permission of Holt,
Rinehart and Winston, Inc., and The Society of Authors: Houghton Mifflin Company,
Inc., and William Heinemann Ltd., publishers, for excerpts from the following works by
Randolph Churchill: *Winston S. Churchill: Youth 1874-1900, Winston S. Churchill:
Youth,* Companion Volumes Part I (1874-1896) and Part II (1896-1900), *Winston S.
Churchill: The Young Statesman, 1901-1914;* Houghton Mifflin Company, Inc., for
excerpts from the following works by Winston S. Churchill: *The Gathering Storm, Their
Finest Hour, The Grand Alliance, Triumph and Tragedy,* used by permission of the
Houghton Mifflin Company, Inc.; Houghton Mifflin Company, Inc., for excerpts from
Winston S. Churchill, The Challenge of War, 1914-1916 by Martin Gilbert, reprinted by
permission of the publisher; G. P. Putnam's Sons, Inc., and the Canadian publisher,
McClelland and Stewart, Ltd., Toronto, for excerpts from *Blood Sweat and Tears* by
Winston S. Churchill, used by permission of the American and Canadian publishers;
Charles Scribner's Sons, Inc., for excerpts from the following works by Winston S.
Churchill: *The Aftermath, The World Crisis,* Volumes I and II, used by permission of the
publisher; Charles Scribner's Sons, Inc., and The Hamlyn Publishing Group, Ltd., for
excerpts from the following works by Winston S. Churchill: *Amid These Storms,* and
My Early Life; used by permission of Charles Scribner's Sons, Inc., and The Hamlyn
Publishing Group, Ltd., publishers; George G. Harrap and Company, Ltd., for excerpts
from *Marlborough, His Life and Times,* Volume I by Winston S. Churchill, used by
permission.

For my Mother and Father

CONTENTS

Illustrations follow pages 128 and 256

INTRODUCTION

WHAT WINSTON CHURCHILL said of Russia—"She is a
riddle wrapped in a mystery inside an enigma"—was true of himself. He
was a very strange phenomenon indeed. The image he left on the world
was simple, for he was the man with the lion's roar and the indomitable
spirit, fixed forever in the attitude of defiance. This was the legend, and
there was enough truth in it to make the legendary figure convincing.
The confusions of his life were forgotten in the contemplation of the
man who seemed so uncomplicated, so forthright, so ebullient, so
determined, so daring. We forget that he was very complex, very
devious, suffered from prolonged bouts of melancholia, which he called
"black dog," and that his daring was sometimes so foolhardy that it was
almost suicidal. A strain of madness ran through his family and he
needed to search himself continually to be sure he was untouched by it.
His father died insane. One of his daughters committed suicide. Too
often for his own comfort his round cherubic face was a mask for
desolation and despair.

What is strange about Churchill is his strangeness. He was not—or
not very often—what he seemed to be. He looked like a small, well-bred
Englishman, but there was very little that was essentially English in
him. In spirit and attitude he more closely resembled an American

frontiersman, for whom it was always high noon. He was a gambler thirsting for danger, determined at all costs to place himself in situations so dangerous that only great luck or great adroitness would enable him to escape. The stakes were high; glittering prizes were within his reach, and he went after them with a cold eye and a casual ruthlessness. He had a frontiersman's feeling for the great possessions just beyond the horizon. His pale blue eyes were lit with the flames of conquest, and he saw himself in the European tradition of Great Commanders. His heroes were Cromwell, Nelson and Napoleon, and all through his life he kept a white porcelain bust of Napoleon on his desk.

His friends, even his close friends, were a little afraid of him, for they never knew where he would strike next. Lord Beaverbrook, who was his closest friend, wrote that "Churchill on top of the wave had in him the stuff of which tyrants are made," and feared his sudden savagery. In 1910, when Churchill was Home Secretary, he gave orders to the troops to shoot down striking miners and dock workers, and gloried in the killings. Afterward he was always a little surprised that Labour Members of Parliament distrusted him. There was an unreasoning core of violence in him. The British people detected this very early in his career, and for almost twenty years, from 1921 to 1939, he was given positions like Minister for the Colonies and Chancellor of the Exchequer, where he could do no damage, and for a good part of this period he was allowed no executive position at all.

For a man who was so ambitious the years he spent in the wilderness were the most galling. He wanted fame, glory, all those things that had been given to his ancestor, the Duke of Marlborough. Life was a game to be played on his own terms, which were not the terms normally laid down by gifted men. He wanted everything. First, he wanted to be a commander of armies, to be a conqueror and king-maker, directing the destinies of whole peoples and whole continents, and deciding the fate of the world for centuries to come. They were not small claims on history. Secondly, like Julius Caesar, he wanted to be the historian of his own deeds, the chronicler of his own legend, so that future generations would see him as he wanted to be seen. In this way he would furnish himself with a passport to posterity.

All this happened as he wanted it to happen, sometimes with breathtaking ease. Those staggering and implausible ambitions derived from a lonely and embittered childhood given over to dreams. At school, at the age of nine, he learned defiance. It was the most important lesson he ever learned. He learned the lesson from schoolboys who threw cricket balls at him, forcing him to hide behind a tree, until it occurred to him that life was not worth living in hiding, and so he went out and faced the balls at the risk of his life. He defied a ferocious, bullying headmaster who beat his pupils until the blood flowed over their bare bottoms, and he did it in the only way possible. He seized the headmaster's straw hat and trampled on it until it was nothing but splinters. He had a raw elemental courage, but there was reasoning behind it. He told a friend that when he was hiding behind the tree, he carefully weighed the chances of being hit and argued with himself about the shame and dishonor of concealment. He went on to defy every powerful person who crossed his path.

He was scarcely out of school, where he was nearly always at the bottom of his class, when he set his ambitions in order. He knew even then what he wanted to accomplish, and almost the least of his aims was to become a field marshal and a prime minister, a combination so rare and improbable that it defied all logic. Nevertheless he became prime minister and appointed field marshals at his pleasure.

As a subaltern in Bangalore in South India he came briefly under the influence of Buddhism, and thereafter the Buddhist concept of Annihilation was never far from his mind. In Bangalore he wrote his only novel, *Savrola*, and an extraordinary document called "The Scaffolding of Rhetoric," in which he showed to his own satisfaction that the orator alone possessed the key to power. "Of all the talents bestowed upon men, none is so precious as the gift of oratory," he wrote. "He who enjoys it wields a power more durable than that of a great king. He is an independent force in the world. Abandoned by his party, betrayed by his friends, stripped of his offices, whoever can command this power is still formidable." This was the thunderclap. From this moment in October, 1897, when he was not yet twenty-three years old, he knew the way to be followed. The power of kings lay in his grasp and he would use it to the uttermost. But there was nothing in the document to suggest that oratory should be used for any purpose except his own advancement. There was not a word about the morality of power. Alcibiades, orator and traitor, might have spoken in the same vein.

Power for its own sake, the greatest possible acquisition of power, this was the spur, but it was also the solace. There were failures all along the line, and sometimes they suggested a grotesque incomprehension of the forces at work. Sometimes, too, he turned failure to his own advantage. When he made errors they were catastrophic, and he passed them off as temporary aberrations or accidents not to be repeated, and went on repeating them. He was not one of those who learn from their errors. On subjects like the history of Asia he was blindly ignorant and seemed to rejoice in his ignorance. His faults like his virtues were on a massive scale.

He was one of those who bent history to their will, but in spite of the hundreds of thousands of pages of documents and memoirs now available, there are still mysteries about him. He possessed prophetic gifts. The historian, confronted with such gifts, can only despair, for he has no way of measuring prophecies. Ralph Hawtrey, who was Lloyd George's brilliant private secretary, remembered that in 1910 or 1911 Churchill spoke about the coming war in tones of absolute conviction. He knew exactly what would happen. The war, which would embrace all of Europe, would come to an end with a decisive battle fought in the Middle East, and the Commander in Chief of the Allied forces would be Churchill himself. Having defeated all his enemies he would return to England in triumph. Lloyd George, who was then Chancellor of the Exchequer, pondered this extraordinary prophecy for a moment and said: "And where do I come in?"

That, of course, was the problem. Where did anyone come in? Churchill was accustomed even then to winning all the victories and leaving nothing to anyone else. As it happened, the prophecy was oddly capricious, for it was Lloyd George who became Prime Minister in World War I and presided over the victory celebrations at Versailles, and Churchill had to wait another twenty years before he was granted the same opportunity of fighting a victorious war. It was as though Churchill's prophetic telescope saw very clearly what lay ahead but mistook the time and the occasion. The future had opened out to him, but it was the wrong future, even though the prophecy came true.

We are tempted to discount the gift of prophecy as we discount the Pentecostal gift of tongues. It has no place, we tell ourselves, in modern biography. Nevertheless Churchill genuinely believed he possessed the gift and was buoyed up by it, although it sometimes manifested itself erratically, inopportunely and unexpectedly. Prophecy was a flickering lamp that sometimes blazed up in full strength and died away again until it was no more visible than the glowing ashes. Cromwell had seen a white specter which declared that he would become "Sovereign of England." That, too, was a form of prophecy. In these dangerous waters Churchill swam at ease, abandoning himself joyfully to the waves.

There were other dangerous seas in which he swam joyfully. He was preoccupied with those miraculous swift changes of fortune which are brought about by brilliant trickery and sleight of hand. Empires have fallen because someone has suddenly pulled away the foundation stone that supported the whole edifice. Churchill was captivated and enchanted by these sinister designs. A skilled fencer in his youth, he had studied the subtleties of the feint, the lunge, the beat, and—perhaps most important of all because it is often so effective—the maneuver called the bind, which consists of nothing more than a light tap on the opponent's blade at the right moment. The effect of the tap is to deflect the blade when it is most threatening and open the way to an unexpected thrust at the heart. A light tap can destroy a man, just as a note of music can shatter a wine glass. The world, as Churchill saw it, was at the mercy of those strange and unpredictable forces that confuse and destroy. Cunning, silence and darkness were formidable weapons to be used in defense of the empire against the barbaric hordes beyond the pale. Unfortunately history teaches the lesson that it is precisely the barbarians who are most skilled in devising these stratagems. Churchill saw no reason why these weapons of surprise and cunning should be left to the barbarians. He was descended from the first Duke of Marlborough, who had employed similar weapons with notable success against the French armies, and was himself an uncommonly gifted student of stratagems. Churchill delighted in the new, the unknown. New shapes of mines and countermines, new explosives, new ships, new armored shields, new engines of destruction, all these fascinated him. Although he possessed no mechanical ability and could not have mended a child's electric train, he could sketch out what he wanted, leaving to the experts the task of filling in the mechanical details. Wars were won by sudden obliterating thrusts which seemed to come out of nowhere. The enemy must die without knowing what had killed him. In *The World Crisis*, written shortly after World War I, Churchill described the mind of the ideal military commander:

> There is required for the composition of the great commander not only massive common sense and reasoning power, not only imagination, but also an element of legerdemain, an original and sinister touch, which leaves the enemy puzzled as well as beaten.

There is no evidence that Hitler ever read *The World Crisis*. If he had read it, he might have realized that he was confronted with a far more dangerous opponent than he had ever contemplated. Churchill was the master of the sinister touch, the inventor of stratagems, the cherub with the bloody ax. Churchill knew his way through the dark woods. He had, as we shall see later, much more in common with Hitler than one would like to believe.

Throughout his life he was haunted by the concept of the Great Man. He believed firmly in "greatness," a rare attribute given to the chosen few. One day, walking through Devonport Dockyard with Admiral Sir John Fisher, he turned solemnly and dramatically toward the admiral as though he had some important information to impart. Standing quite still, he said: "You are a Great Man." The admiral was understandably impressed by the intelligence of the much younger man who had perceived what had long been obvious to himself. Fisher believed in many strange things. He had some illusions about the British being the lost tribes of Israel; he thought all soldiers were nincompoops; he had pondered the words of Jeremiah: "Seekest thou great things for thyself? Seek them not." Churchill preferred Gibbon to Jeremiah, and like Gibbon he saw the world at the mercy of the Great Commanders.

"All great men are bad men," wrote Lord Acton. They are bad for many reasons. They must crush others in order to reach their state of eminence; they must kill in order to achieve a lasting fame; they must corrupt and exploit in order to make others obedient to them. They suck out the energies of the people to inflate themselves and embark on massacres in order to achieve a respectable place in history. They adore applause and like opera singers they will pay a claque to give it to them. They are never content with a small parcel of glory; they must gather it all to themselves.

Worst of all is the corruption inherent in all the processes of power: the steady dehumanization which leads the Great Man to lose sight of people as people, to see them as shapes covered with a gray film, all equally vulnerable, obedient to his wishes and existing only for his pleasure. Then, seeing that they are so obedient and that everything functions well, he regards himself as irreplaceable and destroys or attempts to destroy everyone who disagrees with him. In our own time we have seen more Great Men than we can count, and the question arises whether the world can survive them.

I have called this book *The Great Man: A Portrait of Winston Churchill* because he was obsessed with the concept of the "great man" from a very early age and continued to ponder his own "greatness" until shortly before his death. Within the framework of a short and formal biography I have sought to search out the springs of his action and behavior, to discover what kind of man he was and what led him to traffic in "greatness." I believe the chief clues are to be found in his childhood, in the greatly neglected self-portrait in his novel *Savrola* and in the little-known essay "The Scaffolding of Rhetoric," which he wrote while writing the novel. Thereafter his mind and direction were formed, and he was already an old man when history provided him with the opportunity to act out the violent dreams of his youth.

That he was "great" in his own terms seems undeniable; for a brief while he strode the world like a colossus. But it would be more true to say of him that he was a tragic figure, blinded by ambition until at last ambition consumed him in its fires and he was left powerless while in power during his second premiership. To say that he was a tragic figure is not to demean him. It is to put him in his proper place above the littleness of the "greatness" he espoused and cherished, thinking it had been given to him to protect the largest empire the world had ever seen, only to find himself presiding over its ruins.

Battle Royal

The battle was bloody: the event
decisive. The woods were pierced:
the fortifications trampled down.
The enemy fled.

THE ANCESTORS

WHEN WINSTON CHURCHILL remembered his ancestors—and he did not remember them rarely—there came to mind the vision of a noble tree standing alone in the parkland in the high noon of an English summer. The tree was splendidly armed with great branches and festooned with brilliantly colored leaves, and in power and magnificence it rivaled all other trees in the kingdom. The branches bore the names of the landed aristocracy who had wielded power over England for generation upon generation—the Marlboroughs, the Spencers, the Sunderlands, the Villiers and many more. They were all lords of the earth touched with a kind of divinity and, therefore, not to be confused with common men.

But these family trees were sometimes daringly imaginative, the fruit of much patient learning and many curious subterfuges. Not all the branches had been authentically grafted on the tree. An earlier Winston Churchill, who lived in the reign of Charles II, imagined he was descended from Otho de Leon, Castelan of Gisor, whose son Wandrill, Lord of Courcelle, was one of the companions of William the Conquerer during the invasion of England. Wandrill's descendants adopted the style and title of Lords of Currichill or Chirechile and settled in Somerset, where they lost their fiefdoms during the reign of

19

King Stephen, to regain them during the Barons' War, and to lose them again during the reign of Henry VIII. Of the ancient and heroic lineage of his family the earlier Winston Churchill had not the slightest doubt, but his assertions were barren of proof. He claimed the right to a coat of arms showing a silver lion rampant against a dark ground, which he supposed to be the badge of Otho de Leon, and in 1661 King Charles II graciously permitted him to add a red cross on a white ground as a sign of royal favor. He had hoped for greater favors, and in a rage he added without any authority at all an uprooted oak and the motto *Fiel pero desdichado*, meaning "Loyal but miserable," to signify his displeasure and his fall from grace. Three years later he was knighted, for the King had relented, but Sir Winston Churchill felt that he deserved even greater honors and the motto remained, a perpetual reminder of his shattered hopes of advancement.

Garrulous, absurd, immersed in heraldry and genealogy, the author of a weighty tome on the divine right of kings, Sir Winston Churchill spent the greater part of his life in the anterooms of the great nobles of King Charles' court. He did small favors for them and received small rewards. History would have forgotten him entirely if he had not produced a son, John Churchill, who became the great Duke of Marlborough. Unaccountably the duke retained his father's coat of arms: Otho de Leon's silver lion, the red cross, the melancholy motto and even some vestiges of the uprooted oak.

The English nobility delight in the pageantry of heraldry, for it serves to increase the distance that separates them from common folk, who have no dazzling flags and coats of arms to display. But very often the heraldic emblems with their crowned and crested helms repose on fictions. Edward Harly, who knew the Churchill family well, asserted that there was no truth at all in Sir Winston Churchill's noble connections. "John Churchill's great-grand-father," he wrote, "was a blacksmith who worked in the family of the Meggs."

With John Churchill, Duke of Marlborough, Marquis of Blandford, Baron Churchill of Sandridge, Baron of Aymouth in Scotland, Prince of the Roman Empire, Knight of the Most Noble Order of the Garter, possessor of many more titles and appurtenances—for honors flocked around him like gaily plumaged birds—the fantasies of the father hardened into fact. Sir Winston Churchill, dreaming of a remote and unattainable aristocracy, spent his days weaving legends about imaginary ancestors. His son was made of sterner stuff: He was the aristocracy in action and had no need for ancestors. Superb, disdainful, fiercely acquisitive, a reckless and brilliant soldier, an even more reckless and brilliant peculator, treacherous whenever it suited his purpose, a master of intrigue and of swift changes of direction, he was larger than life and possessed the instincts of a conqueror. It would be absurd to describe him as immoral and ruthless; he would not have known what the words meant. His peculations began early; so did his military experience. He joined a regiment of Guards as ensign, distinguished himself at Tangier, and returned to London to discover that there were ways of entering court society which his father had never dreamed of. Barbara Villiers, Duchess of Cleveland, was one of King Charles' innumerable mistresses and the mother of a large brood of illegitimate children. Some were sired by the King, others by the King's courtiers, and the last, a daughter, was sired by the young and handsome ensign just returned from Africa. For his pains the Duchess presented him with a stud fee of £4,500, a princely sum in those days, which he was able to invest in an annuity of £500. The story was told that the King once found them in bed together and tiptoed away after addressing a mild rebuke to the ensign. "You are a rascal," the King said, "but I forgive you, for you do it to get your bread."

John Churchill was prepared to go to any lengths to establish himself at court. His sister Arabella was equally determined to advance in society and although she possessed a rather plain face, she became the mistress of James, Duke of York, who was later to become King James II. An invitation to go out riding with the Duke of York precipitated the affair, for she succeeded in falling from her horse in such a way as to leave no doubt about the beauty of her body. Anthony Hamilton recounted the incident in a book entitled *Memoirs of the Count de Grammont:*

> Miss Churchill lost her seat, screamed out, and fell from her horse. A fall in so quick a pace must have been violent; and yet it proved favorable to her in every respect; for, without receiving any hurt, she gave the lie to all the unfavorable suppositions that had been formed of her person, in judging from her face. The duke alighted, in order to help her: she was so greatly stunned, that her thoughts were otherwise employed than about decency on the present occasion; and those who first crowded round her found her in a rather negligent posture: they could hardly believe that limbs of such exquisite beauty could belong to Miss Churchill's face. After this incident it was remarked that the duke's tenderness and affection for her increased every day; and, towards the end of winter, it

appeared that she had not tyrannized over his passion, nor made him languish with impatience.

Two daughters and two sons were born to Arabella Churchill and the Duke of York. The sons were ennobled, one becoming Duke of Berwick, the other Duke of Albemarle. Raised and educated in France, the Duke of Berwick became an officer in the army of Louis XIV and rose to become a Marshal of France. In command of Franco-Spanish armies in 1707 he won the decisive victory at Almanza which established Philip V on the throne of Spain. The battle won by an Englishman was fought against an English army led by a French general. In courage and ruthlessness the Duke of Berwick was regarded as the equal of his uncle, John Churchill, the Duke of Marlborough.

Without any fortune and living on their wits, John and Arabella Churchill, when scarcely out of their teens, had forged for themselves places of eminence, or at least of notable influence, at court. Soon they were joined by a third courtier, Sarah Jennings, a maid-in-waiting in the household of the Duchess of York and an intimate friend of Princess Anne, the daughter of James, Duke of York, by an earlier marriage. Sarah Jennings was as ambitious as John Churchill, and like him she knew her way through the intricate mazes of court life. She was pert, ebullient, rosy-cheeked, unlike Arabella, who was pale, cautious, and given to self-doubt. Sarah Jennings married John Churchill, and the hard, unyielding core of one was reinforced by the equally hard, unyielding core of the other. Together they would fight like tigers to acquire money, honors and high positions. The tigress was worthy of the tiger.

John Churchill was one of those men who would advance in whatever government he chose to serve. When James II came to the throne, he became one of the King's closest advisers, helped to suppress Monmouth's rebellion and was made a baron. When James II's Catholicism threatened to bring about a civil war in England, John Churchill corresponded with William of Orange and cunningly baited the traps into which James II fell. When William of Orange became King William III, John Churchill was made an earl. In 1702 William III died and was succeeded by Queen Anne, the former Princess Anne who had shown so much affection for Sarah Jennings. Under Queen Anne John Churchill was made Duke of Marlborough.

Sarah Churchill dominated the Queen, while John Churchill dominated the Grand Alliance of European powers determined to cast off the yoke of Louis XIV; and his victories at Blenheim, Ramillies, Oudenarde and Malplaquet were as much the result of brilliant feats of diplomacy designed to keep the alliance together as of brilliant strategies. His soldiers adored him, because he was braver than they were. To the kings and great officers of the European powers he spoke naturally as an equal. When he was not fighting his enemies, he was busily undermining them on the field of diplomacy. To Sarah's dismay he was constantly traveling across Europe on self-imposed missions, conferring with the Emperor in Vienna, winning over the King of Sweden and conciliating the Dutch in Holland. He was offered the Governor-Generalship of the Dutch Netherlands, which he refused, and after Blenheim he was offered a principality within the empire, which he accepted; and to his many honors there was added that of a princely crown of the Holy Roman Empire. This crown and the double-headed black eagle of the empire were his own additions to the coat of arms so industriously and imaginatively assembled by his father.

His victories threw his shadow across Europe. The French were terrified of him; the Dutch, the Austrians, the Germans, the Swedes and the English were in awe of him. Only Sarah could manage him, and sometimes managed him too well, for she used her own exalted station to advance his cause so stridently that she made enemies where previously there had been only friends. Queen Anne finally wearied of her importunities, and thirty years of close friendship ended abruptly, like the clicking of a fan. Sarah, too, had enjoyed high positions and possessed her own apartment in St. James's Palace. She had been Keeper of the Privy Purse, Groom of the Stole and much else, and was now reduced to being a suppliant who must communicate with the Queen with formal letters of protestation and appeals for mercy, which were left unanswered. The tigress had overreached herself, and the tiger, too, was in disgrace. Accused of peculation he went into exile in Holland and Germany to wait out the years of the Queen's life. When she died in 1714 after a reign of twelve years, her children dead, aware that she was the last of the long Stuart line and that some hapless German prince of the House of Hanover would inevitably become her successor on the throne, an age died with her. The Duke of Marlborough returned to England to receive from the hands of the new King, George I, a warrant restoring him to all his former offices, but too late, for during the last six years of his life he was senile. He died on June 16, 1722, shortly after celebrating his seventy-second birthday. His sister Arabella died eight years later at the age of eighty-two. **Sarah,** unyielding and truculent to the end, outlived all her friends and died at last in 1744 at the age of eighty-four.

Marlborough's monument was Blenheim Palace, built on the site of the ancient royal manor of Woodstock, the gift of Queen Anne, at the expense of a grateful nation. Nothing like this palace had ever existed before in England and nothing like it was ever built again. It disdained elegance; it radiated power; and in its formality and rigidity, its controlled violence and senseless accumulation of vast spaces, and its strange daring, it resembled an abstract portrait of the man magnified to his ultimate extent. Blenheim Palace is too large to be lived in by anything except an army of occupation. Sarah wanted Sir Christopher Wren to be the architect. Marlborough, with a surer instinct, demanded the services of Sir John Vanbrugh, playwright and architect, who could be trusted to produce a palace which would defy all classical proportions and somehow resemble simultaneously a man, an army on the march and a triumphal archway. "He had no brightness—nothing shining in his genius," wrote Lord Chesterfield, meaning that he had no wit, no charisma. He was a man consumed by ferocious ambition, and sometimes his vast palace seems to be ambitious to rise twenty times its own height into the sky and embrace the whole landscape.

John Vanbrugh slyly announced that he was creating "a Monument to the Queen's glory," but the glory belonged only too demonstrably to Marlborough alone. At the four corners stand four great towers, and on each tower there are four astonishing finials carved out of stone, each representing a ducal crown perpetually resting on the flames of an exploding grenade. Sixteen crowns, sixteen grenades! Blenheim Palace was more royal than royalty, and no one was permitted to forget that Marlborough was not only a Duke but a very uncommon Duke, equal or perhaps superior to a King. He could at least claim to be royal on the grounds that he was the legitimate Prince of Mindelheim by gift of the Emperor Joseph I. To this day the Dukes of Marlborough claim to be princes of the Holy Roman Empire as hereditary rulers of the tiny principality of Mindelheim, where Marlborough spent no more than a single day. The inhabitants of that small Swabian market town have long since forgotten that they were once ruled by an English prince.

Blenheim Palace was a monstrosity which grew over the years until it became even more monstrous, more forbidding and more impossible to live in. Sarah kept the builders working long after Marlborough had died, and as though it were necessary to commemorate him even further, she ordered the erection of an enormous column topped with his effigy. This was called the Column of Victory, as though there were not enough memorials of victory within and around the palace.

On the Column of Victory Sarah inscribed the ringing words: "The battle was bloody: the event decisive. The woods were pierced: the fortifications trampled down. The enemy fled." But among the Dukes of Marlborough there were to be no more great warriors. They became gamblers, eccentrics to the point of madness, Regency bucks and wastrels. They were men who would have amounted to nothing without their wealth and titles, and they amounted to very little with them. The name of Marlborough continued to be spoken with awe by people who remembered the first Duke, but for his descendants there was little more than polite contempt.

Since Marlborough's only son died of smallpox, a special act of parliament was passed settling the Duke's many titles on his daughters and their issue. Thus after the Duke's death his daughter Henrietta, Lady Godolphin, was allowed to call herself Duchess of Marlborough. The line then passed through another daughter, Anne, Countess of Sunderland, to her son, Charles Spencer, who was regarded as the third Duke of Marlborough, since his aunt Henrietta had preempted the title which would have belonged to the second Duke. From Anne all the future Dukes of Marlborough were descended. From her husband Charles, the third Earl of Sunderland, came the Spencer family name, which was henceforth to be associated with the Dukes of Marlborough.

Charles Spencer, the third Duke, was pitifully undistinguished. He had a commonplace appearance, spoke through his teeth and said very little, and was bullied by his wife. To escape from her he settled in London, where he gambled for high stakes, or took part in foreign wars, where he distinguished himself by being undistinguished. He was present at the Battle of Dettingen, where he commanded a brigade of foot guards. The battle is chiefly remembered because it was the last occasion on which a King of England actively engaged in battle. When his horse fled from the front lines, King George II jumped off its back and went running forward, waving his sword and shouting hoarsely in German, the only language he knew. Charles Spencer fought neither well nor very badly. He became Lord Privy Seal and Master General of the Ordnance, but these were largely honorary positions. As the reigning Duke he was entitled to receive all the heirlooms, but Sarah during her lifetime refused to give him Marlborough's jeweled sword of

honor "for fear that he would pick out the diamonds and pawn them."
He died of dysentery while campaigning in Germany in 1758, having
been Duke of Marlborough for a quarter of a century.

His son George, born in 1738, was Duke of Marlborough for fifty-
eight years. The family blood was running thin; he was sensitive,
over-refined, lacking in self-confidence. He had a passion for rare gems
and collected them feverishly, and he was addicted to astronomical
observations and calculations. These were lonely pursuits, and he was a
lonely man. For preference he remained within the walls of Blenheim
Palace. Horace Walpole came for a visit and reported that it was "the
palace of an auctioneer who has been chosen King of Poland and
furnished his apartments with obsolete trophies, rubbish that nobody
bid for and a dozen pictures that he had stolen from the inventories of
different families." This was not quite fair. George was one of those
delicately retiring people who cannot stand the sunlight and immerse
themselves in esoteric studies. He employed cataloguers to produce
huge catalogues of his vast collection of gems, and these catalogues,
beautifully bound and expensively printed, were sent to all the
crowned heads of Europe. He employed Capability Brown to landscape the grounds and reshape the lake and sold many of his art treasures
to pay for his many schemes for restoring the palace. Romney and
Reynolds were commissioned to paint family portraits. His wife, born
Caroline Russell, daughter of the fourth Duke of Bedford, predeceased
him, and he spent the last six years of his life living in seclusion in a
corner of the palace.

His son and grandson, the fifth and sixth dukes, married into the
family of the Earls of Galloway. George, the fifth duke, was a rakehell
and a Regency rip, with a high sense of his own importance. He
obtained a royal license to change the family name from Spencer to
Spencer-Churchill, "in order to perpetuate in his Family a Surname to
which his illustrious ancestor the said John the first Duke of Marlborough &c by a long series of transcendant & heroic Achievements
added such imperishable Lustre." Like his father, he was a collector,
but he had no interest in astronomy or gems. He collected exotic birds
and was enthralled by the Orient. He built a Japanese drawing room
with murals showing an Indian tiger hunt. A mysterious and imaginary
East excited the Regency imagination, and one can only surmise with
what grave difficulty he resisted the temptation to provide Blenheim
with an Oriental dome.

George was continually in debt, but that did not prevent him from creating a host of new gardens and something he called a Rock Garden where the gateway consisted of an enormous rock which moved at a touch and revealed a fantastic grotto. He ruled over Blenheim for twenty-three years and died nearly bankrupt.

His son George Spencer-Churchill ruled for only seventeen years. Once, Captain Gronow, a celebrated diarist of his time, drove with him in his coach, which was fitted out with a cupboard containing an excellent lunch and many different wines and liqueurs. In another cupboard there was a secretaire with a desk and writing materials and a pocketbook containing fifty £1,000 notes borrowed the previous day from a moneylender against a post-obit on his father's death to the amount of £150,000. George Spencer-Churchill explained:

> You see, Gronow, how the immense fortune of my family will be frittered away. But I can't help it; I must live. My father inherited £500,000 in ready money and £70,000 a year in land; in all probability when it comes to my turn to live at Blenheim, I shall have nothing left but the £5,000 a year on the Post Office.

The sum of £5,000 a year on the Post Office had been granted to the Dukes of Marlborough in perpetuity by Queen Anne.

When he became the sixth Duke, George Spencer-Churchill attempted to put his house in order. He became a sportsman, enjoyed fishing, shooting and yachting, and presented himself as a sedate landowner conscious of his responsibilities, and was made Lord Lieutenant of Oxfordshire, an honor which would never have accrued to his flamboyant father, who kept a mistress, Matilda Grover, who became the sole executrix of his will. The sixth duke's three marriages, first to the daughter of the Earl of Galloway, then to the daughter of Viscount Ashbrook, and finally to a niece of the Earl of Galloway, produced seven children, and when he was dying and bedridden, there were still young children around and he feared for their future. His affairs were in a terrible state and he took the easy way out by burning all his documents, so that no one was ever able to investigate his financial affairs. He died in 1857, and in his will he urged that no more than £100 should be spent on his funeral expenses.

The sons of wastrels sometimes learn from their father's follies. John Winston, the seventh Duke of Marlborough, was a staid, prim, penny-pinching man, who might have become a parson if he had not been a duke. He was deeply religious in the Victorian manner and much

concerned with the relations between the Church and the State. He
spoke and wrote sonorously; his letters to his sons read like sermons. A
photograph taken shortly before he became Lord Lieutenant of Ireland
shows him standing against a lectern, wearing a long black frock coat
and checkered trousers. He has a broad forehead, a small stubby nose, a
long upper lip, and a mouth turned down at the corners, and there is
about that heavy face something that reminds you simultaneously of an
Irish yokel and a heavy-handed schoolmaster. Unlike his father, who
was noted for his good looks, the seventh duke had no redeeming
features: he was the embodiment of the complete Victorian—stern,
uncompromising, ugly. His wife, Frances Anne, was equally ugly, and
in her photographs resembles a decayed washerwoman dressed up in
brocades.

The six generations since John Churchill had seen the Marlborough
blood thinning out until almost nothing of it remained. Through
Blenheim Palace his descendants wandered like ghosts impatient for
glory and overawed by the glory that had departed. Sumptuous balls
and sumptuous meals followed one another; duchesses and countesses
visiting the palace wore their tiaras; and the children of the family were
given panniers so that they could distribute the leftovers to the poor
during their afternoon promenades through Bladon and Woodstock.
Meanwhile the seventh Duke made resolute efforts to make ends meet,
selling off occasional paintings and the entire collection of gems which
the fourth Duke had assembled at great expense from all over Europe.

The Duchess was kept busy childbearing, producing on an average
one baby every two years over a period of twenty-one years. There
were five sons and six daughters. Three of the sons died in infancy, and
neither of the two remaining sons reached the age of fifty, while all the
daughters were long-lived. The male line was evidently weak, the
female line strong. On February 13, 1849, the Duchess gave birth to her
third son, who was christened Randolph Henry Spencer-Churchill. Her
first son, George, became the eighth Duke of Marlborough and the
second son Frederick died in infancy; thus Randolph was second in line
for the dukedom.

He grew into a curiously unprepossessing schoolboy, with his father's
long upper lip, protuberant eyes, and scowling expression. At Eton he
was known as "Gooseberry Churchill." Pug-faced, jug-eared, his head
too small for his body, he inspired very little respect and was often the
butt of the schoolboys. To survive, he cultivated quick wits and a sharp
explosive tongue together with a classic disdain for the lower orders.

There was a fire in him, but it was fueled by desperation, for he lived in terror of his father. His chief preoccupation when he went up to Oxford was hunting, and he therefore missed the first class honors which he thought he deserved by right of his wits and his wide reading.

Lord Randolph Churchill was the style he adopted, but he was more generally known as "Randy" Churchill, and there were worse epithets. His devastating wit was chiefly turned on his social inferiors; he was the master of the contemptuous phrase. He seemed to be a throwback to the fifth Duke, the Regency buck, but lacked the Regency grace of manner. To conceal the long upper lip, he grew an enormous walrus mustache which gave him a distinctive appearance, and he wore high-heeled shoes to improve his height. The unprepossessing schoolboy became a brilliant, erratic and vengeful politician, who climbed to extraordinary heights. By sheer will power and intricate maneuvering he became Chancellor of the Exchequer at the age of thirty-seven, and within a year he fell from grace to spend the rest of his short life in the political wilderness. He died of general paralysis of the insane brought on by a syphilitic infection. He was only forty-five.

This strange, wayward man, all fire and awkwardness, shone like a meteor and fell like a spent rocket. His virtues, such as they were, brought him to high position; his vices destroyed him. He believed deeply in the inherent right of the aristocracy to rule the people of England and he imagined there was some special virtue in being descended from the Dukes of Marlborough, although all except the first had been nonentities. He was an aristocratic cad, which is to say that he was the most despicable of men, and he had the fighting instincts of a bantam cock, which showed that there was some merit in him.

He was the improbable father of Winston Churchill.

THE AMERICAN COUSINS

For the british aristocracy the United States was a country to be visited only in extreme need or extreme provocation. For centuries delicate aristocratic threads had been spreading across Europe, linking the titled families together, so that the families themselves acquired a supra-national character. A French duke might marry a son to one of the princesses of an ancient German principality and a daughter to an English lord, and it would not occur to him that he was weakening the principle of aristocracy: he had merely arranged his affairs "within the family." The family was powerful; it owned most of Europe; after God and royalty it was the arbiter of human destiny, for if it was a little less self-perpetuating than God, it was established more permanently than the kings who sometimes tumbled from their thrones. The aristocracy owed its power to relentless theft and plunder over the centuries and had no intention of returning the land to the people. There was a Communist International, and there was also an International of the aristocracy. They held together and were impregnable.

When the aristocrats turned their eyes to the United States, they found themselves in a quandary: there was no one they could speak to. The Americans were vulgar, ill-humored, lacking in manners, shockingly ignorant about the privileges of the aristocracy. The delicate web did not reach across the Atlantic. But in the middle years of the nineteenth century and especially in the years following the American Civil War there emerged an American aristocracy of wealth which began to make serious overtures to the European and chiefly the British aristocracy. Why this should have happened is a problem which has puzzled generations of moralists and sociologists. American heiresses flocked across the Atlantic to receive titles in exchange for their dowries. Huge fortunes derived from war profiteering, railroads, steel mills, gold mines and oil wells were showered on an effete and dying race of aristocrats.

The heiresses descended upon Europe like conquering armies and the aristocracy put up very little resistance. Mrs. William K. Vanderbilt, daughter-in-law of old Commodore Vanderbilt, decided that her daughter Consuelo should bear a distinguished, and if possible an excessively important title. She was a forceful, one might say tyrannical woman, and it did not concern her that Consuelo might not like the English aristocracy. Mrs. Vanderbilt's choice was narrowed down to the heirs of the Marquis of Lansdowne and of the Duke of Marlborough. At the age of eighteen Consuelo ventured the statement that she did not really like either of them but slightly preferred Marlborough. Mrs. Vanderbilt immediately went to work, arranged the financial settlement, and saw that her daughter was well and truly married to Marlborough. It was a marriage of convenience. It was convenient for Mrs. Vanderbilt, who had the satisfaction of writing letters addressed to Blenheim Palace, and it was convenient to the Marlboroughs who were in need of the marriage settlement. Consuelo's husband made the point that he would never so demean himself as to visit America and he would go to bed with her only for the purpose of producing a son. Consuelo's first interview with the formidable Dowager Duchess of Marlborough was accompanied by a fierce waving of an ear trumpet and the minute inspection of her figure. "Your first duty is to have a child and it must be soon, because it would be intolerable to have that little upstart Winston become Duke," announced the Dowager Duchess. "Are you in a family way?"

In time Consuelo became the ninth Duchess of Marlborough and the mother of two handsome boys, but the marriage was a failure. The Duke was cold, fastidious, and unyielding in his contempt for her American origins. As she tells the story in her reminiscences, she was butcher's meat laid out on the block. She masked her unhappiness by doing good works among the neighboring villagers, and finally divorced the Duke to marry a French colonel who loved her passionately, adored her beauty, and took her to live on a cliff near Monte Carlo facing the Mediterranean. She had detested the vast cold halls of Blenheim Palace, but there was no coldness in the rambling house on the cliff. The Marlboroughs were grateful to her. She had done her work well. Others can also be grateful to her, for if Winston Churchill had become the tenth Duke of Marlborough, it is unlikely that he would have become Prime Minister in 1940.

Winston Churchill's American cousins had little in common with Consuelo Vanderbilt, the heiress of millions. Jennie Jerome inherited little from her father, who had gone through so many fortunes that he had lost count of them by the time he lay dying in Brighton, worn out by a life of enjoyable excesses. His last words, as he lay in a big brass bed in a rented apartment, were: "I have given you all I have. Pass it on."

From his mother Churchill inherited all that was best in him: gaiety, endurance, courage, a love for bright colorful things, a quick wit, an abrupt daring, a capacity for improvisation and a refusal to countenance defeat. From his father he inherited a strange contempt for the people he regarded as his inferiors and the familiar Marlborough desire to seize all the glory for themselves. Yet he was more like Jennie than Lord Randolph. He had her brazenness and even some of her vulgarity—for she could be very vulgar when she chose—and his physical beauty when he was young seemed to come directly from her, with no trace of his father's curiously bulbous features. We think of him as an Englishman deeply rooted in English ways, but if we study him carefully we shall see that he was far more American than English, with traits of character which were essentially American.

With great care the American genealogists have combed through the records to establish his American ancestry. There are gaps here and there, and not all of his ancestors are known. We learn that they were farmers, blacksmiths, seamen, tailors, merchants, salt-makers, and all of them had their roots in New England, especially in Massachusetts and Connecticut. They had names like Timothy Jerome, Hasadiah Smith, Increase Allen, Thankful Stow, Aurora Guthrie and Gamaliel Phippen. They were of the earth earthy, and not many of them in the early years came to any prominence. We see them against the white clapboard houses of the New England countryside and few of them lived in the large towns. They were sturdy, robust, independent people, who are remembered because they wrote their wills and because their possessions were sometimes listed at great length for the benefit of their survivors. New England is dotted with their tombstones.

Churchill's earliest American ancestors were John Cooke and Francis Warren, both of the Mayflower Company, but for convenience we may start with Timothy Jerome, a sergeant in a train band, born about 1688. He came to New England from the Isle of Wight about 1709. He may have been descended from Huguenot stock, and it is just possible that he was descended from the Reverend William Jerome who was burned at the stake under Queen Mary. When we see him first he is living in Windham, Connecticut, in 1713. Four years later with his wife Abigail he settled in Wallingford, Connecticut, where he fathered seven children: Isabel, Timothy, Zerubbabel, William, Abigail, Elizabeth and Samuel. (Zerubbabel probably got his name from the text "Now be strong, O Zerubbabel, saith the Lord" in *The Book of Haggai.*) He lived well, acquired slaves and died in 1750. Abigail married again and survived him by twenty years, dying in 1771 in her eighty-third year.

An inventory of Timothy Jerome's estate shows that he became a man of considerable wealth, his most valuable property consisting of four slaves, who were called Pomp, Rose, Jenny and Prince. The slaves were valued at £1,000. The remainder of the estate, including his clothes, furniture and pots and pans, amounted to £710. He left "a red vest of baize, a black vest of callimanco, a mixed colored coat and vest worth £17, a silk handkerchief, two fine shirts, a new beaver hat, seven punch bowls, a large cask, a churn, a jack knife, a dough trough, an iron kettle, a looking glass, a large pottle, a large Bible, four black chairs and a plain table." His youngest son Samuel, born in 1728, did better, and became a landowner in Stockbridge in Massachusetts. He was well on in years when he joined the Berkshire County Militia and fought in the Revolutionary War. He was known as a strong Presbyterian. Aaron, his fifth son, married Betsy Ball, who was related to George Washington's mother. Samuel Jerome remained a sergeant, but Aaron became a lieutenant, and Aaron's son Isaac became a captain. Isaac's son Leonard did even better. He became a financier, part owner of the New York *Times,* a Wall Street speculator, owner of a racing stable, promoter of a racecourse, American consul in Trieste and the lover of Jenny Lind. He was the grandfather of Winston Churchill, who was thus six generations removed from Timothy Jerome, the sergeant of a train band from the Isle of Wight who became a slave owner.

But if a man goes back six generations, he discovers that he has already acquired a hundred and twenty-four ancestors. The Jerome family, which gradually rose to wealth and respectability, was only a very small part of Churchill's ancestry. The Murrays, the Willcoxes, the Halls, the Beaches and many others fed into the stream. Lieutenant Reuben Murray was a small landowner who served in Colonel Charles Burrall's Connecticut Regiment during the Revolutionary War. He was a pamphleteer, a balladeer and something of a swell until he settled down and married Sarah Guthrie, a Scottish girl. Their daughter Aurora married Captain Isaac Jerome. From the Murrays and the Guthries came Churchill's Scottish streak, his red hair and perhaps his longevity, for Reuben's father died at the age of ninety and his grandfather at the age of eighty-two. Aurora lived to be eighty-two and her marriage to Captain Isaac Jerome lasted for fifty-nine years.

Leonard Jerome married Clarissa Hall, the daughter of Ambrose Hall and Clarissa Willcox, whose father, grandfather and great-grandfather were all blacksmiths in Dartmouth, Massachusetts. Ambrose Hall is a shadowy figure; he is said to have been tall and striking and to have accumulated some wealth. He was a New York state assemblyman during the last tragic year of his life. In the summer his wife died after giving birth to his sixth daughter and he followed her to the grave a few weeks later. All his daughters were dark-featured, with high cheekbones, raven-black hair, and dark eyes, and according to the family tradition there was Iroquois blood in the family, but no one was quite certain where it originated.

There was one well-known story that Ambrose Hall, a morose and wealthy bachelor, went hunting in the virgin forests of Massachusetts one day in 1816 and came to the door of David Willcox's cabin to beg for a drink. He was greeted by the settler's sixteen-year-old daughter of an Iroquois mother, "brown and lithe," and of great beauty. "Wait for me, I shall come back," Ambrose said, and he was as good as his word. A month later he rode back through the forest, claimed her, and made her his wife.

Unfortunately nearly everything is wrong about the story. We know that Anna Baker, who married David Willcox, was born in Nova Scotia, where there were no Iroquois Indians. We know that David Willcox and Ambrose Hall were both living in Palmyra, New York, and that the marriage of the twenty-one-year-old Clarissa Willcox and the forty-one-year-old Ambrose Hall took place on Christmas Eve, 1817. Nevertheless the family tradition should not be totally discarded. Somewhere along the line there may have been an infusion of Iroquois blood and perhaps it came from David Willcox's grandmother, Meribah, the wife of Eleazur Smith, a small landowner in Dartmouth who married her about 1740. Nothing is known about Meribah's parents, but the name has a suspiciously Indian ring about it.

On April 5, 1849, Leonard Jerome married Clarissa Hall in Rochester. He was thirty-two and his bride was twenty-four. He never regretted the marriage and Clarissa loved him throughout her life, even though he was often unfaithful to her. She gave him four daughters: Clarita, Jennie, Camille and Leonie. Leonard gave her all the money she wanted, a town house, innumerable Negro servants, and a place in society. She flourished quietly, rarely complained over her husband's love affairs and lived for her daughters. Leonard Jerome was a *bon vivant*, a good horseman, with an eye for actresses and female singers, for whom he built a small opera house for private entertainments, and he made many fortunes on the stock exchange, lost them, and made them again.

He was a handsome man with a long drooping freebooter's mustache, and he had the air of a pirate chieftain. Sometimes, wearying of New York, he would go to Europe and settle down briefly to a life of leisure. Thus, shortly after his marriage, he spent a little more than a year in Trieste where he rejoiced in the title of United States Consul, an office which paid little but permitted him the entrée into Austro-Hungarian Society, gave him the opera house as a suitable meeting place for his female friends, and provided him with the opportunity to sail his yacht and exercise his Lippizaner stallions. He had brought his wife and his young mistress with him. This was Clarissa's first taste of aristocracy, and for the rest of her life she remained passionately loyal to the aristocrats who attended her salons. Leonard Jerome had a lesser opinion of them and complained that they generally talked nonsense in languages he did not understand.

The Trieste episode ended abruptly after sixteen months and the entire family returned to New York. His second daughter Jennie, named after Jenny Lind, was born at 8 Amity Street, Brooklyn, on January 9, 1854. The rented house on Amity Street suggested that money was running short, but he made his third or fourth fortune three years later by selling short during the great panic of 1857. Clarissa sighed for her aristocrats, and to humor her he set off for Paris with his family. His money gave him the entrée to the court of Napoleon III. Clarissa established a new salonattended the Emperor's soirées, tried unsuccessfully to learn French, and was admired for her grave dark beauty. Leonard grew bored, thought of spending the summer on the Isle of Wight, where at least he could go yachting, and soon returned to New York, where he built a vast six-story mansion on Madison Square with a ballroom in white and gold. Attached to the house were his stables and private theater where the fountains flowed with champagne and eau de cologne.

Leonard Jerome was one of the bold barons of the American nineteenth century. His friends and rivals were August Belmont and Cornelius Vanderbilt, who could rarely outdistance him in the art of conspicuous consumption. He adored luxury, as Clarissa adored the aristocracy. Yachting, horseracing, opera-going and the pursuit of women filled the time he could spare from moneymaking. But as he grew older, he grew careless, lost money on a prodigious scale, plunged too deeply in the stock market, acquired a vast surplus of railroad stocks and was unable to unload it on the market except at a loss. Telling his family nothing about the disaster, he came to Paris, where he found Clarita at eighteen and Jennie at fifteen growing into beauties. He was sorry he had daughters, but if he must have them he demanded that they should be wildly beautiful, like his mistresses.

The empire of Napoleon III was dying of the same disease which brought about the fall of the Bourbons—extravagance and futility. Clarissa thought she was hobnobbing with the most powerful and talented people in Europe, but the courtiers of Napoleon were pathetically incompetent; their power rested on fictions, and they remembered nothing. A forged telegram, a sudden declaration of war, and Napoleon III fell into all the traps cunningly laid by the Germans. Leonard was in New York when the Jerome ladies escaped to Deauville and then to a London winter, which Jennie regarded with distaste, for a fog had settled on the city and it seemed unlikely that she would see the sun again. The ladies fled again, this time to Cowes in the Isle of Wight, where there was sunlight and yachting. They rented a modest villa called the "Villa Rosetta" and settled down to wait the coming of Leonard Jerome, who was interested in the fate of his Paris town house which had been expensively furnished and in addition possessed the greater part of his art collection. The Commune ruled over Paris, but he had no difficulty crossing the lines, crating his furniture, his silver, his tapestries and brocades and paintings, and shipping them to America. It was all labor lost, for the ship sank in mid-Atlantic. Paris, though pockmarked with shell holes and half starving, was still the city the Jeromes loved most, and so they all visited again in the autumn of 1871.

Jennie was fending off suitors by the score; she rode in the Bois de Boulogne; she attended balls in London and regattas in Cowes, and was serious and frivolous by turns. In the autumn of 1873 she attended the trial of Marshal Bazaine at Versailles. Marshal Bazaine had been the Commander in Chief of the French army during the Franco-German war. An incompetent general, he had led the Army of the Rhine to surrender to the Germans just at the moment when he might have fought his way through the German lines and joined up with the levies of the National Defense Council and saved Paris. By surrendering 140,000 troops he lost the war. His communications with the Germans became known, and though treachery was never fully proven, there was sufficient evidence to place him on trial. Jennie watched closely, and she remembered Maître Lachaud, the marshal's advocate, pointing dramatically to the accused and exclaiming: "You only have to look at him to know that he is not a traitor—he is an imbecile." It is a verdict that describes many generals and many politicians.

A few weeks earlier, at Cowes, Jennie had met and almost immediately accepted the proposal of marriage of young Lord Randolph Churchill. The date was August 12, 1873, and the occasion was a dance given on board HMS *Ariadne* in honor of the Prince and Princess of Wales and the Tsarevich and Tsarevna of Russia. Clarissa Jerome and her daughters were naturally invited. Just as naturally Jennie at nineteen was the belle of the ball. In her coquettish way she smiled briefly at the young man with the too large head and the heavy mustache who kept gazing at her dreamily while standing apart from the crowd. Finally Lord Randolph could stand it no more and asked one of his friends for an introduction. Since this was a dance, they danced. Lord Randolph danced badly and asked her not to dance but instead to talk, and because he was very positive and insistent, she agreed to spend the rest of the evening talking to him. They were still talking in some hidden part of the ship when Clarissa Jerome went in search of her daughter later in the evening.

What did Jennie see in Lord Randolph? He was small, his eyes bulged out of his head, his mustache was too vehemently concealing a weak mouth. He was awkward and abrupt in his movements, excessively vain and forthright in his opinions. He had been a lord since the age of eight when his father inherited the dukedom, and he carried himself with the appropriate arrogance. Jennie, who knew the habits of the aristocracy and was not inconvenienced by them, took all this in her stride. One suspects that what she saw in him was something that always attracts high-spirited young women—the sense of excitement and danger. His ambitions were so excessive, he was so obviously heading for a fall, and was so vulnerable, that she instinctively felt the desire to protect him.

Clarissa Jerome was induced to invite Lord Randolph to dinner the following day at the Villa Rosetta. Clarita and Jennie played duets for him on the piano, Lord Randolph talked in his quick, nervous, explosive voice, Clarissa listened with a growing feeling of uneasiness which only increased when Jennie asked her mother to let Lord Randolph come to dinner again the following evening. No one had ever refused Jennie anything, and accordingly Lord Randolph made his second visit to the Villa Rosetta. By this time it had become evident that Jennie and Lord Randolph were hopelessly in love and the full armory of weapons of the combined Marlborough and Jerome families would not prevent them from marrying.

In a mood of elation and despair Lord Randolph returned to Blenheim to ponder the extraordinary change in his circumstances. He was in love with a splendid young woman about whom he knew little more than that she was passably rich, had spent a good deal of time in Paris, was beautiful enough to attract the attention of the Prince of Wales, who had also been dancing on the ship, and had promised herself to him. While he was absolutely determined to marry her and would allow nothing to get in his way, he was well aware that his father would raise objections. She was a commoner, she was an American, she was therefore loud and vulgar like all the Americans. Lord Randolph, treading warily, unburdened himself to his brother, who thought he was quite mad but the madness would pass, and to his father, who was horrified, especially after he had made some discreet inquiries and learned that Leonard Jerome was a financial adventurer who had lost more fortunes than he had retained. Leonard Jerome, it appeared, was one of those flashy New Yorkers who build up their fortunes by speculation on the stock exchange and the purchase of heavily mort-gaged real estate; he was not respectable; he was beyond the pale.

There was even worse to come: some skittish verses, fifteen quatrains altogether, entitled "An Elegy on Marriage," written by his brother Blandford in mockery of Randolph's desire for marriage. Blandford knew his brother well; there were stinging references to Randolph's weakness for pretty girls; and in a rage Randolph copied out the poem and sent it to the Prince of Wales with a request for his royal inter-vention. The Prince of Wales promised to do what he could to make Blandford behave more reasonably.

Jennie wrote to her father, who knew his daughter well and feared that she was capable of making a shipwreck of her affections. He would have liked her to marry an American; he would not object to an Englishman, and he was decidedly against her marrying "a Frenchman or any other of those Continental Cusses." Jennie could wind her mother and father round her fingers; she was determined to have Randolph.

The Duke of Marlborough disapproved of the match, but his disapproval meant very little in the face of his son's tempestuous insistence. Lord Randolph's greatest failing was a lack of will power but he made up for it by an almost grotesque irascibility and vehemence. What he wanted he got by making a nuisance of himself, and he made so much nuisance that the Duke finally capitulated. It was a grudging capitulation, and there was a grudging marriage settlement. Leonard Jerome was asked to provide £50,000, which would produce £2,500 a year, and in the event of Jennie's death half of this sum would go to Lord Randolph and the other half would revert to Leonard Jerome. The Duke of Marlborough provided £20,000, which would produce £1,000 a year. The despised American was paying more than his fair share. The truth was that the Duke was quite poor, having an income of barely £40,000, out of which he had to pay for the upkeep of Blenheim Palace, a hundred servants, four or five carriages and provide for his two sons and several daughters.

The discussion between the Duke and Leonard Jerome was acrimonious. The Duke held by his lordly principles and demanded that Lord Randolph should have control of all the money. Leonard Jerome wanted Jennie to have some money of her own, if it was only a little pin money. Finally it was agreed that Jennie should be entitled to keep £600 for her own use. All through this correspondence Leonard Jerome kept his temper, but the Duke of Marlborough's determined financial voice can be heard in all the letters written by his solicitors. The final details of the marriage settlement were arranged only on the eve of the marriage.

Lord Randolph wanted to become a politician, and the opportunity presented itself in the spring of 1874, when new elections were announced and he secured the nomination for the family borough of Woodstock. He had no difficulty securing the nomination, which was in the Duke's keeping. Lord Randolph had to be coached to make his election speech, which he read from notes buried at the bottom of his top hat. The top hat being placed upside down on the table, he gave the

impression of someone myopically peering down at the table while
loudly imploring his constituents to elect him. There were some catcalls, but not so many as he feared. It scarcely mattered. The Marlboroughs were popular, and the Duke took the precaution of taking
over the Woodstock hotels and hostelries for election day, dispensing
free liquor to anyone who promised to vote for Lord Randolph. In this
rather fraudulent way he became a Member of Parliament.

The marriage of Lord Randolph Churchill, MP, bachelor of the
parish of Woodstock and the county of Oxford, and Miss Jennie Jerome,
spinster of the city of Brooklyn, took place at the British Embassy in
Paris on April 15, 1874. The best man was Francis Knollys, the secretary of the Prince of Wales, and the bridesmaid was Jennie's sister
Clarita. Jennie wore a white satin gown with a long train trimmed with
Alençon lace, white satin shoes, white gloves, a white tulle veil and a
white corsage at her breast, all this whiteness wonderfully setting off
her dark features, her dark eyes and dark hair.

Leonard Jerome had come to Paris to give the bride away and to
arrange for the enormous trousseau, which consisted of twenty-three
Paris dresses and huge quantities of house linen. There were not very
many presents. Jennie received a pearl necklace from her father and a
pearl and turquoise locket from the Prince and Princess of Wales. The
wedding service was brief and perfunctory, but they enjoyed a hearty
wedding breakfast and Jennie was glad when she could change into a
blue-and-white striped traveling gown for the honeymoon.

The Duke and Duchess of Marlborough did not attend the wedding:
it was beneath their dignity.

The Study Of Defiance

One day I shall be a great man
and you shall be nobodies, and
then I will stamp and crush you.

AN IMPERIOUS BOYHOOD

THE ANNOUNCEMENT IN the *Times* was very brief and said only: "On the 30th Nov., at Blenheim Palace, the Lady RANDOLPH CHURCHILL, prematurely, of a son."

Winston Leonard Spencer-Churchill came rushing into the world at half past one in the morning in a rather small bedroom just off the main porticoed entrance hall of Blenheim Palace. Jennie had sustained a fall while out with a shooting party on the previous Tuesday, and a rough ride in a pony cart on Saturday evening had brought on labor pains. There was no time to reach her own bedroom far away in the intricate maze of the palace, and she was taken to this small room converted into a ladies cloakroom for the St. Andrew's Day ball which was given every year by the Duke of Marlborough. Here she remained all of Sunday in great pain, refusing to take chloroform, attended by the local doctor and a bevy of titled ladies led by the Duchess of Marlborough. There was no layette. The baby's clothes were borrowed from a local solicitor's wife who was expecting a child. The doctor from Oxford could not come; the doctor from London came too late. Finally, in the early hours of Monday morning, the baby was born.

He was dark-haired, dark-eyed, perfectly formed, and the possessor of a powerful pair of lungs. The Duchess was shocked by the noise

produced by such a small object. In time he would have very light blue
eyes and his hair would grow in long, luxuriant, reddish-gold curls. He
had a button nose, a firm chin, a pleasant smile, a look of abundant
health. Lord Randolph wrote that he was "a wonderfully pretty child."
Jennie slept badly and had to take sleeping drafts. She kept to her bed,
and Blenheim Palace settled down to the lengthy preparations for
Christmas.

Early in the New Year Jennie and Lord Randolph returned to their
London house and threw themselves into a whirl of social activities.
Although a Member of Parliament, Lord Randolph rarely attended the
House of Commons; he was too busy making his social rounds, giving
parties, attending races and engaging in extra-marital affairs, like
nearly everyone else in the set surrounding the Prince of Wales, the
future Edward VII. The London season began on May Day and continued through the summer. There were house parties nearly every
weekend; dinners and balls followed one another; there were receptions to be attended at the foreign embassies; and the kings and queens
of Europe descended on London during those long summer months
when life for the rich consisted of an endless round of frivolity and
entertainment. In this way Jennie met the King of Greece, the Tsar of
Russia, the Empress Elizabeth and the Crown Prince Rudolf of Austria.
She also attended an audience given by Queen Victoria at Windsor
Castle. The Queen was so taken by Jennie's beauty that she leaned
forward and pulled Jennie to her, kissing her on the cheek. Jennie was
so paralyzed by the royal kiss that instead of curtseying to the attendant
nobilities surrounding the Queen, she found herself smiling idiotically
and making little bobbing movements to everyone in sight. But in
general she was well aware of her duties in the inner circle of British
society and knew exactly how to behave. But to behave well in the
Prince of Wales' set meant that one had to be available to the Prince,
who demanded as a matter of principle that all his desires should be
satisfied. Lord Randolph was fiercely jealous, and when the Blandford-
Aylesford scandal broke out he behaved with his customary recklessness and with a deep-centered rage against the Prince, which could
only be explained by his belief, whether well-founded or otherwise,
that the Prince had taken advantage of his beloved Jennie.

The morals of the Prince of Wales were those of the pigsty. He was
fat, stupid and possessed a bullying temper. On occasion he could
display a monarchical arrogance that was taken for dignity and a
drunken exuberance that could be taken for conviviality. He was,

however, faithful to his innumerable mistresses and continued to correspond with them affectionately long after they had left his bed. Among his conquests was the beautiful Countess Aylesford, who became the mistress of the Marquis of Blandford when Lord Aylesford accompanied the Prince of Wales to India. The Marquis of Blandford was Lord Randolph's elder brother.

Up to this moment there was nothing in the least remarkable about the situation. Blandford simply abandoned his wife, moved his horses to a hunting inn close to the country house of Countess Aylesford, and every night he slipped into her house and every morning returned to the inn. He was not a man who took precautions, and the servants knew what he was doing. There he remained from the autumn of 1875 to the beginning of 1876, when the Prince of Wales and Aylesford returned from India. Aylesford claimed to be outraged, and the Prince of Wales gave it as his opinion that he should immediately sue for divorce, citing Blandford as the corespondent. He also announced that Blandford should divorce his wife and marry the Countess. These were simple solutions to an intolerable predicament, but they were not quite the solutions that Blandford had in mind. At this point two unexpected things happened. The Countess gave birth to a child, and Blandford came into possession of the love letters written by the Prince to the Countess. Lord Randolph saw the letters and apparently made copies of them. He went around London telling his friends that he "held the Crown of England in his pocket," and he showed the letters to the Princess of Wales, warning her that if Aylesford sued for divorce, the Prince would inevitably be subpoenaed to give evidence in court, and if the letters were published the Prince "would never sit on the throne of England."

Lord Randolph had a considerable affection for his brother, but this affection was not sufficient to explain his fury, his almost maniacal behavior. The Prince sent his private secretary, Francis Knollys, to challenge Lord Randolph to a duel to be fought with pistols in France. Lord Randolph, who had no particular prowess at shooting, decided that nothing was to be gained by a duel with one of the best shots in England. He replied contemptuously that he would fight any nominee but would not raise a sword against his future King. Queen Victoria was appalled and said so. She believed strongly, against all the evidence, that the Prince's letters to the Countess were innocent. Jennie, realizing that something had to be done very quickly, suggested that the time had come for Lord Randolph to visit America.

They sailed for New York. It was summer now; a heatwave hung over the Eastern states; they slaked their thirst by eating melons until there came a time when they seemed to be constantly picking the melon seeds from their teeth. They visited Niagara Falls and were royally entertained by Leonard Jerome, who told them that a little yachting at Newport would take their minds off their troubles. When they returned to London, they learned that Benjamin Disraeli, the Prime Minister, and the Duke of Marlborough between them had succeeded in softening the Prince's heart. Two things were necessary: Lord Randolph was to make an abject apology to the Prince, and he must leave the country until it had all blown over. Disraeli, who was genuinely fond of Lord Randolph, suddenly appointed the Duke of Marlborough to be Viceroy of Ireland and it was especially requested that Lord Randolph should accompany his father as his private secretary.

In this oddly contrived manner, in an atmosphere of dark suspicion and royal censure, a new and thoroughly incompetent Viceroy of Ireland was appointed.

The Duke and Duchess of Marlborough with their entourage, which included the two-year-old Winston, made their public entry into Dublin on January 9, 1877. The London *Times*, which rarely made mistakes when enumerating the titles of the nobility, included among the members of the viceregal party the name of Lord Winston Spencer-Churchill. It was almost the first time Winston appeared in print and he was given the wrong label. His father, as the second son of a Duke, possessed a courtesy title; Winston had none.

Soon the Duke and Duchess were established in the Viceregal Lodge in Phoenix Park, and Lord Randolph was established with his family in the Little Lodge, a stone's throw away. Jennie threw herself into a year-long round of festivities and hunting parties; she hunted every winter with the Meath and Kildare hounds, went snipe shooting in County Mayo and trout fishing in Galway and Connemara. She liked the Irish, but above all she liked hunting. She was quite reckless, took many falls and was good-humored whatever happened. Once her gray crashed broadside into a heavy gate and she was thrown into a ditch. Lord Randolph rushed to see what had happened, expecting to find her crushed beneath the horse, and then, seeing that nothing very much had happened to her, he seized her flask of whiskey and drained it. It became a standing joke that Jennie had the fall and Lord Randolph had the whiskey.

But it was more than a standing joke: this was Lord Randolph's

standard behavior. Exasperating, excitable, more than half mad, he was
continually committing absurd errors of taste and judgment. He had
been sent to Ireland to get him out of the way, but he insisted on
remaining in the limelight. From time to time he would return to
London and deliver violent, vituperative speeches in the House of
Commons, denouncing the government's Irish policy and the crimes
committed in the name of progress. Since he was the son of the Viceroy
of Ireland, the government wondered at the impropriety of his speeches
and went on to wonder whether they represented the opinions of the
Viceroy. The Duke of Marlborough knew his son, disclaimed any prior
knowledge of Lord Randolph's opinions, and wrote: "The only excuse I
can find for Randolph is that he must either be mad or have been
singularly affected with local champagne or claret." In fact, he was
drinking heavily and he was also going mad.

For Winston, growing up in the care of his nurse at Little Lodge,
Lord Randolph was a stern, abrupt, forbidding figure who possessed no
fatherly qualities and was totally indifferent to the existence of his son.
His mother was less forbidding, but he saw her just as rarely. Usually she
appeared in a tight-fitting riding costume, sometimes spattered with
mud, or radiant in a long evening gown, her dark hair piled up so that
she could wear high above her forehead the enormous diamond star
which she had mysteriously chosen for her badge, her emblem, her brief
coronet. "She shone for me like the Evening Star," he wrote of her
many years later. "I loved her dearly—but at a distance." Lord
D'Abernon, who met her at the Viceregal Lodge, wrote that when she
appeared at official receptions all eyes were turned to her when she
made her entrance, and she had "more of the panther than of the
woman in her look." What especially distinguished her was her vitality,
her delight in life, her joyous faith in life and all its benefits. Her skin
was so dark that they sometimes called her "Black Jane."

Winston's first coherent memory went back to the unveiling of a
statue in Dublin by his grandfather. The statue had been erected to
honor General Sir Hugh Gough, later Viscount Gough, the hero of the
murderous Sikh wars in the forties of the last century. Scarlet-coated
cavalrymen were drawn up near the statue, and Winston remembered
them vividly. He also remembered the old Viceroy tugging at the string
that pulled away the brown, shiny sheet hiding the statue, and then his
grandfather proclaimed the virtues of the great soldier, one of the
pillars of the Indian empire, saying: "and with a withering volley he
shattered the enemy's line." The four-year-old boy knew all about

volleys, for during his morning walks his nurse took him past a firing range in Phoenix Park.

These early memories of scarlet-coated cavalrymen and a famous general depicted in bronze were burned into his consciousness and never forgotten. He remembered, too, being taken to Emo Park, the seat of his distant relative Lord Portarlington when he was four or four and a half, and seeing after a lengthy drive across the estate a white stone tower. Someone told him that it had been blown up by Oliver Cromwell. He learned that Cromwell had blown up many things "and was therefore a very great man."

He remembered other things, especially a drum and a bunch of keys. Thomas Burke, the Under Secretary at Viceregal Lodge, had once walked across from his office to the Little Lodge to present Winston with a drum. The boy had an affectionate memory of the drum, but none of Thomas Burke, who was murdered by Fenians hiding in the bushes of Phoenix Park a few years later. As for the keys, they belonged to the manager of a theater where a pantomime was being shown. They had promised to take Winston to the pantomime, but the theater went up in flames and it was said that nothing was left of the manager except his bunch of keys. Winston was promised as a consolation a visit to the burned-out theater. He saw the ruins, demanded to see the keys and was disturbed to discover that the demand was not well received.

His life as a child would have been unbearably lonely if it had not been for his governess, Mrs. Elizabeth Ann Everest, a widow, who resembled the Rock of Gibraltar. She was the one perfect thing in his unsatisfactory boyhood, full of sympathy and good common sense, surrounding him with a protective cloak of affection. She was a personage in her own right and had been known to stand up against the dictatorial Duchess of Marlborough and win her battles. Winston called her "Woom" or "Woomany." She was born at Chatham, in Kent, and she would say that Kent was "the garden of England." Kent, with its capital at Maidstone, with its orchards of plum trees and cherry trees, its strawberries and raspberries, was worth all of Ireland, a country which she found deplorably lacking in orchards.

Mrs. Everest was the center of his life, the one person to whom he could speak his intimate thoughts. She had high standards of morality. People were born in order to do good; they had no right to do wrong. One of her favorite expressions, which Winston remembered all his life, was: "Where there's no sense there's no feeling." What she meant was quite clear to the growing boy: insensitivity to others showed a demonstrable lack of intelligence. Above all, it was necessary to be a person of feeling, of generosity and imagination. Aristocratic disdain was not to be countenanced; rudeness of any kind was not to be tolerated. She was forty-two when she entered the household and took charge of the one-year-old Winston. Previously she had been the nurse and governess of Ella Phillips, the daughter of the Reverend Thompson Phillips of Carlisle. Winston never met "little Ella," but he learned a great deal about her, what she liked to eat, how she said her prayers and what was good or bad about her. Since he had no playmates, the imaginary Ella became his companion, present at all meals, an object of everlasting affectionate conversation.

The Duke of Marlborough spent three years as Viceroy of Ireland and was lucky to leave before the great troubles broke out. He was Viceroy during the famine of 1878 and aided the Duchess in founding the Irish Relief Fund, which ultimately amounted to £135,000. For her indefatigable zeal and devotion, with which she successfully labored to relieve the distress in Ireland, she was rewarded by Queen Victoria with the Victoria and Albert Order, Third Class.

The days when Jennie rode to hounds on a little brown mare vanished into the Irish mists; the Viceroy became Duke of Marlborough again; Lord Randolph settled in his town house in St. James's Place next door to the house of Sir Stafford Northcote, the leader of the opposition, an unremarkable and kindly old gentleman who little knew that he was living next to a hornet's nest. Sir Stafford had many reasons to dislike his neighbor during the following years. Lord Randolph had found a cause which he called "Tory Democracy." It was the purest demagoguery and it had its seeds in Lord Randolph's unreasoning hatred of Gladstone and his unsubstantiated belief that he could put together a program which would appeal to the newly enfranchised masses. He had no program, but he possessed a vituperative tongue and a small following in the House of Commons. He was a master of drab invective. He denounced the aged and venerable Gladstone as "a purblind and sanctimonious Pharisee." Gladstone was known as the Grand Old Man, or G.O.M. Lord Randolph took to calling him the "Grand Old Woman." His fury, his denunciations, his strange appearance with the enormous head and rolling, bulging eyes, brought him some contemporary fame; he was one of the most caricatured men in England; the public enjoyed the spectacle of a politician working himself up into a paroxysm of invective. It was almost as good as the music hall. They called him "Little Randy" and "Yahoo Churchill." They also called him "Grandolph Churchill," which made him into a Grand Old Man but with a difference.

His political star was rising. It would shine briefly and then go out with a suddenness which delighted his enemies and numbed his friends. Meanwhile he had fathered another son, John Strange Churchill, who became a stockbroker and lived all his life under his brother's shadow. Lord Randolph was living in style, betting heavily, drinking heavily, hunting a good deal and presiding over the fortunes of the Primrose League, which was founded in 1883 to promote the principles of "Tory Democracy." The League was curiously undemocratic. It had its Chancellor, its Grand Officers, its Knights Harbingers, its Dames, its local meeting places which were called Habitations. Lord Randolph traveled across the country and made rousing speeches to the Primrose Leaguers, wearing a primrose in his buttonhole, denouncing Gladstone, Sir Stafford Northcote and all the pygmies who thought Britain could survive without "Tory Democracy." But what exactly was "Tory Democracy"? No one seemed to know, though it was sometimes explained as the kind of democracy that would bring the Tories to power. Lord Randolph was aiming for power, and he hoped the Primrose League would be the wave of the future.

Winston saw little of his father, but it was impressed upon him that Lord Randolph was a great man who would one day become Prime Minister of England. His delight was to play with his toy soldiers. He had accumulated a vast army amounting to fifteen hundred toy soldiers, all of them British, organized into an infantry division with a cavalry brigade. His brother Jack, six years younger and scarcely removed from the crawling stage, was allowed to possess a small rabble of colored troops without any heavy artillery. The battles were ferocious. The colored troops were shot down with pebbles or drowned by pouring water on them. Peas were shot at them, forts were stormed, bridges were destroyed. The advantages always lay with the British troops.

When playing with the toy soldiers palled, there was always Mrs. Everest to comfort him and read to him. She was his sheet anchor, the one person he was permitted to love unrestrainedly, his moral counselor, his confessor. At her knees he learned the lessons that survive: to do good, to hate the Pope, to fear the Fenians and to honor the King. When he was annoyed with her, he would think up something very wicked, like "Go and worship idols!" Even as a child he had a way of looking at people with a disconcerting stare. But on the whole the lessons she had taught him took root. Once he was given an air gun, shot and killed a small bird, and was so overwhelmed with remorse that he wept at bedtime. Eighty years later he would still weep if he saw a dead bird lying on the ground.

The man was present in the boy, who was garrulous, sentimental, commanding, impatient of authority and conscious that he was different from other boys, if only because he frequently visited Blenheim Palace and was knowledgeable about his distinguished ancestors. Clement Attlee, who became Churchill's successor as Prime Minister, first learned about Winston's imperiousness from one of his sisters. Lord Randolph Churchill employed a certain Miss Hutchinson tutor his son. Miss Hutchinson was also tutoring the Attlee girls. One day a maid came into the room and asked Miss Hutchinson if she had rung the bell. Winston stepped forward and said: "I rang. Take away Miss Hutchinson, she is very cross." Lady Barlow remembered another curious incident that occurred in 1882, when he was eight years old. A children's party was being held at Bruton Street. Winston was enjoying himself when a footman interrupted the children's games and said: "Your nurse has called for you, sir."

"Tell her to wait," Winston said in his haughtiest manner.

Lady Barlow was suitably impressed and asked him whether he really meant what he said.

"Everything and Everybody waits for me," Winston answered.

But of course Everything and Everybody did not wait for him. Neither Lord Randolph nor his mother waited for him, nor was it in his nature to keep Mrs. Everest waiting for more than a few minutes. This was his public posture, a childish attempt to be in full command of a situation with servants around him to do his bidding. His pride was a defensive mechanism. The private posture was very different, and more subtle. He yearned for affection, wept frequently, lost himself in dreams of great military victories and was terrified of pain. He was growing up very fast in a world which he found almost incomprehensible. He had realized very early that there was something unsatisfactory about life, something poisonous, uncalled for and not in the least desirable. Its name was Death.

THE SHADOW OF
THE SCHOOLMASTER

THE ROUND-FACED BOY with the red hair who looks so nonchalantly out of the early photographs was not quite what he seemed to be. Outwardly he was gay and amusing, the possessor of a happy streak of impertinence. Some boys called him "Copper Top," and he had no objection to their familiarity, although on occasion he would cultivate the air of a *grand seigneur,* and then impertinence would become insolence; at such times he was more difficult to handle. He was an affectionate child. His affections were centered on his mother and on Mrs. Everest, the one so remote and the other so close. He was also affectionate to his toy soldiers and he had a great liking for his clothes, for at a remarkably early age he showed a disposition to regard clothes with the utmost seriousness. One day, arriving at a children's party in a terrible temper, he shouted: "I knew it was all wrong! And it is!" A young lady at the party attempted to soothe him. "My clothes!" he replied. "I told them they were all wrong, and of course they are!"

But that was the outward person; the inner person was prey to doubts and fears which even Mrs. Everest could not dispel. There was death; there was pain; there was suffering. Above all, there was death. Mrs.

Everest was like an old English oak tree with deep roots and massive branches and ample shade, but even in her shade he could not escape the fear of death.

The first stirring of the fear took place when he was five years old, when he heard about the Tay Bridge disaster in Scotland. An express train traveling at full speed across the bridge suddenly shot off the rails in the midst of a storm and plunged into the river. The bridge had buckled under the weight of the train. There were no survivors. The newspapers were full of the incident, the banner headlines announcing TERRIBLE ACCIDENT IN SCOTLAND. *The Illustrated London News* showed an artist's version of the train flying through the air, the passengers scattering like chaff through the windows, the air lit by lightning flashes, the bridge collapsing, the angry river waiting below. The boy was fascinated by the tragedy. Death took the form of a crumbling bridge, a train in mid-air, people catapulting from a great height into the water. The Tay Bridge disaster terrified him and filled his nightmares, and there was no accounting for it. He learned by heart some verses that appeared in *Punch:*

> Who is in charge of the clattering train?
> The axles creak and the couplings strain;
> And the pace is hot, and the points are near,
> And sleep has deadened the driver's ear;
> And the signals flash in the night in vain,
> For Death is in charge of the clattering train.

Two years later, in the summer of 1881, there was another tragedy. He was staying with Mrs. Everest's sister at Ventnor on the Isle of Wight when a storm came up. That night HMS *Eurydice* with a complement of three hundred soldiers returning from the South African wars foundered against the cliffs and was sunk. Once again the boy was confronted with sudden, improbable death, the sense of unappeasable horror. Once there had been a great ship, and now there were only three black masts rising above the surface of the sea. Divers were sent down, and returned terrified by the sight of the drowned soldiers whose flesh was being eaten away by the fishes. Crowds gathered on the cliffs to watch the corpses as they were towed slowly to shore, and the boy remembered that they had all doffed their hats in sorrow. Years later he wrote that the thought of the soldiers nibbled by fishes left a scar on his mind.

These two tragedies had much in common: The machinery fails, men drown. Some years later Winston wrote a short story in which he attempted to exorcise his fear of death. Inevitably it was the story of a man who met his death by drowning.

Death, and the horror of death, haunted him while he was still very young, and they would remain with him throughout his life. He was a prey to melancholia, which he called "black dog." At such times he became aware of what the poet Leopardi called the *infinita vanita del tutto*, the nothingness of life and all human ambitions, and he seemed to sink under the weight of his own futility. These moods would pass, and sometimes his melancholia acted as a spur to ambition.

When the time came to send him to school, Lord Randolph decided that he should go to St. George's School, Ascot, which was housed in a large mansion called Sunningdale House. Winston entered the school shortly before his eighth birthday. He was being weaned from Mrs. Everest and hated it. His letters from the school were full of desperate appeals for visits which were rarely answered. Plump "Copper Top" with his strutting walk, his slight lisp, and impertinent airs was to become a foil for schoolmasters and schoolboys alike. He was miserably unhappy.

From Mrs. Everest he had learned how to read and write; he could add, subtract, divide and multiply. His handwriting, which later became careless and very nearly indecipherable, was bold, clear, and well-rounded. He had developed a passion for English verses with a *tum-ti-tum* rhythm and could recite them endlessly. He had also developed a passionate hatred for authority in all its forms.

Now authority appeared in one of its darkest forms in the person of the headmaster, the Reverend Herbert William Sneyd-Kynnersley, whose improbable name concealed vague aristocratic connections. He was a tall, thin, angular man with a ferocious aquiline nose, beady eyes and red Dundreary whiskers, who habitually wore a white tie and the black clothes appropriate to a clergyman. Absurdly vain and arrogant, and possessing meager intellectual attainments, he prided himself on the fact that he had built up a school suitable for the sons of the rich and the aristocratic, provided with all the modern conveniences. There was electric light, a rarity in those days, for few private houses were then lighted with it. Parents visiting the school would ask permission to switch on the light. There was a swimming pool, a chapel, an excellent kitchen and immense playing fields set among pine woods. The classes were small, and limited to ten students, and the masters wore gowns and mortarboards. Each schoolboy had his private cubicle. The furnishings in the red-brick schoolhouse were solid and commodious.

In theory the schoolboys were granted the utmost freedom. One schoolboy was placed in charge of the electric generator, another edited *The Gazette,* the school magazine, and a third was responsible for discipline in the dormitories. Every term the headmaster organized "expeditions," which might include a visit to the theater, an excursion to Eton or a ramble through the neighboring countryside. Parents were told that no punishments were administered. In fact punishments were administered on a graduated scale. For a small infraction a schoolboy would be ordered to remain silent at meals for a week; for a somewhat larger infraction he was flogged unmercifully.

Winston arrived at the school with his mother on a dark November afternoon, in time for five o'clock tea with the affable headmaster who had mastered the art of entertaining aristocratic women and knew exactly how to put them at ease. Winston was not at ease, and his teacup was threatening to spill over the carpet. When his mother left him and he heard the carriage wheels dying away along the driveway, he knew already that he had been abandoned to the wild beasts. Henceforth survival was everything. But how does one survive when the wild beasts make no secret of their intentions?

He was an indifferent scholar, made few friends and was bad at games. Excellence at games might have saved him; physical strength might have helped him; a clammy obedience might have commended him to his teachers. Having none of these, he dreamed his life away, paid as little attention as possible to his lessons, and attempted to pass unobserved. His reports have survived. He was nearly always at the bottom or near the bottom of his class. His spelling was "weak," his compositions were "feeble," his geography and history "very erratic—sometimes exceedingly," his drawing was "very elementary," his French was "not very good." In the first school report which covered only November and early December, 1882, the headmaster observed: "Very truthful, but a regular 'pickle' in many ways at present."

He was not entirely truthful, for he wrote separate letters to his mother and father announcing that he was very happy at school, when in fact he was weighed down with misery, and only the prospect of the Christmas holidays gave him any happiness.

The following year was probably the worst he ever endured. While his teachers noted his increasing ability at mathematics, they detected very little improvement in anything else. His conduct was generally described as "troublesome." The report for the weeks from March 1 to April 9, 1884, described his conduct as "exceedingly bad." The Reverend Sneyd-Kynnersley peppered his reports with the word "exceedingly," for he was a man of many excesses, but nothing could be worse than "exceedingly bad." Winston was becoming a nuisance; he was late for classes twenty times; he was not upholding the scholastic reputation of the school; and the schoolboys, who were clannish and priggish, had no use for him. If he was not the most unpopular boy in the school, he was very close to it.

There were, of course, some pleasurable moments: cooking chestnuts in winter, chasing butterflies in summer, going on excursions and listening to the headmaster reading from Dickens every evening before bedtime. The real life of the boys was concerned with the periodical "rages" which swept across the school like epidemics. One year everyone was collecting postage stamps, another year it was caterpillars or lizards or grass snakes or toads. There were also private theatricals in French, school concerts and chess tournaments. A parent who visited the school would have imagined that it was scarcely to be distinguished from Eton. Those well-scrubbed boys in black ties, dark coats, gray flannel trousers, all wearing black caps emblazoned with a red Maltese cross, were studiously polite to their elders and wore an air of innocence. Unhappily they were corrupt, and so were their masters.

The most corrupt of all was the Reverend Sneyd-Kynnersley, who enjoyed a private Saturnalia every Monday morning. The Saturnalia was carefully choreographed. The schoolmasters in their black gowns sat on the dais, with the schoolboys arranged on chairs below. Suddenly, from behind a blood-red curtain stamped with black fleurs-de-lis, the headmaster appeared, resplendent in a silk gown, and took his place on the dais. It was the signal for the ordeal to begin.

The masters recited the names of the schoolboys with their new order in class corresponding to the tests performed during the previous week. Any distinctions they had merited, and any failings, were duly recorded. The schoolboys changed their places according to their marks, playing a kind of silent musical chairs under the watchful eye of the headmaster sitting at his high desk. They were in terror of him, for no one knew who would be chosen for punishment, and the power to punish was his, and his alone. He surveyed each class in turn and pronounced judgment. The hapless schoolboy who had committed an insignificant crime was hauled off to the headmaster's study where a wooden box covered with rough black cloth served as the execution block. Two senior boys forced the victim down and pulled off his trousers. The headmaster, fortified by a glass of Marsala, then attacked the boy's bare buttocks with a birch rod, inflicting fifteen to twenty cuts, until the flesh was streaming with blood. Roger Fry, the artist and art critic, had the misfortune to be one of the senior boys who took part in many of these Monday morning Saturnalias. He remembered that the headmaster was totally merciless, used all his force, drew blood with the second or third blow and sometimes had cause to regret his vehemence. He wrote:

> Generally of course the boys endured it with fortitude but sometimes there were scenes of screaming, howling and struggling which made me almost sick with disgust. Nor did the horrors even stop there. There was a wild red-haired Irish boy, himself rather a cruel brute, who whether deliberately or as a result of the pain or whether he had diarrhoea, let fly. The irate clergyman instead of stopping at once simply went on with increased fury until the whole ceiling and walls of his study were spattered with filth. I suppose he was afterwards somewhat ashamed of this for he did not call in the servants to clean up but spent hours doing it himself with the assistance of a boy who was his special favorite.

Inevitably Winston was among those who were summoned to the headmaster's study. He suffered several beatings. On one occasion he was flogged for taking sugar from the pantry. Maurice Baring, the distinguished novelist and expert on Russian affairs, entered St. George's School shortly after Winston left it, and reported that Winston had already become a legend at the age of ten, because instead of showing the slightest repentance he had taken the headmaster's straw hat from where it hung over and door and kicked it to pieces. "His sojourn at this school had been one long feud with authority," Maurice Baring wrote, adding that the schoolboys had little enough sympathy for him.

At the end of the summer term in 1884 Winston left St. George's school never to return. He wrote that he detested the school and everything about it, and had learned nothing of any value. Yet that miserable school dominated by a headmaster who was a pervert and a sadist and perhaps half insane had taught him a lesson of surpassing value and importance, which he never forgot. In loneliness and despair he had cultivated the art of defiance. He would never give in. He would yell, shout, fight, punch and kick the headmaster's hat to pieces. He would, as far as he could, make life intolerable for his oppressors, and there was to come a time when his study of defiance was to prove of inestimable value to western civilization. Speaking to schoolboys in October 1941, when Great Britain was fighting alone against Hitler, he said: "Never give in! Never give in! Never, Never—in nothing great or small, large or petty—never give in except to convictions of honor and good sense!"

Thereafter his schooldays were less unpleasant. The Misses Thomson, two elderly sisters, kept school in Brighton on the south coast and genuinely liked the unruly boy whose conduct still left much to be desired. The few surviving reports show that he was at the bottom of the class in conduct, but was doing surprisingly well in English, classics, drawing and French, being among the first seven or eight in his class. He collected sea anemones, went riding and swimming, learned vast quantities of poetry by heart, and for the first time became interested in writing essays. Then in March, 1886, he caught a cold which turned into pneumonia, and his life hung in the balance. Lord and Lady Randolph Churchill rushed to the bedside to find him unconscious and scarcely breathing. Within a month he had recovered, but this brush with death left upon him scars which never completely healed. Death, which had haunted him when it took the form of a sunken ship or a train hurtling over a bridge and falling into the Tay River, now assumed a more personal and sharply pointed form; it became a familiar presence always ready to spring at him.

The Misses Thomson were both extremely intelligent women, but many things about Winston perplexed them. He was erratic, excitable, unpredictable, and while they were fond of him, they were also a little frightened by him, by his strangeness and by his recklessness. Quite suddenly, for no apparent reason, he would explode with excitement and just as suddenly the excitement would come to an end. Meanwhile he was advancing in his studies and applying himself doggedly to learning Greek and Latin, and while he never knew Greek well, he knew enough Latin to take pleasure in reading Caesar's *Commentaries* and Vergil's *Aeneid*. He could read the simpler passages of Herodotus without too much difficulty, liked geometry, enjoyed mathematics and was developing some skill in French. He had all the makings of a good student, but his unpredictable temperament kept getting in the way.

According to the family tradition he would have gone to Eton. His father and grandfather were Etonians, and it was expected that he would follow in their footsteps. Happily—because Eton applies a veneer to a schoolboy which endures throughout most of his adult life—he escaped this fate and went to Harrow, which stands on a hill in the outskirts of London. His doctor had pointed out that the elevated position of Harrow would be better for his lungs damaged by a long bout of pneumonia. Dr. Welldon, the headmaster at Harrow, was agreeable, but first it was necessary to pass a simple entrance examination to test his ability in Greek, Latin, algebra, geometry and arithmetic. He was well coached by the Misses Thomson, and it was felt that the entrance examination would present no difficulties.

In March 1888, when he was thirteen years old, he journeyed from Brighton to Harrow in the company of Miss Charlotte Thomson. He was in a subdued mood, conscious that much was demanded of him. She was a little alarmed, thinking that he might be overcome by the excitement of the occasion; he was capable of anything when excited. Her fears were justified. Confronted by a dozen lines of Latin to be translated into English, he suffered a strange blackout and was completely unable to make any translation at all. The boy who had been translating Vergil and Caesar for over a year suddenly found that he knew no Latin at all. On the paper he delivered up to the examiners there was only his name and a few blots. Sick with nervous excitement, he announced later to Miss Thomson that it was quite impossible for him to translate Latin because he had never before done any translations. Miss Thomson knew very well that this was untrue, but she did not argue with him. In later years he liked to say that he had never troubled to learn Latin and Greek, and was thus able to devote himself to the mastery of English, but this too was a polite fiction.

The examination in Latin was a total failure; he did better in Greek, algebra, mathematics and geometry. The examiners found some merit in him. Dr. Welldon, a kindly man, invited Winston and Miss Thomson to lunch and was impressed. Partly because he was the son of Lord Randolph Churchill and partly because he obviously possessed some excellent qualities, Winston was allowed to enter Harrow. He was placed in the bottom form of the school, and since he signed his name Winston Spencer-Churchill, and S comes low in the alphabet, he was the very last and least schoolboy at Harrow. In all the processions that filed across the schoolyard, he trailed in the rear. Even when he decided to sign himself Winston S. Churchill, thus considerably improving his alphabetical position, the school continued to regard him as Spencer-Churchill.

His scholastic position was no better, and he remained obstinately at the bottom of the class. "I am very lazy," he wrote to his mother, as though laziness excused everything. Neither Henry Davidson nor Robert Somervell, the two schoolmasters who chiefly dealt with him, felt that they understood him. He was not willfully lazy; it was as though laziness held him by the throat. He kept losing his books, came late to the classroom, studied in short bursts and then abandoned study altogether, and was so regular in his irregularity that he drove his teachers to despair. Yet he possessed a native intelligence. "As far as ability goes he ought to be at the top of his form, whereas he is at the bottom," wrote Henry Davidson to Lady Randolph Churchill at the end of the summer term, adding, "I do think it is very serious that he should have acquired such phenomenal slovenliness."

Nevertheless he was learning to write and was already addicted to grandiloquent phrases. In May 1888, a month after entering Harrow, he was asked to write an essay on "Palestine in the Time of John the Baptist."He began quite sensibly with a physical description of Palestine:

> At the time of John the Baptist Palestine's physical features were the same as they are now—The even coast line with its only projection of any importance, Mt Carmel, forms the Eastern boundary of the Levant. A range of mountains running parallel to the coast, East of which the country slopes down to a depth of several hundred feet below the level of the sea—The river Jordan which passes through the Lake of Gennesareth & the Dead Sea. So shall they be till hoary Time be merged in boundless Eternity.
>
> At the time of John the Baptist Palestine lay at the feet of the Roman, who was then at the apex of his glory.

"Hoary Time," "boundless Eternity" and "the apex of glory" were characteristic Churchillian phrases, to be savored and rolled on the tongue like the sweetest of strawberries. Soon he was composing essays for older boys, which he dictated while pacing across the room. These essays came to an end when a schoolmaster grew suspicious, recognizing the Churchillian cadences in the work of a boy who had never previously shown the slightest proclivity for ornate adjectives. He had also discovered that he possessed a phenomenal memory and thought nothing of learning a thousand lines of poetry by heart.

But school was not only learning; he joined the Rifle Corps, enjoyed gymnastics and swam regularly in the school's vast open-air swimming pool. One day, seeing a small boy standing at the edge of the pool in a meditative mood, Winston attacked him from behind and pushed him into the water. Then to his surprise he realized that the boy was swimming powerfully to the pool's edge and would soon be clambering out of the water. Winston fled, but was overtaken and hurled into the deepest part of the pool. When he scrambled out, he realized that he was in danger of further punishment. Jeering schoolboys pointed out that the boy he had pushed into the water was Leopold Amery of the Sixth Form, head of his House, captain of the Harrow gymnastics team, a redoubtable football player and one of the leading lights of the school. Many honors had fallen to him, and in addition he was possessed of formidable strength. Winston approached him with trepidation, expecting a truly merciless punishment. Trembling, he said: "I am very sorry. I mistook you for a Fourth Form boy. You are so small." This was not quite the apology Leopold Amery expected, and Winston seemed to be in even greater danger. He said quickly: "My father, who is a great man, is also small." Leopold Amery laughed, and soon the incident was forgotten.

About the same time Winston was "fagging" for one of the senior students, Nugent Hicks, who later became Bishop of Norwich. A fag's task was to run errands promptly and in general to act as an obedient slave of his master. Winston was not an especially good fag, and Nugent Hicks found it necessary to upbraid him from time to time and even to administer an occasional swishing. After one swishing, received in resentful silence, Winston said cheekily: "I shall be a greater man than you."

"You can have two more for that!" said Hicks.

The theme of "the great man," which preoccupied Winston's mind throughout the remaining years of his life, had now received its first public expression. Like the deep-throated tones of a double bass it would reverberate at longer or shorter intervals until the end.

He was not always getting into mischief: he was writing occasional letters in *The Harrovian* and composing verses. The letters were hortatory, like undelivered speeches. He vigorously attacked the management of an athletic exhibition held in the school gymnasium. A letter in *The Harrovian,* signed "Junius Junior," shows a certain Churchillian resonance. He wrote:

> What I ask, and what the school asks—and will ask—is: Why do so few boys do anything? Why was the performance watched from the gallery

by two members of the School Eight? . . . All these things that I have
enumerated serve to suggest that there is something rotten in the state of
Denmark. I have merely stated the facts—it is not for me to offer an
explanation of them. To you, sirs, as directors of public opinion, it
belongs to lay bare the weakness.

There was a good deal more of it, and Leo Amery, the editor of *The
Harrovian*, added an editorial note: "We have omitted a portion of our
correspondent's letter which seemed to us to exceed the limits of fair
criticism."

Winston enjoyed excess. He wrote a "Commemorative Ode to
Influenza," which was unnecessarily long—it extended to twelve stan-
zas—and inevitably diverged from the subject. He had had a bad attack
of influenza, and in the poem it amused him to give it back to the
French, who had no doubt originated "the vile, insatiate scourge," and
to the Germans, the Russians, and all the other Continental peoples,
who were in some way responsible for it. Influenza was being treated in
the light of his political beliefs. He was pleased when the epidemic
reached Calais:

> *In Calais port the illness stays,*
> *As did the French in former days,*
> *   To threaten Freedom's Isle:*
> *But now no Nelson could o'erthrow*
> *This cruel, unconquerable foe,*
> *Nor save us from its guile.*

He was less pleased when the epidemic reached England where "it
ravaged far and wide/ Both village, town and countryside." But
gradually the favoring winds of an English spring swept the epidemic
away, and England was left serene and unblemished, having survived
this disaster as it had survived so many others. In the peroration he
celebrated the Empire:

> *God shield our Empire from the might*
> *Of War or famine, plague or blight*
> *And all the power of Hell,*
> *And keep it ever in the hands*
> *Of those who fought 'gainst other lands,*
> *Who fought and conquered well.*

He wrote the "Commemorative Ode to Influenza" when he was fifteen. In 1940, fifty years later, he would be making speeches on the same theme.

Meanwhile, Winston remained at the bottom of his form, proudly and obstinately declaring his insignificance, his slovenliness, his lack of elementary discipline. His chief delight was to learn 1,200 lines of Macauley's *The Lays of Ancient Rome* by heart. To his mother he wrote that he expected to come out first in French, and English and Roman history, and among the first six in Latin and Greek. But such statements were merely pious hopes. Lord Randolph, invited to attend the Speech Day celebrations, did not come. He had long ago come to the conclusion that his elder son would amount to very little.

In his loneliness Winston was continually writing letters to his mother and father, urging them to visit him, and there would be the inevitable letter beginning: "I was very disappointed at you not being able to come down." On rare occasions Mrs. Everest was permitted to visit Harrow. He loved her deeply, escorted her round the school, showed her the same loving attention he would have shown to his mother and kissed her openly, to the amusement of his fellow Harrovians who thought it absurd that a grown-up boy should kiss his old nurse. A suitable punishment was devised: he was thrown on his bed, and the mattress was folded over him until he was nearly asphyxiated. Then hot and cold water were poured on him. Even more complicated tortures were being prepared, but the providential arrival of the Reverend Fred Searle, an under-master, put an end to them. Winston, his face beetroot-red, rose from the bed with his clothes clinging to his skin and immediately launched into an oration, shouting and screaming at the boys who had been attempting to drown him and suffocate him. "One day," he screamed, "I shall be a great man and you shall be nobodies, and then I will stamp and crush you!"

There was not the least doubt that he meant what he said. Rage, defiance, misery and prophecy combined to form an exhilarating witch's brew; he was recognizably the same boy who had torn the Reverend Sneyd-Kynnersley's hat to pieces. When he lovingly accompanied Mrs. Everest through the school, he was probably performing the bravest act of his life, for he knew the consequences. But one does not pass school examinations by courage, and no one quite knew what to do with him. "My only consolation is that your conduct is good, and that you are an affectionate son—but your work is an insult to your intelligence," his mother wrote to him. Fred Searle genuinely liked him and invoked God's blessing on him. Mrs. Everest, remembering his lungs, continually warned him against getting wet. Everyone except his grandfather Jerome was worried about him. "Let him be," wrote Leonard Jerome. "Boys get good at what they find they shine at." What Winston shone at was unbridled courage, and soon it became evident that he might after all make a good soldier.

Harrow at this time had an Army Class designed to prepare school-boys for the entrance examination at the Royal Military Academy at Sandhurst. He was a good shot and was learning to fence; he enjoyed the rather primitive military games conducted at school; and he was already something of an expert on war, having learned to deploy his lead soldiers with considerable skill. Lord Randolph concluded that since Winston showed no aptitude for anything else, he might as well be allowed to enter the Army. Unfortunately the entrance examination to Sandhurst involved a knowledge of elementary mathematics and Winston had forgotten most of the little mathematics he ever knew. He failed twice in the examinations for Sandhurst; the "comical hieroglyphics" of mathematics proved too much for him, and he was sent to Captain James' famous "cramming school" in London in the hope that he would catch up with his studies. Captain James complained that Winston was immensely talkative and spent far too much time attempting to teach his teachers instead of listening to them. Finally he succeeded in mastering sines and cosines by sheer will power, and then by luck, shortly before sitting for the examination, he guessed the questions that would be asked of him. Failure at the third attempt would have been disastrous.

Just before he entered the "cramming school" there occurred a strange event which throws some light on the quality of his courage. On January 10, 1893, when staying with his aunt, Lady Cornelia Wimborne, on her estate near Bournemouth, he was playing with two boys in the pinewoods near the sea when he found himself on a small wooden bridge thrown across a ravine, and suddenly he observed that the boys who were hunting him had divided their forces and now stood at each end of the bridge. At all costs it was necessary to avoid capture. There were some young pine trees growing in the ravine, and it occurred to him that it would be perfectly possible to slide down one of the pine trees. No doubt the branches would snap off and thus break his fall. He flung himself off the bridge and fell thirty feet onto hard ground, and was unconscious for two days. He had ruptured a kidney and was in bed for two months.

This was imaginative daring of a high order: a decision taken quickly and thoughtfully, and also reasonably, if the data could be relied upon. Unfortunately, as he observed later, "the argument was correct; the data were absolutely wrong." It was not the first time he had suffered punishment for defiance of natural laws, nor would it be the last. He was an instinctive gambler who enjoyed taking risks even when his own life was at stake. Some months later, while on a holiday in Switzerland, he and another boy rowed out across Lake Leman in a small sailboat, threw off their clothes and went swimming. The wind rose, the sailboat drifted away, and whenever they drew close to it, the wind sprang up and carried it still further away. Their very lives depended upon reaching the boat. "Death was swimming in the water at our side, whispering from time to time in the rising wind," he wrote when describing the incident. Just in time, and by the purest luck, Winston caught up with the boat and was able to row back to rescue his companion. Yet he enjoyed "the dull yellow glare of mortal peril that had so suddenly played around us." To defy danger, to keep death at arm's length, but only at arm's length, quickened his feeling for life. He was happiest in the midst of storms. He was one of those who must live as often as possible in a state of exaltation. At all costs his father and mother must be made aware of his existence; the boy who was at the bottom of the class must excel *by other means*. The jump into the ravine was a crucial indication of the kind of person he was: with courage and exuberance and a craving to be known went a dangerous recklessness, a suicidal defiance of death. Such men sometimes live long lives.

It seemed then that he had all the makings of a soldier and would probably be killed in some obscure frontier post of the British Empire. But to become a soldier at all it was first necessary to enter Sandhurst. Characteristically, he nearly failed. There were 389 candidates, and he came ninety-fifth, too low on the list for an infantry cadetship; he was thought good enough for a cavalry cadetship. His marks were curious: 72% for geometrical drawing, 68% for freehand drawing, 64% for English history, 62% for mathematics, 62% for English composition, 61% for French, 41% for chemistry, and 18% for Latin. What had saved him on this third attempt was his skill at drawing.

Winston telegraphed his success to his father and received a reply calculated to diminish his exuberance. He was told that he was a failure for missing the infantry and that he had no reason to plume himself; he was reminded that he was addicted to a "slovenly happy-go-lucky harum-scarum kind of work" and would probably continue to work in the same way despite all the advantages he had received and despite his own boasting. He was a fool and a discredit to his family, and was likely to become a social wastrel, who would inevitably lead "a shabby, unhappy and futile existence." Winston had his own ideas. It was true that he had entered Sandhurst by the skin of his teeth; it was true that he had never worked very hard; it was true that he detested examinations. No doubt there were defects in his character. But Sandhurst was where he wanted to be. He had always hoped to be a soldier, and now at last he was a soldier in the army of Queen Victoria.

THE FOOTLOOSE SOLDIER

Sandhurst, the military college for young officers in the British Army, was an astonishingly beautiful place built around a once famous country house. There were trees everywhere, a large lake, lawns and playing fields. It seemed to be deep in the countryside, but was in fact within easy distance of London. A few miles away was Aldershot, where full-scale military games were played. Wellington College, founded in honor of the Duke of Wellington, was close by, and as though to point a mysterious moral there was another important disciplinary institution in the neighborhood, the Broadmoor Prison for the Insane. Amid the rolling hills of Berkshire life could be lived pleasantly and generously. Except for Reading there were no large towns in the county, and there were villages which still seemed to be sleeping through the seventeenth century.

Sandhurst was an aristocracy of young officers, most of whom came from those schools known as "public schools," although they were private, reserved for the rich and the influential. At Sandhurst Winston found young men belonging to his own class. They affected a crisp military tone and an air of conscious superiority, and could be recognized by their military stride and their indifference to normal human preoccupations. They saw themselves as the future guardians of a vast and expanding empire. They wore brilliant uniforms, and on rare occasions, when invited to visit the Staff College at Camberley, which was only a mile away, they could see the even more resplendent red-tabbed uniforms of the future officers of the Imperial General Staff.

Winston was in his element, and if there were some things like parade ground drilling which he did not especially like—he was so bad at drill that he was kept in the "awkward squad" for several months—there were so many things he adored that he was in danger of floating away on a cloud of the purest happiness. No longer was he confronted with periodic examinations in Latin, French or mathematics. Instead he could continue to do exactly what he had done when he was playing with his lead soldiers at Blenheim Palace, but on a larger scale. He was learning tactics and strategy, the art of fortifications, map making, military law and military administration. He was acquiring and reading an impressive library of books devoted to the art of war and the history of recent wars. The American Civil War, which introduced strange new tactics, and the Franco-German War of 1870, which toppled Napoleon III from his throne and brought about the union of the German Reich under the Hohenzollern Emperor, were studied in intricate detail on the blackboard, together with imaginary wars and those future wars which would doubtless exclude the use of the bayonet, the hand grenade or the bomb, for it was generally agreed that future wars would be dominated by machine guns, which were still called Maxim guns, and the unfortunate soldiers would be too far away from one another to see the whites of their eyes.

Education at Sandhurst was a curious mixture of primitive, medieval and modern. In the intervals of learning how to fill sandbags, Winston was taught the use of the lance and how to conceal the iron spiked balls called *chevaux de frises*, both used by the ancient Babylonians. He was also learning the use of the *fougasse*, a primitive land mine formerly used by the Florentines in the fourteenth century. An English comic artist of superb gifts was to call himself Fougasse in memory of those mines. Indeed there was something irremediably comic in the education offered at Sandhurst to the young gentlemen cadets who had only to look at the map to know that there could be no more wars. The British Empire, painted red on the maps, circled the entire globe.

Lord Randolph's complaints had previously centered on Winston's laziness, his refusal to study. Now that the son had succeeded in entering Sandhurst, he had a further reason for complaint. By failing to enter the infantry he had become a greater charge on his father, who could ill afford to keep the boy in horses. Winston needed two official chargers and two hunters; in addition he would soon be demanding a string of polo ponies. He solved the matter in his own way by hiring horses from the local livery stables and running up bills on the strength of his future commission. He was learning the pleasures of debt. Mess bills mounted up. There were extra expenses for grooms and their uniforms; and he was beginning to pride himself on the cut of his expensive riding jackets and jodhpurs. He was so determined to become a first-class rider that he took special riding lessons with the Royal Horse Guards at Knightsbridge Barracks in London. He was a gentleman cadet and a gentleman rider, learning to drink and smoke and carouse with the best of them, indistinguishable from the other young officers at Sandhurst.

One day, while in his second term, he lost the gold watch given to him by his father. It was one of those completely meaningless and stupid incidents which should properly have been forgotten. Lord Randolph was incensed. He was still incensed when Winston explained that as the result of his efforts the watch had been recovered:

> While walking along the Wish Stream I stooped down to pick up a stick and it fell out of my pocket into the only deep place for miles.
>
> The stream was only about 5 inches deep—but the watch fell into a pool nearly 6 feet deep.
>
> I at once took off my clothes and I dived for it but the bottom was so uneven and the water so cold that I could not stay in longer than 10 minutes and had to give it up.
>
> The next day I had the pool dredged—but without result. On Tuesday therefore I obtained permission from the Governor to do anything I could provided I paid for having it all put straight again.
>
> I then borrowed 23 men from the Infantry Detachment—dug a new course for the stream—obtained the fire engine and pumped the pool dry and so recovered the watch. I tell you this to show you that I appreciate fully the value of the watch and that I did not treat the accident in a casual way. The labour of the men cost me over £3.

Winston's cumbrous ingenuity—who else would summon a detachment of infantry, a fire engine crew and a fire engine to pump out a pool six feet deep?—tells us a great deal about the workings of his mind and his fear of his father's wrath. The letter written in the spring of 1894 tells us something more. He was showing that he could command a clean-cut and expressive narrative style. For the first time we are aware that he might become a writer.

There was, however, very little to suggest that he would spend many years of his life writing books and nothing at all to suggest that he would become Prime Minister. His instinct was to enjoy himself with an exquisite selfishness. He attended weekend parties in the houses of his aristocratic relatives; he liked to socialize, to hunt, to play polo and to cut a fine figure in his riding clothes. He was not tall—the medical records at Sandhurst give his height as five feet six and a half inches— but he had lost the baby fat of his school days and was developing into an extraordinarily handsome young man with a subtle refinement of features. He had a broad forehead, large glowing eyes, a straight nose, a firm chin and lips that were petulant and sensual. His profile did not compare with his full face, but it was evident that he had inherited his mother's beauty.

Weekend parties in country houses toward the end of Queen Victoria's reign were outwardly decorous. In theory the young women were chaperoned; in theory, too, the young men were virtuous. Wherever possible these house parties were built around the presence of some especially distinguished guest who set the tone and led the dances. If Edward, Prince of Wales, was the principal guest, no woman was safe and the best wines in the wine cellar were soon depleted. Winston became a willing guest at these house parties where there were never enough young bachelors. Handsome, elegant and witty, he was in danger of being invited to all the house parties within a three-hour railroad journey from Sandhurst.

At weekend parties Winston sought out high government officials and soldiers who would help to advance his military career. Colonel John Brabazon, an impoverished Irish landlord, who was an intimate of the Prince of Wales and a cavalry officer of great distinction, attracted Winston's attention. The colonel was powerful, and there was much to be learned from this man who had won so many medals in the colonial wars that he permitted himself to wear only the most important. He wore a fiery mustache and a goatee, although the wearing of a goatee was against the Army Regulations. In addition he had a fashionable lisp. The story was told that when he was waiting for the train at Aldershot, he asked the station master: "Wheah is the London twain?" "It has gone, Colonel." "Gone? Bwing another!"

Colonel Brabazon took Winston under his wing. The young man's talent for reaching out for the top proved fruitful. He was doing well in his studies, although he found it difficult to master map making and was noted for his unpunctuality. For the first time, too, he delivered a rousing political speech. This event took place on November 3, 1894, in a music hall in Leicester Square in the heart of London. It appeared that a certain Mrs. Ormiston Chant, of the London County Council, was busily protesting against the morals of the young people who crowded the promenade at the Empire Theatre. They drank to excess, they were noisy, they flirted openly, and it occurred to her that morality would be protected by dividing the men from the women by an awning and a balustrade. This was done, and in addition, the bar in the promenade was closed down. Churchill asked for a drink and was told there was none to be found. Discovering that the Empire Theatre was given over to a deadly sobriety and an unpleasing separation of the sexes, he scrambled onto the velvet-covered top of the railing separating the auditorium from the promenade and made an inflammatory speech.

"Where," he shouted, "does the Englishman in London always find a welcome? Where does he first go when, battle-scarred and travel-worn, he reaches home? Who is always there to greet him with a smile, and join him in a drink? Who is ever faithful, ever true—the Ladies of the Empire Promenade!"

This speech, the first he ever made in public, was greeted with violent applause. At Churchill's prompting a happy mob tore down the awning and smashed the balustrade to pieces and the terrified management ordered drinks to be served to its victorious patrons. The small, red-haired youth in evening clothes had the feeling that he had done well for his country by invoking freedom, the Magna Carta and the rights of man, and he was last seen in a hansom cab, shouting boisterously to the crowd, delighted by the sensation he had caused. The newspapers described the incident the next day but failed to mention Churchill's name.

A few days later he made another speech, this time in private. He organized a dinner, and Richard Harding Davis, the American writer and traveler, was included among the guests. Davis discovered that the purpose of the dinner was to celebrate those of Churchill's friends and acquaintances who "were under twenty-one years of age, and who in twenty years time would control the destinies of the British Empire." Churchill made an impassioned speech in honor of the future rulers, among whom he included most of the people sitting around the table, and just as previously he had lauded the Ladies of the Empire Promenade, so now he paid homage to the Young Men of the Empire. Davis was obscurely aware that Churchill was the only person present who was likely to disturb the destinies of the Empire. His account of the youthful Churchill was published in a book called *Real Soldiers of Fortune* in 1906.

In December Churchill took his final examination at Sandhurst, passing out twentieth in a class of 130. He was now twenty, no longer the boy at the bottom of the class, but a jubilant young officer of the Fourth Hussars with the world at his feet. But his joy was short-lived, for on January 24, 1895, on a day when London was carpeted with snow, Lord Randolph Churchill died of syphilis and general paralysis of the insane in his London house. The son who had scarcely known his father and had never understood him reached the deathbed in time to hear him murmuring, "Have you got your horses?"

Lord Randolph Churchill's death was a shattering blow to his son; for Jennie it was a release from a slow agony of scandal and misery. She had known for three or four years that he was dying and that the disease was incurable. In the summer of 1894, with astonishing bravery, she accompanied him on a world tour, partly in order to remove him from London and partly in the hope that a change of air might somehow cure his disease. They visited New York, traveled across Canada, spent a few days in San Francisco, sailed to Japan, Hong Kong, Singapore and Rangoon, and were back in England shortly before Christmas. All the time he was a slobbering, squeaky-voiced ghost of himself, continually speaking about his great importance, sometimes threatening her with a revolver, demanding continual attention. They traveled with a lead-lined coffin, for no one expected him to survive the journey; and when they reached London, he was delirious and beyond help.

Lord Randolph Churchill was buried in Bladon Churchyard near Blenheim Palace. There was the inevitable memorial service in Westminster Abbey, and Dean Farrar, the author of *Eric, or Little by Little*, presided. In the course of time a statue of him was erected in the chapel at Blenheim, facing the baroque tomb of the first Duke of Marlborough. The life-size marble statue of Lord Randolph bears an inscription lamenting his death at the early age of forty-five "after a lingering illness patiently borne." This ghostly statue has only the faintest resemblance to the man who had once been Chancellor of the Exchequer and who might, but for an inexplicable defect of character, have become Prime Minister.

There was another death that year that hurt Winston even more deeply. Mrs. Everest died during the summer from peritonitis. He had seen her a few days earlier as she lay in bed—the calm, strong face showing few signs of illness. He came hurrying to her through a rain-storm, and because she was always afraid he would catch cold, she was not satisfied until he had removed his coat and dried it thoroughly. He set out to find a good specialist in Harley Street and brought him to the bedside. She seemed to rally, but on the next day when he returned he found her sinking. He remained with her until she died during the night. "Death came very easily to her," he wrote. "She had lived such an innocent and loving life of service to others and held such a simple faith that she had no fears at all, and did not seem to mind very much." He made all the funeral arrangements, attended the funeral and then returned to his military duties, the glittering weekend house parties, the cavalry parades, the powerful lords and ladies of the land.

Through all the years of his life he would remember Mrs. Everest. She had been the one woman who loved and consoled him in his youth, whose comforting presence concealed an anxious concern for his wel-fare. He described her in his novel *Savrola,* as the housekeeper who waits upon the imperious revolutionary leader. "She had nursed him from his birth up with a devotion and care which knew no break. It is a strange thing, the love of these women. Perhaps it is the only disinterested affection in the world." Her death left him heartbroken and he kept her photograph with him all his life. In time he came to resemble her, for soon the oval, aristocratic face grew round like hers, his chin grew firmer, his lips more compressed and his eyes larger. If you place a photograph of Mrs. Everest against a photograph of the older Churchill, it is as though they were mother and son.

That summer the Fourth Hussars left Aldershot and took up quarters in Hounslow's old barracks, nearer the center of London. The life of a cavalry officer was a leisurely one; he was allowed five months' leave each year. Cavalry officers were expected to spend the winter months fox hunting. Churchill thought there were better and cheaper ways to spend the winter. Máximo Gómez and José Martí were spreading revolution against the Spanish on the island of Cuba, and it occurred to him that he might combine a pleasant holiday in the West Indies with a grandstand view of the military operations of the Spanish garrison which was attempting to suppress the rebellion. Sir Henry Drummond Wolff, the British ambassador in Madrid, intervened on his behalf and he was provided with a letter of introduction from the Spanish Minister of War to General Arsenio Martínez de Campos who commanded the Spanish army in Cuba. His expenses were few, and the *Daily Graphic* agreed to pay for any dispatches he wrote from the front. Early in

November 1895, he set out lightheartedly for Cuba by way of New York and Tampa, accompanied by his friend Reginald Barnes, a fellow officer of the Fourth Hussars.

New York proved to be almost as adventurous as Cuba. For a week the two subalterns were entertained by Bourke Cockran, known as the "Tammany Tiger," an Irish-American of prodigious oratorical skills. He was a man with a heavy, ugly, granite-hewn face and powerful shoulders, and he lived in ostentatious luxury in a mansion on Fifth Avenue. Since he had been a close friend of Leonard Jerome and had no children of his own, he went out of his way to smother young Churchill with advice and affection. Was there anything he would like to see? Churchill would like to inspect West Point. It was arranged immediately. He would like to visit the ironclad cruiser *New York,* which was then in the harbor. This, too, was arranged. On subsequent days Churchill saw the forts guarding New York, visited fire stations and attended a murder trial, sitting beside the judge on the bench. He was surprised that the judge wore neither robe nor wig, and no one wore uniform. The murderer, the judge, the attorneys, the warders and the jury were all in ordinary clothes, and the courtroom like any other room. "There seems to be no such thing as reverence or tradition," he wrote. "But they manage to hang a man all the same, and that after all is the great thing."

Between visits with the Vanderbilts and suppers at the Waldorf, there were long sessions in Cockran's library. Over excellent brandies Cockran dilated on the subject of government, fiscal responsibility and the art of oratory. He was a spellbinder, and Churchill asked him how one trained oneself to keep an audience of thousands enthralled. Cockran answered that it was very simple: All that was needed was to transform oneself into an organ. Every word must be organ-strong, clearly enunciated, and in addition there must be the huge, wavelike rhythm of organ notes. It was easier for Cockran with his Irish brogue than for Churchill, who spoke with the slurring accents of the well-bred Englishman and suffered from an impediment which made it difficult for him to pronounce *s* and *th.* Cockran read out his speeches in his voice of thunder and Churchill was deeply impressed. Cockran liked to express himself in vast, rolling generalities. To the end of his life Churchill remembered many of Cockran's phrases. "The earth is a generous mother," Cockran would declaim in those vibrant organ notes. "She will provide in plentiful abundance food for all her children if they will but cultivate her soil in justice and in peace." Churchill liked the phrase so much that he continually repeated it in his own speeches until his wife threatened to leave him if he said it again.

In this way Churchill learned his first lesson in oratory from a corrupt Tammany boss.

Churchill and Barnes went off to the war in Cuba in great style, for Cockran provided them with a private stateroom on the train to Tampa and for thirty-six hours they lived in great comfort. From Tampa they sailed to Havana, where they were treated like great dignitaries, envoys of a mighty power. General Martínez de Campos was at Santa Clara and accordingly they set off to meet him. The guerrillas were operating near the railroad, and the train was therefore equipped with armor plating: if the guerrillas began to shoot, all you had to do was to throw yourself on the floor. Churchill was keyed up, for the railroad carriage smelled of war. Campos was friendly and entrusted them to a young lieutenant who suggested that if they wanted to see the fighting they should join the column of General Valdez, who had already left for Sancti Spiritus. Churchill was all for riding out and overtaking the general, but the young lieutenant warned him that while a column can ride through guerrilla-infested country, two men cannot. "Fifty horsemen can go where they please," he explained. "Two cannot go anywhere." So it was arranged that Churchill and Barnes should go by train to Cienfuegos, then by sea to Tunas and then by train to Sancti Spiritus, which they would probably reach before the arrival of General Valdez. They found Sancti Spiritus to be a godforsaken small town, very unhealthy, with a raging epidemic of yellow fever, and smallpox as well. They spent the night in a filthy tavern, and the next evening General Valdez marched into the town at the head of a column of 3,000 foot soldiers, two squadrons of cavalry and a mule battery. Since the guerrilla forces of Máximo Gómez in the neighborhood were thought to number about 4,000 men, General Valdez was outnumbered and could expect to see some brisk fighting.

Churchill liked the look of the soldiers with their dark, sunburned faces, thick beards, sombreros and double bandoliers. They all wore white pajamas and most of them were barefoot, but they looked like men who would acquit themselves well in battle. There was no nonsense about them. At dawn, when the earth was dripping with dew, the long Spanish column crept snakelike through clammy forests and rolling fields, and punctually at nine o'clock in the morning came the order to halt for breakfast and a siesta. The horses were offsaddled, the hammocks were slung between the trees and the whole column except

those on guard duty went to sleep for four hours in the heat of the day.
Churchill found that he enjoyed the Cuban cigars; he also enjoyed the
siesta; for the rest of his life he was addicted to both. He also developed
a lifelong affection for Spaniards.

There were a quarter of a million rough Spanish peasants in uniform.
They were in barracks in all the important towns; they guarded the
railroads and the blockhouses; they formed columns and marched
endlessly through the forests in search of the enemy who burned the
canefields, shot from behind hedges, wrecked trains, destroyed
property, fired into the camps where men were peacefully sleeping in
their hammocks and otherwise behaved in the manner of guerrillas.
Churchill, with his profound sense of the importance of property, found
the guerrillas tiresome, even though in the last resort they must be
credited with being courageous fighters for their freedom against an
alien power. Churchill found himself in a quandary. He admired the
Spanish soldiers and he was impressed with the fact that Spain was
spending her treasure in order to put down the insurrection. On one
side was General Valdez, resplendent in his white uniform and gold
braid, the representative of law and order, and on the other were the
nameless and invisible peasants determined to destroy colonial rule.
Churchill found a useful formula for dealing with the problem. "I
sympathize with the rebellion—not with the rebels," he wrote later.
Meanwhile he enjoyed the company of the general who was putting
down the rebellion. They marched for several days without coming
upon any trace of the enemy but with the eerie sensation that they were
being continually watched.

At last on the morning of November 30, 1895, his twenty-first birthday, fighting broke out in the small fortified village of Arroyo Blanco.
The low mists clung on the ground. He was sitting on his horse and
gnawing a chicken when a volley rang out from the edge of a forest. The
horse immediately behind him gave a bound. Soldiers rushed to the
edge of the forest, but found only some spent cartridge cases. Churchill
turned his attention to the wounded horse:

> It was a chestnut. The bullet had struck between his ribs, the blood
> dripped on the ground, and there was a circle of dark red on his bright
> chestnut coat about a foot wide. He hung his head, but did not fall.
> Evidently, however, he was going to die, for his saddle and bridle were
> soon taken from him. As I watched these proceedings I could not help
> reflecting that the bullet which had struck the chestnut had certainly

passed within a foot of my head. So at any rate I had been "under fire." That was something. Nevertheless, I began to take a more thoughtful view of our enterprise than I had hitherto done.

A few days later there was a more formal engagement. It began just as Churchill, Barnes and two Spanish officers who had been bathing in the river were putting on their clothes. They rushed back to the camp to find bullets falling all over it, the deep notes of the Remingtons in the hands of the guerrillas contrasting oddly with the staccato rattle of the magazine rifles of the Spanish. Thousands of bullets were fired, but very few people were hurt. The fighting lasted about half an hour and suddenly broke off. The guerrillas, wrote Churchill, "went off carrying away with them the wounded and dead, with which it was hoped they were not unprovided." The last words are puzzling, for they showed an unexpected animosity toward the guerrillas. Then, having written five dispatches for the *Daily Graphic,* he left Cuba forever. He had not covered himself with glory, but for the first time he had watched men being killed in battle.

He returned to England to enjoy what remained of the winter season: the balls, the dinner parties, the weekends in the country houses, the strange frenzied gaiety of the last years of the Victorian era. Second lieutenant Churchill, aged twenty-one, veteran of the Cuban war, became a determined partygoer and was often accompanied by his mother, who could have been taken for his glamorous elder sister. He was a frequent visitor at weekends at Lord William Beresford's estate near Dorking. There he met General Sir Bindon Blood, the descendant of Thomas Blood, who had stolen the Crown Jewels from the Tower of London in the reign of Charles II. Blood had led many punitive expeditions in the Northwest Frontier of India, and Churchill extracted from the general a promise that if ever he commanded another expedition on the Indian frontier he would let his young friend ac-company him. There, too, at a dinner party given for the Prince of Wales Churchill arrived twenty minutes late, having missed the train. The Prince of Wales was fuming because Churchill was the fourteenth guest and he refused to sit thirteen at table; and when at last Churchill arrived, he received from the Prince of Wales the withering rebuke: "Don't they teach you to be punctual in your regiment, Winston?"

In this way Churchill met all the influential people of his time and took pains to cultivate them. He was likable, fresh-faced, eager for compliments, knowledgeable on many matters, ferociously ambitious.

Yet in spite of all his social advantages he was getting nowhere. He was a subaltern in a not very distinguished regiment. He wanted to be a Minister of the Crown with power to order the destiny of the nation, and he thought he could achieve this ambition by feats of great boldness, suitably rewarded by medals, on the battlefield. The path was mapped out: first, military glory, then a seat in Parliament, then a ministerial position. Shortly before his regiment left for India he wrote to his mother beseeching her to use all her influence to have him sent to a front where he could earn his spurs:

> The future is to me utterly unattractive. I look upon going to India with this unfortunate regiment—(which I now feel so attached to that I cannot leave it for another)—as useless and unprofitable exile.
>
> When I speculate on what might be and consider that I am letting the golden opportunity go by I feel that I am guilty of an indolent folly that I shall regret all my life. A few months in South Africa would earn me the S.A. medal and in all probability the company's Star. Thence hot foot to Egypt—to return with two more decorations in a year or two—and beat my sword into an iron despatch box. Both are within the bounds of possibility and yet here I am out of both. I cannot believe that with all the influential friends you possess and all those who would do something for me for my father's sake—that I could not be allowed to go—were those influences properly exerted.

His own and his mother's efforts proved to be quite useless, and he went off with his regiment to Bangalore in southern India, where there was no fighting, no opportunity for military glory and no prospect of a ministerial dispatch box. Arriving in Bombay Harbor and being ferried to the dock, he leaned out of the wherry bringing him to shore, seized a heavy iron ring on the side of the dock, and half dislocated his shoulder with the result that he was troubled with his right shoulder for all the remaining years of his life.

Bangalore might be a place of unprofitable exile but it had its own pleasant rewards. It was 3,000 feet above sea level; the mornings and evenings were fresh and cool; and in the pink and white stucco house where he lived with two fellow officers there was an abundance of servants including a butler, two valets, two gardeners, three water carriers, four washermen, one watchman and five or six grooms to look after the horses and ponies. He cultivated roses on a massive scale, collected brilliantly colored butterflies, played polo every afternoon and lived the life of a perfect sybarite. His duties were minimal but sometimes included supervising practice at the rifle butts. Once a bullet ricocheted off the iron target and a small fragment entered his hand, giving him the only wound he ever received. Other officers went down with malaria and typhoid fever, but Churchill remained in remarkably good health, suffering an occasional bruised knee at polo but being otherwise unharmed.

He was also beginning to give himself an education by reading extensively. From November to May he read steadily for four or five hours every day. He read Plato's *Republic,* Gibbon's *The Decline and Fall of the Roman Empire,* Macaulay's *Essays* and his *History of England,* Lecky's *History of European Morals,* Winwood Reade's *The Martyrdom of Man* and Schopenhauer's *Essays.* Gibbon and Macaulay especially impressed him, and though he rejected the gloomy conclusions of Schopenhauer and Winwood Reade, his mind was always to be colored by a kind of visionary pessimism. In the end all action is vain; all empires perish; death wins. Nevertheless there was honor in performing great deeds and death's victory was perhaps as vain as man's temporary triumphs. From his reading he hammered out a philosophy of life which he expressed briefly: "After all, a man's life must be nailed to a cross either of Thought or Action." It is not a very workable philosophy because it totally obscured the boundaries between Thought and Action. He chose Action but informed it with as much Thought as he could muster. He still aimed to cover himself with military glory in South Africa and Egypt, and perhaps—for the idea was at last beginning to occur to him—to write his own accounts of his great deeds. But after nine months in Bangalore, having read much but accomplished no action whatsoever, he found he was entitled to three months accumulated leave and returned to London, stopping on the way for two weeks of leisurely wandering in Italy and visiting Rome to pay tribute to the ghost of Gibbon.

He stayed only a few weeks in England, for while attending Goodwood races in July he opened a newspaper and saw that fighting had broken out on the Northwest Frontier and General Sir Bindon Blood was in charge. Churchill promptly telegraphed the general, reminded him of his promise, and received a reply saying that there were no vacancies on his staff but he was welcome to join the expedition as a war correspondent. In a high state of excitement Churchill hurried across France and Italy, caught the Indian mail steamer at Brindisi and was back in Bangalore by the middle of August to report to the colonel of his regiment. *The Daily Telegraph* agreed to pay him £5 a column for his dispatches and *The Pioneer* of Allahabad, which had been Rudyard Kipling's newspaper, also agreed to publish them. The colonel gave him leave of absence and almost immediately he was traveling by train to the Northwest Frontier, a journey of more than 2,000 miles. He was very happy, for there was going to be a big war and he would be in the thick of it. Everything happened as he wanted it to happen except that there was no big war, only a series of small bloody skirmishes.

General Sir Bindon Blood entertained the young war correspondent at dinner in his encampment on the edge of the Mamund Valley. Sometimes the tribesmen fired joy shots into the camp, and for a while during dinner it was thought advisable to eat in darkness. Churchill was told he could accompany one of the brigades advancing into the valley on a punitive expedition. The army which had marched off 1,200-strong for some reason became dispersed and Churchill found himself at the head of the valley with a small group consisting of four British officers and about eighty-five Sikhs. They reached a small, abandoned mud-walled village. It was eerily quiet and obviously something had gone wrong. The captain of the company came up and said: "We are going to withdraw. You stay here and cover our retirement." The British officers and the Sikhs seemed to regard this as a perfectly normal order. The captain went away, and once more they waited for something to happen. Ten minutes passed. Nothing happened. Then the long silence was interrupted by distant screaming and shouting, and suddenly all the hills and rocks above them seemed to be infested with tribesmen "dropping from ledge to ledge like monkeys down the branches of a tall tree." They flowed down the mountainside, and when they were a hundred yards away Churchill decided that it was no longer possible for him to be a passive spectator. He was lying on the ground beside a Sikh armed with a Martini rifle, and he took the rifle and began firing. The battalion adjutant came up and told them they would have to fall back. This was a difficult task, and it might have been safer to fight it out. A British officer was spinning round, his face a mass of blood, his right eye cut out. Two Sikhs carried him down the slope, and one of them was wounded in the leg and began screaming, but what Churchill chiefly remembered was how strange he looked when his turban fell off and his long black hair streamed over his shoulders. The adjutant, a heavy man, was wounded; his bearers, seeing the Pathans advancing on them, dropped him; and the adjutant was left to the mercy of a Pathan who hacked at him with a sword. This was more than Churchill could bear, and he advanced on the Pathan with his drawn sword sharpened to a razor edge, and then thought better of it and drew out his revolver and fired several shots at the tribesman who vanished behind some rocks. Somehow the small company of Sikhs withdrew, carrying their wounded, leaving behind them one dead British officer and a dozen dying Sikhs to be cut to pieces by the enemy. Churchill with his usual good luck was unharmed. This was his only serious engagement with the enemy. In the following days he accompanied the troops as they fanned out across the valley and leveled the mud-walled villages, filled up the wells, burned the crops, cut down the trees and destroyed the reservoirs of the villagers in a wide-sweeping punitive action. The tribesmen had suffered too many losses to fight and they remained high up in the hills.

Churchill's book on the brief campaign, called *The Story of the Malakand Field Force,* amounts to nearly four hundred pages in the only available edition. He was not spreading himself thin, for the book is an attempt to set the campaign in historical perspective, to give color and depth to the strange events on the frontier. It was deservedly successful, and since it was read by many influential people in the government it fulfilled his purpose. He had hoped to distinguish himself on the battlefield and to earn a medal. He received no medal, but in his dispatches Sir Bindon Blood praised "the courage and resolution of Lieut. W. L. S. Churchill, 4th Hussars, the correspondent of the *Pioneer* newspaper with the force, who made himself useful at a critical moment."

He was back in Bangalore in October, playing polo, attending to his roses and collecting butterflies. He was writing hard, revising the articles he had written for the *Daily Telegraph* and *The Pioneer* to shape them into a book. He began a novel, and sketched out in considerable detail an article called "The Scaffolding of Rhetoric," which was designed as a scaffolding for his own oratorical skills. His wide reading during the previous winter was bearing fruit and he was now thinking his own thoughts and hammering them into shape. The article on oratory is a remarkable document, for he is writing for the first time on a subject that was later to engross him. He wrote:

> Of all the talents bestowed upon men, none is so precious as the gift of oratory. He who enjoys it wields a power more durable than that of a great king. He is an independent force in the world. Abandoned by his party, betrayed by his friends, stripped of his offices, whoever can command this power is still formidable. . . .

The orator is real. The rhetoric is partly artificial. Partly, but not wholly; for the nature of the artist is the spirit of his art, and much that appears to be the result of study is due to instinct. If we examine this strange being by the light of history we shall discover that he is in character sympathetic, sentimental and earnest: that he is often as easily influenced by others as others by him. Indeed the orator is the embodiment of the passions of the multitude. Before he can inspire them with any emotion he must be swayed by it himself. When he would rouse their indignation his heart is filled with anger. Before he can move their tears his own must flow. To convince them he must himself believe. His opinions may change as their impressions fade, but every orator means what he says at the moment he says it. He may be often inconsistent. He is never consciously insincere. . . .

First of all a striking presence is necessary. Often small, ugly or deformed he is invested with a personal significance, which varying in every case defies definition. Sometimes a slight and not unpleasing stammer or impediment has been of some assistance in securing the attention of the audience, but usually a clear and resonant voice gives expression of his thoughts.

He went on to examine six principal aspects of oratory: correct diction, rhythm, accumulation of argument, analogy, examples and deliberate extravagance of language. The short, old words were best. The cadences should be long, rolling and sonorous. The argument should consist of a series of facts all pointing in a single direction, all vividly depicted and marshaled so that the audience is led irresistibly to a single conclusion. Apt analogies were essential and the wildest extravagances were permitted in order to inflame the imagination of the audience. He gave as an example to be imitated the Earl of Chatham's speech on the excise bill:

The poorest man may in his cottage bid defiance to all the forces of the Crown. It may be frail; its roof may shake; the wind may blow through it; the storms may enter; the rain may enter—but the King of England cannot enter! All his forces dare not cross the threshold of the ruined tenement.

Rhetoric, in Churchill's view, was the key to the hearts of men, a mysterious faculty that demanded the utmost skill and an iron scaffolding. He was well aware that evil men could use their powers of oratory for evil purposes:

The orator who wished to incite his audience to a deed of violence would follow his accumulative argument, his rhythmical periods, his vivid word-pictures, by a moderate and reasonable conclusion. The cooling drink will be withheld from the thirsty men. The safety valves will be screwed down and the people will go out into the night to find the expression of their feelings for themselves.

This was cunning of a high order, for he showed that it was perfectly possible for the orator to incite to deeds of violence without in the least declaring his real aims. All he had to do was to leave them with a feeling of total frustration—the cooling drink withheld from them. When printed in the newspapers, the speech would not look like incitement to violence; nevertheless the city was burned down and he had provided the spark. Churchill thought there were safeguards against such provocation, but there are none. Hitler showed that he was possessed of this power to inflame the masses by enlarging on their frustrations. Without these safeguards, Churchill suggested that rhetoric would long since have been adjudged a crime.

Fame was the quarry; oratory and military glory would, he felt, bring him the fame he desired. He was still, at twenty-two, a subaltern in Bangalore eating his heart away. Another year passed before he was permitted to engage in martial exploits. The scenario was being repeated. Once more he was on home leave when he heard the announcement that a punitive expedition was about to be sent into the Sudan. At all costs he was determined to join it. He had useful allies including Lord Salisbury, who was Prime Minister and Foreign Secretary. Lord Salisbury had read *The Story of the Malakand Field Force* with approval, and Churchill quite properly asked for the Prime Minister's assistance in getting him sent to the Sudan as a member of the expeditionary forces or as a war correspondent. A telegram was sent to Sir Herbert Kitchener, the Commander in Chief of the Egyptian Army, who replied that he did not want Churchill at any cost. Churchill's friend Lady Mary Jeune, a well-known hostess of the time, then appealed to the Adjutant General, Sir Evelyn Wood, who was not on the best of terms with Kitchener. Wood gave his permission and seconded him to the 21st Lancers, while the *Morning Post* offered him £15 a column. There was no time to seek the permission of his colonel in Bangalore. In August he was in Cairo. On September 2, at dawn, 20,000 British troops met an army three times their number on the field of Omdurman. The Dervishes attacked, but Kitchener's artillery smashed and cut to pieces the huge wave of men carrying banners, and those who survived the artillery were met with disciplined volleys of rifle fire. They wavered and broke, and as they began to fall away and scatter, the 21st Lancers were ordered to charge them and complete the rout. This was the last classic cavalry charge in the history of British warfare. There were four squadrons of lancers—400 men and horses—surging across the plain with leveled lances. Suddenly they found themselves in a broad nullah where the enemy had prepared an ambush. Churchill, cut off from the main force, watched a Dervish hurling himself on the ground. He wrote:

> My first idea therefore was that the man was terrified. But simultaneously I saw the gleam of his curved sword as he drew it back for a ham-stringing cut. I had room and time enough to turn my pony out of his reach, and leaning over on the offside I fired two shots into him at about three yards. As I straightened myself in the saddle, I saw before me another figure with uplifted sword. I raised my pistol and fired. So close were we that the pistol itself actually struck him. Man and sword disappeared below and behind me. On my left, ten yards away, was an Arab horseman in a bright-colored tunic and steel helmet, with chain-mail hangings. I fired at him. I pulled my horse into a walk and looked around again. . . .
>
> There was a mass of Dervishes about forty or fifty yards on my left. They were huddling and clumping themselves together, rallying for mutual protection. They seemed wild with excitement, dancing about on their feet, shaking their spears up and down. The whole scene seemed to flicker. I have an impression, but it is too fleeting to define, of brown-clad Lancers mixed up here and there with this surging mob. The scattered individuals in my immediate neighborhood made no attempt to molest me. Where was my troop? Where were the other troops of the squadron? Within a hundred yards of me I could not see a single officer or man. I looked back at the Dervish mass. I saw two or three riflemen crouching and aiming their rifles at men from the fringe of it. Then for the first time that morning I experienced a sudden sensation of fear. I felt myself absolutely alone. I thought these riflemen would hit me and the rest devour me like wolves. What a fool I was to loiter like this in the midst of the enemy! I crouched over the saddle, spurred my horse into a gallop and drew clear of the *mêlée*.

He was leading a charmed life, but others were less lucky. The Lancers lost nearly a quarter of their strength in men and horses. The Dervishes hacked and mutilated the bodies of the Lancers who fell into their hands, and carried off their own wounded. Three days later, after burying their dead, the 21st Lancers were on their way to Cairo.

Out of his short experience in the Sudan came thirteen dispatches to the *Morning Post* and a full-length study of the campaign called *The River War*, which was published in two stout volumes. Once again, as when he was writing *The Story of the Malakand Field Force*, he was attempting to describe much more than the engagement in which he took part. It was to be a history of British intervention in the Sudan with his reflections on imperialism and the attendant dangers and advantages of conquest, and of all his books it is the most carefully written and the most scholarly.

Running to wars, experiencing brief encounters with the enemy, and then writing enormous volumes about the background of these wars had become part of the constancy of his youth. In the following year came another brief engagement. This time he accomplished what he set out to accomplish and almost by accident became world famous.

In October, 1899, he sailed to South Africa to report the Boer War as a special correspondent for the *Morning Post*. He was to receive £250 a month and all expenses paid. Within two weeks of his arrival he was captured by the Boers. A month later he escaped into Portuguese East Africa, and nearly every newspaper in the world carried the news of his escape. He had made the headlines at last.

Both in the Mamund Valley and at Omdurman he was caught in an ambush, and here in South Africa he was caught in his third ambush. He was traveling in an armored train out of Estcourt on November 15, 1899, on a mission of reconnaissance. The train was charging round a curve when it ran into a big rock placed on the line. The engine was in the middle of the train with three cars in front and two more behind. The three front cars were derailed, the last of them completely blocking the line. Churchill took command of the engine while Captain Haldane commanded the troops on the train who were defending themselves against the well-directed fire of the Boers. As a war correspondent, Churchill had no business taking command of anything, but since the engine driver had been struck by a shell fragment and it was obviously necessary to try to push the derailed cars off the line so that the train could return to Estcourt, he did what duty told him to do. He gave orders to the engine driver, succeeded in pushing the derailed cars completely off the line, and at the end of an hour had freed the engine and tender so that it could return to Estcourt with the survivors and some forty men wounded in the engagement. He was still directing the operations of the train when he saw two men in plain clothes on the line. At first he thought they were platelayers, but they were Boers. A few moments later a horseman rode up and aimed at him from a distance of forty yards. Churchill's hand went to his belt for the Mauser pistol which he carried in spite of the fact that he was a war correspondent and therefore not permitted to carry any weapon at all. Fortunately it was not there, and seeing that there was nothing to be done he raised his hands in surrender. His captor was a Boer farmer called Louis Botha, who was soon to become the first president of the Union of South Africa.

Many others from the train were captured, and soon Churchill was under detention in the State Model Schools in Pretoria, which had been converted into a prison for British officers. The prison was guarded by about forty police with ten of them permanently on duty on the four sides of the enclosure. The police were armed and none of the British officers had escaped. Churchill was determined to escape, but he was in a strange depressed state, sometimes ebullient but more often morose, as though he could not yet bring himself to believe that he was a captive and was terrified by the prospect that he might be imprisoned for a long time. He was reading John Stuart Mill's book, *On Liberty*, with its heady arguments demonstrating man's right to liberty of opinion even if everyone in the world is against him; and thus fortified, on the night of December 12 he slipped over the wall, made his way through Pretoria unrecognized, and after walking for two hours in the open country, he clambered onto a slow-moving train and found refuge in a car full of empty coal sacks. He slept for a while and awoke with the realization that he was in danger of being caught when the coal sacks were taken off the train. He jumped off the train, found himself in some woods, and spent the day wandering near the railroad line, not knowing what to do, trusting to chance and the mysterious beckonings of the unconscious. He had sometimes played with the planchette, a wheeled board provided with a pencil, and with his hand holding the pencil he had written strange sentences without conscious direction or effort. So it was now. He wandered about in uncertainty but with the certain knowledge that he was making for safety. At dusk he came to a house near a coal mine and decided to knock. The door was opened by an Englishman, and he had come to the only house owned by an Englishman within twenty miles.

"I want help," he said. "I have had an accident."

At first the Englishman seemed bemused, and then when Churchill admitted his identity he went into action. At great risk to himself he decided to conceal Churchill in a mine shaft. Other Englishmen worked in the mine and they were taken into the secret. The alarm had already gone out and the Boer Government was offering a reward of £25 for his capture dead or alive:

WANTED

Englishman twenty-five years old, about five feet eight inches tall, of indifferent build, walks with a slight stoop, pale appearance, red-brown hair, small mustache barely perceptible, talks through the nose, cannot pronounce "s" properly and does not know any Dutch.

Except for the height it was a good description, but Churchill was always to remain a little offended at the thought that he was worth no more than £25. John Howard, his host, concealed him well, and since he had a number of bales of wool to consign to Lourenço Marques in Portuguese East Africa, it was decided to hide him among the wool sacks and Charles Burnham, who ran the company store, was deputed to travel on the same train and keep watch over the cargo. In this way, in the late afternoon of December 19, he arrived in Lourenço Marques to discover that a steamer was sailing for Durban the same night. When he reached Durban he discovered that his escape was known all over the world. He promptly wrote an article for the *Morning Post* in which he described his escape, but without mentioning Howard, Burnham and the others who had assisted him, for they would have been arrested if their assistance had become known.

At Durban he was received with acclamation as the hero of the hour. Sir Redvers Buller asked: "Is there anything I can do for you?" and he answered at once: "Give me a commission." So he became a lieutenant in the South African Light Horse, known as the Cockyoly birds because of the spray of feathers in their wide-brimmed hats. He was present at the relief of Ladysmith and then joined Lord Roberts in his slow advance on Johannesburg and Pretoria. With the help of a French miner called Lautré, who served as a guide, he bicycled through Johannesburg when it was still occupied by the enemy. It was not all derring-do, for there were bloody battles at Spion Kop and Diamond Hill where the British fared badly. Then it was all over and he was back in England to attend his mother's wedding to George Cornwallis-West and to stand for Parliament in the "Khaki Election." He won his seat handsomely. Already he had told many people that he would become Prime Minister of Britain and now even that was within his reach.

He was a young man in a hurry, and to those who knew him well he would explain that he was forced to hurry because he did not expect to live very long. His father had died at forty-five and it was likely that he would die at about the same age.

George Stevens, the war correspondent who met him on the ship returning from Omdurman, described him as "the youngest man in Europe. He is ambitious and he is calculating, yet he is not cold—and that saves him," Stevens wrote. "At the rate he goes, there will hardly be room for him in Parliament at thirty or in England at forty." Stevens also noted his failings: He could not laugh at himself, he had a steady flow of conversation which resembled an endless speech to a vast audience, he was grossly immodest, and he had few real friends. He was a man at the mercy of his soaring ambitions. Already he had achieved many of them. He was a Member of Parliament; he had acquired as much fame as he could reasonably deal with; he had seen many battles, and written several books. Only one prize remained, and he would wait forty years until it was given to him. Since for him this prize was the only one worth having, he regarded all those forty years as being spent in the wilderness.

THREE BOOKS

Between march, 1898, and February, 1900, Churchill published three books which originally appeared in magazines and newspapers, and in addition he published a short story called "Man Overboard—An Episode of the Red Sea." All of them in their different ways shed light on his character, his fears, his ambitions.

The short story, which appeared in *Harmsworth Magazine* in 1899, is a slight work, carefully constructed, but without any pretensions to literature. Originally Churchill had hoped it would be published in Alfred Harmsworth's *Daily Mail*, which had a wider circulation. Lady Randolph, who acted as his literary agent, appears to have had some difficulty in getting it published. When it finally appeared, it was spread out over three pages of the magazine with drawings by Henry Austin to fill out the space. To distinguish him from the well-known American writer Winston Churchill, he signed himself Winston Spencer Churchill and there was a cautionary footnote: "As by a very remarkable coincidence there are two Winston Churchills, both writers, we may mention that this Mr. Churchill is the son of the late Lord Randolph Churchill."

The story is interesting because it is a reworking of an experience he had felt very deeply when he was visiting Switzerland in his schooldays and nearly drowned in Lake Leman. In the story a man on a mail steamer traveling through the Red Sea feels uncomfortably hot while his fellow passengers are crowding round the piano and singing lustily. Suddenly he decides to walk out on the empty deck. He smiles, smokes a cigarette, enjoys the music from a distance and leans against a railing, which snaps, so that he falls backwards into the sea. He shouts for help, but no one on the ship can hear him. From far away comes the singing:

> *Then-I-say-boys,*
> *Who's for a jolly spree?*
> *Rum-rum-tiddley-um,*
> *Who'll have a drink with me?*
> *Fond of a glass now and then,*
> *Fond of a row or noise.*
> *Hi! Hi! clear the way*
> *For the Rowdy Dowdy Boys!*

As he swims after the ship, hoping it will stop and send out a lifeboat, the man who only a few minutes before was perfectly content with life realizes that he is suddenly caught up in a terrible drama. Sobbing quietly, in the misery of fear, he continues to swim mechanically in the wake of the ship until at last the faint yellow stern light vanishes from sight, and he knows he will never be found. Exhausted, he decides to die.

> He threw up his hands impulsively and sank. Down, down he went through the warm water. The physical death took hold of him and he began to drown. The pain of that savage grip recalled his anger. He fought with it furiously. Striking out with arms and legs he sought to get back to the air. It was a hard struggle, but he escaped victorious and gasping to the surface. Despair awaited him. Feebly splashing with his hands he moaned in bitter misery—
> "I can't—I must. O God! let me die."
> The moon, then in her third quarter, pushed out from behind the concealing clouds and shed a pale, soft glitter upon the sea. Upright in the water, fifty yards away, was a black triangular object. It was a fin. It approached him slowly.
> His last appeal had been heard.

So ends Churchill's first and last short story, and it is perhaps significant that it should be concerned with physical death in one of its most savage and bloody forms, and that he carefully left it to the reader's imagination to fill out the cruel details. Death haunted him and a peculiarly sharp awareness of death was never far from him.

In *Savrola*, his only novel, written when he was a young Lancer in India, death is present in a more histrionic form. Churchill, describing a revolution in Laurania, a Mediterranean republic apparently situated on the northern shores of Africa, but possessing in its physical features a certain resemblance to Cuba, paints death as the evil but inevitable fruit of revolution. Death is what happens to conspirators and the luckless crowds caught in the crossfire. The chief conspirator is Savrola, the somewhat aristocratic thirty-two-year-old leader of the National Party, rich and elegant, possessing a town house in a fashionable part of town with a glass-walled observatory on the roof. To this observatory it is his habit to come at the end of a day's work to gaze upon the splendors of the stars and to ponder the insignificance of mankind. His expensive, electrically driven astronomical telescope was his talisman, and his secret vice, for no one else was permitted to gaze into it. Savrola has no faith in mankind, which is doomed to vanish on a cooling planet. Nevertheless he believes profoundly in power, in the necessity for great men to arise and dominate their circumstance. The telescope is directed at the planet Saturn, while Savrola contemplates the extinction of the universe:

> He thought of the future of Jupiter, of the incomprehensible periods that would elapse before the cooling process would render life possible on its surface, of the slow, steady march of evolution, merciless, inexorable. How far would it carry them, the unborn inhabitants of an embryo world? Perhaps only to some vague distortion of the vital essence; perhaps further than he could dream of. All the problems would be solved, all the obstacles overcome, life would attain perfect development. And then fancy, overleaping space and time, carried the story to periods still more remote. The cooling process would continue; the perfect development of life would end in death; the whole solar system, the whole universe itself, would one day be cold and lifeless as a burned-out firework.
>
> It was a mournful conclusion. He locked up the observatory and descended the stairs, hoping that his dreams would contradict his thoughts.

Savrola was the prey of many mournful thoughts, yet as Churchill depicted him he was a very credible Hamlet in modern clothes. He had the tragic vision, but he was also the man of action, caught up in the unreasoning desire to prove himself and to leave a mark on history. "Ambition was the motive force and he was powerless to resist it," Churchill writes of Savrola. "Vehement, high and daring was his cast of mind." We soon become aware that Laurania has acquired its own Churchill and that the novel is an astonishingly accurate projection of his own political activities written long before he had embarked on a political career. It is not only that Savrola is Churchill, but he is Churchill seen with candor and intelligence and in three dimensions. Churchill had been given the rarest of gifts—the gift of prophecy.

When the story opens, the people of Laurania are in a rebellious mood as they crowd into the great square outside the Parliament House. For five years they have lived under the dictatorship of President Antonio Molara, but at last the dictator has had a change of heart. The dictator has agreed to hold elections, but at the same time he has taken measures to mutilate the registers of citizenship and disenfranchised half the electorate. This has become known to the crowd just at the moment when the presidential carriage, led by four horses and an escort of Lancers, enters the square. The president's life is in danger, and when someone at the back of the crowd fires a revolver in the air, the Lancers charge and foot soldiers shoot into the crowd. A few moments later the square is empty except for forty bodies lying in pools of blood.

The president, well pleased with himself, drives into the courtyard of his palace and congratulates the officers of his guard, especially a young subaltern who had given the order to fire. He was twenty-two years old, and could hope for speedy promotion. Then the president enters the palace where the mosaics in the great pillared hall tell the ancient story of Laurania:

> . . . the foundation of the city; the peace of 1370; the reception of the envoys of the Great Mogul; the victory of Brota; the death of Saldanho, that austere patriot, who died rather than submit to a technical violation of the Constitution. And then coming down to later years, the walls showed the building of the Parliament House: the naval victory of Cape Cheronta, and finally the conclusion of the Civil War in 1883.

At this point the reader becomes aware that there are strange similarities between Laurania and London, and these similarities become even clearer when Lucile Molara, the young and beautiful wife of the dictator, gazes out of the palace at the ships in the harbor and the gardens of the city. The author seems to be standing in Parliament Square and seeing London through a soft Mediterranean haze.

Savrola himself is a latecomer on the scene. He was not present during the shooting outside the Parliament House, and when we first encounter him he is attempting to calm the members of his own National Party, who are outraged by the shooting and talking about revenge. Savrola, instead, talks about giving the dictator enough rope to hang himself. Instead of a popular uprising with all its inevitable bloodshed, Savrola prefers to embark on a conspiracy with the aim of striking terror into the heart of the dictator. Having delivered himself of his views, he returns to his apartment to enjoy a lonely supper in his well-stocked library. Churchill describes the library with a glance at his own bookshelves in Bangalore:

> The room was lit by electric light in portable shaded lamps. The walls were covered with shelves, filled with well-used volumes. To that Pantheon of Literature none were admitted until they had been read and valued. It was a various library: the philosophy of Schopenhauer divided Kant from Hegel, who jostled the *Memoirs* of St. Simon and the latest French novel; *Rasselas* and *La Curée* lay side by side; eight substantial volumes of Gibbon's famous *History* were not perhaps inappropriately prolonged by a fine edition of the *Decameron*; the *Origin of Species* rested by the side of a black-letter Bible; *The Republic* maintained an equilibrium with *Vanity Fair* and the *History of European Morals*. A volume of Macaulay's *Essays* lay on the writing-table itself; it was open, and that sublime passage whereby the genius of one man has immortalised the genius of another was marked in pencil. *And History, while for the warning of vehement, high, and daring natures, she notes his many errors, will yet deliberately pronounce that among the eminent men whose bones lie near his, scarcely one has left a more stainless, and none a more splendid name.*
>
> A half-empty box of cigarettes stood on a small table near a low leathern armchair, and by its side lay a heavy army revolver, against the barrel of which the ashes of many cigarettes had been removed. In the corner of the room stood a small but exquisite Capitoline Venus, the cold chastity of its colour reproaching the allurements of its form. It was the chamber of a philosopher, but of no frigid, academic recluse; it was the chamber of a man, a human man, who appreciated all earthly pleasures, appraised them at their proper worth, enjoyed and despised them.

The serpent's sting comes with the last two words. Savrola is the archromantic with a revolver always within reach. He possesses no

books in the Lauranian dialects, but contents himself with the English
classics, German philosophers, Plato and two books in French,
precisely the books which Churchill was reading in Bangalore. Almost
the room portrays the man, the young artist whose "vehement, high,
and daring nature" would seem inevitably to lead him to a spec-
tacularly romantic death.

But in fact nothing like this happens, for Savrola is one of those who
survive all dangers and indeed he finds strength in the pursuit of danger.
Like Churchill, who wrote to his mother at this time: "I am more
ambitious for a reputation for personal courage than for anything else
in the world," Savrola will endure all dangers and take the most
exquisite pleasure in his own survival. He will dare the utmost, but to
what end? This is the question that absorbs him. If only fame were
eternal, if only there was some meaning to life, if only the stars in their
courses had not assured him of the nullity of all living things! The
romantic hero expresses a fashionable nihilistic philosophy which is
derived partly from Schopenhauer and partly from Churchill's inability
to acquire even a glimmer of Christian faith.

News of Savrola's speech reaches the dictator, who announces that it
is absolutely necessary to bring about the downfall of the revolutionary.
"Wanted—a Delilah!" he declares, and a Delilah is close at hand in the
person of Lucile, whose beauty is only one of her many weapons. To
serve her husband she agrees to attempt to compromise Savrola and to
ferret out his secret intentions at a reception given in honor of the King
of Ethiopia. The reception is described jauntily. We encounter the
British ambassador, Sir Richard Shalgrove, K.G., the youthful Countess
of Ferrol and the Princess of Tarentum. The King of Ethiopia leaves
early, being horrified by the low dresses of the unveiled women,
Churchill having confused the Christian Lion of Judah with an Arab
Sultan. Once the King of Ethiopia is out of the way, Lucile maneuvers
Savrola into the quiet garden of the presidential palace for a tête-à-tête.

Savrola has no intention of revealing his secrets. Instead he embarks
on a general survey of his hard-won philosophical nihilism, the inevitable decay of all societies under the sun and the equally inevitable
annihilation of all mankind in an extinct universe. The argument is
spirited and conclusive. Here is Savrola arguing on behalf of total
extinction:

> "Ultimately the dominant race will degenerate, and as there will be
> none to take its place, the degeneration must continue. It is the old

struggle between vitality and decay, between energy and indolence; a
struggle that always ends in silence. After all, we could not expect human
development to be constant. It is only a question of time before the
planet becomes unfitted to support life on its surface."

"But you said that fitness must ultimately triumph."

"Over relative unfitness, yes. But decay will involve all victors and
vanquished. The fire of life will die out, the spirit of vitality become
extinct."

"In this world perhaps."

"In every world. All the universe is cooling--dying, that is—and as it
cools, life for a spell becomes possible on the surface of its spheres, and
plays strange antics. And then the end comes; the universe dies and is
sepulchred in the cold darkness of ultimate negation."

"To what purpose then are all our efforts?"

"God knows," said Savrola cynically, "but I can imagine that the
drama would not be an uninteresting one to watch."

Such were Savrola's conclusions uttered in a dark garden under the
stars, and Lucile was sufficiently intrigued by them to ask for more.
"We are consequential atoms," Savrola announces portentously, but he
is not sure what the consequences are. Lucile suggests that after death
all the mysteries will be resolved. Savrola answers: "If I thought that, I
should kill myself tonight out of irresistible curiosity." He has taken her
measure, revealed no secrets, and shown himself to be a man of high
moral purpose and philosophical calm. Lucile is gradually falling in
love with him.

Savrola, well aware of the effect he has produced on her, goes off to
contemplate the next step of the drama of the people versus a dictatorship. He decides to deliver a rousing speech that will bring
everything to the boil. We are well-informed about the composition of
his speeches, for Churchill describes it at considerable length with a
proper feeling for cadence and alliteration.

His speech—he had made many and knew that nothing good can be
obtained without effort. These impromptu feats of oratory existed only in
the minds of the listeners; the flowers of rhetoric were hothouse plants.

What was there to say? Successive cigarettes had been mechanically
consumed. Amid the smoke he saw a peroration, which would cut deep
into the hearts of a crowd; a high thought, a fine simile, expressed in that
correct diction which is comprehensible even to the most illiterate, and
appeals to the most simple; something to lift their minds from the

material cares of life and to awake sentiment. His ideas began to take the form of words, to group themselves into sentences; he murmured to himself; the rhythm of his own language swayed him; instinctively he alliterated. Ideas succeeded one another, as a stream flows swiftly by and the light changes on its waters. He seized a piece of paper and began hurriedly to pencil notes. That was a point; could not tautology accentuate it? He scribbled down a rough sentence, scratched it out, polished it, and wrote it in again. The sound would please their ears, the sense improve and stimulate their minds. What a game it was! His brain contained the cards he had to play, the world the stakes he played for.

What a game it was! Suddenly we become aware that Savrola is gambling for high stakes—the world. We are not told why the opposition leader of a rather small country on the Mediterranean littoral hopes for so much, the world being so vast and human ability so small. What Savrola meant by the world is perhaps no more than world fame. Nevertheless it appears that his ambitions are limitless: this "consequential atom" will dominate all other atoms if he can.

The dreams of the young officer at Bangalore were not small dreams. He had never in his life delivered a political speech, unless we include the wild oration delivered at the Empire Theatre against the Purity Campaign of Mrs. Ormiston Chant during his final year at Sandhurst. Yet he had thought a great deal about speechmaking, and as he describes Savrola at work in 1888, he might be describing Churchill at work in 1940. In just this way—painfully, slowly, elaborately, arranging the words so that they will give the impression of effortless ease—did Churchill compose his speeches. Strangely, the very themes of Savrola echo the themes of Churchill in wartime England. Here is Savrola addressing a vast crowd of his followers at the city hall of Laurania:

> When I look at this beautiful country that is ours and was our fathers' before us, at its blue seas and snow-capped mountains, at its comfortable hamlets and wealthy cities, at its silver streams and golden cornfields, I marvel at the irony of fate which has struck across so fair a prospect the dark shadow of a military despotism.

It is not, of course, a good speech, because the sense of urgency is lacking. But the essential elements are all present, and we can almost hear the rasping voice as it fastens on the words "the dark shadow," pauses, then spits out the words "of a military despotism." Savrola spoke for an hour at the city hall and thought it the best speech he had ever delivered. He had held the audience spellbound, confounded his opponents within the Nationalist Party and thrown Lucile, who was present, into a state bordering on delirium, so swept away by the vigor and brilliance of his speech that she scarcely knew where she was and totally forgot her promises to her husband. Savrola collapses into a chair, drinks some water, and shivers uncontrollably under the stress of his emotions, while the crowd cheers wildly for five minutes.

As the excited mob pours out of the City Hall, Lucile is carried off her feet and a "dark burly man" jabs her in the breast with his elbow. She screams, there are cries for help, and Savrola jumps off the platform to go to her assistance. She is, of course, heavily veiled, but he recognizes her. He has the presence of mind to cry out: "Why, Mirette, my little niece! How could you come alone to such a crowded place at night!" Then, while Lucile leans on his arm, he walks down the steps to the waiting carriage. "Where to, Sir?" asks the coachman. "Home," he replies, and the stage is set for another tête-à-tête between the dictator's wife and the tribune of the people.

But before this happens, a new and sinister element has entered the scene. Two men of foreign aspect, members of a secret society determined to use the Nationalist Party for their own purposes, are heard discussing the speech. "He is a good tool to work with at present," says one of them in his most conspiratorial manner. "The time will come when we shall need something sharper. He has no sympathy with the cause. What does he care about the community of goods?"

Thus the Communist conspiracy makes its first entry on the stage of Laurania. We learn the name of the leading conspirator, Karl Kreutze, and it is evident that he has a following among the workers and threatens the position of the "great Democrat" Savrola. Savrola will have nothing to do with Kreutze, and Churchill, having brought him on the stage, finds little for him to do. Finally he is permitted to murder the dictator. He is a *deus ex machina*, felt rather than seen, implacable and terrible as he hovers on the wings of the stage.

We know from Churchill's letters to his mother that the first eighty pages of the novel were written without any difficulty, freshly and easily. The characters came vividly to life and the incidents followed one another in a credible order. We believe, or half believe, in Molara, Lucile and Savrola, and as the novel progresses we come to believe in the reality of Laurania. But after writing the chapter where Savrola takes Lucile home, Churchill laid the novel aside for some weeks, and when he returned to it, he had apparently lost the thread and was compelled to improvise. Suddenly we hear that HMS *Aggressor* (12,000 tons displacement, 14,000 horsepower, armed with four eleven-inch guns) is steaming toward Laurania's African port, and that the British collier *Maude* has been deliberately sunk in the Suez Canal to prevent the Lauranian fleet from steaming to the rescue of its only African port. HMS *Aggressor* and the British collier are soon forgotten, and a more fateful enemy appears in the shape of an invasion force of 2,000 men advancing across the frontier under the command of General Strelitz. Exactly where the general has come from, and why he is invading Laurania are not clear. The dictator sends more than half of his available troops to meet the invader, and Savrola, now President of the Executive Committee of the Council of Public Safety, takes charge of the revolution. Or rather, he sleepwalks through the revolution, having removed himself from "the blue-white fires of ambition" to find himself pondering the vanity of all actions. When everything is considered, he asks himself, what is there left except "an unabsorbed residuum of pure emptiness"?

It is a sensible question, but it remains unresolved. The revolution breaks out, Molara's palace guard is hurled back by the revolutionaries, Lucile has another secret meeting with Savrola and in the midst of it Molara himself appears, and the city is given over to street fighting. Molara returns to the presidential palace and when the palace surrenders he walks down the steps unarmed. Shots ring out, Molara falls, and a man in a black suit steps forward to deliver the *coup de grâce.* "The back and left side of the skull behind the ear was blown away, and the force of the explosion, probably at close quarters, had cracked all the bones of the face, so that as the skin was whole, it looked like broken china in a sponge bag."

Savrola, horrified, turns on the murderer, Karl Kreutze, the man in the dark suit.

"It is not murder," Kreutze explains. "It is an execution."

Savrola strikes the man across the face with his cane; someone else cuts the murderer down with a sword; and Savrola makes a speech to quieten the crowd and at a dramatic moment lifts his blood-stained left hand, so that they can see that he too has been wounded in the fighting. He wins the people over, becomes their undisputed leader and would have remained in Laurania but for the unexpected arrival of the Lauranian fleet. The admiral in command of the fleet is loyal to the dictatorship of Molara and threatens to bombard the city unless Savrola retires from the scene. He goes into exile, taking Lucile with him. We are informed that the illustrious exile who had won freedom for his people and was deserted in the hour of victory later returned to rule over the ancient city he had loved so well.

Part fairy story, part prophecy, part cautionary tale, *Savrola* remains an enigma. As a novel it fails, for the second half of the novel is so disorganized that it boggles the imagination. HMS *Aggressor*, General Strelitz, the admiral of the Lauranian fleet, and even Karl Kreutze all have the appearance of having been forced into the book "for good measure" or to fill up the empty pages, and having invented them, Churchill has no idea what to do with them. The story progresses by fits and starts to the sound of crackling gunfire and the drumbeat of revolution. Yet from the beginning Churchill seems to have had in mind a revolution that failed and swallowed up its great leader. Savrola, when we first see him, is a doomed man who wears his doom with a proper theatricality. When we see him last, he is the savior of his country, the heroic exile who returns to resume his rightful place in the history of Laurania, but this homecoming takes place offstage in a footnote added at the last moment to round off the story. We remember him as the doomed hero, the romantic aesthete of revolution, dreaming his life away and writing those immaculate speeches which will, he believes, bring him to power and eminence.

Most young writers write their autobiographies. Churchill, at the age of twenty-four, was projecting himself into the future, seeing himself with quite extraordinary clarity as he would be twenty, thirty, forty years hence. But the novel was not only a prophetical tract; it was also a carefully argued statement on the nature of power, or rather of the futility of power. Again and again the theme of futility is pronounced with absolute conviction. Savrola is contemplating the moment when he will let loose the revolutionaries on the city, horrified by the thought of the inevitable bloodshed and his own responsibility for it. At the thought of this crime about to be visited on innocent people, he tells himself: "There are sins, sins against the commonwealth of mankind, against the phenomenon of life itself, the stigma of which would cling through death, and for which there was pardon only in annihilation."

In later years Churchill rejoiced in the exercise of power. For many years he occupied positions of responsibility; people were simply objects he manipulated to maintain and increase his power; he became hardened to suffering, even when the suffering arose manifestly as a result of his errors. In his youth he was more generous toward the suffering. Savrola could think of the stigma which outlasts death and receives its ultimate pardon in annihilation. This concept was essentially Buddhist and owed something to Churchill's reading of Buddhist literature. By the time he left India he had abandoned the position reached by Savrola after so much hard and desperate thinking; henceforward he would find all wars justified if they were fought by the British.

Savrola, written in the early months of 1898, was Churchill's second full-length book. The first was *The Story of the Malakand Field Force,* describing the campaign fought on the Indian frontier in the summer of 1897. Much of this area was once a Buddhist sanctuary inhabited by yellow-robed monks and their followers. About 400 A.D. the Chinese pilgrim Fa Hien traveled through these valleys and found the monks still living there. Churchill, who had read Fa Hien's story of his pilgrimage in the translation of James Legge, was agreeably surprised to come upon the ruins of the ancient monasteries, the red-brick rubble on the hills. And since Fa Hien took pleasure in relating the miraculous legends associated with Buddha, Churchill took equal pleasure in quoting them with an appropriate measure of disbelief.

In *The Story of the Malakand Field Force* Churchill describes the forays and skirmishes at which he was present and others where he was not present but heard authentic accounts from the officers who took part in the fighting. He enjoyed the fighting—he was very lucky and bullets seemed to take the trouble to curve round him whenever they were aimed in his direction—and was puzzled and saddened by the killing. Brave men died horribly, and he often pondered their deaths and came to the conventional conclusions:

> To some the game of war brings prizes, honour, advancement, or experience; to some the consciousness of duty well discharged; and to others—spectators perhaps—the pleasure of the play and the knowledge of men and things. But here were those who had drawn the evil numbers—who had lost their all, to gain only a soldier's grave. Looking at those shapeless forms, coffined in a regulation blanket, the pride of race, the pomp of empire, the glory of war appeared but the faint and unsubstantial fabric of a dream; and I could not help realizing with Burke: "What shadows we are and what shadows we pursue."

It was not, of course, quite so simple; there was also the question of the responsibility for all that killing. He found the answer—or part of it—in a speech given at the Guildhall in 1892 by Lord Salisbury, who described the frontier wars as "the surf that marks the edge and the advance of the wave of civilization." The tribesmen of the frontier were savages who needed to be tamed before they were permitted to enter the *imperium britannicum.* Their lawlessness must be punished, their villages must be burned, their rifles must be surrendered, their crops must be destroyed, and all this so that they should receive the benefits of civilization. Unfortunately they continued to fight whenever British columns marched into their territory, and they went on fighting even when they were defeated. Churchill tells the story of the cavalry returning to camp and proudly displaying their blood-stained lances. "How many?" someone asks. "Twenty-one," replied an officer. "But they are full of fight." They were always full of fight because their lands were being invaded.

Sometimes, as he pondered the ravages of imperialism, Churchill's historical mind, fed on Gibbon and Fa Hien, would look back to the time when the Roman Empire was in disarray, and civilization was on the verge of collapse. Alaric the Goth, Attila the Hun and Genseric the Vandal surged across Europe, sacked Rome and reduced entire cities to rubble, and while all this was going on there existed in what is now the Northwest Frontier of India a superbly peaceful civilization and "a placid people, thriving, industrious and intelligent, devoting their lives to the attainment of that serene annihilation which the word *nirvana* expresses." This was the mystery: that civilizations come to birth, grow to maturity, and die, leaving almost no trace behind.

So he would look out in the few days he spent on the Northwest Frontier for the ruined temples and try to imagine what life was like in the days before the Pathans came down from the hills. He thought of the Pathans as a wild, murderous people, although they were reasonably peaceful when the British left them alone. He half admired them and was sorry they had to die. Here Churchill describes a dead Pathan who was found propped against a stone beside a little pool:

> He had been an ugly man originally, but now that the bones of his jaw and face were broken in pieces by the bullet, he was hideous to look upon. His only garment was a ragged blue linen cloak fastened at the waist. There he sat—a typical tribesmen, ignorant, degraded, and squalid, yet brave and warlike; his only property his weapon, and that his countrymen had carried off.

The pages of Churchill's early books are full of portraits of the dead.

Usually he applauds them for their courage in much the same way that he applauds wounds—they are "glorious deformities." He describes the dead so that they seem very real, but surprisingly he has no gift for describing the living. He is happiest when he is describing men en masse, when they are on parade or when they are advancing across the plains or leaping down the hills of the Mamund Valley. He thinks continually in terms of squadrons and regiments, of lines of force moving across the landscape, and sometimes he seems to be lost in contemplation of wars fought with toy soldiers like those he played with in his childhood.

Sometimes a vivid description in his original dispatches will become strangely diffuse when it appears in a book. New emotions color the half forgotten past, when he writes from memory without consulting his dispatches. Here is the description of a dead Boer in the original dispatch sent to the *Morning Post*:

> Here by the rock under which he had fought lay the field cornet of Heilbronn, Mr. de Mentz—a grey-haired man of over sixty years, with firm aquiline features and a short beard. The stony face was grimly calm, but it bore the stamp of unalterable resolve; the look of a man who had thought it all out, and was quite certain that his cause was just, and such as a sober citizen might give his life for. Nor was I surprized when the Boer prisoners told me that Mentz had refused all suggestions of surrender, and that when his left leg was smashed by a bullet had continued to load and fire until he bled to death; and they found him, pale and bloodless, holding his wife's letter in his hand.

In the book we see Mr. de Mentz rather differently, and the sense of pity amid the horror of war has vanished. He wrote:

> De Mentz! The name recalled a vivid scene—the old field cornet lying forward, grey and grim, in a pool of blood and a litter of empty cartridge cases, with his wife's letter clasped firmly in his stiffening fingers. He had "gone down fighting"; had had no doubts what course to steer. I knew when I saw his face that he had thought the whole thing out. Now they told me there had been no man in all Heilbronn more bitterly intent on the war, and that his letters in the *Volksstem*, calling on the Afrikanders to drive the English scum from the land, had produced a deep impression.

Churchill is describing the same man, but how different are the two portraits! One is charged with pity, the other with contempt and hate.

It is a strange transformation, hinting at a dichotomy of the soul. Churchill's humanity was at war with his sense of imperial mission. In the first dispatch the man is to be praised for his courage and high resolve, and in the second version he has become an object of scorn because he fought the British and lost.

The River War, the huge volume devoted to the Sudan, had the same virtues and vices as *The Story of the Malakand Field Force.* The immense canvas is spread out before us; the intricate details are marshaled in proper order; and the sweep of events is described with intellectual passion. He immersed himself in a library of books and obtained the services of no less a personage than Lord Cromer, the British Agent and Consul General in Egypt, serving with all the powers of a Viceroy, as his adviser and editor. This was almost as though a very young American officer had written an account of the war in Europe and obtained the services of General Marshall as adviser and editor. It was a considerable feat in itself.

In the original edition Churchill attacked Kitchener bitterly for his insensitivity to the living and brutality toward the dead. "General Kitchener, who never spares himself, cares little for others," he wrote. "He treated all men like machines." Churchill was incensed because Kitchener gave orders that the head of the Mahdi, the prophet of the Dervishes, should be removed to Cairo in a kerosene tin as a war trophy; at his orders, too, what remained of the body was thrown into the Nile. This was not, Churchill felt, the proper way to deal with a genuine prophet who was also a remarkable military commander. The Mahdi had not been killed at Omdurman; his body had been dug up. Kitchener could have replied that General Gordon had suffered a similar fate at the hands of the Mahdi and that this was one of the punishments to be inflicted on the rebellious Dervishes. Churchill's diatribes against Kitchener were not wholly insincere, but since Kitchener at the beginning of the campaign had put him in charge of a decrepit mule and two donkeys, his rage also served the purposes of revenge.

The River War is colored with the bright, torturing sun of the Sudan. He describes the Dervish empire and the fall of Gordon and the Sudanese invasion of Abyssinia and how they cut off the head of the Abyssinian king and brought it in triumph to Omdurman, and the pace is quick and the colors glow. But here and there, and often unexpectedly, there comes that same feeling of helplessness before the forces of history that haunts *The Story of the Malakand Field Force.* Here, in *The*

River War, Churchill communes with himself on the ultimate corruption of all civilizations, however beautiful and however good:

> All great movements, every impulse that a community may feel, become perverted and distorted as time passes, and the atmosphere of the earth seems fatal to the noble aspirations of its people. A wide humanitarian sympathy in a nation easily degenerates into hysteria. A military spirit tends towards brutality. Liberty tends to license, restraint to tyranny. The pride of race is distended to blistering arrogance. The fear of God produces bigotry and superstition. There appears no exception to the mournful rule, and the best efforts of men, however glorious their early results, have dismal endings, like plants which shoot and bud and put forth beautiful flowers, and then grow rank and coarse and are withered by the winter.

He was saying perhaps no more than that all things perish, but he was saying it with a note of terror in his voice, having seen the process at work and gazed deep into the black pit, which was not nirvana. All his life he was to be haunted by that terror, that sense of the impermanence of things, even the impermanence of the British Empire.

Savrola, The Story of the Malakand Field Force and *The River War* show Churchill in fine fettle and indeed they are the best of his early books, and perhaps the best of all his books. We see the mind breaking loose and making its own discoveries, before the arts of the orator softened the shapes of his prose. In time they would be followed by biographies of Lord Randolph Churchill and of the first Duke of Marlborough, works of incredible length and prolixity, and by histories of the two world wars, which were even longer. He also wrote two books on the Boer War called *London to Ladysmith* and *Ian Hamilton's March,* but they lack the skill and excitement of his books on the Northwest Frontier and on the Sudan. There is a slackening of intensity, an absence of ideas, with only here and there a spark of the essential excitement.

He had been a writer, and a very good one in his time. Now he was to become a politician, thirsting for power, speaking in speeches and utterances, and issuing orders. He had studied oratory even more passionately than he had studied the art of writing. Henceforth the orator, "who wields a power more durable than that of a great King," would take precedence of the writer who attempts to understand the world and come to terms with it. His aim was to become the master of England and the British Empire, and in those days—for he was very young—it seemed to be the easiest thing in the world.

Sagittarius Rising

Ambition was the motive force, and he was powerless to resist it. He could appreciate the delights of an artist, a life devoted to the search for beauty, or of sport, the keenest pleasure that leaves no sting behind. To live in dreamy quiet and philosophic calm in some beautiful garden, far from the noise of men and with every diversion that art and intellect could suggest, was, he felt, a more agreeable picture. And yet he knew that he could not endure it. Vehement, high, and daring was his cast of mind.
—SAVROLA

A MINISTER
OF THE CROWN

HE WAS YOUNG, red-haired, fresh-faced, with something about him that resembled the youthful Napoleon whom he revered, and as he stood up in the House of Commons for the first time, there was an air of expectancy, for much was expected of him. It was a rather solemn occasion, for the House was in mourning for Queen Victoria who had died on January 23, 1901. It was now February 18, the new King Edward VII was on the throne, and the House was debating the Boer War. Lloyd George had just spoken against the British generals, particularly Kitchener, who had been conducting the war with astonishing ruthlessness. He spoke bitterly and passionately about the useless slaughter and stopped abruptly, as though in mid-passage, to give Churchill an opportunity to speak. When Churchill rose to deliver his maiden speech there was more than the usual excitement.

Dinner was over, the parliamentarians were still returning from the dining room, the gallery was full of elegantly dressed ladies leaning forward on the hard benches in order to hear better, and the House itself, lit by gas jets, was in its normal state of disarray with the frock-coated members half reclining on their seats, some of them with their top hats tipped over their foreheads. The huge golden mace, sign of the King's sovereignty, rested on the Speaker's table. In the distance,

very faintly, there could be heard the *clop-clop* of carriages and hansom
cabs making their way across New Palace Yard. White shirt fronts
gleamed in the gaslight. Huge shadows raced across the walls. As
always during the late evenings of a long debate, there was a subdued
creaking sound made up of whispers, the unfolding of newspapers, the
crackling of starched shirts and the strange noises of the night.

Churchill looked up at his mother and half a dozen Marlborough
relatives sitting in the Ladies' Gallery and embarked haltingly on his
speech, which had been carefully, perhaps too carefully, prepared. He
had no gift for speaking extempore. He had written it out and learned it
by heart, and in his hands there were a few notes to help him on his way.
He was terrified that quite suddenly, without warning, he would find
himself at a loss for words, his memory gone, his ideas dried up. But this
terror only spurred him on, and he seemed to have no care in the world
once the original hesitation had passed.

He spoke as a twenty-six-year-old veteran of the South African War,
and he was well aware of the importance of the occasion. The speech
must be memorable; he must strike hard, make oratorical points and
have the House on his side. He must disassociate himself from Lloyd
George, the Welsh radical, and at the same time, since his sympathies
were with the Boers, he could not disassociate himself too much. His
long quarrel with Kitchener was over, and nothing would be gained by
a direct attack on that eminent personage. He must therefore strive to
stake out a middle position, reinforcing Lloyd George one moment and
defending Kitchener the next, at the same time offering a program of
reconciliation and generosity to the defeated. The speech was a masterly exhibition of walking a tightrope.

First, there was the slap at Lloyd George:

> I do not believe that the Boers would attach particular importance to
> the utterances of the honourable member. No people in the world
> received so much verbal sympathy and so little support. If I were a Boer
> fighting in the field—and if I were a Boer I hope I should be fighting in the
> field—I would not allow myself to be taken in by any message of sym-
> pathy, not even if it were signed by a hundred honourable members.

The Irish Members of Parliament, who had always strenuously opposed the war, cheered when Churchill said: "If I were a Boer I hope I
should be fighting in the field," and Joseph Chamberlain, the
archimperialist, turned to his neighbor and said: "That's the way to

throw away seats!" Churchill had slapped at Lloyd George, but it was not a heavy slap. He proceeded to defend Kitchener, but without too much conviction. No doubt Kitchener had been heavy-handed; no doubt many farmsteads had been burned; and then (and this was curious) Churchill went on to say that the German army had not been prevented by any considerations of humanity from throwing its shells into the dwelling houses of Paris and starving the inhabitants so that they lived on rats. Modern war was barbarous, and we must accept it as it is. "From what I saw of the war—and I sometimes saw something of it—I believe that as compared with other wars, especially those in which a civilian population took part, this war in South Africa has been on the whole carried on with unusual humanity and generosity."

Meanwhile, he asked that more and more troops should be sent to South Africa to prosecute the war until the Boers were forced to lay down their arms. In defeat this "brave and enduring army" will receive all the honors of war and their small independence will be merged into "the larger liberties of the British Empire." They must be treated with generosity by a civilian administration which, at the end of the war, will immediately replace the military government. He had a deep respect for the Boer farmers who were "a curious combination of the squire and the peasant," and he said it had saddened him to see these farmers ordered about by young subaltern officers.

Before he sat down Churchill expressed his gratitude for the indulgence the House had shown him. "It has been extended to me, I know, not on my own account, but because of a splendid memory which many honourable members still preserve."

The speech was a triumph: it pleased the newspapers, it pleased the Tories and the Liberals, and it pleased Churchill. He had staked out his independent middle ground successfully, without giving offence to anyone except perhaps Joseph Chamberlain. A few minutes later he was introduced to Lloyd George in the smoking room. "Judging from your sentiments you are standing against the light," Lloyd George remarked. Churchill answered: "You take a singularly detached view of the British Empire."

In retrospect Churchill's speech delivered on February 18, 1901, appears to flow like the waters of a fountainhead. He would deliver the same speech with minor variations for the rest of his long parliamentary career, which spanned sixty-four years, exactly the same number of years that Queen Victoria reigned. The glorification of war, the sanctity of the British Empire, the necessity for generosity toward the vanquished, the celebration of his own prowess: these were the elements that endured. He did not believe he was standing against the light. On the contrary, he believed that he was looking toward the sunrise.

Overnight he became a "character," closely watched, his appearance, his clothes, his walk, his habits minutely examined in the newspapers and commented upon lengthily in the clubs. It was observed that he spoke with a pronounced lisp, that he possessed some of the mannerisms of his father, that he was more clever than his father. He would go far. Those who knew him better saw that he was happiest when he walked alone and that he would always be restless unless he was in a position of supreme authority. His ambition was to become Prime Minister while he was still young. Partly this was because he saw himself as the most brilliant intelligence in politics, but it was also because he felt the deep-seated need to succeed where his father had failed. The shadow of his father walked by his side.

In his second speech, delivered on May 13, 1901, Churchill deliberately seized upon the issue, the Army Estimates, that had ruined his father's career. Mr. St. John Brodrick, the Secretary of State for War, had introduced a scheme for the creation of three new army corps which would be made available for service overseas. Churchill reminded the House that it was precisely on the subject of army extravagance that his father had spoken fifteen years before when he was Chancellor of the Exchequer; and for his vehement opposition to extravagance he had been destroyed. "I am very glad," he said, "the House has allowed me after fifteen years to lift again the tattered flag I found lying on a stricken field." He pleaded for economy. It was much better to put all the available money into building up a navy, thus preserving England from the necessity of fighting wars on land. He saw already that a European war would be a war of peoples as well as of armies, and the coming wars would be more hideous than any in the past. His words, spoken at the beginning of the century, were strangely prophetical and had a fateful ring:

A European war cannot be anything but a cruel, heartrending struggle which, if we were ever able to enjoy the bitter fruits of victory, must demand, perhaps for several years, the whole manhood of the nation, the entire suspension of peaceful industries, and the concentrating to one end of every vital energy in the community. . . . In former days, when wars arose from individual causes, from the policy of a Minister or the passion of a King, when they were fought by small regular armies of professional soldiers, and when their course was retarded by the difficulties of communication and supply, it was possible to limit the liabilities of the combatants. But now, when mighty populations are impelled against each other, each individual severally embittered and inflamed—when the resources of science and civilization sweep away everything that might mitigate their fury, a European war can only end in the ruin of the vanquished and the scarcely less fatal dislocation and exhaustion of the conquerors. Democracy is more vindictive than Cabinets. The wars of people will be more terrible than those of kings.

The prose is Macaulay updated to incorporate softer Victorian rhythms, but the urgency and the thought belonged to Churchill. A new theme had been added to the elementary themes announced earlier. He was not the first to say that the next European war would take the form of total war, peoples against peoples, but he was the first to insist on the primacy of the Royal Navy as the guardian of Britain's shores. The London *Times* thought the son was repeating "the most disastrous mistake of his father's career." But when Lord Randolph had called for economy and resigned with a sense of brooding outrage because his advice was not taken, he was the Chancellor of the Exchequer; Churchill was merely a backbencher and the veriest neophyte. He had no following, he was regarded as too ambitious and too aggressive, and was not popular in the House; and he was without any office or any immediate hope of office. He had already marked out his own middle road between the Liberals and the Conservatives, sniping at both. His aim from the beginning was to broaden the middle ground and force both the Liberals and the Tories to the wall. He would have his own party and lead it to victory; and when, forty years later, he achieved something very close to his aims and became Prime Minister of a government that included both Conservatives and Socialists, he still occupied the dangerous and uncharted middle ground, the shadowless territory which had no historical traditions and associations and was therefore unstable, surviving only as long as he was in power and by a series of miracles.

But the Churchill who first entered Parliament was far from being a dominant personality. He had shocked the House with two electrifying speeches, but thereafter the electricity failed. He was personable, he knew everybody, he was a "coming man," he cut a splendid figure in society, and Lord Rosebery prophesied that he would become Prime

Minister. But the House distrusted him, and his political fortunes advanced at a snail's pace. By the autumn of 1902 he was spending most of his time on a work which, he thought, would bring him enduring fame—a biography of Lord Randolph Churchill.

Lord Randolph Churchill has been described as "one of the three or four outstanding political biographies in the language." The statement was made by Churchill's son Randolph and is not entirely unprejudiced. It is not really a biography at all. Instead, Churchill collected all the available documents and speeches, printed them at vast and insatiable length in their proper order, and added a commentary written in a style which reveals nearly all his literary vices and few of his virtues. Churchill made no serious effort to discover the springs of his father's character. He passes over the tragedy of Lord Randolph's life in a way which would lead no one to suspect that he died insane. Lady Randolph is a ghostlike figure in the distance, rarely mentioned. There is scarcely any life flowing through the book: the documents are worm-eaten, the speeches echo like the wind in distant corridors, and the commentary is pretentiously ornate. Here Churchill describes the mood of Lord Randolph on the eve of his downfall:

> He was often—and seemed to be, more often still—in things political a hard man, reaping where he had not sown, severe to exact service and obedience, hasty in judgment, fierce in combat; and many a black look or impatient word had been remembered against him by those of whose existence he was perhaps scarcely conscious. Friends he had in plenty—some of them true ones; but, for all the personal charm he could exert at will, his manner had added to his enemies. Venerable Ministers saw a formidable intruder who had entered the Cabinet by adventurous and unusual paths. Austere Conservatives shrank from this alarming representative of the New Democracy. Worthy men thoughtlessly slighted, tiresome people ruthlessly snubbed, office-seekers whose pretensions had been ignored, Parliamentary martinets concerned for party discipline, all were held in check only as long as he was powerful. His position had been won by the sword, and he must be armed to keep it.

Churchill wrote page after page in this way, far removed from the direct manner of his novel *Savrola* or his reports from the battlefield. It was a leisurely age, and this was leisurely prose with a vengeance. It was also sometimes ridiculous, for beyond Lord Randolph there appeared the shadowy outlines of the Duke of Marlborough, and sometimes Churchill confused one shadow with the other. Lord Randolph had not won his place by the sword and it was a hopeless task to make him into a hero.

What Churchill was attempting to do was to discover the father he had never known. In all his life he had enjoyed only three or four long talks with his father, and these talks had not added very deeply to his knowledge of the man. He was under the illusion that Lord Randolph had achieved greatness by sheer force of character; instead he had achieved his high position by intrigue, bombast and violent ambition. Since the original premise was false, the portrait of Lord Randolph was completely distorted. Churchill was not describing a man but a monument, not unlike the life-size marble image of Lord Randolph in the chapel at Blenheim, in flowing robes, white as chalk, the features smoothed out to an unaccustomed perfection like an angel in a cemetery.

The extraordinary Aylesford-Blandford episode in which Lord Randolph gratuitously insulted the Prince of Wales and showed compromising letters to the Princess of Wales is dismissed cavalierly and in such a way that the honor of Lord Randolph remains unsullied. Churchill wrote: "Engaging in his brother's quarrels with fierce and reckless partisanship, Lord Randolph incurred the deep displeasure of a great personage." This was deliberate distortion; nor was it the only occasion that Churchill distorted facts for his private purposes.

The book, which was finally published in January 1906, in two enormous volumes, had a moderate success. Churchill was pleased with the advance payment for the book which amounted to £8,000, a stupendous sum at the time and equivalent in purchasing power to about $60,000 in modern money. The advance payment was a tribute to his fame and to the cleverness of his new agent, Frank Harris, who received a commission of £400. Frank Harris was not yet the author of the scurrilous five-volume autobiography *My Life and Loves*, which was to bring him posthumous fame. He was a brilliant editor and writer of short stories with a swashbuckling manner and an agile tongue, and he had therefore much in common with Churchill.

Henceforth Churchill, as he told Frank Harris, was free "from care and fear." He could do as he pleased, secure in the knowledge that his wealth, earned by his pen, was sufficient for his purposes. He had never felt the need to be an obedient Member of Parliament who would run at the bidding of a Party whip; wealth gave him independence; he would do as he pleased. In May, 1904, having grown weary of the Conservatives, he crossed the floor of the House of Commons and joined the Liberals. This was risky, for the Conservatives were unforgiving and would regard him as a traitor to the cause. In 1906, the year that saw the publication of the biography of his father, fortune favored him. The Liberals won a landslide victory over the Conservatives, winning 401 seats against 157, and now, as one of the leading members of the Liberal Party, he claimed a ministerial award. He was appointed to the post of Under Secretary for the Colonies.

This was the first of many ministerial posts, and there came with it two luxuries which gave him enormous pleasure. He needed a private secretary and found one in the person of the young scholar Edward Marsh, a small, gentle man with a pair of beetling eyebrows which would have been ferocious if it were not that the man himself was incapable of ferocity. He was a homosexual with a piping voice, exquisite manners and extraordinary self-control. He was also a connoisseur of modern paintings and literature, a friend of poets, a distinguished translator and a man of immense erudition. For thirty years, until he resigned in 1937, Edward Marsh served Churchill like a knight-errant serving his king. This was the first luxury.

The second was a six-month holiday tour of Africa described as an official visit, and therefore paid for by the Crown. With Edward Marsh beside him he traveled in leisurely fashion to Malta, Cyprus, and then through the Suez Canal to Mombasa. The ship carrying him was HMS *Venus,* a cruiser transformed temporarily into a passenger ship and placed by the Admiralty under Churchill's orders; it would go wherever he wanted it to go, and stay in port as long as he wanted it to stay. It was an ideal method of conveyance, and in a rather lordly fashion he took full advantage of it.

From all the places he visited he sent streams of long memoranda to the Government. The Treasury, the Foreign Office and the Colonial Office were bombarded with reports, minutes, observations, memoranda and annotations on previous memoranda, not altogether to the liking of his superiors. Sir Francis Hopgood, the Permanent Under Secretary of the Colonial Office, was incensed and sent a memorandum to Lord Elgin, who was Churchill's immediate superior with the title of Secretary of State for the Colonies. Hopgood observed that Churchill was meddlesome, unpredictable and absurdly demanding. "He is most tiresome to deal with and will, I fear, give trouble—as his father did—in any position to which he may be called," wrote

Hopgood. "The restless energy, uncontrollable desire for notoriety and the lack of moral perception make him an anxiety indeed!"

Such was Hopgood's verdict, but Edward Marsh, who labored to transcribe Churchill's endless reports, thought Churchill vastly entertaining and the soul of morality, always on the side of the angels and the oppressed. On one particular day, in the sweltering heat of the Red Sea, Churchill kept Marsh working for fourteen hours on those interminable reports with scarcely a murmur of protest.

In those days most of East Africa was a British colony, and Churchill was greeted like visiting royalty. Large areas of East Africa were being ruled by District Commissioners, English boys in their twenties dressed in khaki shorts, shirts and puttees, good-humored and perfectly at ease, never troubling to ask themselves why a solitary Englishman should find himself acting as the governor, judge, executioner and adviser to so many thousands of Africans. Churchill was deeply impressed by the evidence of the *pax britannica* in working order, and his views on the British Empire were permanently colored by his leisurely safaris in the interior. He went hunting, brought down a rhinoceros, and was taken on a lion hunt which produced no lions but did produce a couple of ferocious wart hogs which charged with tails erect and tusks gleaming. They were shot down, or, in Churchill's words, "they met a fate reserved for a king." He made observations on the tribes he encountered. Of the Kavirondo tribe he wrote: "They have a very strong prejudice against the wearing of clothes, which they declare lead to immorality; and no Kavirondo woman can attire herself even in the most exiguous raiment without sullying her reputation." His attitude toward the Africans was one, common in his time, of undisguised paternalism. As bearers and guides they were kindly, obedient and resourceful. Thinking of the Asiatics, mostly Indians, who had settled in these regions, and of the Africans who had lived there since time immemorial, he spoke of their immense services to the happiness and material progress of the world once they had been harnessed to modern civilization; and he seems to have thought the Asiatics would act as a stimulus to the Africans. The horrors of the tsetse fly were coming to an end; the railroads were on the march; power was being generated from the rivers. "It is no good trying to lay hold of Tropical Africa with naked fingers," he wrote. "Civilisation must be armed with machinery if she is to subdue these wild regions to her authority. Iron roads, not jogging porters; tireless engines, not weary men; cheap power, not cheap labour; steam and skill, not sweat and fumbling; there lies the only way to tame the jungle—more jungles than one." And again: "Let us be sure that order and science will conquer, and that in the end John Bull will be really master in this curious garden of sunshine and deadly nightshade."

He was fascinated by Africa and by Africans. He drove through the streets of Nairobi to find the sidewalks lined with warriors with hair matted with red and yellow earth, brandishing spears adorned with ostrich feathers. At Kampala the roads were thronged with men and women in white robes, and they crowded round him and applauded him. At length the procession arrived at the gates of the palace of Daudi Chewa, the King or Kabaka of Uganda, who was eleven years old, simply dressed in a flowing black robe edged with gold and a little white gold-rimmed cap. The palace was made of elephant grass. Churchill and his party first tasted syrup from tiny bowls, and were then led into the presence of the Kabaka, who was too young and too nervous to say anything more than "yes" or "no" in a soft, low voice. The boy was handsome and distinguished, very much a king. On the following day there was a war dance, with two or three thousand men, naked and painted for war, rushing frantically to and fro to the beating of drums; and Churchill observed that not one in ten of them had a spear, and they were all conscious of performing a charade. The truth was that the Baganda people were gentle-mannered, peaceful and excessively polite. Someone had called them the Japanese of Africa, and Churchill has a delightful description of two Baganda as they pass one another along the road:

> They begin to salute each other as soon as they come within earshot. "How are you?" cries the one. "Who am I that you should care to know?" cries the other. "Humble though I be, yet I have dared," rejoins the first. "But say first how are *you*," continues the second. "The better for the honour you have done me," is the answer. By this they have already passed each other, and there is only time for the Parthian affability, "The honour is mine, and I shall treasure it," and a quavering of delicately-modulated, long-drawn "A—a—a's" of contentment and goodwill which gradually die away in the distance, leaving neither of them the worse circumstanced, nor the better informed.

Leaving Kampala, Churchill went by steamboat to Jinja, where the Nile flows out of Lake Victoria over the Ripon Falls; and seeing the falls

Churchill began to contemplate the turbines which one day would gin all the cotton and saw all the wood of Uganda. It hurt him that all that power was going to waste, and he composed another long memorandum for the Colonial Office and wondered whether Providence had not intended Uganda, with its pacific and industrious people, without classes, to be ruled according to the principles of State Socialism. There were no European vested interests; the British administration was "personally disinterested"; a purely Communist state could come into existence overnight. The only difficulty lay with the choosing of the Governor. For the first and last time in his life Churchill thought of Communism as a beneficent form of government, and perhaps significantly the thought occurred to him in the country of a boy-king while deafened by the roar of the Ripon Falls, a vast green slope of water plunging down to the foaming rapids "fringed by splendid trees and pools from which great fish leap continually in the sunlight." Almost it was Paradise.

So they continued with their long safari—at the end of each day Churchill announced: "Sofari sogood"—and every day, as they marched from one encampment to another or rode in a motor launch, they were assailed by new splendors. There were birds as bright as butterflies, and butterflies as big as birds. He ran after the butterflies with his net— swallowtails, fritillaries, admirals, tortoise shells, peacocks, orange tips—but those were the English names and they were more beautiful than any English butterflies. He had had a passion for butterflies when he was a child, and this journey through Uganda only reinforced his passion. But he was dismayed when he discovered that the butterflies crowded over dead and putrescent animals, so that, as they slaked their hunger, he had only to lean over and pluck them gently with his fingers. "They come in such gay attire to eat such sorry meat," he wrote in one of the best phrases in the short book he wrote about his African journey.

Here in tropical Africa he encountered the theme that had absorbed him in India when he was writing *Savrola* and *The Story of the Malakand Field Force*—the way all things enter into corruption and annihilation. He became the spectator of "an intense convulsion of life and death." The soil, bursting with irrepressible vegetation, let loose a terrible struggle for survival, reproduction and decay locked in infinite embraces. It was a humbling experience; he observed it, as he said, with a secret aversion; and then forgot about it in wonder of the brilliantly colored butterflies at their sickening meals. Jauntily he continued his travels.

After his Indian and Egyptian travels Churchill rarely permitted himself the luxury of describing landscapes, but *My African Journey,* which was based on articles written for the *Strand* magazine, is full of such descriptions. He reveled in the sights and colors of Africa. The fish eagle, "glorious in bronze and cream," sunning himself on the tree tops and watching for a prey, had something in common with Churchill himself as he surveyed the plains and mountains of Africa. Nearly ten years would pass before he took up a paintbrush and splashed his first canvas with paint, but already he had developed an artist's eye.

He marched through forests and saw processions of ghostly elephants, and once, near the water he saw the famous white rhinoceros "with the long, thin horn of his rare tribe upon him," as he walked in stately grandeur from his evening bath. At another time he watched two wild boars playing at fighting in a glade and gazed openmouthed at a dozen splendid waterbuck browsing on the crest of a ridge. Then he was sailing up the White Nile to find Omdurman again and Khartoum, now a smiling civilized city with schools and shops and thriving industries, so changed since he was last there less than ten years before that he felt he had seen the justification for the British Empire. The streets were lit by electricity; there were tramways; there was a railroad station, and the train would take him to Cairo.

Tragedy struck at the end of the journey. George Scrivings, his English servant, died within fifteen hours of Asiatic cholera, and Churchill found himself once more standing by an open grave in Khartoum. After the battle of Omdurman it had been his task to bury the soldiers of the 21st Lancers who had died of their wounds during the night. Africa, which had shown him so much splendor, had wrung his heart at the last.

He returned to London in January, 1908, to find the Prime Minister, Sir Henry Campbell-Bannerman, gravely ill. He died, Herbert Henry Asquith became Prime Minister, and Churchill, after fighting two by-elections in quick succession, losing in Manchester and winning in Dundee, became President of the Board of Trade, a position previously occupied by Lloyd George. Here he established trade boards composed of impartial committees which determined minimum wages and hours in each industry and went on to establish labor exchanges, where the unemployed could go in search of jobs. Beatrice and Sidney Webb, the Fabian Socialists, had suggested the labor exchanges and he worked closely with them. Beatrice Webb was a tall and stately bluestocking who knew more about statistics than about life; her husband Sidney was an odd, dwarfish, bearded man who possessed an even greater love for statistics. Lenin had translated one of their books on social reform; Churchill put their ideas into practice. For a very brief period Churchill became the darling of the Socialists.

As always, he was difficult, impulsive, generous and brash. Cock of the walk, he worked miracles, and people were sometimes offended when he crowed about them. He lectured everyone about everything. He even lectured Sir Edward Grey on foreign politics, saying, "The longer I live, the more certain I am I know all there is to be known." Grey commented: "Winston, very soon, will become incapable, from sheer activity of mind, of being anything in a Cabinet but Prime Minister."

Others—and they were very numerous—thought him ignorant, dangerous and bumptious. Lady Lugard, the wife of Lord Lugard, a great West African colonial administrator, said he was "so obviously ignorant in regard to colonial affairs and at the same time so full of personal activity that the damage he may do appears to be colossal." At a dinner party given by Lady St. Helier in honor of Lady Lugard, Churchill met Clementine Hozier, the twenty-three-year-old daughter of Sir Henry Hozier and granddaughter of the tenth Earl of Airlie. She had a beautiful, oval, classical face, exquisite manners, a slight tartness, and no money. She was earning a little pocket money by giving French lessons. She found herself sitting beside Churchill at the dinner, and was not especially impressed by him. He asked her whether she would read his life of Lord Randolph Churchill if he sent it to her. She agreed to read it and he forgot to send it. They met again some days later, and like many others she found herself surrendering to his "dominating charm and brilliancy." The Duke of Marlborough invited her to visit Blenheim Palace. There the trap was sprung, and Churchill proposed to her when they were taking shelter from the rain in an ornamental temple overlooking the lake. She accepted at once. The proposal was offered during the late afternoon of August 11, 1908; it was published officially in the London *Times* four days later, and the marriage took place almost exactly a month later at St. Margaret's, Westminster. The day of the wedding coincided with the Eucharistic Congress, which was being held nearby, and the streets were crowded with sightseers, some coming to see the wedding couple, some coming to see the bishops and clerics at the congress, and some coming to see both.

Wilfred Scawen Blunt, who arrived late at the wedding, found the church so crowded that he had to be given a seat up front with the bride's relatives. He thus obtained an excellent vantage point. He wrote in his diary: "The bride was pale, as was the bridegroom. He has gained in appearance since I last saw him, and has a powerful if ugly face. Winston's responses were clearly made in a pleasant voice, Clementine's inaudible."

They enjoyed a reasonably happy marriage, and if it was not quite as happy as Churchill liked to say it was, it was because they were both dominating personalities. Clementine was strong-willed, hot-tempered, violently jealous and profoundly loyal to her husband. If any woman looked admiringly at her husband, she was immediately up in arms; and any politician who attacked him became her instant enemy. No one in her presence was permitted to speak against her husband or his political friends. Once, when she was staying at Blenheim Palace, she heard the Duke of Marlborough make some slighting remark about Asquith. She immediately packed her bags, leaving the palace without another word. She was the perfect wife for a politician, being herself a political animal, though somewhat more liberal than her husband. He called her Cat, and she called him Pug.

Five children were born of the marriage, four girls and one boy. Diana was born in 1909, Randolph in 1911, Sarah in 1914, Marigold in 1918, Mary in 1922. Marigold died when very young. It was a close-knit family, but the children were nearly unmanageable and a little frightened of their father, who demanded obedience, spoke interminably about himself, and grew visibly ill-tempered if the children spoke haltingly. "Say what you have to say, say it clearly or don't say it at all," was the family commandment. No one was physically punished, but they were so much in awe of their father that his quiet anger was worse than punishment. Churchill could not tolerate noises when he was thinking, and he had a special horror of whistling. The children therefore were reduced to long silences. They whispered, crept stealthily about the house and clapped their hands to their mouths when they felt they were about to explode in a fit of coughing or giggles. A dripping tap, a distant hammering, the noise of a gramophone sent Churchill into a towering rage.

It was not that he was unsympathetic to them; it was simply that he could not stand small talk, and most children talk small. They were all handsome and well-mannered; they were spirited and energetic; he liked to watch them, but at a distance. Like most fathers, he had a special affection for his youngest daughter, whose clear-cut chiseled features were most like his own when he was young.

In 1910 he moved from the Board of Trade to the Home Office, a catchall ministry, roughly equivalent to the ministry of the interior in other governments. Churchill was in charge of the police, prisons and reformatories, supervised the liquor trade, issued ordinances on safety in factories, administered the Channel Islands and ruled on privileges. He had a hundred other duties, none of them clearly defined, though nearly all of them were in some way related to law and order. His liberal ideas had run their course, and he proved to be a stern policeman, a skillful and obdurate strikebreaker, a determined enemy of women's suffrage and an ineffective prison reformer.

As he climbed higher up the ministerial ladder, he found himself inevitably reaching out for more and more increments of power. Power, naked power, delighted him, and in the Home Office he had as much power as a man could reasonably desire. He had the power to commute death sentences, and though his conscience wrestled manfully with every death sentence that crossed his table, he usually permitted the sentence to be carried out. He was one of the very few ministers of the Crown who had ever been imprisoned, and he had, therefore, some sympathy for prisoners, disliked the thought of solitary confinement, and believed that political prisoners should be treated more gently than common criminals. When he visited prisons, he sometimes reduced the sentences of a few selected prisoners. Boy prisoners fascinated him. He would ask why they were there, and they answered they had been stealing. Such forthrightness demanded a reward, and he sometimes reduced their sentences on the spot. John Galsworthy's play *Justice* brought tears to his eyes; he asked for a meeting with Galsworthy; and he wrote long memoranda on prison reform, with surprisingly little effect. He had spent less than a month in prison in Pretoria. If he had spent a long time in prison, he might have become a more memorable Home Secretary.

In November, 1910, 30,000 coal miners went on strike in the Rhondda and Aberdare valleys of South Wales. On November 8 a column of strikers stormed the pithead in the village of Tonypandy and destroyed some shops. They had legitimate reasons for striking, but Churchill showed no interest in their reasons. Law and order must be established. When the chief constable appealed for help, Churchill sent a thousand Metropolitan policemen to Glamorgan and placed them under the command of General Sir Nevil Macready who was seconded from the War Office with orders to put down the strike even if it meant bringing out the military and killing people. Predictably the general called out the local troops. According to Macready's official report the soldiers did nothing more than use "a little gentle persuasion with the bayonet." The strikers, charged on one side by policemen with truncheons and on the other by soldiers with fixed bayonets, had a different version of the affair. Two miners were killed, and many were injured. Churchill said later that he had little sympathy for the mine owners and he regarded the miners as upright, peaceable men who had been sorely tried by events. But he sent troops against them and they never forgave him.

Churchill enjoyed battles. Marching men, flags, drums, military music, the booming of guns and the whistling of bullets, all these physically excited him. A little more than a month after Tonypandy it was given to him to superintend a battle in a miserable street in London.

ON THE EVE

At ten thirty on the night of December 16, 1910, a strange event occurred in Houndsditch in the East End of London. The owner of a fancy goods shop reported to the police that he had heard suspicious rapping or hammering noises in the house next door, and six policemen arrived to investigate. This was an unusually large number of policemen for such a routine investigation, but the police were being cautious. The second house from the fancy goods shop contained a jeweler's shop, and it seemed possible that the hammering sound was made by thieves attempting to break into the jeweler's shop. Then, as now, the London police were armed only with truncheons.

A police sergeant went up to the house whence the sounds had come and knocked on the door. Surprisingly, one of the thieves opened the door a little, and then vanished. The sergeant pushed the door wide open and found himself in a gaslit room with no one in sight. Three constables were waiting outside the front door, and there were two more at the back of the house. Suddenly there was the sound of a pistol shot, and the sergeant fell dead in the doorway. In the space of a few seconds all six policemen lay dead or seriously wounded, and the thieves had escaped from the house under cover of darkness. One of the thieves, Georgy Moruntseff, had been wounded by an accidental shot from one of his accomplices. He succeeded in making his way to the house of two women friends, who summoned a doctor in the early hours of the morning. He died before daybreak, leaving behind a Browning automatic pistol, a dagger and a violin.

In those days armed robbery was a rare occurrence, and the public was stunned by the murder of the policemen. Churchill, as Home Secretary, was particularly disturbed, because the matter fell within his jurisdiction. He ordered an inquiry and arranged that the dead policemen be accorded a public funeral at St. Paul's Cathedral, their flag-draped coffins lying below the high altar during the memorial service. At all costs it was necessary to ensure that the Metropolitan police realized that they had the backing of the government. To do less was to admit failure and to encourage more armed robberies.

The police had their own espionage system in the East End of London, and they soon arrived at the conclusion that they were dealing with something more frightening than a gang of robbers. Rumor pointed to the existence of a Russian revolutionary society composed of about twenty conspirators under the leadership of "Peter the Painter," a mysterious personage who may have had no existence at all. The police had no doubt that they were dealing with Russian revolutionaries who were well-armed and desperate to accomplish their revolutionary aims. It was said that they were anarchists and that most of them were Letts from Baltic Russia. What chiefly mattered was that they were armed with Browning automatic pistols, which were considerably more lethal than ordinary pistols and revolvers.

During the Christmas holidays nothing more was heard about the Russian revolutionaries. Then, at ten o'clock on the morning of January 3, 1911, Churchill, who was in his bath, was surprised by an urgent tapping on the door and the news that he was wanted immediately on the telephone by the Home Office. Wrapping a towel around himself, he hurried to the telephone. The message, as he remembered it, ran somewhat as follows: "The anarchists who murdered the police have been surrounded in a house in the East End—No. 100 Sidney Street —and are firing on the police with automatic pistols. They have shot one man and appear to have plenty of ammunition. Authority is requested to send for troops to arrest or kill them."

Churchill immediately gave permission for the use of troops, and a detachment of Scots Guards from the Tower of London was soon on its way to Sidney Street. He then dressed and hurried to the Home Office, where he learned that a full-scale siege was already taking place in

Sidney Street, with the police firing into the house with shotguns procured from a local gunsmith. A police inspector had been shot dead. There was so much firing from the house that it was believed that about a dozen revolutionaries had transformed it into a fortress during the night. Churchill wanted to know more, but very little further information was available. Finally, at about half past eleven, having consulted at length with his advisers, he decided to investigate the matter himself and if necessary take command of the operations. He was well within his rights, as Home Secretary. Above all, it was necessary to boost the morale of the police, who had lost four officers and constables to the revolutionaries.

In later weeks Churchill was criticized for appearing on the scene, as though he were deliberately seeking notoriety. Dressed in a top hat and a fur-lined overcoat with an astrakhan collar, he was indeed a notable figure as he moved quickly through the shabby streets of Stepney until he had reached a vantage place sufficiently close to the house so that he could have a good view. At an inquest held some days later, he explained that he had driven down from the center of London without any intention of interfering with the work of the police. "I was only there to support them in any unusual difficulty as a covering authority," he declared. This was true, but it was only part of the truth. He had come, as a responsible officer of the Crown, to see with his own eyes the defeat of the revolutionaries, whose numbers were unknown, though men spoke of a dozen or twenty armed men barrricaded within the house.

He arrived with a large entourage, which included his secretary, Edward Marsh, the Chief of the Criminal Investigation Department of Scotland Yard, the Commissioner of Police, and the head of the political section of Scotland Yard. Other dignitaries, like Lord Knutsford, the chairman of the London Hospital, had also appeared, to share in the excitement. But inevitably it was Churchill who attracted the attention of photographers and cameramen, who cranked their movie cameras by hand in the early beginnings of the newsreel. They all took shots of Churchill slipping quickly across an embattled street or sheltering in top-hatted splendor in doorways. When these newsreels were shown a few days later at the Empire Theatre, there were, according to Edward Marsh, "howls of execration." These, too, were undeserved. For once Churchill was doing his duty, and only his duty.

He was making intelligent suggestions: calling up a couple of field guns from the Royal Horse Artillery depot in St. John's Wood, discuss-

ing the possibility of sending sappers to mine the house, and demanding, when the police threatened to storm the house, that at least they
should provide themselves with steel shields. He knew where they
could be found—at Woolwich Arsenal. The Scots Guards had set up
Maxim guns and sharpshooters were posted on neighboring roofs, while
several hundred armed policemen surrounded the house. Preparations
were being made by the police to storm the house by breaking through
the doors and windows and smashing through the roof, when it was
observed that wisps of smoke were curling out of a shattered upper
window. The house was plainly on fire. Soon there was more smoke, and
then flames and the crackling of wood. The house was burning from the
top, but the revolutionaries were still shooting through the shattered
lower windows. It was now about half past one in the afternoon, and
Churchill had been on the scene for about an hour and a half.

For another hour Churchill watched the slow burning of the house,
and then a surprising thing happened. A horse-drawn fire engine drove
up and the captain of the firemen insisted that it was his duty to put out
the flames. Churchill disagreed, saying that it was absurd that the
firemen should endanger their lives, while the captain replied that he
was under orders to put out any fire that took place within his district
and no one had ever stopped him from putting out fires before. The
argument grew heated, until Churchill pointed out that as Home
Secretary he was ultimately responsible for the conduct of the fire
brigade. He promised the captain that he would be permitted to put
out the fire if it spread to any of the neighboring houses, but he was on
no account to enter the burning house.

When the house was nothing but a burned-out shell, Churchill returned to the Home Office. He had done what he set out to do, and
saved some lives, and prevented the captain from endangering the lives
of the firemen, or so he thought. Later he learned that a falling wall had
injured five firemen, two of them seriously. Later still he learned that
two charred bodies had been found in the ruins. They were identified as
Fritz Svaars and Jacob Vogel, both believed to be members of "Peter
the Painter's" revolutionary society. No other bodies were found, and
there was some doubt whether in fact Svaars and Vogel were revolutionaries. Of "Peter the Painter" there was no trace. Churchill, who
enjoyed mythologies, came in time to believe that "Peter the Painter"
was "one of those wild beasts who, in later years, amid the convulsions
of the Great War, were to devour and ravage the Russian state and
people." Here, in the East End of London, he had been within a few

yards of one of those strange East European conspirators who hold the destiny of empires in their hands.

There was not an atom of proof that "Peter the Painter" existed outside of Churchill's imagination. "The wild beasts who devour and ravage" haunted him, as the wild beasts of the *Apocalypse* had haunted the medieval mind. They were the dark-browed, bomb-throwing Socialists and Communists of the lands bordering on the Russian empire, who had vowed to overthrow the Russian state and all other states. Churchill had never encountered them except in novels, including his own novel *Savrola*, with its sketchy and not very believable portrait of Karl Kreutze, the Number One of the Secret Society, the man in the black suit, who shot down the former president of the Republic of Laurania on the steps of his palace. In *Savrola* the archconspirator is a contrived figure who meets a contrived death; first Savrola slashes him across the face with a cane and then a lieutenant cuts him down with a sword. Karl Kreutze died ignominiously, and came to life again in the imaginary "Peter the Painter."

Unknown to Churchill, the real conspirators, the men who overthrew the Russian empire, had met in London for three weeks of conferences in the spring of 1907. They did not throw bombs; they went about their affairs quietly and studiously; and when Plekhanov opened the conference, which took place in the Brotherhood Church in Southgate Road, Whitechapel, he was dressed in a morning coat, a high white collar and a silk tie. Lenin, Stalin, Trotsky, Kamenev, Litvinov, Zinoviev, Rykov, Gorky, and three hundred more Russian revolutionaries attended the conference, and scarcely one of them resembled the image of the revolutionary that Churchill had formed in his mind. They were dressed soberly and could be taken for bourgeois gentlemen from the continent who had come to London for a change of air.

Churchill thought the revolutionaries most dangerous to England came from Russia, Poland and the Baltic states. In this he was wrong, for the most dangerous revolutionaries were to be found in the mines and factories of England, where men worked at starvation wages and had no recourse in Parliament. From time to time they went on strike, and Churchill sent the police and the military to force them back to work. There were dock strikes and railroad strikes in August, 1911. Churchill acted with his customary vigor; the strikes were broken by armed soldiers; the disgruntled workmen returned to their jobs, vowing vengeance. As the years passed and nothing was done to redress the wrongs inflicted upon them, the temptation to come out in open revolt grew greater. Wealth poured into England from the colonies and from India, but very little of it reached the working man. These were the dangerous years, when only the outbreak of the First World War saved the country from bloody revolution.

As Home Secretary, Churchill was an unmitigated disaster, for he relied on weapons to solve social questions and had not the least idea what the common man was thinking. Ramsay MacDonald, the leader of the Labour Party, reminded him: "This is not a mediaeval State, and it is not Russia. It is not even Germany. We have discovered a secret which very few countries have hitherto discovered. The secret this nation has discovered is that the way to maintain law and order is to trust the ordinary operations of a law-abiding and orderly-inclined people." One of the tragedies of Churchill was that he continued to regard England as a medieval state.

In July, 1911, a German gunboat, the *Panther,* armed with eight three-inch guns, anchored off the coast of Morocco opposite the small, sleepy fishing port of Agadir. There were only a few mud huts and some goats, and on that hot summer day on the Atlantic coast it appeared that nothing of any importance had happened. The fishermen mended their nets, the Germans sent a small landing party on shore, and just as quietly they returned to their gunboat. What they were doing was of no great significance in itself, but in terms of the existing balance of power in Europe they were doing something of very great significance, for they were challenging the French protectorate of Morocco which had begun when French troops entered Fez earlier in the year. It was a deliberate and calculated insult to France, a warning to the world that Germany would not tolerate the expansion of the French empire in Africa. It was a threat uttered in those bleak and monotonous tones used by one colonial power when disputing with another. And there were many who thought they heard at Agadir the first drumbeat of the coming war.

The Kaiser, who had ordered the dispatch of the gunboat to Agadir, was a man who rarely concealed his intentions. He had made it abundantly clear that the German army at his orders would soon be on the march and that the German navy would blast out of the sea any navy opposing it. He called himself "the Admiral of the Atlantic" and praised the German army for its invincibility. Like Hitler later, he saw himself as a profoundly gifted strategist who knew exactly how to conquer his neighbors. For the French and the Russians he had only contempt, but for the British he retained a lurking respect, perhaps

Imperial War Museum, London

Winston Churchill, age seven

Lord Randolph Churchill, a
caricature by H. Furmiss
*National Portrait Gallery,
London*

Jennie Churchill
The Bettmann Archive

Churchill, the young subaltern

Paul Popper

Imperial War Museum, London

Churchill with one of his early airplanes, about 1912

Churchill at the headquarters of the French 33 Army
Corps, with General Emile Fayolle, 1915

Imperial War Museum, London

Churchill, painted by
Guthrie, about 1910
*Scottish National Portrait
Gallery*

Edward Marsh, painted
by Oswald Birley, 1949
*National Portrait Gallery,
London*

Eisenhower and Churchill, Christmas Day, 1943

Archbishop Damaskinos and Churchill, December, 1944

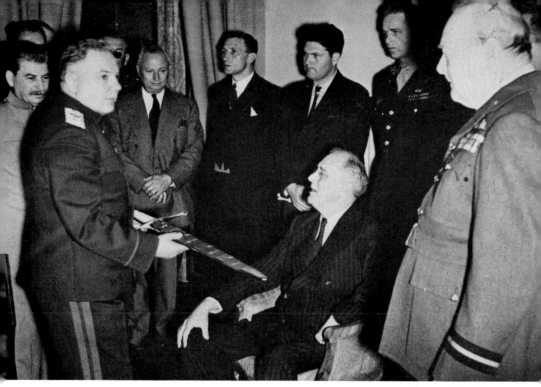

Presentation of the Stalingrad Sword at Teheran,
December, 1943

Paul Popper

Stalin and Churchill during Yalta Conference,
February, 1945

Paul Popper

Churchill in the bombed House of Commons
Paul Popper

because he was half English, his mother being Princess Victoria, the eldest child of Queen Victoria.

The Agadir crisis came at the height of the London season in the most glorious summer in living memory. Karsavina danced at the Palace Theatre, Nijinsky and Pavlova at Covent Garden, and all the great houses of London were vying with one another in the splendor of their balls, receptions and dinner parties. Churchill appeared at a fancy dress ball wearing a red Venetian cloak and a half-mask. It was a uniform well-suited to a man who liked to disguise himself but not in such a way that he would be unrecognizable. Agadir had shaken him. Cynthia Asquith remembered that he talked incessantly about matters far removed from his duties at the Home Office and seemed to think he would soon be called upon to direct vast armies against the foe. He brooded eloquently and with a frightening intensity, and sometimes it was "as if the weight of the world and of his own destiny were on his already bowed shoulders." The Agadir crisis passed, but the Kaiser had delivered a shock which was like a wound, and was well-satisfied with himself.

Churchill was growing weary of the Home Office, where he had earned a deserved unpopularity. What interested him above everything else was the coming war with Germany, the mechanics of battle, the deployment of lines of force on the map—particularly the map of France, where, he thought, most of the fighting would take place. On August 13, 1911, while still at the Home Office, he completed a lengthy and detailed memorandum which he called "Military Aspects of the Continental Problem." In something of the same spirit, Isaiah might have called his prophecies "Some Aspects of the Jewish Problem." For what Churchill accomplished in the memorandum was nothing less than prophecy of a peculiarly disturbing kind. It was deadly accurate. Once the battle was joined, he foresaw to the precise day and almost to the precise hour the sudden shifts and revolutions of the war. In *The World Crisis* he wrote modestly that it was, of course, only an attempt to pierce the veil of the future and to conjure up in the mind a vast imaginary situation. The attempt was astonishingly successful. He wrote:

MILITARY ASPECTS OF THE CONTINENTAL PROBLEM
MEMORANDUM BY MR. CHURCHILL

August 13, 1911

The following notes have been written on the assumption that a decision has been arrived at to employ a British military force on the Continent of Europe. It does not prejudge that decision in any way.

It is assumed that an alliance exists between Great Britain, France and Russia, and that these Powers are attacked by Germany and Austria.

1. The decisive military operations will be those between France and Germany. The German army is at least equal in quality to the French, and mobilises 2,200,000 against 1,700,000. The French must therefore seek for a situation of more equality. This can be found either before the full strength of the Germans has been brought to bear or after the German army has become extended. The first might be reached between the ninth and thirteenth days; the latter about the fortieth.

2. The fact that during a few days in the mobilisation period the French are equal or temporarily superior on the frontiers is of no significance, except on the assumption that France contemplates adopting a strategic offensive. The Germans will not choose the days when they themselves have least superiority for a general advance; and if the French advance, they lose at once all the advantages of their own internal communications, and by moving towards the advancing German reinforcements annul any numerical advantage they may for the moment possess. The French have therefore, at the beginning of the war, no option but to remain on the defensive, both upon their own fortress line and behind the Belgian frontier; and the choice of the day when the first main collision will commence rests with the Germans, who must be credited with the wisdom of choosing the best possible day, and cannot be forced into decisive action against their will, except by some reckless and unjustifiable movement on the part of the French.

3. A prudent survey of chances from the British point of view ought to contemplate that, when the German advance decisively begins, it will be backed by sufficient preponderance of force, and developed on a sufficiently wide front to compel the French armies to retreat from their positions behind the Belgian frontier, even though they may hold the gaps between the fortresses on the Verdun-Belfort front. No doubt a series of great battles will have been fought with varying local fortunes, and there is always a possibility of a heavy German check. But, even if the Germans were brought to a standstill, the French would not be strong enough to advance in their turn; and in any case we ought not to count on this. The balance of probability is that by the twentieth day the French armies will have been driven from the line of the Meuse and will be falling back on Paris and the south. All plans based upon the opposite assumption ask too much of fortune.

4. This is not to exclude the plan of using four or six British divisions in these great initial operations. Such a force is a material factor of significance. Its value to the French would be out of all proportion to its numerical strength. It would encourage every French soldier and make the task of the Germans in forcing the frontier much more costly. But the

question which is of most practical consequence to us is what is to happen after the frontier has been forced and the invasion of France has begun. France will not be able to end the war successfully by any action on the frontiers. She will not be strong enough to invade Germany. Her only chance is to conquer Germany in France. . . .

Three years later it would all happen as Churchill said it would happen. He gave the twentieth day of mobilization as the day on which the French armies would be driven from the Meuse, and in a later passage he proclaimed that the German army would be fully extended on the fortieth day on all fronts, and so it happened. The gift of prophecy is rarely given to Home Secretaries. In those days Churchill was in a strange, exalted mood, seeing himself somehow lifted above all other members of the Cabinet in authority over armies and navies, imagining that in some mysterious way he had been chosen as the war leader who would command the British forces in their final battle somewhere in the Middle East.

No doubt some of this exaltation was derived from Lord Fisher, the former First Sea Lord, now retired, who combined a harsh practical sense with a fervent belief that the British were the Lost Ten Tribes of Israel and that the *Book of Revelations* was an unfailing guide to world history. He had thus reached the conclusion that Armageddon would be fought in October, 1914, and the British race would then come into its larger inheritance. Churchill had met Fisher in 1907 and had been properly impressed.

About the time Churchill was writing his prophecies, he was also sending soldiers to put down the railroad and dock strikes. More workmen were killed; he did not care; at all costs law and order must be preserved. In London, Liverpool and Llanelly the soldiers fired at the strikers, and in thirty other places there were serious confrontations between the soldiers and the strikers. Lloyd George, sickened by the killing, patched up a settlement with the strikers and immediately telephoned the news to Churchill. "I'm very sorry to hear it," Churchill barked. "It would have been better to have gone on and given these men a good thrashing." Then he hung up the telephone and went off for a game of golf.

The strikers were a nuisance: they were vermin, and they interfered with his meditations on the coming war.

He spent a long weekend at the house of Lady Frances Horner in

Somerset. He had known her for many years, and once when she asked him after one of his interminable self-absorbed silences what he was thinking about, he answered: "I am thinking about a *diagram.*" That remark had brought their friendship to a temporary end, but it had since been revived. The Horner family descended from the Little Jack Horner of the nursery rhyme. They were kindly and generous, and owned in the quiet village of Mells one of the most splendid Tudor manor houses in England. Here Churchill rested from the labor of murdering strikers. It was high summer, the bees were humming, the light drowsed on gray stone walls, and he should have been content. But he was not content. He could think of nothing else but the peril of war, and wandered restlessly in the smiling countryside under the shadow of the Mendip Hills. Suddenly he remembered some lines from A. E. Housman's *Shropshire Lad:*

> On the idle hill of summer,
>   Sleepy with the sound of streams,
> Far I hear the steady drummer
>   Drumming like a noise in dreams.°
>
> Far and near and low and louder
>   On the roads of earth go by,
> Dear to friends and food for powder,
>   Soldiers marching, all to die.

The poem haunted him, and there was no escape from its menacing beat. He was resting on a hilltop, and it seemed to him that the valleys were full of marching soldiers and there was nothing he could do to prevent them from going to their deaths.

In the following month he went to stay with the Asquiths in a house on the East Lothian coast of Scotland. Asquith had taken up golf and was seriously concerned to improve his game, and consequently Churchill was invited to accompany him on his golfing expeditions. Lord Haldane, the Secretary for War, was staying nearby and frequently came over. Asquith, the pure parliamentarian, Olympian and aristocratic in appearance, though his father was a cloth manufac-turer, confronted Haldane, the son of a signet writer, a hugely fat and ungainly man who spent his free hours studying German philosophy and discussing it in a high and squeaky voice. Asquith was fifty-nine,

---

° Housman had written "Sleepy with the flow of streams." Churchill, who had a prodigious memory for poetry, sometimes misremembered.

Haldane was fifty-five, Churchill was thirty-six. All of them had heard the steady drummer and were aware that great changes were needed in the army and navy to prepare them for the coming war. Haldane wanted to go to the Admiralty, and suggested that Churchill should take over the War Office for a year or two, and then Haldane would resume as Secretary for War, leaving Churchill in charge of the Admiralty. Churchill, seeing the Admiralty so close to his grasp, wanted the Admiralty now. The younger Pitt once proclaimed that patience was the most important quality of a statesman, but Churchill lacked all the arts of patience. He used all his wiles on Asquith, and was aided by Asquith's daughter Violet, his golfing companion, who was half in love with him and knew that he wanted the Admiralty above all things. Churchill was insistent; Haldane doubted Churchill's ability; and so for some days the debate continued with all the advantages on the side of the younger man, who was staying in the Prime Minister's house and constantly dancing attendance on him. Finally Asquith surrendered. They were playing golf when Asquith abruptly decided to let Churchill have the Admiralty. When they returned to the house in the early afternoon, Violet Asquith was preparing a tea party. "I don't want tea—I don't want anything—anything in the world!" Churchill exclaimed. "Your father has just offered me the Admiralty!"

So he had, but it would be fairer to say that Churchill had taken it by force, breaking down the resistance of Asquith and Haldane by the impetuosity of his attack and the violence of his self-assertion. He had been a roving and not especially brilliant Under Secretary for the Colonies, a statesmanlike President of the Board of Trade, and a calamitously incompetent Home Secretary. And Haldane wondered what virtues he possessed to take command of the Royal Navy at a time when it needed to be violently reorganized and placed on a war footing. If the war came within the next few weeks, before Churchill had learned the basic elements of his job, then the choice would be disastrous. Give him three or four years, and he might make an excellent First Lord of the Admiralty.

Churchill had no doubt about his ability to command the navy. His sense of the justice of the appointment was confirmed that same evening when he opened the large Bible in his bedroom at random and read the words of *Deuteronomy:*

> Hear, O Israel: Thou art to pass over Jordan this day, to go in to possess nations greater and mightier than thyself, cities great and fenced up to heaven.

A people great and tall, the children of the Anakims, whom thou knowest, and of whom thou hast heard say, Who can stand before the children of Anak!

Understand therefore this day, that the Lord thy God is he which goeth over before thee; as a consuming fire he shall destroy them, and he shall bring them down before thy face; so shalt thou drive them out, and destroy them quickly, as the Lord hath said unto thee.

Armed with these words, which seemed so appropriate and so full of presages of greatness and great victories, Churchill embarked on his career as First Lord of the Admiralty.

Edward Marsh, his perennial secretary, who accompanied him to the Admiralty, observed an abrupt change in him. "He has completely changed his character in some ways," Marsh observed, "and has come out with a brand new set of perfect manners and a high standard of punctuality." Nevertheless, the swashbuckling continued, for Churchill soon took possession of the Admiralty yacht *Enchantress* and dashed about on well-publicized visits to naval establishments. He swept out three of the four Sea Lords, explaining that many were set in their ways, that they were bound to disagree with his innovations, and that he had come to the Admiralty "with the clear intention of having an entirely new Board of my own choosing." Prince Louis of Battenburg, who had married a granddaughter of Queen Victoria and had no other special claim to prominence, became First Sea Lord. As his Naval Secretary he appointed Rear Admiral David Beatty, who had been in command of a gunboat on the Nile shortly before the battle of Omdurman and had tossed a bottle of champagne to the young Churchill from the quarter-deck. Beatty was a hard-riding horseman, a fine shot, a man about town, and the husband of the heiress of the Marshall Field department store in Chicago. He was a man of Churchill's own kind, brash, domineering, quick-witted and superbly self-confident. At the time he became Naval Secretary he had been retired from the navy on half pay for refusing to accept a command which he regarded as beneath his dignity.

When Churchill became First Lord he knew very little about the navy, but he learned fast. He sent for Lord Fisher, who was living in retirement in Italy, and bombarded him with questions and received vehement replies to all of them. Fisher was even more daring than Churchill; the old, crusty, retired First Sea Lord, whose letters ended "Yours till charcoal sprouts" or "Yours to a cinder," had the Nelson touch. He became the presiding genius of the new navy. New ships, new kinds of ships, came into existence. Fisher wanted fifteen-inch guns, and so fifteen-inch guns were made. Fisher wanted speed, and this could be obtained only by converting coal-burning ships to oil, which had the additional advantage of permitting ships to be fueled at sea. But Britain had risen to power in the industrial age because its immense coal beds could be harnessed to machinery. Where was the oil? Churchill set up a Royal Commission on Oil Supply, appointed Fisher as the chairman, and superintended the creation of the Anglo-Persian Oil Company with an original investment by the British Government of £2,200,000. The cost of the new navy mounted at a prodigious rate. When Churchill presented his naval estimates to the Cabinet at the end of 1913, the cost was £49,000,000, a sum which left the Cabinet gasping.

Churchill's attitude toward the Royal Navy was proprietorial. He loved it, cherished it, studied its history, its capability, its tactics and strategies with a consuming passion, and since he loved it so much, he could also be highly disrespectful. The story was told that at a meeting in the Admiralty in 1913, someone objected to his untraditional approach to naval problems. "The tradition of the navy!" he exploded. "Do you know what is the tradition of the navy? I will tell you. Rum, sodomy and the lash—that is the tradition of the navy! Good morning, gentlemen!" Fisher, who began his naval career as a midshipman, possessed a similar disrespect for naval traditions.

Fisher loved to sing hymns from Keble's *Christian Year,* and there was one line that especially attracted him: "The dusky hues of glorious War," and he liked to fling the words at Churchill. "Don't fiddle about armour; it is really so VERY silly!" he wrote. "There is only ONE defence and that is SPEED!" Churchill agreed, and the fastest, costliest and most sophisticated fleet known to history came into existence at Churchill's orders.

Meanwhile, of course, the Germans were building warships at an alarming pace, and the naval race threatened to exhaust the treasuries of both countries. Churchill made a speech explaining patiently that a fleet was a necessity for Britain, a luxury for Germany. In the translation the words *Luxus-Flotte* has connotations absent in the luxury fleet, which only made matters worse, and when Churchill seriously proposed a year-long holiday from naval shipbuilding, the Germans greeted the proposal with icy silence. The Kaiser received through Sir Ernest Cassel a secret memorandum from Churchill urging him to believe in the powers of patience to resolve all quarrels. The British, he explained, could not but view German naval expansion with alarm; surely there must be an end to the race! But there was no end. The two powers were on a collision course, and the probability of a war between Britain and Germany became greater with every passing month.

It was a time when the utmost caution was necessary, and no one was cautious. Churchill gloried in his navy and continued to make provocative statements which alarmed the Germans and to hold war games designed as shows of force, which alarmed them even more. On both sides provocation became a way of life. Lord Haldane made an official visit to Berlin to inquire into German intentions and received from the hands of the Kaiser the new German Naval Law, which outlined a staggering expansion of the German navy. Immediately afterward, in the spring of 1912, Churchill ordered a naval review off Portland with 150 warships, and the Royal Yacht in attendance. It was a massive display of force. Maneuvers of great complexity and ingenuity took place in sight of the naval attachés of a dozen nations, and Churchill observed with delight the effect produced on foreign observers by these majestic warships as they loomed through the mist. Among those foreign observers were many German officers.

The navy became Churchill's religion, his pride, his sole occupation. In the thirty-two months between his appointment as First Lord and the outbreak of the war, he spent eight months, a quarter of the total, on the *Enchantress.* He was traveling incessantly, so that the Cabinet had some difficulty in keeping up with him. Official duties were not allowed to interfere with more pleasurable occupations, and he permitted himself long Mediterranean cruises. Landing at Athens in the days before the Parthenon had been artificially restored for the benefit of tourists, he considered and then rejected the idea of sending blue jackets to set up the tumbled columns for the benefit of posterity; and, landing at Syracuse and standing in the vast Greek theater, he regaled his companions with a long account of the ill-fated Sicilian Expedition which led to the total annihilation of the Athenian invasion army and the loss of the Athenian fleet. Athens fighting Sicily could be compared with Germany fighting England, and Churchill had seriously studied the lessons of that war which had taken place 2,325 years before. He believed almost as an article of faith that the German army and the German navy would suffer the same fate as the Athenians.

During the spring and summer of 1913, when there could already be felt the shuddering in the sky which announces a coming war, Churchill drew up a series of hypothetical constructions describing the first months of the war in prophetical terms. One of these constructions was written as a diary, others—there were altogether four of these works, which he described as "exercises of the imagination"—were drawn up like position papers. The diary, which he called "The Time Table of a Nightmare," described the first twenty days of the war in precise and graphic detail from the moment when the Germans occupy Liège on April 1 by simply racing into the city in automobiles to the surrender of the German commander of the invasion force somewhere in the suburbs of London on April 20, whereupon the second phase of the war begins.

The style of "The Time Table of a Nightmare" corresponds very closely to the style of *Savrola* and especially to the concluding chapters of the novel, when civil and foreign war break out simultaneously in Laurania. A German invasion army lands at Harwich under cover of the guns of German battleships and cruisers, while almost simultaneously two German battle cruisers and forty destroyers occupy Scapa Flow and close the Pentland Firth before proceeding to establish a destroyer base at Balta Sound in the Shetlands. On the following day the British fleet steams up the Channel, comes in sight of the German fleet off Harwich and pursues it back to German waters. In effect, the Germans turn tail and flee, escaping punishment because they are faster than the British ships. The British fleet then bombards Harwich, while the German invasion army advances on Colchester and Chelmsford. Simultaneously a British expeditionary force of five divisions lands in France.

By 10 P.M. on April 3 the British blockade of Harwich is complete, but during the night German destroyers darting across the North Sea play havoc with the blockade. Five of the best armored cruisers of the British fleet are sunk or holed by torpedoes, but most of the German destroyers are lost in the engagement. Harwich lies open to the enemy.

An army of 45,000 German infantry equipped with sixty guns and ten days' supplies and emergency rations moves on London, the advance guards forging ahead on bicycles. The grave threat to London while the British Expeditionary Force is being transported to France leads to serious riots.

> *April 7, Afternoon.*—Serious rioting in London to prevent the departure of troops. Enormous crowds, converging on Westminster, were repeatedly charged by the mounted police, and finally fired on by the two battalions of Guards which had been assigned to the duty of protecting

His Majesty's person. From this time on the movement of troops to the south was increasingly hindered by the population, who endeavoured everywhere to prevent the departure of troop trains by invading the lines, tearing up the rails, or laying themselves in front of the engines. Continued collisions between the military and the people at all points of entrainment and detrainment reported.

Saturday, April 8.—German army marches south from Chelmsford to the line Harlow-Ongar-Billericay.

In spite of the delays on the railroads through ignorant popular manifestations, the transportation of the army continues, though many units and portions of units are delayed.

Sunday, April 9, 3:40 P.M.—House of Commons: Leader of the Opposition asks the Government what steps they propose to take to protect London, and particularly whether some part of the expeditionary army should not be employed for that purpose . . .

April 9, 11 P.M.—Government defeated by 617 votes to 22. Ministry resigns. New Ministry formed. Sole object and policy: "To save London."

German advance guards reach Waltham Abbey, Romford, and Woolwich. Continuous street fighting commences at all points of contact.

Monday, April 10, 3 A.M.—All transportation of troops to the Continent stopped . . . Orders given to concentrate all regular troops on London. German army continues its advance in three divisions, fighting their way through the suburbs of London, being resisted by the civil population, and large numbers of Territorials without organisation of any kind, and reinforced piecemeal from hour to hour by the regular units brought back from the south . . .

April 10, 8 P.M.—German advance definitely arrested on the line Tottenham-Dagenham-Woolwich.

Tuesday, April 11.—Germans completely invested in the triangle Tottenham, Woolwich, Romford.

British forces reorganizing on all fronts . . .

Friday, April 14.—German raiding column from Blyth enters Newcastle, the North having been completely denuded of troops by the supreme need of London . . .

April 14, 4 P.M.—Great battle on the line of the Meuse begins. British troops on the left (mainly infantry) heavily engaged . . .

Saturday, April 15.—Total defeat of the French and the Franco-British left on the line of the Meuse . . .

April 16, 17, 18, and 19.—French armies and remnants of the British force in full retreat from the line of the Meuse.

Enemy near London still holding out.

Newcastle raiders fortifying themselves practically unmolested.

No serious operations against the enemy in the Shetlands possible pending the settlement of the London business.

All British warships are riveted to the vital task of preventing further disembarkations.

April 19, Midnight.—German Commander-in-Chief near London offers to capitulate on terms of being conveyed out of the country. He states his ability to hold out for several weeks more, and declares that rather than surrender at discretion he will shoot the 10,000 prisoners who are in his hands, and destroy all the plant of Woolwich Arsenal.

Terms accepted. . . .

Such, in brief, was "The Time Table of a Nightmare," to which Churchill attached quite extraordinary importance. It is a strange document, intensely personal, written as though he were observing a war in a state of hallucination. Much of the excitement derives from the diary form, but there is no doubting Churchill's conviction that the war might develop in this way and perhaps only in this way. Yet nothing of the kind happened, nor was it likely. The fantasy is out of control; memories of the bombardment of Laurania in *Savrola* mingle with the projected German bombardment of Harwich; and the longest paragraph, the center pin, of the entire fantasy is devoted to the rioting by Londoners who are shot down by two battalions of Guards with the sole object of protecting the King's life. Churchill seems to delight in the rioting and the consequent punishment. The bloody-mindedness which led Lloyd George to call him "the Minister of Civil Slaughter" is still in evidence. He was, in the modern phrase, attempting to think the unthinkable, but this time the gift of prophecy had been removed from him and he was deadly wrong.

All through these months he was in a curiously manic mood, so sure of himself and so certain of his powers that he seemed to be ridden by demons. Lord Riddell remembered a conversation with Churchill in January, 1913. "I think I know the English people," Churchill said. "The old Cromwellian spirit still survives. I believe I am watched over. Think of the perils I have escaped." By "the Cromwellian spirit" he meant the demonic, visionary Cromwell who walked surefootedly along the paths laid out by destiny, as described by Thomas Carlyle in *Heroes and Hero-Worship* in the chapter "The Hero as King." Like Fisher, he felt he was divinely protected.

For many years Cromwell had absorbed his imagination, and now that he was First Lord of the Admiralty, it occurred to him that one of the new battleships should be named *Oliver Cromwell,* and he submitted this name to King George V, who had succeeded his father, Edward VII, in 1910. King George V was by training a sailor and took a special interest in his navy. He rejected the name *Oliver Cromwell* for a battleship when it was submitted in 1911, and because Churchill was insistent he summoned his First Lord of the Admiralty to a private meeting, where he made his objections quite clear. If England had been a republic, there might have been some justification for naming a ship in this way, but England was a monarchy and the reigning monarch did not think highly of regicides. But in the following year Churchill submitted the name again. There was an acrimonious correspondence, the King refusing, Churchill insisting. Churchill's arguments were devious, supported by the testimony of historians and buttressed by his own unyielding belief in the propriety of his choice. He wrote: "The great movement in politics and religion of which Oliver Cromwell was the instrument was intimately connected with all those forces which, through a long succession of Princes, have brought His Majesty to the Throne of a Constitutional and a Protestant country. The bitterness of the rebellions and the tyrannies of the past have long ceased to stir men's minds." But King George V was still stirred by the fate of King Charles I and in no mood to surrender. He adamantly refused to let any battleship be called *Oliver Cromwell.* Nor, for various reasons, did the King approve of *William Pitt* and *Ark Royal,* the flagship of the fleet that defeated the Spanish Armada. Churchill protested, hinted that he possessed ministerial privilege and could go ahead and name the ships according to his own wishes, and received from the King's secretary, Lord Stamfordham, a severe letter of reproof.

Churchill's obsession with Cromwell lasted throughout his life, apparently beginning in his early childhood. Some of the best pages in his *History of the English-Speaking Peoples* are devoted to the study of that strange, calm and frenzied genius. Cromwell was the type of "the great man," the popular hero and warrior whose name resounds in history. At times of crisis Churchill inevitably returned to the contemplation of the hero who sometimes seemed even larger than the Duke of Marlborough. One day in 1943 Churchill was entertaining Harold Macmillan in Cairo. The war had passed its turning point, and he was confronted with the specter of Russia overrunning Europe, one monstrous regime apparently about to replace another that was slowly being strangled to death.

"Cromwell was a great man, wasn't he?" Churchill asked.

"Yes, sir, a very great man," Macmillan replied.

"Ah, but he made one terrible mistake," Churchill went on. "Obsessed in his youth by fear of the power of Spain, he failed to observe the rise of France. Will that be said of me?"

Thus the trinity was established in his mind: Cromwell-Marlborough-Churchill. Cromwell, who had permitted the rise of France, Marlborough, who had brought France low, Churchill, who had permitted another power to rise threateningly over Europe.

So he thought of himself as the man of destiny, the eye of the hurricane directing the movement of vast and terrifying forces, his five-sworded hands stretched across Europe and all the seas patrolled by the Royal Navy. He was almost insanely proud, and at the mercy of his demons.

THE FIRST LORD

WHEN THE WAR broke out in the summer of 1914, the fleet was ready. Out of enthusiasm, self-indulgence and a vast pride in the Royal Navy, Churchill had conjured up a fighting force so powerful that it was inconceivable that any other navy or combination of navies could stand up to it. In controlled firepower, in tonnage, in maneuverability, in excellence of design, these warships represented to a quite extraordinary degree the might of the British Empire which girdled the globe, and it was not his fault that the fleet served little purpose and only once, briefly and indecisively, met the German High Seas Fleet head on.

The exciting days for the navy came at the beginning of the war. The fleet had already been mobilized for over two weeks when the war broke out, following a test mobilization carried out at Churchill's orders in the middle of July. The test mobilization culminated with a grand review off Spithead with the King taking the salute from the Royal Yacht. There was nothing especially sinister in the test mobilization; it was cheaper than holding maneuvers in the North Sea. On July 20 the London *Times* had a small item of information: "Orders have been given that the First Fleet, which is concentrated at Portland, not to disperse for manoeuvre leave for the present. All vessels of the

Second Fleet are remaining at their home ports in proximity to their balance crews." Churchill had ensured that this rather cryptic message appear in the *Times* so that it would come to the attention of the German Embassy and thus to the Kaiser. The great fleet of more than seventy ships was being held together off the Isle of Wight, but though it was the largest and most powerful fleet ever assembled in one place, it was quite useless where it was. By July 29 Churchill and Prince Louis of Battenberg, the First Sea Lord, had decided that the First or Grand Fleet should move quickly to the east coast, and that night the fleet sailed without lights through the Dover Straits to vanish in the mists of Scapa Flow.

Although Churchill gloried in war in the abstract and liked to say that the story of the human race is war, he was certain that this war would produce unimaginable horrors and must be prevented. The Cabinet did not want war; the people did not want it; only the Kaiser and the Emperor Franz Josef appeared to want it with any passion. At a Cabinet meeting Churchill proposed a conference of all the European kings to settle all the outstanding issues. Nothing came of the proposal, and step by step, as though deeply fascinated by the prospect of doom and the extinction of European civilization, the Kaiser and Franz Josef together with their ministers succeeded in digging the pit into which Europe fell.

When the war came, Churchill proposed to enjoy it. The fleet was ready, and he used it with the utmost efficiency to protect the troops that were sent to France, with the result that thirteen British army divisions were transported to France by the end of November. Fighting the German fleet was another matter. The only major battle, fought off the coast of Jutland, was inconclusive, both sides claiming a victory. Instead of sea battles there were sudden raids, brilliant skirmishes, interminable errors. The first British naval engagement in the war took place on August 5, 1914, the day after war was declared, when the light cruiser *Amphion* sank the German minelayer *Königin Luise*, took the survivors on board, and shortly afterward was struck by one of the minelayer's mines. This kind of thing was to be repeated endlessly. The fates preserved the big fish intact, but all the little minnows were gobbled up.

The fast German battle cruisers *Goeben* and *Breslau* were prowling the Mediterranean. British and French ships were available to engage them and blast them out of the water. Confused messages came from the Admiralty; neither the British nor the French were in time to prevent the German battle cruisers from slipping through the Dardanelles to the safety of the Turkish ports.

Toward the end of the month the British mounted a sudden naval raid on the Heligoland Bight. It was a brilliantly daring operation, but once again the Admiralty issued confused orders. Happily, three German cruisers were sunk and three others damaged, and not a single British ship was lost. Admiral David Beatty received full credit for the operation, and the Admiralty planners, who deserved no credit at all, were exonerated. It was the first engagement which could be described as a victory, and in the following month came the first serious defeat, off the Dogger Bank. The cruiser *Aboukir* was sunk by a torpedo from a submarine, and while the survivors were clinging to the wreckage, two other cruisers, the *Cressy* and the *Hogue,* came to their rescue and were sunk by the same submarine. There were 800 survivors, but more than 1,400 were drowned.

So it went on in dingdong fashion throughout the war: small defeats, small victories, while the great battle fleets remained in their closely guarded harbors. Churchill's navy was proving to be an expensive luxury.

Meanwhile, the war on land was going badly, with the Germans throwing their whole strength against France with the aim of annihilating French military power. The French army was falling back on Paris, the Channel ports were dangerously exposed, and Churchill was calmly waiting for that famous fortieth day, when he expected German lines to be fully extended and the counterattack to begin. The rapid German advance on the Channel ports was of special interest to the Cabinet, because if the Germans established themselves in Calais, then the danger of invasion became crucial. They were moving in the direction of Antwerp, the largest of the Belgian ports, and at all costs it was necessary to stop them or at the very least to delay their advance. Crucial decisions had to be made, but as far as the Channel ports were concerned, no one was making them. Churchill decided that he would have to take a hand in this perilous situation and he set up a detachment of naval airplanes at Dunkirk in the hope of bombing any German troops who came within range of his airplanes. To the alarm of Asquith, who felt that the First Lord of the Admiralty should be dealing with ships, Churchill was continually running over to Dunkirk to inspect these airplanes and to discover new uses for them. He decided to send airplanes to bomb the zeppelin sheds at Cologne and Düsseldorf, and although the airplanes were sent out, no harm was done to the zeppelins, for the bombs failed to explode. Churchill consoled himself with the thought that the principle had been established: the sheds were vulnerable, and it was much better that the zeppelins should be destroyed on the ground than when they were flying over London.

By the beginning of September the Belgians were being hard pressed at Antwerp and Sir Edward Grey, the Secretary of State for Foreign Affairs, received an urgent appeal for help. Kitchener thought the Belgians were exaggerating the danger; Churchill thought every effort should be made to go to their aid. By the end of the month it had become evident that Antwerp would be unable to hold out without massive aid from both the French and the British. Grey and Kitchener were in conference on the evening of October 2, 1914, discussing the flood of appeals from the Belgian government. While they were talking, Churchill was on a special train taking him to Dover and so to Dunkirk to inspect a marine brigade which was falling back to the coast from the French town of Cassel. The train was halted and ordered to turn back, and Churchill learned that he was wanted immediately at Kitchener's house. The conference was still going on when Churchill arrived. He was told that Antwerp was now within range of the German guns, that the Belgian government intended to abandon the city and retire to Ostend, and although the Belgians thought they could defend the city for five or six days, it was believed that all resistance would come to an end when the government left. The position of Antwerp, Belgium's most powerful and well-defended fortress, seemed hopeless.

From Bordeaux, where the French government had taken refuge, came news that the French were preparing to send two territorial divisions, together with artillery and cavalry, to Antwerp as quickly as possible. They were also preparing to launch an offensive in the neighborhood of Lille with the object of causing a retreat by the German forces investing Antwerp. The question was: How long could Antwerp hold out? Asquith was in Cardiff and could not be reached. Decisions had to be made quickly. Since all arrangements had already been made for his journey to Dunkirk, Churchill suggested that he carry out his original plan and race from Dunkirk to Antwerp by car. While there he could make his estimate of the real danger threatening the city, communicating his findings by telephone or telegraph. With luck he would be able to reach Antwerp some time during the following morning. He left Kitchener's house at about 1:30 A.M. and he reached

Antwerp early in the afternoon. Alexander Powell, the correspondent
of the *New York World*, who happened to be present outside Belgian
army headquarters when Churchill arrived, recorded the scene:

> At one o'clock in the afternoon a big drab-colored touring-car filled
> with British Naval officers drove down the Place de Meir, its horn
> sounding a hoarse warning, took the turn into the Marché aux Souliers on
> two wheels, and drew up in front of the hotel. Before the car had fairly
> come to a stop the door of the tonneau was thrown violently open and out
> jumped a smooth-faced, sandy-haired, stoop-shouldered, youthful-
> looking man in undress Trinity House uniform. There was no mistaking
> who it was. It was the Right Hon. Winston Churchill.
>
> As he darted into the crowded lobby, which, as usual in the luncheon
> hour, was filled with Belgian, French and British staff officers, diploma-
> tists, Cabinet Ministers, and correspondents, he flung his arms out in a
> nervous characteristic gesture, as though pushing his way through a
> crowd. It was a most spectacular entrance, and reminded me for all the
> world of a scene in a melodrama where the hero dashes up, bare-headed,
> on a foam-flecked horse, and saves the heroine, or the old homestead, or
> the family fortune as the case.may be.
>
> While lunching with Sir Francis Villiers and the staff of the British
> Legation, two English correspondents approached, and asked Mr.
> Churchill for an interview.
>
> "I will not talk to you," he almost shouted, banging his fist down upon
> the table. "You have no business to be in Belgium at this time. Get out of
> the country at once!". . .
>
> The Burgomaster stopped him, introduced himself, and expressed his
> anxiety regarding the fate of the city. Before he had finished Churchill
> was part way up the stairs. "I think everything will be all right now, Mr.
> Burgomaster," he called in a voice which could be distinctly heard in the
> lobby. "You needn't worry. We're going to save the city."

At that moment Antwerp was in a hopeless situation. The outer forts
were falling one by one, as the enormous German howitzers reduced
them to rubble. The water supply was cut off. There were almost no
supplies—scarcely any guns, the ammunition was running out, military
telephones, searchlights and entrenching tools were in short supply,
and, worst of all, the soldiers were becoming dispirited. Churchill soon
realized that there was something even worse than the fall of Antwerp:
the whole Belgian army might fall into the trap the Germans were
preparing for it. The only safe line of retreat ran parallel to the Dutch
frontier. Although two Belgian divisions and a cavalry division were

protecting this line of retreat, there was no guarantee they would be successful. Churchill asked for a last-ditch effort. Could they hold out for three days? For six days? For ten days? Fired by his enthusiasm, they answered that they could hold out for three, were pretty certain they could hold out for six, and would try for ten, provided that reinforcements came quickly. Churchill telegraphed to London for two naval brigades to be routed to Antwerp by way of Dunkirk with five days' rations and 2,000,000 rounds of ammunition.

He inspected the defenses. It was the typical Belgian terrain—flat, a few trees and bushes, much of the land under water, the trenches a foot deep in water, the lines very thinly held. "Where are the bloody men?" he asked, and was told that the defenders were few and the enemy numerous. High in the sky hung the German kite balloons. There was no infantry action, but from time to time there came the dull roar of heavy artillery in the distance.

Churchill waited impatiently for a reply from London and made his own plans for assuming command of the defenses. He had wanted this more than he had wanted anything else—the command of an army, a battlefield of enormous significance, a breakthrough which would have the effect of routing the German army back to its frontiers. He was very serious about this, and telegraphed to Asquith a request to be allowed to remain at Antwerp with "the full powers of a commander of a detached force in the field," by which he meant that he would have the rank of a Lieutenant General. Since his previous rank was that of a Lieutenant of Hussars, this considerable promotion caused an outburst of laughter at the Cabinet meeting where it was discussed. Kitchener was in favor of giving Churchill full powers; Asquith demurred; he wanted a general with some experience of generalship in Antwerp. Accordingly, a general was sent out, but Churchill remained in command. Suddenly, from all directions, help began to arrive at Antwerp. A French division was embarking at Le Havre; two British naval brigades and 8,000 French marines were on their way; and from England the British Seventh Division and the Third Cavalry Division were sent across waters infested with submarines to Ostend and Zeebrugge, where they disembarked on October 6. There was the danger that all these forces might be trapped. The danger was recognized, but the risk had to be taken to give the Allied forces time to reorganize and meet the German drive against the Channel ports. So the Belgians dug themselves in, the French and the British relief columns hurried to the burning city, and every morning King Albert of the Belgians and

Churchill presided over the War Council and deliberated about fortresses, defenses, escape routes, supplies and succour for the population terrorized by the shells from the German howitzers. Only a miracle could have saved Antwerp, and no miracle came. Churchill's dream of taking command of an army that would hurl the Germans back across Belgium faded; he became a spectator. He wore a cloak and a yachting cap and smoked the inevitable cigar as he toured the front lines, a strange visitor from another planet, oddly gentle now, for there was nothing much that could be done except to hold out for a little while longer against the overwhelming guns of the enemy.

Many of the men in the naval brigade were only partly trained. Some had never held a rifle in their hands; their officers had no ammunition for their revolvers; and there were no bandages, no medical supplies. Rupert Brooke, the poet, was one of those raw, green recruits thrown into the lines. He describes the first night he spent in a garden near an abandoned chateau on the outskirts of Antwerp: "Little pools glimmered through the trees, and deserted fountains, and round corners one saw, faintly, occasional Cupids and Venuses—a scattered company of rather bad statues—gleaming quietly. The sailors dug their latrines in the various rose-gardens and lay down to sleep—but it was bitter cold —under the shrubs. I was officer on guard till the middle of the night. Then I lay down on the floor of a bedroom for a decent night's sleep. But by 2 the shells had got unpleasantly near. A big one (I'm told) burst above the garden: but too high to do damage. And some message came. So up we got—frozen and sleepy—and toiled off through the night. By dawn we got into trenches, very good ones, and relieved Belgians."

Most of the naval brigade escaped, but two battalions strayed over the Dutch border in the darkness and confusion, and were interned for the rest of the war. The Belgians fell back on the coast, and the refugees poured endlessly along the roads. Antwerp, which held out until October 10, was nothing more than a fiery skeleton when the Germans entered, to find scarcely ten thousand people remaining in a city of half a million. Churchill returned to London on the sixth, having accomplished nothing. Many years later he would tell General Sir Harold Alexander that Antwerp was one of the major disappointments of his life, for there had come to him a fierce thirst for military glory and he had seen himself as the commander of the armies of the Allies on Belgian soil. His telegram to Asquith asking to be relieved of his duties as First Lord of the Admiralty and to be invested with the rank of a

Lieutenant General was made with the utmost seriousness. A hope had blazed up, and within forty-eight hours it died down.

Sir Edward Grey wrote to Mrs. Churchill that her husband was a hero. "I can't tell you how much I admire his courage and gallant spirit and genius for war," he wrote. "It inspires us all." He was writing to comfort her because she had just given birth to a daughter. But this was not the opinion of the newspapers, which thought that Churchill's intervention at Antwerp was ill-conceived, costly in lives and totally unnecessary. It was said darkly that Churchill had enjoyed himself too much playing the hero; and those who remembered the Sidney Street affair and the shooting of the miners and dock workers thought they recognized the emerging pattern which was to become more clearly recognizable with the fiasco of the Dardanelles. The truth was not quite so clear. That Churchill was dangerous and unpredictable was evident to everyone who knew him; the overmastering ambition was always present; he thirsted after all the glory in the world. But these personal defects, which he regarded as his greatest virtues, were compensated for by his critical intelligence, his wide-ranging knowledge of strategy, his power to inspire enthusiasm. He had not journeyed to Antwerp on his own. Kitchener and Grey had sent him, and the vision of supreme power had come to him only when he was on Belgian soil.

The attacks on him in the newspapers increased, and he pretended to pay no attention to them, though they hurt him deeply. He thought he could outlive the storm, although the newspaper attacks tended to decrease his usefulness in the Cabinet. In *The World Crisis,* written after the war, he offers a favorable portrait of himself surveying the ruins of Antwerp with shells and shrapnel falling all around him and men being killed at his side. He is gallantry incarnate, singlehandedly ensuring the presence of the King and his government in the doomed city for a few days longer. But strangely there is not a word about the desperate plight of the hundreds of thousands of refugees and he forgot to mention that the naval brigade fought ineffectively and was of no use to the defenders, and when they were called out of line they scrambled over one another to reach safety. George Cornwallis-West, who was one of the three husbands of Lady Randolph Churchill, commanded a battalion at Antwerp and Rupert Brooke was one of his junior officers. During the retreat he kept shouting to his men that he was ashamed of their cowardice, but he could not prevent them from falling over one another in their panic.

In human terms Churchill was culpable. It was nothing to him that Antwerp had been destroyed, that the roads were made impassable by the thronging refugees, that he had offered the Belgians the promise of vast reinforcements and not all these reinforcements arrived, and he knew he was making promises he could not keep. He gave no thought to the problem of feeding and caring for the refugees; he was not concerned with people, only with the giant forces at work; and he saw himself as one of the giant forces. Churchill's fondness for himself, and his inhumanity, were only too evident. The fondness would remain; defeats and tragedies would make him more human in time; and the new Marlborough, after his four days in Antwerp, returned to his duties at the Admiralty conscious that he had acted at all times with perfect propriety and with sufficient authority, professing to be puzzled that so many people thought he had acted abominably.

Churchill was not yet a popular figure. He was admired and distrusted, as Alcibiades had been admired and distrusted in Athens. In 1913, on the eve of the war, A. G. Gardiner had published a famous book of biographical sketches called *Pillars of Society*. Of Churchill he wrote prophetically:

> He is always unconsciously playing a part—an heroic part. And he is himself his most astonished spectator. He sees himself moving through the smoke of battle—triumphant, terrible, his brow clothed with thunder, his legions looking to him for victory, and not looking in vain. He thinks of Napoleon; he thinks of his great ancestor. Thus did they bear themselves; thus, in this rugged and most awful crisis, will he bear himself. It is not make-believe, it is not insincerity; it is that in that fervid and picturesque imagination there are always great deeds afoot with himself cast by destiny in the Agamemnon rôle. . . . He will write his name big in the future. Let us take care he does not write it in blood.

But while Agamemnon was the leader of the hosts, Churchill at the Admiralty played the minor roles of troubleshooter and civilian commander of the navy. His troubleshooting was now largely concerned with the "Dunkirk circus," consisting of marines and airmen attached to the Fleet Air Arm, a commando group settled in the region of Dunkirk with unspecified duties. They acquitted themselves well, finally succeeded in blowing up the zeppelin in the shed at Düsseldorf which they had previously attacked without success, and made occasional sallies into German-occupied territory. For a while this was

Churchill's private army, to be enjoyed whenever he had a spare moment to give to it.

Prince Louis of Battenberg, the First Sea Lord, had outlived his usefulness. The idea that a prince of German extraction, however well descended, should be in command of the Royal Navy at a time of war against Germany was not one to give comfort to the people. He was ousted and replaced by the seventy-four-year-old Lord Fisher, whom Asquith described as "a well-plucked chicken." This was an unfair description of a bantam rooster with flaming feathers, as proud and as wildly erratic as Lucifer. Churchill was forty, and Fisher, who was nearly twice his age, sometimes appeared to be the younger man.

Fisher's return to the Admiralty coincided with a major British naval defeat. Admiral Count von Spee, commanding the German Far Eastern Squadron, defeated the smaller fleet of Admiral Sir Christopher Cradock off the coast of Chile on November 1. The cruisers *Monmouth* and *Good Hope* were sunk with all hands and the Germans suffered no casualties at all. Cradock had made every possible mistake. His ships were clearly silhouetted in the afterglow, while the German ships faded into the dark background of the Chilean coast. He was fighting a superior force when he could without difficulty have acquired a superior force of his own by waiting for the old, heavily armed battleship *Canopus* to join him. It was a time for caution and he chose to be foolhardy with the result that 1,500 British sailors went down with their ships. Von Spee could now roam all the world's oceans with the near certainty that his greater firepower gave him mastery of every fleet sent against him. He was master of the Pacific; he could become master of the Atlantic and the Indian oceans as well. Fisher and Churchill ordered the two powerful battle cruisers *Inflexible* and *Invincible* out of Devonport Dockyard, where they were being refitted, to avenge the loss of the *Monmouth* and *Good Hope*. They belonged to the Grand Fleet and were intended for the defense of Britain and for battle against the German High Seas Fleet. Workmen were still on board the battle cruisers; they would have to go too. *Inflexible* and *Invincible,* the heavily armed *Canopus,* and the remaining ships of Cradock's fleet were off the Falkland Islands in the South Atlantic when Von Spee's fleet blundered into them. This time the British had overwhelming firepower. In a running battle four of Von Spee's capital ships were sunk, and the fifth was sunk later. Cradock was avenged; and in the Admiralty, where long faces had been the rule, there was now the first glow of triumph. The battle of the Falkland Islands seemed to be a presage of victory.

But while the high seas had been cleared, or nearly cleared, of German ships, and the German navy at the orders of the Kaiser, who called himself the All Highest War Lord, remained in the safety of its harbors with only rare and tentative appearances in the North Sea, victory was denied to the Royal Navy. Churchill and Fisher prayed for more battles like the Falkland Islands, but there were none. In the mists of the North Sea a battleship might emerge briefly only to vanish again. Traps were laid; sometimes the Germans entered the traps, but the doors were not closed in time, and the mists protected them.

In that somber winter Churchill grew pale and wan; life, for him, was scarcely worth living unless there was a victory a day. The dynamo seemed to be burning itself out in frustrations. He was attending to everything, giving orders on everything, arguing about everything. One day, late in the evening, he summoned Admiral Hall, the Director of Naval Intelligence, to his office. Churchill began to discuss something, the discussion became a monologue, and Admiral Hall found himself confusedly wondering why Churchill was so convincing when it was clear that his arguments were unsound; and soon he began to murmur to himself: "My name is Hall, my name is Hall . . ."

Churchill frowned and said: "What's that you're muttering to yourself?"

"I'm saying that my name is Hall," the Admiral replied, "because if I listen to you much longer I shall be convinced that it's Brown."

"Then you don't agree with what I have been saying?"

"First Lord, I don't agree with one word of it, but I can't argue with you."

Then he left Churchill's office and went to bed.

Fisher, too, was beginning to feel the strain. He wrote to Admiral Jellicoe on December 20, 1914:

> *Please burn at once*
> My beloved Jellicoe—I find much difficulty in snatching even a few moments in which to write to you—Winston has so monopolised all initiative in the Admiralty and fires off such a multitude of departmental memos; *(his power of work is absolutely amazing!)* that my colleagues are no longer *"superintending Lords,"* but only *"the First Lord's Registry"!* I told Winston this yesterday and he did not like it at all. Yours always
> FISHER

Churchill possessed that quality known in the days of the Italian Renaissance as *terribilità*. He was fascinated by large and dangerous exploits, the larger and more dangerous the better. He liked to drive himself unmercifully, and he liked to drive everyone with him unmercifully, and like the "terrible prince" of the Renaissance it was necessary for him to intrigue continually, to hold many secrets, and to have few friendships. Antwerp and the Dunkirk Circus, the battle of the Falkland Islands and some skirmishes in the North Sea had only whetted his appetite for violent action. Suddenly, on the horizon, there appeared an opportunity to break through the circle of frustrations and to use the fleet in a massive blow against the enemy, and he welcomed it with open arms.

THE HAPPY WARRIOR

DURING THE LAST days of December, 1914, the Grand Duke Nicholas, Commander in Chief of the Russian armies, sent a desperate appeal for aid to Great Britain. What he feared most of all was the German spring offensive and he urged the British to mount a diversion as close to Russia as possible, otherwise there would be a disaster.

The message came as no surprise to the British War Council which had been set up a month earlier to coordinate the war effort. Russia was in dire straits; her ammunition was giving out; her soldiers had been so roughly mangled by the Germans that already, in the fifth month of the war, with a long winter ahead, she seemed to be exhausted. Something had to be done, and done quickly, and hopefully it would be done without diverting troops from the Western Front. Churchill, who had wanted to attack Gallipoli on the declaration of war and had been overruled, now thought again about that long mountainous peninsula, only a few miles wide, which lay on the European side of Turkey. Here, forgotten for five months, was the diversion that would help the Russians and might bring about a sudden alteration in the course of the war.

He was not, of course, alone in this belief. Lord Kitchener and Admiral Fisher had pondered an attack on Gallipoli, and there had been some brief general discussions which were soon abandoned because of more pressing needs elsewhere. No fronts were stable; the Allies were suffering setbacks everywhere; all were confronted with imminent disaster. The Grand Duke Nicholas' message was therefore both a cry of despair and a ray of hope. Suddenly, when everything was going badly, there came the realization that the opening of another front might lead to victory.

On January 2, 1915, Kitchener wrote a letter to Churchill in which he attempted to clarify his own ideas. Nothing, he thought, would be gained by attempted landings in Syria or Asia Minor, and he seriously doubted whether anything effective could be done to help the Russians in the Caucasus. "The only place that a demonstration might have some effect in stopping reinforcements going East would be the Dardanelles. Particularly if, as the Grand Duke says, reports could be spread at the same time that Constantinople was threatened." But having written this, he added as a kind of postscript: "We shall not be ready for anything big for some months." On the same day he telegraphed to Sir George Buchanan, the British ambassador in Petrograd: "Please assure the Grand Duke that steps will be taken to make a demonstration against the Turks." Thus a promise was made, and it came with all the authority of the man who dominated the War Council. Kitchener was Secretary of State for War, but he was much more. He was virtually the Commander in Chief of the British armies and of the home front, not quite a dictator, but the one person who was regarded as essential for the successful conduct of the war. If he failed, no one else could be expected to succeed.

In later years Churchill would be credited with the responsibility for the disaster at Gallipoli. The truth was that he was one of many who sensibly and seriously weighed the issues, accepted the risks, and gave the orders. The ultimate responsibility lay with Kitchener.

Among those who had worked over plans for an attack on Turkey was Lord Fisher, the First Sea Lord, who thirsted for action and was never content with delaying tactics. His letters with their abrupt scorings and underlinings, whole sentences in capital letters, and strange Latin tags, revealed his explosiveness. As for the Dardanelles, he wanted to go the whole way, *totus porcus*. He thought Marseilles should become the staging port for a Turkish Expeditionary Force which would land at Haifa and Alexandretta, while the battleships were attempting to force the Dardanelles. He was not quite clear how these two forces would join up, but he was certain that the attack on Turkey was both possible and desirable. He wrote a long letter to Churchill outlining the scheme, the most important sentence being appropriately written in capital letters: "I CONSIDER THE ATTACK ON TURKEY HOLDS THE FIELD!—but ONLY if it's IMMEDIATE! Fisher's sense of urgency was communicated to Churchill who telegraphed to Vice Admiral Sir Sackville Hamilton-Carden, in command of the British warships in the Eastern Mediterranean, on the same day, asking whether the Dardanelles could be forced by ships alone. Carden answered that they might be forced "by extended operations with a large number of ships," and by this he meant that they would have to reduce the forts and the gun positions overlooking the straits and a very large fleet would be necessary to run this gantlet. Plans were made for providing him with a suitable fleet and an encouraging message was sent by Churchill to the Grand Duke Nicholas.

Quite suddenly there was an impasse. Fisher got cold feet. He had a proper respect for the German High Seas Fleet and he wanted all available forces held in reserve for the expected naval battle in the North Sea which would no doubt have a decisive effect on the war. Churchill believed the ships could shoot their way through the straits and threaten Constantinople; it was to be a naval operation entirely. Fisher, still thinking of his Turkish Expeditionary Force, wanted an army to accompany the fleet. There were quarrels and recriminations, until Kitchener decided that the situation in France was safe enough to send troops to the Dardanelles after all, and General Sir Ian Hamilton was sent to investigate the situation on the spot. Kitchener admired Ian Hamilton, who had been his chief of staff in South Africa, and trusted him implicitly. He was Kitchener's man. Churchill, who now held most of the strings of the Dardanelles campaign in his hands, saw Ian Hamilton off at the railroad station, asked casually whether he would be seeing copies of the general's reports, and learned that they would be sent to Kitchener and no one else. He was beginning to feel left out in the cold.

Ian Hamilton arrived off the Dardanelles just in time to witness the first disastrous attempt to force the straits. On March 18, 1915, the battleships advanced into the straits and blasted the forts with their heavy naval guns. It was a magnificent clear day, and throughout the morning everything went well. Altogether eighteen naval ships, including a French squadron, took part. The forts answered the fire of the ships maneuvering in the straits, but caused very little damage. One fort after another blew up or ceased firing, and by the early afternoon it appeared that the Allied naval forces were masters of the straits. But just before two o'clock the *Bouvet,* a French battleship, struck a mine and sank within two minutes, leaving only a raging black cloud of smoke to witness that it had ever existed. Two hours later two British battleships were struck by mines; one sank, the other was severely crippled, and Admiral De Robeck who had taken charge when Admiral Carden fell ill decided to call off the engagement. Minesweepers had already been sent into the straits and all known enemy mines had been swept up. The sudden, mysterious appearance of mines where none were expected and the loss of three battleships had sent De Robeck into a panic. He consulted Ian Hamilton and concluded that the only thing to do was to wait for the arrival of more battleships and of the troops which were being assembled by Ian Hamilton from Egypt and elsewhere. It was also necessary to find a more effective means of dealing with the minefields. The army for the combined operation would not be ready until the middle of April.

Churchill was furious. "Celerity" was Napoleon's watchword; it was also Fisher's; it was also Churchill's. The long delay which would permit the enemy to bring up reinforcements, the knowledge that De Robeck had not really understood the mission entrusted to him, the immense difficulties which would attend a combined operation, all these things reduced him to a state bordering on despair, and he was even more despairing when he learned that Fisher favored the delay and the combined operation. He prepared a telegram urging De Robeck to continue the attack, to force his way through the Dardanelles, and to attack the Turkish fleet in the Sea of Marmora. There must be no delays. But the telegram, when it finally went out, gave the admiral the final decision, for the War Council, which always viewed Churchill with alarm, was not prepared to issue a direct order. Fisher was wavering. "You are very wrong to worry and excite yourself," he wrote to Churchill. "Do try to remember that we are the lost ten tribes of Israel. We are sure to win!!!" But this kind of assurance was not calculated to appease Churchill's unhappiness. From secret agents in Turkey he had learned that the Turks, like the Russians, were suffering from a severe shortage of ammunition, were losing heart and were preparing to abandon Constantinople. The attack must come now. Later would be too late.

All the evidence made available after the war seemed to show that Churchill was justified: the condition in Turkey was even worse than he had suspected. A sudden raid on Constantinople would have had a catastrophic effect. The German General Liman von Sanders, who was about to take command of the Turkish army, announced that Turkey would be saved "if the English will leave me alone for eight days." The English gave him a whole month, and when at last Ian Hamilton's troops landed on a hostile shore, they were outnumbered by the enemy who had accurately guessed where they would land, how they would be supported and exactly how they would operate.

From his office at the Admiralty Churchill looked out at the Dardanelles, where it seemed to him that "a wall of crystal, utterly immovable" towered over the straits. But the wall was not made by human hands. It had been created by the inertia, the hesitations and the caution of the War Council itself. The combined operation, which seemed so eminently safe, proved to be an excursion into futility and irretrievable ruin. The losses of British, Australian and New Zealand troops were so vast that they were kept secret until after the war.

In later years Churchill surmised about what would have happened if the fleet had anchored off the Golden Horn with its guns trained on Constantinople. He thought that Turkey would probably have been knocked out of the war, that all the countries of the Balkans would have joined the Allies, that the way would have been open to send ammunition to the Russian armies, that Russian wheat would have poured through the Dardanelles to feed Britain and France and that the Russian Revolution would not have taken place. These were bold surmises, and as always he was prepared to believe that a mysterious veil hovers over the conclusions of battles. Liman von Sanders thought that with luck and a little time the Turks would have put up a stout defense even if the fleet had appeared off Constantinople. No one knows what might have happened; it is certain that nothing could have been worse than what did happen.

In his history of the Dardanelles campaign in *The World Crisis* Churchill presents himself for the most part as a man of calm and calculating judgment, logical and cool, confronted by an indecisive War Council and an irascible, unpredictable Fisher. It is true that Fisher kept wavering, that the War Council was chiefly concerned with winning victories in the West and that Kitchener was never completely convinced that the naval operation would be successful. But part of the failure must be laid at Churchill's feet. His abrupt manner, his absolute conviction that he and he alone was the possessor of the golden keys, his self-absorption and intellectual vanity, were not calculated to make friends. *Hubris* was riding for a fall.

He was a close and intimate friend of Fisher, but there were large shadowy areas where there could be no agreement between them, where in fact real communication became impossible. Fisher's beliefs rested on the hard rock of congealed fantasies, which were not the same as Churchill's fantasies. He genuinely believed that the British were the lost ten tribes of Israel, that the Royal Navy was under the special protection of God, and that the British Empire was the divinely inspired instrument of world rulership. General Gordon had even wilder beliefs and they had not prevented him from becoming a brilliantly successful general. But Fisher's fantasies lay close to the surface and he made no effort to conceal them. When he resigned it was because he lacked ultimate faith in Churchill, who belonged to the devil's party without knowing it. And when Churchill wrote one of his most brilliant letters urging Fisher to stand firm, Fisher replied that in the past he had given only "unwilling acquiescence" to Churchill's plans and was coming very quickly to the conclusion that he could no longer tolerate the role of an involuntary confederate. Churchill's letter, written on May 11, had the quality of his great speeches during the Second World War. He wrote:

> We are now in a very difficult position, whether it is my fault for trying, or my misfortune for not having the power to carry it through, is immaterial. We are now committed to one of the greatest amphibious enterprises in history. You are absolutely committed. Comradeship, resource, firmness, patience, all in the highest degree will be needed to carry the matter through to victory. A great army hanging on by its eyelids to a rocky beach and confronted with the armed power of the Turkish Empire under German military guidance: the whole *surplus* fleet of Britain—every scrap that can be spared—bound to that army and its fortunes as long as the struggle may drag out: the apparition of the long-feared submarine—our many needs and obligations—the measureless advantages, probably decisive on the whole war, to be gained by success.
>
> Surely here is a combination and a situation which require from us every conceivable exertion and contrivance which we can think of.

At the War Council held two days later Fisher declared that "he had been against the Dardanelles and had been all along." It was not true, but it contained a sufficient portion of truth to be convincing. Churchill afterward asked him what he meant: Was it fair that the First Sea Lord

should obstruct the taking of the necessary measures at the Dardanelles
and then turn round when things went wrong and say: "I told you so!"
Fisher replied: "I think you are right—it isn't fair." That same night
Churchill played his worst card. On his own responsibility, in order to
encourage the entry of Italy into the war, he issued an order commanding four cruisers to enter the Mediterranean forty-eight hours
before the time originally arranged. He worked into the night and
usually returned to the Admiralty late into the morning. Fisher arrived
punctually early in the morning to find the order on his desk. Across it
Churchill had written: "First Sea Lord to see after action."

The fatal words, the fatal insult, had been committed to paper, and
there was no turning back. Fisher refused to serve under Churchill any
more. He wrote on May 16: "YOU ARE BENT ON FORCING THE DAR-
DANELLES AND NOTHING WILL TURN YOU FROM IT—NOTHING . . . *You will
remain* and I SHALL GO—It is better so." His resignation, which coincided with a crisis about high explosive shells, brought down the
government. As a price for consenting to act under Asquith in the new
government, the Conservatives demanded that Churchill should be
dismissed from the Admiralty. At the last moment, just before the
dismissal became effective, Churchill learned that the German High
Seas Fleet had emerged from its safe harborage into the North Sea and
he ordered the British fleet to action stations. It seemed that the great
naval battle to decide the issue of the war was imminent. Churchill
remained in the Admiralty, aware that he had received a last minute
reprieve and that very soon he would be in a position to give the
Cabinet a message of incalculable importance. But having emerged,
the German High Seas Fleet, which had been sent out only to guard the
minelayers busily sowing mines along the Dogger Bank, retreated to
safety. The reprieve was no reprieve. He was dismissed from office.

Kitchener came to console him and to ask him what he intended to
do. Churchill replied that he had not the least idea. The formidable
Kitchener then offered him a supreme accolade: "Well, there is one
thing at any rate they cannot take from you. The Fleet was ready." In
the months to come Churchill would remember these words sometimes
with bitterness, sometimes with happiness.

Of the three men who had taken leading roles in directing the war,
Fisher had resigned and Churchill was dismissed; only Kitchener
remained, and he was soon to die when the ship taking him to Russia
was sunk off the coast of Scotland. Fisher, with his heavily lidded eyes,
his harsh, aggressive features, his brilliant and erratic ideas, passed into

obscurity. Churchill, too numbed to think out his next move, thought it extremely likely that he would be doomed to lesser positions for the rest of his life.

He had not learned his lesson; he still thought he was right; and it seems never to have occurred to him that "First Sea Lord to see after action" was like the small, angry stone over which giants stumble to their deaths. Some newspapers were jubilant. There were many who were weary of this showman of the one-man show. "Mr. Churchill is still his own Party, and the chief of the partisans," wrote one news-paper. "He still sees himself as the only digit in the sum of things, all other men as mere cyphers, whose function it is to follow after and multiply his personal value a million-fold." There was some truth in this judgment. His violence, his rudeness, his self-assertiveness were remembered against him. Sympathy went out to Fisher, but there was little for Churchill. It was felt that he had cooked his own goose.

The real fault, which Churchill never accepted, was his pride. He scarcely listened to the opinions of others. All wounds would be healed if he could bless them, all arguments would be resolved if he was permitted to address himself to them. When he was exhausted after a long day's work, then all that was tyrannical in him emerged in de-structive fury. The same pattern became visible in World War II. At the end of a hard day he lacked judgment.

Churchill dramatized his sufferings when he was dismissed from office. It seemed to him that England had suddenly become vulnerable because he was no longer there to defend her. "I am the victim of political intrigue! I am finished!" he declared. He was not finished. They gave him the minor post in the Cabinet reserved for people who have outlived their usefulness but need to be appeased by a semiofficial position. It was called the Chancellorship of the Duchy of Lancaster and no official duties were attached to it, but in addition they also gave him a seat on the War Council, which gave him the opportunity to argue on policy while depriving him of the opportunity to issue com-mands. He said later that when he left the Admiralty, he thought he would die of grief. Yet he had little reason to be grief-stricken, for the seat on the War Council was a tribute to his vast abilities and he could scarcely in defeat have received a great honor.

John Burns, the trade union leader who had risen to high office and resigned at the outbreak of the war, wrote in his diary on the eve of Churchill's dismissal:

It looks as if poor Winston was doomed to go. In a way a great pity. He is patriotic (not in the Johnsonese sense). He is energetic and at times inspired to great thoughts and noble expression, but at heart he is dictatorial and in his temper demoniacal (note his look coming from Admiralty in papers); he alternates in his passions between blood lusts against the foreigner, and brain storms against his rivals which would be better if they burst upon them instead of devouring himself. I have always been fair, at times indulgent, to him and I see his displacement with regret, because he is brave.

He was not quite as brave as John Burns would have it. To everyone he met he spoke of himself as one who had been ill-used by ungrateful politicians. He carried on a private vendetta against Asquith, the prime minister, without realizing that Asquith had been his chief supporter, an untiring defender of all his actions and designs upon the Dardanelles. When Asquith offered to let him remain in Admiralty House because his income was now greatly reduced, he refused indignantly on the grounds that a gentleman does not accept a gift from an enemy. He was venomous and passionate, and induced his wife to be just as venomous and passionate, for she swore that her greatest pleasure would be to dance on Asquith's grave. (Neither of them knew that Asquith had just received the greatest blow he had ever received in his life; for many years he had been in love with Venetia Stanley and she had just rejected his offer of marriage and announced that she would marry Edwin Montagu.)

In this partial retirement Churchill took up painting, having come upon one of his children's paint boxes. With a canvas, an easel and a paint box he began to work hesitantly; he had gone so far as to put a little blue blob of paint on the snow-white canvas when his neighbor, Lady Hazel Lavery, arrived by the purest chance to observe him with a small paintbrush surveying the canvas in trepidation. The little blue blob was about the size of a bean. He seemed incapable of doing more. Lady Lavery seized the big paintbrush, cried: "What are you hesitating about?" and went to work, splashing intriguing colors on the canvas. Thereafter he was on his own. He enjoyed the colors, splashing them with happy fury. For the next forty years painting was his avocation, his solace and his joy.

He was not a very good painter or even a very remarkable one. He could never paint a portrait; when he placed people in his landscapes they had neither bones nor flesh; but he could paint flowers and landscapes with conviction, and his one minor masterpiece was a painting of goldfish in a pool he had lovingly built for them. His interiors are usually unsuccessful, for the walls tend to cave in and the floors rise at abrupt angles. But give him vast sweeping spaces, streaming skies, and a foreground of many planes, with trees to break up the foreground, and he is in his element. Small, constricted landscapes, though he painted many of them, were generally failures, and his paintings of bottles, which he called "bottle scapes," were no better, but his larger landscapes are nearly always pleasing. He reveled in colors. He could dominate vast spaces, but little spaces disturbed and annoyed him. Humanity had little place in the painter's imagination. The paintings reveal perhaps more of himself that he would have liked to have known. He wrote a spirited account of his introduction to painting which he called *Painting as a Pastime,* which was finally published in the *Strand Magazine* in 1921. The title was a misnomer. For Churchill painting was far more than a pastime; it was a lifeline when things went wrong.

The months passed, the war went on, and Churchill still possessed little influence on events. His vendetta against Asquith was pursued relentlessly and with surprisingly little effect. He occasionally made speeches and sometimes there can be detected in embryo the great organ chords that would be heard in World War II. Here he is still proclaiming the necessity of forcing the Dardanelles in November, 1915, after nearly a quarter of a million casualties had been suffered there:

> Take Constantinople; take it by ships if you can; take it by soldiers if you must; take it by whichever plan, military or naval, commends itself to your military experts, but take it, and take it soon, and take it while time remains.

He was learning the truth, which he found intolerable, that England could get on very well without him. The government listened to him and then went its own way. Since he was obviously unwanted, he decided to prove himself on the field of battle. In November he went to France, where he was not especially welcomed at the 2nd Battalion of the Grenadier Guards. On a bitterly cold afternoon he was told by his colonel: "I think I ought to tell you that we were not at all consulted in the matter of your coming to join us." The adjutant added: "We have found a servant for you, who is carrying a spare pair of socks and your

shaving kit. We have had to leave the rest behind." The newly appointed Major Churchill was soon in need of wading boots, two pairs of
khaki trousers, a sheepskin sleeping bag, a periscope (most important),
and three face towels. He wrote to his wife to send them. He showed
himself to be a cautious, sensible soldier with a perplexing habit of
going off to meet high officials without notice. Inevitably he rose
rapidly in the chain of command and within a few weeks became a
brigadier general. This appointment however was never confirmed; it
was vetoed by the Cabinet, and once more Churchill suspected the
hidden hand of Asquith, who had in fact been one of those who vetoed
it, fearing a revolt by the backbenchers, who would claim that
Churchill had insufficient experience of military affairs. Instead he was
given an infantry battalion of the Royal Scots Fusiliers, and as battalion
commander ruled over thirty officers and seven hundred men. When
news of his appointment reached the battalion, the officers discussed
the advantages and disadvantages of a mutiny.

It was not that Churchill was disliked by the officers; it was simply
that they were well aware that he would "ginger up" the battalion and
make his presence felt. This he proceeded to do in the worst way
possible, for having arrived at battalion headquarters he took lunch
with his officers, said nothing whatsoever during the lunch, and afterward went around the table looking each officer straight in the eye.
Then he said: "Gentlemen, I am now your commanding officer. Those
who support me I will look after. Those who are against me I will break.
Good afternoon, gentlemen."

It was a bad, a deplorable, beginning. But if he was stern to the
officers, he was kinder to the men and took pleasure in reducing their
punishments and did his best to make life comfortable for them. He still
acted like the First Lord, a little distant, a little too certain of his
importance. Once when they were moving up to the front, a soldier
wondered apprehensively what the Germans might do to the battalion if
they knew that Churchill commanded them. He was quite serious when
he answered: "If they knew I was in the line they wouldn't send over a
few shells like this. They would turn on all their guns and blot the place
out." His fame walked beside him on the battlefield.

Not that he saw very much fighting or took very much interest in the
squalid details of trench raids and hand-to-hand fighting. Sometimes
shells exploded near him, and he would comment with a painter's eye
on the rich colors of the smoke rising from a ruined church or from a
house. The smoke from the church was brick-colored, patched with

black and white; sometimes the smoke was red, sometimes purple. With his easel planted just outside the abandoned convent which was his headquarters he painted a scene of desolation—leafless trees, torn roofs, skies smudged with black smoke—and his wartime painting closely resembled the paintings being made by Adolf Hitler, stationed some thirty miles away at Wytschaete, where he was a dispatch runner attached to the headquarters of a Bavarian regiment. Churchill's paintings then and later showed a curious lack of stability; the walls are always about to fall down and the earth tilts dangerously.

Meanwhile he was very happy with the war. In 1909 he had attended the military maneuvers in Germany and shuddered at the sight of massed soldiers moving like machines. "Much as war attracts me," he wrote to his wife during the maneuvers, "and fascinates my mind with its tremendous situations—I feel more deeply every year—and can measure the feeling here in the midst of arms—what vile and wicked folly and barbarism it is." But near the front he was enjoying that strange sense of being outside the world, in a no-man's-land of the mind, where all the ordinary rules of existence were held in suspension. To be famous, to be in the front, to have soldiers jumping to attention, to wear a French poilu's helmet, thus being immediately distinguished from every other British officer—all this was profoundly satisfying. But sometimes the real horror of the war reached down to him:

> Filth and rubbish everywhere, graves built into the defences and scattered about promiscuously, feet and clothing breaking through the soil, water and muck on all sides; and about this scene in the dazzling moonlight troops of enormous bats creep out and glide, to the unceasing accompaniment of rifle and machine guns and the venomous whining and whirring of the bullets which pass over head.

He was writing to his wife and therefore diluting the horrors, but he was very much aware of them. Yet he was more aware of himself, and he noted with approval that "99 people out of every 100 in this great army have to touch their hats to me." Again and again he speaks about the element of chance—if you turn left you are killed or paralyzed for life, and if you turn right you survive to become a major general. Chance ruled. He was content that it was so. Meanwhile he was playing the game with gusto and considerable impatience, for he wanted to be back in politics, where he could make decisions.

Since he was not overwhelmingly popular in the army, he had no difficulty in leaving it in the summer of 1916. He had taken part in no major engagements, seen only a small part of the front, and contributed virtually nothing to the cause of the Allies. He returned to London to resume his political career only to realize that it was ruined beyond repair and only a political cataclysm might pitchfork him into prominence again. For the remainder of the year he lived quietly in a large house on Cromwell Road, Kensington, watching the war from a distance, intriguing for high office and being snubbed at every turn.

In December, 1916, Asquith's government fell and Lloyd George became Prime Minister. Churchill thought his hour had come, but it had not. Lloyd George was superbly intelligent, kindly, and understanding; he carefully read the interminable memoranda Churchill sent to him; but he was adamantly opposed to giving him a ministerial position. Finally, in July, 1917, as the result of much lobbying, Churchill was given the Ministry of Munitions. He had spent twenty months in the desert, and now at last in a mood of savage intensity he found use for his pent-up energy.

He was a competent Minister of Munitions, cautious in his public utterances, subdued in his relations with the Cabinet, from which he was excluded except on the rare occasions when he was invited to discuss munitions problems. In private he was as bellicose as ever, roaring out his opinions on the war on the slightest provocation. One of his unlikely visitors at the ministry was the gentle poet Siegfried Sassoon whose poems against the war in a volume called *Counter-Attack* had raised him to some eminence in literary circles. No two people could have been more different than Churchill and Sassoon, who was a friend of Edward Marsh. It had occurred to Marsh that Sassoon needed a job and that Churchill might consider employing him in the ministry. Sassoon was famous, Churchill was famous, they would therefore get along splendidly.

Churchill was intrigued by Sassoon, had read *Counter-Attack*, and was impressed by the fact that Sassoon was something of a fox hunter. He had a lazy morning in front of him and prepared to give his visitor a good deal of time. Sassoon was alarmed by the great man's evident friendliness and suspected a trap. The trap was soon sprung. Churchill profoundly disagreed with the poet's attitude toward the war and wanted an argument. He would state the case for war; Sassoon would state the case against war; and Churchill in a few well-chosen sentences would demolish it. But Sassoon refused to play and Churchill contented himself with a vast monologue:

Pacing the room, with a big cigar in the corner of his mouth, he gave me an emphatic vindication of militarism as an instrument of policy and stimulator of glorious individual achievements, not only in the mechanism of warfare but in spheres of social progress. The present war, he asserted, had brought about inventive discoveries which would ameliorate the condition of mankind. For example, there had been immense improvements in sanitation. Transfixed and submissive in my chair, I realized that what had begun as a persuasive confutation of my anti-war convictions was now addressed, in pauseful and perorating prose, to no one in particular. From time to time he advanced on me, head thrust well forward and hands clasped behind his back, to deliver the culminating phrases of some resounding period. It was the spontaneous generation of a speech which would probably be fully reported in the press before I was many weeks older.

Churchill's speech came to an end because Edward Marsh put his head around the door and announced that Admiral Fisher was waiting outside, and had indeed been waiting for some time. On the way out the young poet was introduced to the aged admiral—"a small man with a queer Mongolian face, who had obviously come there with lots to say."

Churchill was not content to sit in solemn state in his ministry. He was continually going on inspection trips, flying to France, demanding that the War Cabinet answer the simple question: "What is the War Plan?" and generally creating as much havoc as possible. On his frequent visits to Paris he sometimes encountered Georges Clemenceau, the "Tiger," then in his seventies, vigorous and alert, with the weight of the war on his shoulders, for he was Prime Minister and Minister of War. Clemenceau was the incarnate spirit of victory, totally ruthless and totally in command. Churchill liked to remember that one day at the Ministry of War Clemenceau told him: "I will fight in front of Paris; I will fight in Paris; I will fight behind Paris." Some time later Clemenceau used the same words in a speech. Twenty-two years later Churchill would adapt these words in the most famous of the speeches he delivered during the Second World War.

It was not Churchill's habit to be awed by politicians, but he was awed by Clemenceau, perhaps because he saw in the old fiery Frenchman some of his own virtues. Once Clemenceau told him: "I have no political system, and I have abandoned all political principles. I am a man dealing with events as they come in the light of my experience." This, of course, was Churchill's principle: an unwavering disbelief in any principles whatsoever.

On one occasion Churchill accompanied Clemenceau on a visit to the front. At Beauvais they visited Field Marshal Foch, the generalissimo of the Allied armies, and went on to visit the British headquarters where Clemenceau attended to a wounded horse and attempted to rouse the flagging spirits of some weary British officers. When Churchill gently rebuked Clemenceau for spending so much time under fire, the great Frenchman replied: *"C'est mon grand plaisir."*

America had entered the war; the end was inevitable; and when it came, Churchill felt cheated. He had hoped to play a commanding role like Clemenceau or Foch, directing the armies to victory, returning to England in triumph, and then settling down like his hero Savrola to rule over his countrymen in peace and prosperity. It had not happened, and he was dimly aware that it was partly his own fault that he had spent twenty months of the war without doing anything of any importance. He had made only two contributions to the war: one at the beginning, and one at the end. He had made the Royal Navy ready for war, mobilized it, transferred it successfully from the Channel to the North Sea, and safely transported the troops from England to France. Then, as Minister of Munitions, he had worked successfully to produce tanks on a vast scale—at the end of the war he was planning to construct 10,000 tanks a year and the army was preparing to train 100,000 men in the Tank Corps. Churchill had helped to design the tanks, but he was neither the sole instigator nor the chief defender. Nevertheless, it pleased him to be called "the father of the tank," and he bore a fair share of responsibility for it. Although he always claimed that the Dardanelles campaign was a major contribution to the war and he proudly accepted full responsibility, he was not, as we have seen, the instigator of that unmitigated disaster.

In January, 1919, Churchill was appointed Secretary of State for War and Minister for Air. Significantly the appointment came when the war was over. His chief task was to demobilize the army as speedily as possible at a time when the country was going through a period of violent social stress and disorganization. There was widespread poverty; strikes and mutinies broke out; the red flag was flown in many factories; there was some incendiarism. Lloyd George weathered the storm, refusing Churchill's offer to bring back to England four divisions of the Rhine Army to shoot down the strikers and quell the mutinies. Churchill appears to have been under the delusion that the Rhine Army would have shot down the strikers at his orders, although it was much more likely that the army would have gone over to their side against the government.

Churchill's proclivity for playing with fire and championing lost causes was still strongly in evidence. The Great War was over, but a civil war was being fought in Russia and he now threw all his strength on the side of the White Russian armies against the Red Army. He had developed an insuperable loathing for Trotsky, the Commander in Chief of the Red Army, while retaining a kind of wry admiration for Lenin, whose audacity and intelligence marked him out as one of the Great Contemporaries. In addition, Lenin possessed that "original and sinister touch" which Churchill regarded as the necessary attribute of the Great Commander. British troops were still stationed at Murmansk and Archangel, and there were British liaison officers with Admiral Kolchak and General Denikin. Both generals were urgently in need of armaments and Churchill was ready to supply them on his own responsibility. For eight months he poured weapons and supplies into Russia, and attempted without success to form a British Expeditionary Force consisting of volunteers from the regular army. Most of the weapons and supplies fell into Bolshevik hands, and by the end of the year the White armies had collapsed and the Bolsheviks found themselves in absolute control of a land ravaged by famine. Churchill's intervention in Russia had cost the British taxpayers £100,000,000 to no advantage whatsoever.

In February, 1921, Lloyd George appointed him Secretary of State for the Colonies, where it was thought that he would do less damage. The Middle East was seething with unrest, a bloody uprising had been suppressed in Iraq, there was trouble in French-occupied Syria, and there was no effective government in Trans-Jordan. Churchill summoned a conference in Cairo and attempted, with the help of T. E. Lawrence, "the Uncrowned King of Arabia," to provide solutions to these pressing problems. From Cairo he journeyed to Saqqara on camelback, and not being accustomed to camels he fell off. Lawrence explained that the accident came about because the camel was puffed up with pride for having so distinguished a rider. The Emir Feisal, whom Lawrence had led to victory in Damascus, was made King of Iraq, while his brother, the Emir Abdullah, became King of Trans-Jordan. King-making was a pleasant occupation, but since neither of these Hashemite Emirs possessed any roots in the countries they ruled over, the seeds of more dangerous confrontations were being planted.

Churchill returned to London well pleased with himself, while Lawrence remained in Trans-Jordan as acting governor. Lawrence, although professing to believe that Britain had fulfilled some of its promises to the Arabs, was not so pleased with himself and soon vanished in the vast anonymity of the Air Force, where he served in the ranks.

Soon Churchill, too, vanished from the political scene. In November, 1922, there were general elections. He had represented Dundee in Parliament for fourteen years and imagined that his constituents would remain faithful to him. He did little electioneering, for he was recovering from an operation for the removal of his appendix. The mood of the country had changed, and he went down to overwhelming defeat. "In the twinkling of an eye," he said later, "I found myself without an office, without a seat, without a party, and without an appendix." Once more he was in the wilderness.

The Years of the Locust

The loyal forces in every street and village do not know what to do. The subversive forces are gaining in confidence and audacity . . . Business is at a standstill; prices are rising; the pressure of life upon all classes must inevitably grow greater. Faction is rampant, and winter is at hand.

CHARTWELL

FOR MOST OF his life Churchill had been rootless. He had fought in many countries, occupied many ministerial positions, and lived in many houses and apartments. Now at the age of forty-eight, he found himself thinking more and more about settling down. He wanted a large comfortable house within easy distance of London. There should be a large estate attached to the house where he could roam at will and set up his easel, and preferably there should be no other houses in sight. There should be room enough for his children, their nursemaids, and the small army of servants that always accompanied him. Above all it was necessary that the country house should have a certain splendor in keeping with his own dignity: not Blenheim Palace, but a good solid manor house with himself as the lord of the manor.

Since he was a frequent visitor to Sir Philip Sassoon's palatial country house at Fort Lympne in Kent, he was coming to know Kent well. By chance he heard that Chartwell Manor near the village of Westerham was for sale with eighty acres of woods and parkland. The manor house itself was undistinguished and even ugly, for the previous owner, John Campbell Colquhoun, had converted what was originally a Tudor mansion into a distressingly obvious Victorian monstrosity with gables and bay windows, while most of the front of the house was shrouded in a thick carpet of ivy. It looked like a schoolhouse kept by elderly Victorian spinsters, but it was not the house so much as the rolling valley below that appealed to Churchill. The view of the softly rounded hills and the plunging valley was breathtaking; chestnut, beech and oak grew in profusion; and not far away lay the Weald of Kent. To stand beside the house and to look down the valley is to see a kind of abstract portrait of Churchill himself: breadth, softness, power, easy strength. As for the Victorian monstrosity, this was not a matter which weighed heavily with him. In due course the ivy, gables, bay windows and oriels would be swept away, the house would acquire a new face, new chimneys would be installed, and instead of the former heaviness there would be lightness and grace. Churchill would continue to reshape and remodel the house for the remaining years of his life.

He bought the manor house in November, 1922, for £5,000. This was a bargain, for the standing timber alone was said to be worth £2,000. He was a rich man and could well afford it. Two legacies from relatives—one of £40,000 from his great-grandmother, Frances Anne, Marchioness of Londonderry, and another of about £20,000 from his cousin, Lord Herbert Vane-Tempest—had recently added considerably to his fortune. He was not by any means one of the wealthiest men in England, but he was wealthy beyond the dreams of most men. From investments alone he could count on £5,000 a year. In those days this was a very solid income.

There were many other reasons for acquiring a house in the country. Lady Randolph Churchill died as the result of a fall at the end of June, 1921. She slipped on the stairs at Lady Horner's beautiful gabled manor house at Mells and broke her left leg. The wound refused to heal, gangrene set in, the leg was amputated, and when everyone thought she was well on the way to recovery, the main artery in the thigh of her amputated leg burst, and she bled to death. Two months later Churchill's youngest daughter, Marigold Frances, died of a septic throat. She was only three years old. The double blow, the second coming so quickly after the first, was not something he could bear with equanimity. He was shattered. Like many grief-stricken men he yearned for the solace of the countryside, all the more because he possessed no religious faith. His faith, such as it was, consisted in an enduring belief in England as one of the powers chosen to rule the earth. Why it had been chosen, and why it had (in his eyes) been given primacy over all the other powers, were not matters that greatly concerned him. He knew it was so, and there was no further discussion. But grief remained, tormenting him during all the years to come.

Then there were his four surviving children who also, he felt, needed the country air. In 1922 Diana, the eldest, a beautiful redhead, was thirteen, Randolph was eleven, Sarah was eight and Mary was only a few months old. They were a very close-knit family, happy together, even though the children were a little overwhelmed by a father who insisted that everyone should talk sensibly and to the point. Sarah remembered that as a child, and even later as a young woman, she found it necessary to pause and "straighten out" her thoughts whenever she went to see him, for he became irascible if he had to listen to long involved statements. And sometimes—more often than she wished—she found it altogether simpler to write out a request rather than to confront him in person. A surprisingly great number of letters were written to him by his children when they were living under the same roof.

The truth was that children bewildered him and he had no easy approach to them. There was something animal-like about them; they were tempestuous, irrational, secretive, stridently emotional; they lacked precision. So, jokingly, he gave them animal names. Thus Sarah was known as "Mule," because she was slow, and Mary was known as "Chimp," apparently because she was ugly as a child, although she developed into a good-looking woman with the finest features of any of his children. Clementine Churchill was known as "Cat." The appropriate animal sounds were sometimes heard, and visitors to Chartwell Manor were sometimes mystified by the sound of mewing and braying.

Since the house consisted of a maze of rooms—there were altogether nineteen bedrooms—the children delighted in it, and Sarah, being the most secretive, found innumerable hiding places where she could dream of becoming an actress or weep over an imagined slight. There was a nurse, Miss Maryott Whyte, who was Clementine Churchill's first cousin and a woman of boundless energy, to superintend the children, scold them, wash them, see that they were properly dressed, and to whisk them away whenever they became troublesome to their parents. Churchill believed in the solid virtues of Victorian society, where the Nanny ruled over the children and acted as a buffer between the parents and their offspring. But Miss Whyte was not Mrs. Everest, that mountain of goodness and compassion. Miss Whyte had aristocratic connections; she was sharp; she gave orders; she intimidated. In her eyes order and good manners, not goodness and compassion, were the admirable characteristics of a child.

At first Churchill had not wanted to change anything at Chartwell. It was enough that there was the breathtaking view and a large rambling house, however ugly. Clementine, emerging from the stupor of grief, busied herself with the gardens and the shrubbery. Down came the trees, the tangled ivy was swept away, the suffocating rhododendrons were banished, until Churchill lamented: "If you go on like this, Clemmie, we had better rename the house One Tree Hill." Clementine knew what she was doing. "Creepers tend to undermine the mortar of the house," she explained. "Besides there will be earwigs in the children's bedrooms." Clementine had a far greater practical sense than her husband.

But once the shrubbery and the trees had been cleared, the house began to look strangely awkward and ungainly, and the first tentative beginnings were made to remodel it and shape it, until in the end it came to resemble at a great distance the original Tudor manor house before successive owners had added wings and ornamental decorations. Then Churchill would find himself sitting down at the drawing board with the architect. Walls were removed; new stairways appeared; and a door belonging to the house at nearby Westerham of James Wolfe, the soldier who took Canada away from the French, was exactly copied and set up at Chartwell. Churchill was beginning to develop an architect's eye.

One room on the second floor became his study, where he spent the greater part of his working day. The Victorian ceiling had been removed to reveal the beams and rafters of the Tudor mansion; windows faced east and west; pictures crowded the walls; and photographs in silver frames crowded the large mahogany desk which had once belonged to his father. Here he wrote, facing the fireplace, with a window beside him. Over the fireplace dominating the room was an immense panoramic painting of Blenheim Palace by some unknown eighteenth century artist.

Today Churchill's study can be seen very much as he left it for the last time in October, 1964, a few weeks before his death. A huge banner representing his coat of arms hangs from the rafters, the bright crimson and gold adding a garish, theatrical aspect to the room. But when he worked in it, it was a very ordinary room, quiet, somewhat cut off from the rest of the house, and not especially comfortable or commodious.

Nevertheless the room announced his obsessions, his yearnings, his admirations.

Although the painting of Blenheim Palace dominated the room by its size, it was not the object that first attracted the eye. The object that attracted the most attention was a white porcelain bust of Napoleon which stood squarely on the table, so bright, so gleaming, that it seemed to gather half the light of the room on its shining surface. Churchill had an extravagant admiration for Napoleon, whose works he knew well and whose battles he had examined with minute care. For many years he contemplated writing a life of Napoleon and he had gathered together over a hundred volumes in preparation for the task, but other books kept getting in the way. Among those books, written at Chartwell, were the four volumes of *The World Crisis* and their two sequels, *The Unknown War: Eastern Front* and *The Aftermath*, which were published between 1923 and 1929.

These books are fascinating documents not so much as credible history as because they show the peculiar loops and whorls of Churchill's mind. Like all history-makers who write histories he was very generous to himself, often grossly inaccurate and defensive even when it was totally unnecessary to be defensive. He claims more than his fair share of glory. When he describes the birth of the tank, he assumes as a matter of demonstrable fact that it emerged, like Athena, fully formed from his own brain, forgetting that it was the brainchild of many men. He likes to occupy the foreground, and sometimes depicts himself too large. When he quotes letters and directives, he prints what he wrote and rarely prints the replies, a habit he revived when writing *The Second World War*. If the recipient wrote back: "You're crazy!" we are not told about it.

Nevertheless *The World Crisis* is a wonderfully appealing work full of a kind of adolescent gusto, a sufficient number of remarkable purple passages and a scrupulous feeling for representing a scene in three dimensions. He has the novelist's temper and deliberately cultivates the art of maintaining excitement. "Writing a long and substantial book," he once said, "is like having a friend and companion at your side, to whom you can always turn for comfort and amusement." The key word is "amusement." He enjoyed writing, or rather he enjoyed that curious mingling of mumbling, dictating, revising, reworking, re-dictating and revising all over again, which was his normal method of work. Like Balzac, who rewrote extensively on galleys, Churchill liked to pepper his galleys with multitudinous revisions; unlike Balzac, who could not

afford vast printer's bills, Churchill was inclined to rewrite the rewrit-
ten galleys and then rewrite the third and fourth galleys to the alarm of
the publisher who sometimes found it necessary to call a halt. Churchill
was impenitent. His books sold well. His publishers could afford the
loss. To the end of his writing career he continued to plague them with
monstrous printer's bills.

The reader of the 3,000 or so pages of *The World Crisis* is soon struck
by a singular shift of focus when he comes to write about events where
he was not present and where his authority was not manifested. When
he describes, for example, the Battle of Jutland or the Battle of the
Marne, where he took no part, he is immediately credible. The iris of
the camera opens out, the large landscapes and seascapes appear, we
see the soldiers through the murk of battle and the ships looming
through the mists, and we see them in their proper colors, in three
dimensions and with the appropriate sounds of battle. He was writing
at a time when few war memoirs had been published and the official
histories were not yet available. He owed his information largely to
naval and military friends who had taken part in these actions, and
some of the immediacy of their experience enters his prose. When he
writes about his own experiences, it is always: "I did this . . . I issued this
order . . . I was present . . ." The magnification of the ego is accompanied by excited sounds of applause, and he gets in the way of his own
story.

But these books were not only an attempt to write a more or less
factual history. The scaffolding of rhetoric buttressed the argument and
heightened the effect. These rhetorical passages play the same role as
the chorus of a Greek tragedy: destiny speaks through them. If destiny
sometimes wears the familiar mask of Churchill, this is because destiny
must assume a human face to be convincing. In much the same way the
choruses of *Antigone* wear the mask of Sophocles.

Churchill's rhetoric was either very good or very bad. Either the
rocket soared sweetly into the air or it zigzagged and fumbled. When
he was thinking about things he deeply cared about or deeply feared, he
wrote magnificently, with a natural authority. We have seen that from
his days in India he was obsessed with the idea of annihilation, the
tragedy of all endings. In one of the early chapters of *The World Crisis*
Churchill finds himself wondering what would happen if the Royal
Navy was sunk without a trace—*spurlos versunken*. The thought grips
him, terrifies him, and in a sudden change of direction he discovers that
even this tragedy may have its compensations. He wrote:

Consider these ships, so vast in themselves, yet so small, so easily lost to sight on the surface of the waters. Sufficient at the moment, we trusted, for their task, but yet only a score or so. They were all we had. On them, as we conceived, floated the might, majesty, dominion and power of the British Empire. All our long history built up century after century, all our great affairs in every part of the globe, all the means of livelihood and safety of our faithful, industrious, active population depended upon them. Open the seacocks and let them sink beneath the surface, as another Fleet was one day to do in another British harbour far to the North,° and in a few minutes—half an hour at the most—the whole outlook of the world would be changed. The British Empire would dissolve like a dream; each isolated community struggling forward by itself; the central power of union broken; mighty provinces, whole Empires in themselves, drifting hopelessly out of control and falling a prey to others; and Europe after one sudden convulsion passing into the iron grip of the Teuton and of all that the Teutonic system meant. There would only be left far off across the Atlantic unarmed, unready, and as yet uninstructed America to maintain, single-handed, law and freedom among men.

Guard them well, admirals and captains, hardy tars and tall marines; guard them well and guide them true.

It is not the rhetoric of our time; the scaffolding creaks when he takes a new breath, but there is no doubting the passion and urgency of the vision. Although the rocket wobbles a little, it soars splendidly.

In *The Aftermath* Churchill wrote many pages about Lenin, although he knew very little about him, and that little was mostly wrong. He believed that Lenin suffered from syphilis, that he died murmuring the prayers of the Church and indeed had been murmuring them for many months in his long agony. In Churchill's eyes Lenin was the absolute tyrant, the grand repudiator, the utmost evil, yet undeniably a great man, whose name would be remembered for a thousand years. Of the Russians he said: "Their worst misfortune was his birth: their next worst—his death." Lenin was responsible for more deaths than any man who had lived, and no Asiatic conqueror, not even Tamerlane or Genghis Khan, could match his fame.

As Churchill warms to the task of depicting Lenin, it becomes clear that a certain admiration, even awe, is present. The exceptional will-power and an extraordinary intelligence, combined with total devotion

---

° Churchill was referring to the German High Seas Fleet which was interned at Scapa Flow, south of the Orkneys, at the end of World War I. On June 21, 1919, the fleet was scuttled by the German crews and sank.

to absolute principles, ride him. No one like this has appeared on the world stage before, and please God, nothing like him will appear again. Here Churchill describes Lenin:

Implacable vengeance, rising from a frozen pity in a tranquil, sensible, matter-of-fact, good-humoured integument! His weapon logic; his mood opportunist. His sympathies cold and wide as the Arctic Ocean; his hatreds tight as the hangman's noose. His purpose to save the world: his method to blow it up. Absolute principles, but readiness to change them. Apt at once to kill or learn: dooms and afterthoughts: ruffianism and philanthropy: but a good husband; a gentle guest; happy, his biographers assure us, to wash up the dishes or dandle the baby; as mildly amused to stalk a capercailzie as to butcher an Empire. The quality of Lenin's revenge was impersonal. Confronted with the need of killing any particular person he showed reluctance—even distress. But to blot out a million, to proscribe entire classes, to light the flames of intestine war in every land with the inevitable destruction of the well-being of whole nations—these were sublime abstractions.

It was odd that Churchill should find sublimity in Lenin, and odder still that he should grant to Lenin a religious death. There are errors of fact all along the line, but it scarcely matters. He has said what is essential, with vigor and passion, about a man who was greater and more terrible than anyone in his generation.

As he was coming to the close of his six-volume history of the war Churchill permitted himself some somber conclusions. He believed that history had reached a turning point, and that we had seen the last of the Great Commanders. He wrote with tragic conviction:

[War] has at last been stripped of glitter and glamour. No more may Alexander, Caesar and Napoleon lead armies to victory, ride their horses on the field of battle sharing the perils of their soldiers and deciding the fate of empires by the resolves and gestures of a few intense hours. For the future they will sit surrounded by clerks in offices, as safe, as quiet and as dreary as Government departments, while the fighting men in scores of thousands are slaughtered or stifled over the telephone by machinery. We have seen the last of the Great Commanders. Perhaps they were extinct before Armageddon began. Next time the competition may be to kill women and children, and the civil population generally, and victory will give herself in sorry nuptials to the diligent hero who organizes it on the largest scale.

o   o   o   o   o   o

It is established that nations who believe their life is at stake will not be restrained from using any means to secure their existence. It is probable—nay, certain—that among the means which will next time be at their disposal will be agencies and processes of destruction wholesale, unlimited, and perhaps, once launched, uncontrollable.

Mankind has never been in this position before. Without having improved appreciably in virtue or enjoying wiser guidance, it has got into its hands for the first time the tools by which it can unfailingly accomplish its own extermination. That is the point in human destinies to which all the glories and toils of men have at last led them. They would do well to pause and ponder upon their new responsibilities. Death stands at attention, obedient, expectant, ready to serve, ready to sheer away the peoples *en masse;* ready, if called on, to pulverise, without hope of repair, what is left of civilization. He awaits only the word of command. He awaits it from a frail, bewildered being, long his victim, now—for one occasion only—his Master.

These words, written in 1928, form the peroration of the six volumes in which he had mingled so much history, fantasy and hard thinking. He had started out in life with visions of being a Great Commander, but he had learned that the only Great Commander was mankind irresistibly urging Death to wipe out the human race. "We have seen the last of the Great Commanders," he wrote. It was not quite true. Ironically, in the fullness of time, he would become one of them.

When he sent copies of these books to his friend T.E. Lawrence with a modest inscription saying that he regarded them as potboilers, Lawrence had the last word, "Some pot!" he exclaimed. "I suppose he realizes that he is the only high person since Thucydides and Clarendon who has put his generation unimaginably in his debt."

While he was writing, Churchill was busily engaged in politics and suffering some unexpected reversals. In 1923 he contested a by-election at West Leicester, calling himself a National Liberal Free Trader, and was roundly defeated by a Socialist who became Lord Pethwick-Lawrence and was one of the architects of the freedom of India from the British Raj. Undeterred, Churchill fought another election in the following year in the Abbey Division of Westminster. This time he called himself a Constitutionalist and was opposed by Conservative, Liberal and Socialist candidates. He was defeated again—by forty-three votes. Two defeats in quick succession only made him more certain that he was indispensable to the government, and later in the year he stood for Epping with Conservative support. He won easily and a few days

later, on the advice of Neville Chamberlain, Prime Minister Stanley
Baldwin, appointed him Chancellor of the Exchequer.

He was not on especially good terms with either Chamberlain or
Baldwin, and the appointment came as a surprise. The most surprised
person was Churchill, who had no head for figures and no knowledge of
how to put a budget together. He was accompanied to his new office by
his perennial private secretary, Edward Marsh, who had even less
knowledge of figures. Marsh was by this time a well-known littérateur,
a close friend of D.H. Lawrence and all the rising poets and novelists,
whose works he sometimes edited and whose starved bank accounts he
sometimes replenished from his own pocket. His duties were light and
he spent his days happily translating the verses of La Fontaine into
English. The real work of the Chancellor of the Exchequer was being
done by professional economists, thus permitting Churchill to
complete his history of the war and engage in political mischief.

Lord Ponsonby, who admired Churchill and had affectionate feelings
for Marsh, had some reservations about the new Chancellor of the
Exchequer. "He is so far and away the most talented man in political
life besides being charming and a 'gentleman' (a rarish bird in these
days). But this does not prevent me from feeling politically that he is a
great danger, largely because of his love of crises and faulty judgment.
He once said to me years ago, 'I like things to happen, and if they don't
happen I like to make them happen.' "

Such was Ponsonby's verdict on Churchill in a long letter to Marsh. It
was a just verdict. At the first opportunity Churchill decided to make
things happen.

ALARMS AND EXCURSIONS

At midnight on May 3, 1926, at the orders of the general council of the Trade Union Congress, the work and industry of Great Britain came to a standstill. For the first time in English history there was a general strike.

People awoke the next morning to find that no newspapers were delivered, there were no buses or tramways to take them to work, the trains were no longer running, the gas and electricity works were shut down, the iron and steel industry no longer functioned, the stevedores were no longer working on the ships and the coalpits were deserted. Overnight the face of the country had changed, and time had come to a stop.

In London, where a light mist clung to the ground, there was the eerie sensation that the industrial age had never happened and that in some mysterious manner there had been a return to a bygone age. When the mist lifted, the sky was seen to be unusually clear, for there was no smoke pouring out of the factory chimneys. Outside the factories workmen were clustered in small groups around signs reading: ON STRIKE. They were courteous and respectful to the police who tried to move them away, but they held their ground. Housewives listening to 2 L.O., the London radio station, on the small sets which consisted of little more than a pair of earphones, a threadlike wire called a cat's whisker, and a crystal the size of a child's fingernail, heard faint music and the occasional voice of an announcer saying the government had everything under control.

In fact the government, led by Stanley Baldwin, a slow-speaking, slow-moving man who habitually held a briar pipe to his lips while he attempted to unravel political problems, did not know what to do. He was learned, stolid, crafty, without any rhetorical gifts—he disliked rhetoric—and he had no feeling for the working people. He belonged to the newly risen aristocracy of mineowners and steel manufacturers, and possessed a vast fortune. The strike, which came about as the result of long and fruitless negotiations between the coal miners and the mineowners, who insisted that the miners accept lower wages because it had become increasingly difficult to sell British coal on the foreign market now that Britain had returned to the gold standard, left him curiously unmoved. He had done little to prevent it and much to precipitate it. When it happened, he was half inclined to believe that the Trade Union Congress consisted of revolutionaries determined to overthrow the government. A.J. Cook, the head of the miners' union, was a Communist, but the Trade Union Congress, which issued the strike notices, was run by mild-mannered members of the Labour Party.

A large part of the blame for the strike rested on Churchill, who as Chancellor of the Exchequer had returned Britain to the gold standard to benefit the London bankers. He had not paid any attention to the needs of the workers. John Maynard Keynes, then a brilliant young don at Cambridge, had written a book called *The Economic Consequences of Mr. Churchill,* in which he showed that the Chancellor of the Exchequer was totally lacking in any understanding of economics. "On grounds of social justice no case can be made out for reducing the wages of the miners," he wrote. "The plight of the coal miners is the first, but not—unless we are very lucky—the last, of the Economic Consequences of Mr. Churchill."

Churchill subscribed to the view that the state had no business interfering with the laws of supply and demand, that the mineowners were loathsome profiteers and that the Trade Union Congress was a hotbed of revolutionary Socialists determined to bring down the government. He had many scores to pay against the Socialists, for on two successive occasions he had lost elections to Labour candidates. He had friends among the mineowners; he had none among the mine workers. Baldwin was prepared to wait out the storm. Churchill was determined to crush the Trade Union Congress and send the miners back to work. Against the strikers he proposed to wage implacable war.

In later years Baldwin claimed that his appointment of Churchill as editor in chief of a government newspaper dedicated to breaking the strike was a masterstroke. "The cleverest thing I ever did," he declared, "was when I put Winston in a corner and told him to edit *The British Gazette.*" Absorbed in the task of running a newspaper, Churchill was less likely to interfere in the day-by-day running of the government and the delicate or not so delicate negotiations to bring the general strike to an end. The new newspaper would exhaust his energies.

Churchill delighted in having a newspaper at his command, and directed it as though he were the captain of a battleship firing continual broadsides. "The field of battle is no longer transport but news," he wrote. He commandeered the presses of *The Morning Post,* staffed it with students of printing from London University and whatever compositors he could lay his hands on, wrote the editorials, decided what news should be printed, issued a stream of directives, ordered a submarine crew from Devonport to guard the machines and appointed Admiral Hall, the director of the Intelligence Division in World War I, as his security chief. The Automobile Club was pressed into service to find volunteers to distribute the newspaper. Distribution centers were set up. He planned to have half a million copies of the newspaper published by the morning of May 5.

Stanley Baldwin, who liked Churchill but worried over his capacity to do everything to extremes, thought some guidelines should be prepared. To his close friend, Geoffrey Dawson, the editor of the London *Times,* he said: "For heaven's sake give Winston some tips on how to produce a newspaper. Make it out in a letter to me." Dawson agreed, wrote a long letter on the subject, and in due course received from Churchill an even longer letter explaining how a newspaper should *really* be produced.

Churchill sat at the editor's desk, jauntily waving his cigar, barking out orders and sometimes descending to the press room to admire the huge presses as they poured out thousands upon thousands of copies of what he called "the authoritative government journal," but which was a four-page inflammatory broadsheet designed to terrify the strikers into submission and to rally the public against the strikers. One day when he went down to the press room he found a pitcher of beer beside each man.

"Have they got enough?" he asked.

"Yes, sir."

"Nonsense, nonsense. There is no such thing. Send for more."

Churchill thrust a pound note into someone's hand, and more beer was brought to the press room. It was not a particularly happy moment. He was behaving like a jovial lord of the manor who orders beer for his farm workers at harvesting time with an air of exquisite condescension.

Afraid that the strikers would smash the machinery, he set a heavy guard around the offices of *The Morning Post* and no one was permitted to enter without a purple card duly signed by Admiral Hall. Churchill was given a purple card and presented it to the policeman on duty outside the building. Suddenly it occurred to him that this was a monstrous imposition. He had not presented a card to the police officer standing at the entrance of the Admiralty; why should he do so now that he was the editor in chief of *The British Gazette*? He tore up the card, threw the pieces at the policeman's feet, and said: "You will have to remember, young man, who I am. I don't need the card!"

High-handed and piratical, conscious of his power, strangely excited by the knowledge that he was the spearhead of the attack on the strikers, he behaved with quite extraordinary contempt for the normal rules of human behavior. *The British Gazette* became his mouthpiece, his toy, his battering ram. The strikers were "the enemy," to be remorselessly exposed and finally punished, not so much because they had committed evil but because they were a threat to the entire people who would soon, if the strike were permitted to continue, be reduced to the level of the natives of Africa. He wrote in his first lengthy editorial, which appeared on May 5, 1926:

> Nearly all the newspapers have been silenced by violent concerted action. And this great nation, on the whole the strongest community which civilisation can show, is for the moment reduced in this respect to the level of African natives dependent only on the rumours which are carried from place to place. In a few days, if this were allowed to continue, rumours would poison the air, raise panics and disorders, inflame fears and passions together, and carry us all to depths which no sane man of any party or class would care even to contemplate.
>
> The Government have therefore decided not only to use broadcasting for spreading information, but to bring out a paper of their own on a sufficient scale to carry full and timely news throughout all parts of the country.
>
> *The British Gazette* is run without profit on the authority and, if

necessary, at the expense of the Government. It begins necessarily on a small scale, and its first issue cannot exceed 700,000 copies. It is proposed, however, to use the unlimited resources of the State, with the assistance of all loyal persons, to raise the circulation day after day until it provides sure and sufficient means of information and a guide for action for all British citizens.

Many of these statements were untrue. There had been no violent action by the Trade Union Congress, and the strikers with very few exceptions had obeyed the order of the general council to behave quietly even under extreme provocation. There was no danger of panic arising from lack of news: the London broadcasting station was still operating, *The Daily Mail* was being printed in France and flown into England every day, and the London *Times* continued to be published on its own printing presses, although the first number during the strike consisted of a single typewritten sheet. Churchill declared that the first issue would not exceed 700,000 copies, but the actual print run was 232,000 copies. On the second day *The British Gazette* did better with 507,000 copies. By commandeering a quarter of the paper stocks of the *Times*, Churchill was able to raise the figure to nearly 2,125,000 during the remaining days of the general strike; and his newspaper became a force to be reckoned with. An equally powerful force was *The British Worker* issued by the Trade Union Congress. The newspaper of the strikers was far more moderate in tone, and more accurate. Churchill ordered his staff to produce headlines indicating that the general strike had failed and that life was returning to normal. *The British Worker* more accurately stated that the strike was indeed a general strike and all heavy industries had been closed down. Churchill published a report from a French source saying that the strike was a Bolshevik plot. *The British Worker* said the miners could not live on their wages and the Trade Union Congress was employing the only available weapon to improve their lot. Between *The British Gazette* and *The British Worker* the battle lines were drawn. The argument had become polarized, with no solution in sight.

Churchill's resources were such that he could call on the army, navy and air force. Royal Air Force planes carried the newspaper to northern England; mechanics from Chatham Dockyard helped to repair the machinery when it broke down; soldiers guarded the paper supplies. That the army, navy and air force should be involved in publishing a newspaper which was attempting to inflame the middle classes against the workers was tragic, absurd and very dangerous. Churchill was obviously hoping to spark a revolutionary upheaval, and just as obviously he was thirsting for blood. On his own responsibility he had given orders to shoot the striking miners and dock workers in 1910, and the working classes deeply feared him. In their eyes he was the enemy—implacable, ferocious, capable of every kind of malice. The workers had only to read *The British Gazette* with its palpable lies to realize that he was determined to crush them and to reduce them to servile obedience.

Today *The British Gazette* has a faintly comic appearance. Complete copies are rare, but it has been reproduced in facsimile and the modern reader perusing its headlines can get a feeling of those strangely quiet days when people walked to work and went about their affairs very much as usual, while Churchill thundered about the coming revolution. HOLD-UP OF THE NATION. ASSAULT ON RIGHTS OF THE NATION. ORGANIZED MENACE: THE REAL ISSUE BEHIND THE GENERAL STRIKE. He liked to use the word "menace," though he was himself the most menacing aspect of those times. This was the "bloody-minded" Churchill who emerges at intervals to surprise those who were accustomed to thinking of him as the pudgy aristocrat with the rapier wit. Once more he had become the cherub with the ax.

Strangely, Churchill's periods of extreme tension and violence appeared to come at intervals of about five years. The killing of the miners and dock workers came in 1910. His savage denunciations of those who opposed the Dardanelles campaign and his determination to continue it whatever the cost in lives came in 1915. In 1920, as Secretary of State for War, he worked himself into a prolonged fury over the Russian Revolution and did everything he could to strangle the revolution. Then in 1926 came the General Strike and he threw himself into the war against the strikers with astonishing venom and vindictiveness.

Happily the General Strike came to an end nine days later when the Trade Union Council surrendered to the government. *The British Gazette* went out of business. The last issue, which appeared on May 13, contained a long valedictory article by Churchill celebrating the greatest contribution ever made to British journalism. He wrote:

> Nothing like it has been done before, the world over. If the exceptional occasion provided the inspiration and the opportunity, it also imposed the severest disabilities. What was done represented a triumph of resource and determination over what might well have seemed insuperable difficulties. It is a triumph of which all who had part in it have

a right to be proud, and one which has served equally well two great causes.

It has defeated the attempt to keep the country in the dark during a formidable crisis in its affairs; and it has vindicated the Press against a new conspiracy to muzzle its freedom.

Let us tell the story . . .

And he went on, at great length, to tell the story of how the Chancellor of the Exchequer, with extraordinary presence of mind and working against innumerable difficulties, convinced a small group of men that it was proper to let England know the facts and that they should be printed. He described the long anxious night "of toil and ineffable weariness" which saw the birth of the newspaper and how the key men worked in snatches for seventy-two hours on end, rarely leaving the building, so dedicated they were to the task set before them. These heroic men frustrated "the most formidable and insidious attempt that has yet been made to cripple the freedom of the Press and to withhold essential news from the public." Then came the brief peroration:

> The *British Gazette* may have had a short life; but it has fulfilled the purpose of living.
> It becomes a memory; but it remains a monument.

In fact, it was a monument to one of Churchill's more dangerous follies. He had hugely enjoyed the experience and cherished its memory. Many years later he confessed his pleasure at the spectacle of "a great newspaper office, with its machines crashing and grinding away, for it reminds me of the combination of a first-class battle-ship and a first-class election."

Having constructed his brief monument, Churchill took an extended holiday in Egypt and Greece, and on the return journey paid his respects to Mussolini.

Churchill was still searching for great men, and sometimes found them. He had been engrossed by the study of Mussolini's rise to power: the march to Rome, the sudden emergence of a political army of Blackshirts, a new Roman Empire coming to birth under the sign of the ancient imperial fasces—the ax and the thin rods for inflicting punishment. Mutual friends arranged a meeting with the Italian dictator at the Palazzo Venezia. Mussolini, who admired Churchill, was affable and charming, received his guest kindly and said nothing to alarm him.

There were two lengthy discussions on the state of Europe under the threat of advancing Communism, and Churchill went away with the feeling that he had met one of the truly great men of his time. He said:

> I could not help being charmed, like so many other people have been, by Signor Mussolini's gentle and simple bearing and by his calm, detached poise in spite of so many burdens and dangers. Secondly, anyone could see that he thought of nothing but the lasting good, as he understood it, of the Italian people and that no lesser interest was of the slightest consequence to him.
>
> I am sure that I am violating no confidence when I say that a large part of my conversation with Signor Mussolini and Count Volpi turned on the economic condition of the Italian wage-earner. . . . If I had been an Italian, I am sure that I would have been wholeheartedly with you from start to finish in your triumphant struggle against the bestial appetites and prisons of Leninism. But in England we have not had to fight this danger in the same deadly form. We have our own way of doing things. But that we shall succeed in grappling with Communism and choking the life out of it—of that I am absolutely sure.
>
> I will however say a word on an international aspect of Fascism. Externally your movement has rendered a service to the whole world. The great fear that has always beset every democratic leader or working-class leader has been that of being undermined or overbid by someone more extreme than he. It seems that a continued progression to the left, a sort of inevitable landslide into the Abyss was the characteristic of all revolutions. Italy has shown that there is a way of fighting the subversive forces which can rally the mass of the people, properly led, to value and wish to defend the honour and stability of civilized society. She has provided the necessary antidote to the Russian poison.

Churchill, in fact, held to the belief that Mussolini was defending "the honour and stability of civilized society" long after Fascism had been proved to be nothing more than the theoretical scaffolding for a police state. Mussolini and Churchill had much in common: magniloquence, a sense of imperial destiny, the desire for swift and determined action. They both liked to trample their way across the battlefields of life, seizing the prizes as they fell, and both exulted in their own prowess. Many years later, in a broadcast to the Italian people on December 23, 1940, Churchill said of Mussolini: "That he is a great man I do not deny." It was the supreme accolade, for only those who knew Churchill well knew what he meant when he spoke about "great men." A little more than four years later, when news of Mussolini's execution was brought to him, Churchill revised his estimate of his former friend. "So the bloody beast is dead!" he said.

At various times Churchill had a good deal to say about Mussolini, whose works he read and whose career he followed with interest. He wrote newspaper articles praising him, sometimes with minor reservations. When the dictator with the "gentle and simple bearing" who provided "the necessary antidote to the Russian poison" attacked Abyssinia, Churchill applauded him because he was bent on building an African empire. He believed that Mussolini had a profound sense of imperial mission and a true understanding of his people.

Stanley Baldwin's government ended in the General Election of 1929 and the Chancellor of the Exchequer fell from office. It disturbed Churchill that a Labour government was now in power, but he was even more disturbed by the attitude of the Conservative Party toward him. Finally they had grown tired of him, and they attributed their defeat partly to his strange ineffectiveness as Chancellor of the Exchequer. Baldwin himself found Churchill insufferable. What can one do, he complained, with a Chancellor of the Exchequer who continually interrupts Cabinet meetings with long and brilliant lectures on subjects which have nothing to do with his department? Churchill remained out of office for the next ten years.

He went off to paint in the Canadian Rockies, wrote newspaper articles, pontificated about India and Mussolini—he loathed Indians and was full of admiration for Italians—and finally settled down at Chartwell long enough to write *My Early Life: A Roving Commission*, the most engaging of all his books, telling the story of his life until he entered the House of Commons. He enjoyed reminiscing about his early campaigns, and the enjoyment is infectious. Sometimes the book reads like a boy's story told by George Alfred Henty, whose stories have entertained at least six generations of English schoolboys:

> I heard an order: "Volley firing. Ready. Present." Crash! At least a dozen tribesmen fell. Another volley, and they wavered. A third, and they began to withdraw up the hillside. The bugler began to sound the "Charge." Everyone shouted. The crisis was over, and here, Praise be to God, were the leading files of the Buffs.

The Buffs usually arrive in time, the tribesmen usually fall, the bugles usually sound the "Charge." To the modern reader there is the sense of quite unimportant battles being fought with antiquated weapons, while woolly-haired tribesmen clamber among the rocks and the British troops form impregnable squares. But while in *The Story of the Malakand Field Force, The River War, London to Ladysmith* and *Ian Hamilton's March* Churchill was concerned to tell the story like a good war correspondent without permitting himself to obtrude too much or too frequently, in *My Early Life* he unabashedly focuses on himself even to including at quite preposterous length the congratulatory letters he received from the Prince of Wales, Lord Salisbury, and other dignitaries. But this self-absorption has a quality of innocence. In middle age he was rejoicing in his lost youth: that youth of high adventures in many wars, the writing of many books and the friendship of many important people. He mentions the editors who paid him for the books and the book reviewers whose enthusiasm was sometimes tempered with words of caution. And so he quotes the book reviews.

My Early Life gives the impression of having been dictated rather than written; it is told conversationally, with warmth and good humor. He rarely consulted the books he had written in his youth, with the inevitable result that the student who compares for example the account of the battle of Omdurman in *The River War* with the account of the same battle in *My Early Life* and then again with the account given in his original dispatches, which have survived, finds curious discrepancies. No doubt the early versions are more accurate. But Churchill was perfectly justified in presenting himself as he saw himself more than thirty years later in the bright glare of a capacious and sometimes faltering memory. Only when it came to describing his escape from prison in Pretoria—an event which provoked much controversy—did he repeat what he had written earlier.

Churchill prided himself on his zest and exuberance, but these are not qualities often present in his books. They are present in *My Early Life*, which bubbles with excitement, and they are notably absent in the great six-volume compilation which he called *Marlborough, His Life and Times.* He began writing *Marlborough* in 1931, shortly after the publication of *My Early Life*, partly as an act of devotion toward a revered ancestor, partly in an effort to rebut Macaulay, who had described Marlborough as a sordid amoralist who was intent only to line his own pockets and achieve glory in the process, and partly to fill up his time. It was a labor of love and a labor of justification. The love, amounting to adoration, shines through the book, and the justification provides the occasion for much creaking machinery and strident obfuscation. The portrait of the virtuous Marlborough, which Churchill hoped to present, is totally unconvincing. He wrote:

> It is my hope to recall this great shade from the past, and not only to invest him with his panoply, but make him living and intimate to modern eyes. I hope to show that he was not only the foremost of English soldiers, but in the first rank among the statesmen of our history; not only that he was a Titan, for that is not disputed, but that he was a virtuous and benevolent being, eminently serviceable to his age and country, capable of drawing harmony and design from chaos, and one who only needed an earlier and still wider authority to have made a more ordered and a more tolerant civilization for his own time and to help the future.

The implications were clear: Churchill hoped to show that Marlborough was not only the greatest of English soldiers, ranking high above the Duke of Wellington, but that he was also the greatest English statesman, a paragon of virtue and benevolence, and a man who should have been granted an even wider authority than he possessed, by which Churchill clearly meant that he should have been appointed prime minister of England. This was a tall order and Churchill proceeded to fulfill it as best he could.

"At twenty he made money of his beauty and his vigour; at sixty he made money of his genius and his glory." So Macaulay described Marlborough with the lack of charity he reserved for thieves, peculators and murderers. What especially disturbed Macaulay was that Marlborough was continually capable of committing acts of treachery "with that bland serenity which neither peril nor infamy could disturb." Marlborough's manner, his chilling coldness and his insatiable desire for wealth were to the highest degree offensive to the historian. Others had haughty manners; others desired wealth; others were traitors; others commanded armies; but no one, according to Macaulay, was so triumphantly successful in all these things as that strange marble effigy which called itself the Duke of Marlborough.

Churchill did his best to warm the effigy into life. With all the resources of the muniment room at Blenheim Palace at his disposal, and with the aid of many scholarly authorities of the period, he described the long career of Marlborough at enormous length. He permitted his ancestor a few peccadilloes. Once or twice he is gently reproved for minor errors of judgment. The virtuous, benevolent, titanic being who should have been prime minister comes through unscathed.

Just as Churchill was far more convincing in *The World Crisis* when he described battles he had never seen and political events in which he took no part, so in *Marlborough, His Life and Times* he is more convincing whenever Marlborough is offstage or when he is describing a battle after having patiently explored the half-forgotten battlefield. In the summer of 1932, accompanied by his friend Frederick Lindemann, he set out on a journey of exploration which led him through Holland and clean across Germany to the Danube following Marlborough's victorious march of 1704. He studied Marlborough's battlefields and spent some days in Munich where he met Ernst Hanfstaengl, a huge, bony-faced, laughing journalist, amateur pianist and owner of an art print shop. Hanfstaengl was a close friend of Hitler and invited Churchill to meet Hitler on the following day. According to Churchill the meeting did not take place because Churchill raised some hard questions about the ill-treatment of the Jews. Hanfstaengl, who wrote his memoirs, did not remember the hard questions about the Jews and thought that Churchill, after toying with the idea of meeting Hitler, finally decided that it was inadvisable for political reasons.

For Churchill had seen enough of Germany to be profoundly alarmed. With all his guarded admiration for Hitler, he was aware that the rise of the National Socialist Party to power would alter the balance of power in Europe. Once again, as in Marlborough's time, Europe was on the verge of disaster: new struggles, new combinations of forces, new armaments, new terrors.

He returned to Chartwell to continue working on *Marlborough*. It was a pleasant and not too exacting occupation, and he was in no hurry. The first volume was published in 1933, the last in 1938. There were laudatory reviews, and he had the happy feeling that he had breathed life into a man who had been ill-served by his previous biographers. All Macaulay's charges had been refuted scornfully and vigorously; all opposition was crushed; Marlborough was vindicated. Sitting in the study at Chartwell with the immense painting of Blenheim Palace on the wall, Churchill could claim that he had served his ancestor well, as a knight serves his prince, and nothing more was demanded of him.

In 1930 he was fifty-six, white-haired, fat, with a scholar's stoop and a rambling walk. He did very little exercise, but liked to superintend the workmen on the estate and he had a fondness for bricklaying and was often photographed placing one brick on top of another. Since 1928 he had been a member in good standing of the Amalgamated Union of Building Trade Workers, paying his annual dues of five shillings. In this way he built a tree-top house for his children, devised miniature waterfalls, dammed a lake, constructed a swimming pool heated by two enormous boilers and created very close to the house a small pond which he filled with goldfish; and these gleaming goldfish in the shadowy waters were his constant delight. Black swans were imported from Australia to decorate the lake, and he was enraged when the foxes caught the young swans. He was on affectionate terms with the animals on the estate: badgers, geese, dogs and cats liked to walk beside him; even foxes sometimes accompanied him as he wandered around the estate; and for a brief period a malodorous sheep was his companion.

From his writings and investments he was making £20,000 a year, a huge sum for those days, and inevitably he complained against the exactions of the income tax inspectors. It was a life of leisure and abundant work, of great contentment and growing fear, of responsibility and total lack of responsibility. He attended the House of Commons, made occasional broadcast speeches, painted, wrote books and articles and wondered how long it would be before the government in power gave him another ministerial position. Of those years he wrote: "I lived mainly at Chartwell, where I had much to amuse me. I built with my own hands a large part of the cottages and extensive kitchen-garden walls, and made all kinds of rockeries and waterworks and a large swimming pool which was filtered to limpidity and could be heated to supplement our fickle sunshine. Thus I never had a dull or idle moment from morning to midnight, and with my happy family around me dwelt at peace within my habitation."

THE YEARS OF
THE LOCUST

"A GREAT ROUND white face like a blister. Incredibly aged. Looks like pictures of Lord Holland. An elder statesman. His spirits also have declined and he sighs that he has lost his old fighting power." So Harold Nicolson described Churchill in January, 1930, at the height of the Depression, when the industries of Europe and America were gradually slowing to a standstill and the unemployment figures demonstrated that the governments were incapable of solving the chief problems of the time.

Churchill was out of office and therefore bore no responsibility for the disastrous courses of the government. He was estranged from both Ramsay MacDonald and Stanley Baldwin, and no longer possessed any influence in high places. He was a Member of Parliament, but his occasional speeches were no longer listened to with avidity, and junior backbenchers rustled papers impatiently whenever he rose in the House of Commons. They felt he had nothing to offer them; they had heard it all before, and the time for oratory had long since passed away. He was a spent force, a survivor from the Victorian age, and not to be trusted in the new world of massive unemployment and economic chaos. He was fifty-six years old and his career was over.

History has her own cruel ways of dealing with aging politicians when they are out of office: she throws them away and permits the young to fight like vultures over the corpses. He had spent twenty years in Liberal and Conservative governments, occupied more ministerial posts than any man in England, and sometimes shaped the course of English history. Out of office he was only a shadow of himself.

The National Government, formed by Baldwin and MacDonald in August, 1931, was a patchwork designed to cover up a multitude of sins of omission. There was no common ground between Conservative and Labour, and they could work together only by resolutely disregarding each other's existence. From the wilderness Churchill proclaimed his contempt for the two-headed monster which had emerged to plague the nation, and wondered aloud whether it would not be better to abandon the patchwork altogether and summon a Great Leader to assume command of the destiny of a great imperial power. He was never more contemptuous than when he was in defeat. His speeches and writings that year were chilling in their virulence. He cursed vehemently; he resembled an old drunkard who wanders home from the inn, raging at every tree and shadow and sometimes raising his stick to strike at some innocent wayfarer encountered on the journey. The special objects of his ill-temper were the Labour Party and Mahatma Gandhi, the strange and saintly leader of the Indian separatist movement. About Gandhi he could scarcely talk without foaming at the lips. In a speech delivered in February, 1931, he declared his detestation of Mahatma Gandhi.

> It is alarming and also nauseating to see Mr. Gandhi, a seditious Middle Temple lawyer now posing as a fakir of a type well-known in the East, striding half naked up the steps of the Viceregal Palace, while he is still organizing and conducting a defiant campaign of civil disobedience, to parlay on equal terms with the representative of the King-Emperor.

This was spleen, not oratory, and there was more of it to come. All through the year he inveighed against Gandhi, as though the very existence of the Indian leader was a personal affront to him. That Gandhi should have been invited by the government to attend the Round Table Conference, which was to decide the future of India, seemed to demonstrate the total irresponsibility of the men in power. Was India, the brightest jewel in the British Crown, to be snatched away by "this impudent agitator"? He professed to be terrified by the thought that Gandhi would be permitted to live in London and to attend the conference. He wanted Gandhi arrested and tried for treason. At all costs he must be punished for his acts of defiance.

There were enemies nearer home, and he inveighed against them with the same bitterness and brutal incomprehension of the real forces at work. In his most bloodcurdling manner he demanded that a dictator should arise to sweep the Socialists away. He wrote in October, 1931:

> An anxious and bewildered nation is waiting for Guidance, and not only for guidance, but for Action. The loyal forces in every street and village do not know what to do. The subversive forces are gaining in confidence and audacity.
>
> No one can doubt the malignity of the appeal to class-hatred and revolutionary promptings for which the Socialist Party is now apparently prepared to be responsible. The disturbances in the Fleet and the signs of disorder in great cities are symptoms which none should ignore. Business is at a standstill; prices are rising; the pressure of life upon all classes must inevitably grow greater. Faction is rampant, and winter is at hand. . . .

In England no one paid much attention to these dire warnings uttered in such menacing tones. Few doubted that the world was entering a period of turmoil and unrest, but the causes lay deeper than Socialism and minor disturbances in the fleet. A new age was being ushered in: an age of terror, which would see massacres taking place all over the world.

At first there was only a small cloud on the horizon. In far-off Manchuria, on the night of September 18, 1931, a detachment of the Imperial Japanese Army invaded Mukden, massacred the Chinese garrison troops, and went on to massacre the inhabitants of many of the surrounding villages. The Japanese war for the conquest of China had begun. This was the first war in modern times in which the weapon of massacre was employed. Churchill condoned the outrage. He had affectionate feelings for the Japanese, knew little or nothing about China, and hoped that the effete Chinese civilization would improve as the result of Japanese intervention. "If the Chinese now suffer the cruel malice and oppression of their enemies," he wrote later, "it is the fault of the base and perverted conception of pacifism their rulers have ingrained for two or three thousand years in their people." This was simply not true, and Churchill would have learned that the Chinese had been a warlike people throughout their history if he had consulted a short primer on the Chinese dynasties. China did not interest him, and it was therefore proper that she should be swallowed up by the

Japanese. In the same way he condoned the Italian massacres in Abyssinia and Generalissimo Franco's massacres in Spain.

Weary of Parliament, China, Gandhi and the Labour Party, Churchill set out for a lecture tour in America. He sailed on the *Europa* and reached New York on December 11, 1931, where he was greeted by a crowd of reporters, whom he addressed as "my dear colleagues," for was he not a former reporter and the former editor of *The British Gazette*? He liked to live in style and stayed at the Waldorf-Astoria Hotel. His first public lecture, called "The Destiny of the English-Speaking People," was to be delivered on December 14 at the Brooklyn Academy of Arts and Music. It was never delivered, for on the evening of December 13, on his way from the Waldorf-Astoria to the house of his friend Bernard Baruch at 1055 Fifth Avenue, he stepped out of a taxi at Sixty-seventh Street and was immediately knocked down by another taxi. The taxi driver took Churchill to Lenox Hill Hospital, where he said: "It is all my fault," and then lapsed into unconsciousness.

Mario Contasino, the driver of the taxi, became a tabloid hero by default. He was photographed in the hospital corridor weeping unrestrainedly, telling everyone that an elderly man had darted in front of his cab, and how could he have known that it was Winston Churchill? He had jumped out of the cab in time to hear Churchill saying apologetically: "It is my fault." He appears to have made the same statement many times, and the taxi driver was somewhat calmed by the memory of so many apologies. Churchill was not seriously hurt. He suffered multiple lacerations of the face and nose and a sprained right shoulder. The most important damage was to the shoulder, which had been badly wrenched in India. There were complications owing to a slight attack of pleurisy in the right chest, and his temperature rose to 100.6 degrees. He was given 3,000 units of antitetanus serum.

Churchill employed his time at the hospital to good effect. He wrote an article on the accident, which he called "My New York Misadventure" and sold to a New York magazine for $2,500. In the article he explored one by one the sensations of shock and outrage and misery which accompanied his collision with the taxicab and offered grudging tribute to the human body's resilience. It occurred to him that it was very strange that he had survived and no doubt Providence had her own mysterious reasons for keeping him alive. He wrote:

> There was one moment—I cannot measure it in time—of a world aglare, of a man aghast. I certainly thought quickly enough to achieve the

idea *"I am going to be run down and probably killed."* Then came the
blow. I felt it on my forehead and across the thighs. But besides the blow
there was an impact, a shock, a concussion indescribably violent. It
blotted out everything except thought.

A friend of mine of mathematical predilections has been kind enough
to calculate the stresses involved in the collision. The car weighed some
2,400 pounds. With my evening coat on I could not have weighed much
less than 200 pounds. Taking the rate of the car at thirty-five miles an
hour—I think a moderate estimate—I had actually to absorb in my body
6,000 foot pounds. It was the equivalent of falling thirty feet on to a
pavement. The energy absorbed, *though not, of course, the application of
destructive force,* was the equivalent of stopping ten pounds of buckshot
dropped 600 feet, or two charges of buckshot at point-blank range.

I do not understand why I was not broken like an eggshell or squashed
like a gooseberry. I have seen that the poor policeman who was killed on
the Oxford road was hit by a vehicle traveling at very much the same
speed, was completely shattered. I certainly must be very tough or very
lucky, or both.

As Churchill well knew, he was both tough and lucky. Never in his
life, in all his wars, was he hurt more grievously. It was some months
before he was fully recovered. The accident left him in a state of
complete physical exhaustion.

He left the hospital and returned briefly to the Waldorf-Astoria,
before leaving for a three-week vacation in the Bahamas in the hope of
recovering his strength. Mentally he was vigorous; only the physical
body was injured.

Shortly after his accident a new secretary, Phyllis Moir, a young
English woman, entered his employment, and she has described her
amazement when she saw him for the first time in the palatial apartment in the tower of the Waldorf-Astoria with brightly colored hunting
prints on the wall, trunks and packing cases everywhere, for he was
about to leave for Nassau. He was sitting in an enormous Queen Anne
armchair beside a blazing fire. There was a deep, livid gash on his
forehead, and a large mound of silver-gray ash on his midriff, which had
become an ashtray. There was a Christmas tree in the corner of the
room, red poinsettias, red carnations, lilacs—the room was filled with
flowers. He barked a few questions at her, glanced at her references,
noted that she was related to Sir Ernest Moir, said: "I understand you
are willing to accompany me on my peregrinations," and then abruptly
dismissed her. She did not accompany him on his peregrination to the

Bahamas, but served as his secretary from the day he returned to New York.

That he was brusque, overwhelming, inconsiderate, intolerant and commanding, all this she had learned from her first brief meeting with him. He did not change over the years. In the middle of the night the thought would come to him that he would write a letter on a subject that suddenly seemed to have enormous importance, and Sergeant Thompson, his valet and bodyguard, would be sent to awaken her. Half asleep, she came trembling into the presence: Churchill sitting up in bed, smoking a cigar and reading a book. He then dictated a brief letter to David Low, the cartoonist, pointing out that in recent cartoons the faces of Churchill and Lord Hailsham were indistinguishable, and would he please do something about it. Having dictated the letter, he then dismissed her.

His inconsiderateness, his total lack of any understanding of the needs of others, was sometimes bewildering. On a long train journey, after going to bed in a pullman car, he suddenly demanded that a book should be brought to him. The book was locked in a trunk in the baggage car at the end of the train. Nevertheless it must be brought to him. Sergeant Thompson was ordered to fetch the book, although it was late at night and he was exhausted after a long day's work. He went to the baggage car and learned from the baggagemaster that the trunk was wedged in an inaccessible corner of the tightly packed car. Perhaps Mr. Churchill would wait until the morning. Sergeant Thompson reported this to his employer, who demanded that the baggagemaster be instantly produced before him, all this in a loud voice to the consternation of the other passengers who wanted to sleep. Sergeant Thompson went back wearily to the baggage car, somehow prevailed upon the indignant baggagemaster to accompany him along the full length of the train to confront a scowling Churchill, who demanded the right to put his hands on his own books when and where he needed them. The baggage car was taken to pieces and the book was produced. Churchill had not changed since the day when, attending a children's party and reminded that his nurse was waiting for him, he announced in lordly fashion: "Everyone waits for me."

For his new secretary there were many compensations. Although out of office, and in a mood of daily belligerence against all those who thwarted him, Churchill acted the role of "the great man" with extraordinary élan. He was writing, or rather dictating, letters to everyone of importance, and his secretary found herself filling two shorthand notebooks a day. She noticed that his most overused word was "prod." He was prodding everyone. The Prime Minister, the Duke of Marlborough and a hundred other people of eminence were the recipients of his communications. Miss Moir was deeply impressed. She was also impressed by the huge sums he received for his writings and by the enormous quantities of liquor he absorbed. A glass of dry sherry at midmorning, a small bottle of claret or burgundy at lunch followed by a glass of port at the end of lunch. Then in late afternoon came the first whiskey and soda, the prelude to many more. At dinner there was always champagne followed by port and the finest Napoleon brandy. During the course of the evening there were highballs. And just as he drank well, so he ate well, abhorring frugality and the sins of austerity. For him a picnic was always a feast, with hampers filled with cold game, caviar, hothouse fruits and champagne. He traveled, even in wartime, with elaborate wooden cases filled with magnums of champagne.

No man lived more royally. He had, by habit and desire, acquired the tastes of emperors: the best horses, the best food, the best liquor, the most handsome women around him. Strangely he had very little interest in art, although he admired his own paintings. He liked to say: "Only the best satisfies me."

When he drank, the words flowed, ideas multiplied, exciting prospects opened, and the world with all its subtly changing colors assumed the guise of a beautiful maiden to be conquered by his wiles. His talk consisted very largely of monologues and reminiscences, in sentences constructed on models laid down by Gibbon and Macaulay, stuttering vehemently when he became excited. He was almost incapable of normal conversation. Probably no one has ever talked so much or listened so little.

All this his secretary observed in the intervals of taking dictation. He even talked and dictated in his bath while maneuvering the hot and cold water taps with his toes. He would first whisper and growl the words to himself and then when he had accumulated a whole paragraph he would bawl the words in a resounding voice. Emerging from his bath, with a towel wrapped loosely around him, he would continue to dictate, stimulated by the hot water and the heavily scented soap, and even when he was half dressed, running around the room in his undershirt, pink silk shorts and a bright-red cummerband, the dictating continued.

When he returned to England the Depression was still on, he was still out of office, Hitler was in the ascendant, and the statesmen were groping blindly for solutions to insoluble problems. Hitler now absorbed his attention. In 1932 his son Randolph was one of those who accompanied Hitler during his election campaigns. From conversations with his son, Churchill developed a grave respect and some sympathy for Hitler, which became evident in his speeches and in a chapter on Hitler he wrote in his book *Great Contemporaries*. When he descended on the House of Commons he said very little about Hitler, reserving his thunderbolts for the Indian nationalist leaders, those "evil and malignant Brahmins whose itching fingers are stretching and scratching at the vast pillage of a derelict empire." Such things sound better in a speech than in print, though they are woebegone even in a speech. Too often he seemed to be amusing himself at the expense of Gandhi and Nehru, who were great men, whether he knew it or not.

Churchill's humor was often infuriating, for he could be cruel and biting when he chose. He had read the Restoration dramatists and admired their balanced, casual invective. From his father he inherited the patronizing upper-class humor designed to put his inferiors in their proper place; from his mother came a wit softened by kindness. At his most savage, he was ruthless in the Restoration manner; but what might have been tolerable during the reign of Charles II had become almost intolerable during the reign of George V. Churchill spent long hours polishing his most ferocious barbs, reciting them until every last assonance and every calculated pause had been mastered. It was observed that his humor was always more violent when he was out of office, addressing himself to someone in power.

He had always detested Ramsay MacDonald, the leader of the Socialist Party, who became Prime Minister in the Conservative-dominated National Government of 1931. MacDonald represented the emerging social forces that Churchill was determined to thwart at all costs, but MacDonald was in power and Churchill was in the opposition. To reduce MacDonald to manageable terms, it was necessary to present him as a freak and a monstrosity. On January 28, 1933, Churchill rose in the House of Commons to denounce the Prime Minister as "the Boneless Wonder." He said:

> I remember, when I was a child, being taken to the celebrated Barnum's Circus, which contained an exhibition of freaks and monstrosities, but the exhibit on the program which I most desired to see was the one described as "The Boneless Wonder." My parents judged that the spec-

tacle would be too revolting and demoralizing for my youthful eyes, and I have waited fifty years to see the Boneless Wonder sitting on the Treasury Bench.

This was cruel humor without the saving grace of wit, heavy-handed, scornful, patronizing. He had scored a bull's-eye, but the price was too high, for the Socialists vividly remembered it against him. Since he could not understand Socialism, he contented himself with withering attacks on Socialists. Clement Attlee, the mild-mannered politician who served him faithfully as Deputy Prime Minister during World War II, incurred his wrath by becoming Prime Minister at the end of the war. Churchill thereupon described him as "a sheep in wolf's clothing." When someone described Attlee as a modest man, Churchill replied: "Attlee is a very modest man. And with reason." It was unfair, and he knew it was unfair, but he could not prevent himself from indulging in aristocratic contempt for those he regarded as his social inferiors.

Once in the House of Commons Miss Bessie Braddock, a Socialist member for Liverpool, observed that he was swaying and slurring his words. "Winston, you're drunk," she said. Churchill turned on her furiously: "Bessie, you're ugly, and tomorrow morning I'll be sober but you'll still be ugly." The Conservatives broke up in laughter, but the Socialists were not so easily amused.

Once in 1941, during a debate on the conduct of the war, Aneurin Bevan, who traded many sharp insults with Churchill, said in Parliament: "The government has conceived the war wrongly from the start and no one has more misconceived it than the prime minister himself." Churchill's reply was uttered in the accents of lordly contempt. "You, sir," he declared, "are nothing more than a slave to scurrility."

A wide reading in eighteenth-century literature had given Churchill a taste for the balanced literary insult, but "a slave to scurrility" was not one of his better inventions. The method invited counterattack. When Churchill called Aneurin Bevan "a merchant of disloyalty," which had at least the advantage of introducing a concept more immediately intelligible than a scurrilous slave, there came Bevan's more damning rejoinder: "Better than being a wholesaler of disasters."

When Churchill heard that someone he disliked was indisposed, he remarked: "Nothing trivial, I hope."

Churchill's wit flashed with corrosive fire, but it was often brutal, always self-serving and sometimes totally unfair. He once described

General de Gaulle as "a female lama who had been surprised in her bath." But this tells us more about Churchill than about General de Gaulle, whose wit was also grounded on eighteenth-century literature. Yet there was a great difference between their humors. De Gaulle's humor was ice-cold, Churchill's ran the whole gamut from coarse barrack-room insult to brilliant repartee. De Gaulle, too, was contemptuous of most of mankind.

Churchill's contempt for the Indians was presumably derived from his memory of the days he spent at Bangalore surrounded by obsequious Indian servants. The years had not changed him: he remained patronizing and condescending. When asked whether they were ready for elections, he answered that they were too ignorant to know who they were voting for, and he spoke of those "humble primitives who are unable in 450,000 villages even to produce the simple organization of four or five people sitting in a hut in order to discuss their common affairs." This was not a blind spot; it was an attitude of mind deeply engrained in him, another aspect of his liking for the totalitarian leaders, Mussolini and Hitler. The superior civilization rules the inferior, massive power is necessary to keep the natives in subjection, the empire endures. It never occurred to him that the civilization of India might not have been inferior.

Thus when he talked about Gandhi, it was always with venom and scorn. Gandhi's ugliness offended him; Gandhi's nakedness insulted him; Gandhi's demand for independence threatened him. "Gandhi-ism and all it stands for will, sooner or later, have to be grappled with and finally crushed. It is no use trying to satisfy a tiger by feeding it on cat's meat." He was addressing the Indian Empire Society which was full of people with similar ideas. He went on to paint a dark picture of India if British rule gave way to rule by the Congress Party, "when the British will be no more to them than any other European nation, when white people will be in India only upon sufferance, when debts and obligations of all kinds will be repudiated, and when an army of white janissaries, officered if necessary from Germany, will be hired to secure the armed ascendancy of the Hindu."

In his opinions on India he had few followers, and some of his closest friends opposed him. Alfred Duff-Cooper, for example, regarded Churchill's long-drawn-out and ultimately ineffective fight to prevent India from gaining Dominion status to be the most unfortunate event between the two wars. There were, of course, many far more unfortunate events, and the most unfortunate of all was Hitler.

Churchill, surveying the rise to power of Hitler, was caught in a dilemma. He feared, loathed, and admired the man who had singlehandedly awakened Germany out of her lethargy and made her a dominant power in Europe. His feelings toward Hitler remained ambivalent at least until 1937. If Hitler was not quite a Great Man he was so very close to it, in Churchill's eyes, that it made very little difference. He wrote in 1935:

He has succeeded in restoring Germany to the most powerful position in Europe, and not only has he restored the position of his country, but he has even, to a very large extent, reversed the results of the Great War. . . . The vanquished are in process of becoming the victors, and the victors the vanquished. When Hitler began, Germany lay prostrate at the feet of the Allies. He may yet see the day when what is left of Europe will be prostrate at the feet of Germany. Whatever else may be thought about these exploits, they are certainly among the most remarkable in the whole history of the world. . . .

Those who have met Herr Hitler face to face in public business or on social terms have found a highly competent, cool, well-informed functionary with an agreeable manner, a disarming smile, and few have been unaffected by a subtle personal magnetism. Nor is this impression merely the dazzle of power. He exerted it on his companions at every stage in his struggle, even when his fortunes were in the lowest depths. Thus the world lives on hopes that the worst is over, and that we may yet live to see Hitler a gentler figure in a happier age.

The spectacle of "the gentle Hitler" emerging out of the mists of the future inspires little confidence in Churchill's powers of judgment. This time the gift of prophecy failed him. Nor was he more clairvoyant than the average Englishman. "There is no likelihood of a war in which Great Britain would be involved," he said immediately after Hitler came to power. By November, 1933, like many millions of other people who had seen the newsreels of the Storm Troopers and the Hitler Youth marching through the streets of Germany, he was beginning to wonder where it was all leading to. "They are not looking for status," he observed. "They are looking for weapons, and, when they have the weapons, believe me they will then ask for the return of lost territories and lost colonies." He urged that there should be a revision of the Treaty of Versailles to permit Germany her proper place in the sun. In February, 1934, a year after Hitler came to power, he spoke on air defense and drew a dramatic picture of London vanishing under a black flood of bombs. "We are as vulnerable as we have never been before," he declared, and prophesied that by 1936 Germany would have a far larger air force than Britain. He was haunted by the fear of a sudden preemptive bombardment by air, and in his articles spoke of the tank as an outmoded instrument of war and the submarine menace as equally illusory. The truth was that he was as confused as nearly everyone else. Only Basil Liddell Hart, the military correspondent of the *Times,* had thought out the new forms that war would take. Churchill consulted him rarely, and when Liddell Hart came to him, it was Churchill who did all the talking. "The tank," Churchill announced with all the assurance that comes with the knowledge that he had helped to bring it into existence, "cannot stand up to anti-tank rifles and anti-tank guns." And he believed, as an article of faith, that battleships were impervious to bombing planes.

About this time Frederick Lindemann, a reserved, eccentric and crotchety bachelor, became Churchill's chief adviser on scientific and military affairs. Lindemann was the son of an Alsatian father and an American mother, and his chief claim to fame was that he had worked untiringly to bring the Cavendish Laboratory to a state of great efficiency in the study of low-temperature physics. Independently wealthy, he knew very little about the ordinary lives of people and was contemptuous of the works of other physicists. Churchill had met him in the twenties and continued to meet him at aristocratic house parties, for Lindemann liked aristocrats and was fond of saying that he was only concerned with prominent people. Churchill and Lindemann had much in common. Churchill was especially impressed with the fact that Lindemann, given any problem at all, would instantly take out his slide rule and calculate the answer to four places of decimals. "Lindemann," wrote Churchill, "could decipher the signals of the experts on the far horizons and explain to me in lucid homely terms what the issues were."

Perhaps; but other scientists were considerably less enamored of Lindemann's scientific skills. Lord Rutherford, who knew him well, characterized him as "a scientist *manqué.*" Lindemann had a reputation for vicious infighting when placing his protégés in high position, and his ascendancy over Churchill was regarded then and later as highly dangerous, and perhaps calamitous, by other scientists who did not share his Germanic way of thinking. Nevertheless he was wholly right when he insisted that Churchill should make a direct appeal to the Prime Minister, Stanley Baldwin, to build a more powerful air force, and together with Lindemann, Churchill made a hurried journey to Aix-les-Bains to see Baldwin in the autumn of 1934, after the Night of the Long Knives and the reorganization of the Wehrmacht had shown that Hitler would stop at nothing to enforce his will. But it was not until the following March that Baldwin in his slow, labored way formed the Air Defence Research Council designed to study the problem of Hitler's growing air force.

With an unusual blindness, even in those times when the blind were leading the blind, Churchill continued to hold Mussolini in high esteem. The man he was later to call "Hitler's utensil" belonged to the company of "great men" to be admired, placated, and helped on their way. When Mussolini invaded Abyssinia in October, 1935, Churchill staunchly defended him: The Abyssinians were as primitive as the Indians and deserved to be conquered. While the invasion was taking place Churchill was holidaying pleasantly in Barcelona and North Africa.

As late as October, 1937, Churchill continued to proclaim the abiding genius of Mussolini. He wrote: "It would be a dangerous folly for the British people to underrate the enduring position in world-history which Mussolini will hold; or the amazing qualities of courage, comprehension, self-control and perseverance which he exemplifies." He announced that the invasion of Abyssinia was "a little thing" scarcely worthy of anyone's attention. He had spoken of Mussolini's "gentle and simple bearing" and of the "gentler Hitler" who might one day emerge to surprise Europe. It appeared that gentleness was one of the qualities of dictators armed to the teeth and determined to annihilate their adversaries.

The time of invasions had begun. Abyssinia fell, and then came Hitler's invasion of the Rhineland in the spring of 1936 and Franco's call to arms in Spain in the summer. Churchill approved of Franco, who was a gentleman, unlike the liberals, Socialists and Communists on the other side. In this way, as gullible as all the rest of the statesmen of the democracies but with a healthy fear of Hitler's bombing planes, Churchill confronted the uncertain future.

THE END OF AN AGE

ON JANUARY 20, 1936—a cold, dark, blustery day—King George V died of pneumonia in Sandringham. He was seventy years old and had reigned for more than a quarter of a century. Rudyard Kipling died two days earlier—the King's trumpeter had gone in advance of the King.

George V was one of those men who seem to incarnate an epoch. There was nothing flamboyant about him; he was down-to-earth, stolid, virtuous, possessing a rough good humor and a peppery tongue. With his short, bristling beard he resembled a ship's captain, and only his enormous blue Hanoverian eyes suggested the foreignness in him, for he had little English blood and was descended from the house of Saxe-Coburg-Gotha. His wife, born Princess Mary of Teck, was largely German and Hungarian by origin. The British people thought of them as a characteristically British couple, and they especially admired the King's deeply felt sense of responsibility, as befitted the father of a large family of nations spread out across the world. In theory the innumerable dominions, colonies and protectorates of the British Empire belonged to him; and when, every year at Christmas, he addressed his peoples by radio, calling upon them to live virtuously and prayerfully in comradeship with one another, it was as though some magical rite of passage was being performed. The quiet, assured voice bound the Empire together.

His successor was Edward, Prince of Wales, his eldest son, who came to the throne under the title of Edward VIII. He was then forty years old, but looked much younger with his delicately handsome features and his air of a young man about town. He was an intrepid horseman, spoke French and German fluently, and had traveled through all the countries of the Empire. No prince had ever been more popular. Those who knew him well and admired his daring thought he had all the qualities that would make a great King in the dangerous age of the dictators. Those who knew him better wondered whether he possessed the essential gift of a sense of responsibility. He was far more knowledgeable about world affairs than his father had ever been; he had long ago broken down the barrier that separated the royal family from the people; and he was at ease with soldiers, sailors, workmen and the common people. Nevertheless a doubt persisted. Highly strung, impatient of protocol, determined to lead a normal life amid the inevitable panoply of royalty, he seemed to find his responsibilities irksome and wearying. The emblem of the Prince of Wales consisted of three white feathers and the motto *Ich dien*—I serve. It was gradually becoming apparent that he might not want to serve and would maneuver himself into a position in which service would become impossible.

It was a year of catastrophes: rising unemployment in England, a tidal wave of oppression in the Soviet Union, the Italian armies driving into Abyssinia and the Spaniards engulfed in Civil War. King Edward VIII enjoyed a holiday in the Mediterranean accompanied by Mrs. Wallis Simpson, an American lady who had been divorced by her first husband and was in the process of obtaining a divorce from her second husband. News of the King's holiday on the yacht *Nahwal* was published in the English press, but the presence of his companion was discreetly concealed. In the American press pictures of the King in the company of Mrs. Simpson appeared frequently. Stanley Baldwin, the Prime Minister, became alarmed. If, as it appeared, the King wanted to marry Mrs. Simpson, then this was a matter which would have to be submitted to the government and the governments of the dominions. It was not a matter that depended solely on the King's wishes.

Mrs. Wallis Simpson possessed admirable qualities, but she was not (in British eyes) virtuous, and to imagine her wearing the Crown was to imagine the impossible. Her decree nisi became effective on October

27, and thereafter the drama hurried toward its conclusion. The King was obdurate: he would marry Mrs. Simpson whatever the cost, even if it meant abandoning the throne. A morganatic marriage was acceptable to him, and he was prepared to discuss and to tolerate any constitutional amendment which would permit him to live with her. Baldwin, although devoted to the King, scented danger. A morganatic marriage would inevitably involve a constitutional crisis. The abdication of a popular King was to be avoided at all costs. Queen Mary and the rest of the royal family intensely disliked the lady and refused to entertain the thought of a morganatic marriage but feared to protest too loudly. Among the English people there was a growing feeling that a King who contemplates renouncing the throne for a private pleasure is not a King; and Baldwin, who usually knew what the people were thinking, was gradually accustoming himself to the thought that Edward's younger brother, Albert, Duke of York, would make an admirable King, though he was quiet and retiring and lacked Edward's charm.

Quixotically Churchill threw himself into the fray on the King's side. On December 4 he saw the King and vehemently opposed abdication. He suggested that Edward should bide his time until Baldwin's fury had abated, and he hinted at the formation of a King's Party which would sweep the government into oblivion, thereby making two cardinal errors of judgment, for the King had no intention of waiting and no desire to preside over a King's Party with Churchill acting as party leader. "I do not find people angry with Mrs. Simpson," Harold Nicolson wrote in his diary on the previous day. "But I do find a deep and enraged fury against the King himself. In eight months he has destroyed the great structure of popularity which he has raised." This was not quite true. The people still liked the King; they only wished he would make up his mind and settle the business once and for all; and they detested Mrs. Simpson as an interloper meddling in their affairs, for they felt a proprietorial right over their King.

Churchill had made many grievous errors in his life—errors of strategy, errors of judgment, errorts of tact. Now, brandishing a quiverful of errors, demanding the impossible and the unthinkable, he championed the King in a public statement. He insisted that the government, not the King, should abdicate. "If the King refuses to take the advice of his Ministers, they are, of course, free to resign," he declared. "They have no right whatever to put pressure on him." He represented the King as a man who had no personal access to Parliament or the people, and was therefore doomed to silence. On December 7, when Churchill rose in

Parliament to plead for further delay he was shouted down. It was not the shouting down of a firebrand; they were shouting against him because he seemed to be insulting their intelligence by pleading for a lost cause which was no longer of any great importance. In red-faced anger Churchill rounded on Baldwin and said: "You won't be satisfied until you have broken him, will you?"

Churchill's reasons for supporting the King were deeply personal and historical. He had great affection for the King, and when Home Secretary he had superintended the investiture of the young prince as Prince of Wales at Carnarvon Castle. They had met frequently and enjoyed each other's company. The King could mimic Churchill's speech with extraordinary accuracy. The historical reasons were based on Churchill's study of the time when young John Churchill went to bed with the King's mistress while his sister Arabella slept with the Duke of York. Churchill had no pronounced views on sexual immorality; he was disposed to leave moralizing to others. He had forgotten that the English were profoundly moralistic and out of sympathy with Mrs. Simpson.

His reputation had never been at a lower ebb than during the days when he defended the King. His career was in a shambles and he was regarded as the ultrareactionary, the man on the white horse who came charging to the rescue of Obsolescence, for suddenly King Edward VIII had become obsolete and Churchill himself was no longer a wanderer in the wilderness but in exile in the furthest regions of the wilderness where his enemies, who were numerous, hoped he would be forgotten. It was generally agreed that he had shown himself in his true colors and was quite incompetent.

In May, 1937, Albert, Duke of York, was crowned in Westminster Abbey and thereafter bore the name of King George VI. He was liked and admired but not loved—that would come later. Churchill had no close relations with him. He was spending more and more time at Chartwell, bricklaying, writing articles, lying low. In that year he was invited to meet Joachim von Ribbentrop, the German ambassador, at the German Embassy in London. It was an unhappy meeting, for Ribbentrop was a man who spoke brusquely, with immense self-assurance, on matters about which it would have been wiser to speak gently. Speaking as one elder statesman to another, he outlined a case for an Anglo-German alliance with Germany standing guard for the British Empire in all its greatness and extent provided that Britain would give Germany a free hand in Eastern Europe. What did he mean by Eastern Europe? It transpired that he meant Poland, White Russia and the Ukraine, and to emphasize the point Ribbentrop pointed to the map and outlined the area which needed to be incorporated into the German Reich. Churchill regarded the German claims as preposterous and said so. "In that case, war is inevitable," Ribbentrop said. "There is no way out. The Fuehrer is resolved. Nothing will stop him and nothing will stop us." Churchill did his best to remind Ribbentrop that destiny did not always march with the big battalions. "Do not underrate England," he replied. "She is very clever. If you plunge us all into another Great War, she will bring the whole world against you like last time." "No," said Ribbentrop, "England will not bring the world against Germany." Churchill left the embassy more certain than ever that Germany was bent on more and more conquests.

While Churchill saw the war coming, there was very little he could do about it, for he was out of office. To earn money and to employ himself usefully he began to revive a long-cherished plan of writing a history of the English-speaking peoples. All the preliminary preparations were completed by June, 1938. By September, 1939, he had completed the first drafts of the first three volumes and part of the fourth volume.

There are long, dry pages in *The History of the English-Speaking Peoples*, where Churchill is quite obviously bored. Neither his army of assistants nor the man himself could find much excitement in the reign of King Stephen and Queen Matilda, the early Plantagenets, or the rise of the Tudors to power. For long stretches of the book the fires are banked down and the light glows fitfully. Even Queen Elizabeth is dealt with summarily, and when he describes the reign of Henry VIII the fire glows brightly with his description of the execution of Anne Boleyn and then fades again. There is scarcely any sense of a man wrestling with history. Instead, it is all taken at second or third hand from other historians, patched and pulled together, wrung through a mangle and displayed without enthusiasm. Only about half of the work appears to have come from his own hand, while the dull methodical prose of his assistants appears in every chapter.

The truth was that he lacked the historical imagination; his characters fail to come alive. Even the Duke of Marlborough, who is described at length, fails to be convincing. Churchill describes a well-known portrait of Henry VII in the National Portrait Gallery in London. He describes the King as having "an air of disillusionment, of fatigue, of unceasing vigilance, and above all of sadness and responsibility." It would have been simpler to reproduce the portrait. The cadence is characteristically Churchillian, but one detects that something has gone profoundly wrong. What he has seen in the portrait is not the King with the strange gray eyes but his own self. Disillusionment, fatigue, unceasing vigilance, sadness and responsibility were precisely the characteristics of Churchill in the late thirties, as he waited impotently for the war to begin.

Churchill had always admired Cromwell, and he especially admired Cromwell's speeches. The dictator who ordered the execution of Charles I and ruled England as the Lord Protector, the tyrant who had the sense to employ the great poet John Milton as his secretary, pitiless to his enemies but gentle to all those around him, a good father and family man, was a man after Churchill's heart. He describes Cromwell as "the harsh, terrific, lightning charged being," and as "a giant laggard from the Elizabethan Age," a man born out of his time, possessed of demonic energy and extraordinary farsightedness, whose political conceptions were only to be realized in a later day.

When Churchill writes about Cromwell, the fire burns brightly and the logs crackle and roar. Here is Cromwell after he has seized power:

> One man's will now ruled. One puzzled, self-questioning, but explosive spirit became for a spell the guardian of the slowly gathered work of ages, and of the continuity of the English message.

But here come complexities, for if he was the guardian and protector, what precisely did he protect? Churchill was not quite sure. One moment he is filled with loathing, becomes almost livid, as he contemplates Cromwell uprooting the past, destroying the king, setting the commons against the aristocrats, breaking up the landed estates and burning the title deeds of civilization. Churchill thunders: "If in a tremendous crisis Cromwell's sword had saved the cause of Parliament, he must stand before history as a representative of dictatorship and military rule who, with all his qualities as a soldier and a statesman, is in lasting discord with the genius of the English race." It is vintage Churchill, and it is in direct contradiction with what he has said previously. No matter! There remains the summing up. Here Churchill invents an entirely new and improbable thesis: that Cromwell was indeed the protector of the ancient English traditions precisely because he protected them against himself and Parliament. He writes:

With all his faults and failures, he was indeed the Lord Protector of the enduring rights of the Old England he loved against the terrible weapon which he and Parliament had forged to assert them. Without Cromwell there might have been no advance, without him no collapse, without him no recovery. Amid the ruins of every institution, social and political, which had guided the Island life he towered up gigantic, glowing, indispensable, the sole agency by which time could be gained for healing and regrowth.

Churchill was in love with Cromwell, and was therefore quite capable of saying absurd and contradictory things about him. At the same time he was attempting to unravel the mysteries of dictatorship. He warns us that we would be misled if we believed that the triumph of Cromwell and the Ironsides was a victory for democracy and the Parliamentary system over the Divine Right of Kings and "Old World dreams," by which he means the hopes and aspirations of the pre-Cromwellian Englishmen. On the contrary, Cromwell's triumph was "the triumph of some twenty thousand resolute, ruthless, disciplined, military fanatics over all that England had ever willed or wished." We are far away from the vision of Cromwell as "the guardian of the slowly gathered work of ages." Instead he has become the destroyer, the Fuehrer in command of twenty thousand Storm Troopers.

Churchill wrote these pages on Cromwell in 1938 and 1939, when the thought had already occurred to him that he would be called upon to lead Great Britain against Hitler. He could not guess the stages by which he would be raised to power, but he spoke to his intimates of a feeling amounting to certainty that the people would summon him. He would demand full powers, and become virtual dictator of England. The thought did not seem to oppress him, but seemed to buoy him up. The long years in the wilderness would come to an end in a blaze of glory. The dream which had first intoxicated him when he was scarcely out of his teens would be fulfilled at last.

The pages on Cromwell in *The History of the English-Speaking Peoples* show Churchill wrestling with dictatorship, like Jacob wrestling with the angel. He was not only perfectly aware that he might become the second Cromwell, but he was also, and to a greater degree, aware that dictatorship was destructive of ancient institutions and traditions, and that it was the most dangerous of all methods of government, to be tolerated only as a last resort. Simultaneously fascinated and appalled by it, Churchill both embraced and rejected it, adored it and quarrelled with it, and finally accepted it. "One man's will now ruled. One puzzled, self-questioning, but explosive spirit . . ."

Henceforth Cromwell's speeches were to be absorbed into Churchill's oratory, and in place of the rolling periods of Gibbon and Macaulay there emerged a style closer to Cromwell's—clear, tough and sinewy. Here, for example, is Cromwell talking to Hampden about the need for raising a new army after the indecisive battle of Edgehill. "You must get men of a spirit that is likely to go as far as gentlemen will go," he said, "not old decayed serving men, tapsters and such kind of fellows to encounter gentlemen that have honour and courage and resolution in them." And a little later he spoke of raising an army of "such men as had the fear of God before them and made some conscience of what they did." Churchill's war speeches, which were the best he ever made, involve a mixture of many styles, but the very best of them owe most to Cromwell and Shakespeare.

Meanwhile the war was many months away, and Churchill was still puttering away in the gardens of Chartwell, revising *The History of the English-Speaking Peoples,* and making dire predictions about the inevitability of the war, which few people listened to. He was not alone in prophesying war, and others spoke more urgently. He was drinking heavily, his face alarmingly red, his waistline expanding, his temper flaring up and then subsiding, as he became increasingly aware of the growing hostility toward him not only in government circles but among the people. In drawing rooms and public houses people were saying they did not want Churchill in power even if there was a war—he was too bloody-minded. A. G. Gardiner's famous observation that "Churchill will write his name in history; take care that he does not write it in blood" was remembered. People listened to him with skepticism and more than a little fear, for they had taken his measure in the past and found him wanting. In 1938 he was far from being a popular figure. Many years had passed since he had been in office; he was an elder statesman without a large following; and he was thought to be useful only as a goad to the government of Neville Chamberlain, which was evidently pursuing a policy of "muddling through."

Neville Chamberlain was a much more forthright and intelligent person than he appeared to be. His personal ascendancy over his Cabinet was complete, and he knew exactly what had to be done: to temporize, build up the armed forces, demonstrate his willingness to yield to the legitimate aspirations of Mussolini and Hitler, watch carefully for the first chink in the dictatorial armor. At this juncture

on the sunlit terrace facing the Thames. Those who discussed the speech at all remarked that it was the usual Churchill ranting and should be taken with a grain of salt, they had heard it all before, and there were far too many generalities. They had not heard the music.

"Rouse the nation" was precisely what Chamberlain could not, and would not, do. He descended from a family of leather goods merchants, and he had the mind of an accountant and a salesman. Before becoming Prime Minister he had been a good Minister of Health and twice Chancellor of the Exchequer. All his training conspired to make him a man who would never take needless risks. Writing to his sister long before Czechoslovakia was being threatened, he observed that even if there were a close and firm alliance between Britain and France and some of the smaller powers in Europe, there was simply nothing that could be done to prevent Germany from marching into Prague. He was constantly being badgered by Churchill to take "a clear, decided, bold and unmistakable lead." But, as he reminded his sister, Churchill was not at the head of the government and would not have to bear the consequences. He regarded Churchill's call for action as so much "twaddle." Prudence and caution were the watchwords.

Unfortunately prudence and caution were not enough, and by the end of the year Chamberlain had demonstrated so much ability to be prudent and cautious that he was in danger of conniving at his own defeat. When the Czechoslovak crisis blew up in September, he flew three times to Germany to intercede with Hitler, believing against all the evidence that Hitler was a reasonable man who would listen to reason. Hitler had already drawn up his battle plan against the Soviet Union, and it was essential to him to annihilate Czechoslovakia. He was prepared to humor Chamberlain. He would take a small slice now, a larger slice later. Chamberlain listened to Hitler's rantings about the miseries inflicted on the German-speaking inhabitants of the Sude- tenland, and meekly surrendered. In October the German army marched into the Sudetenland, and Czechoslovakia was now in a far worse situation than if there had been no negotiations. The Munich Pact was the fruit of Chamberlain's prudence and caution. Before leaving Munich, Chamberlain urged Hitler to sign a statement promising that Britain and Germany would continue to negotiate and enter discussions on all matters pertaining to the two countries "and thus to contribute to assure the peace of Europe." Hitler signed the document casually, disdainfully. It meant nothing to him, and it per- mitted Chamberlain to return to England with the promise of "peace in our time." Churchill, less easily buoyed up by illusory hopes, described the negotiations in Germany very simply: "One pound was demanded at the pistol's point. When it was given, two pounds were demanded at the pistol's point. Finally, the dictator consented to take £1 17s 6d and the rest in promises of goodwill for the future."

To his friends Churchill said he felt crushed and impotent. Munich was a total disaster. "I fear," he said, "that this is the end of the British Empire."

Although a Czechoslovak government still ruled in Prague, it was a government virtually without power, at the mercy of Hitler. "All is over," Churchill wrote. "Silent, mournful, abandoned, broken, Czechoslovakia recedes into the darkness."

In a single year Hitler had added more than ten million subjects to his empire by the conquest of Austria and the Sudetenland. He had acquired the Skoda Works, the second most important arsenal in Central Europe. The thirty-five divisions of the Czechoslovak army were now rendered powerless and the fortifications along the frontier were so much useless steel and concrete. The German preponderance of power was now so great that it seemed that no combination of forces could overcome it. "We have sustained," said Churchill at the time of Munich, "a total and unmitigated defeat." There were more defeats to come before Hitler hurled his full weight on France and Poland. In March, 1939, he invaded what was left of Czechoslovakia, thus providing himself with all the resources of a large industrialized country shaped like an arrowhead aimed at the Soviet Union.

Churchill was still busily working on his *History of the English-Speaking Peoples,* but he was becoming increasingly involved in politics. He attended the Bastille Day celebrations in Paris with the soldiers, sailors and marines marching past the President of France, while fighter planes flew low overhead, and was properly impressed. In August, at the invitation of the French army, he was taken on a tour of the frontier to see the extent of the fortifications and the armed might of France, and again he was impressed. He returned to England confident that the French could repel a German attack.

On June 14, exactly a month before he attended the Bastille Day celebrations, he was a guest at a party given by Kenneth Clark. Walter Lippmann, the American columnist, was there, and he reported that the American ambassador, Joseph Kennedy, had announced like Ribbentrop that war was inevitable and Britain would inevitably be defeated. Joseph Kennedy was a multimillionaire who had made many fortunes in many dubious circumstances, and he had become the

American apostle of defeatism. Churchill was indignant. War was perhaps inevitable, but he urged Walter Lippmann to attempt to convince the ambassador that the defeat of Britain was by no means inevitable, and as he sat there, waving his whiskey and soda to the rhythm of his sentences and stubbing his cigar with his free hand, he delivered himself of one of those orations which were to become familiar in later years. He said:

> Supposing (as I do not for one moment suppose) that Mr. Kennedy were correct in his tragic utterance, then I for one would willingly lay down my life in combat, rather than, in fear of defeat, surrender to the menaces of these most sinister men. It will then be for you, for the Americans, to preserve and to maintain the great heritage of the English-speaking peoples. It will be for you to think imperially, which means to think always of something higher and more vast than one's own national interests. Nor should I die happy in the great struggle which I see before me, were I not convinced that if we in this dear dear island succumb to the ferocity and might of our enemies, over there in your distant and immune continent the torch of liberty will burn untarnished and (I trust and hope) undismayed.

This was vintage Churchill of the period: soon the orotund prose would lose its fat in the excitement of war.

He was working at breakneck speed to complete the *History of the English-Speaking Peoples,* but it was becoming increasingly clear that war would come before he had finished it. He was continually seeing scientists, journalists, Members of Parliament, anyone who could inform him about the subterranean movements of power. From his close friend Professor Frederick Lindemann came news of recent German experiments on the harnessing of atomic energy. How far had the experiments progressed? How great was the danger that atomic bombs would fall on London? In a long letter to Kingsley Wood, the Secretary of State for Air, written on August 5, 1939, Churchill wrote with what turned out to be remarkable accuracy that the experiments had not progressed very far, that many years of work and experiment would be needed before the bomb could be perfected, and that the extraction of "a minor constituent of uranium" presented great difficulties. On two matters he proved to be remarkably inaccurate. He thought atomic bombs would not be much more effective than the bombs already in existence and that the Germans would use this new, secret and sinister weapon in their armory of psychological warfare. They did not have it, but they would pretend to have it and thus threaten and intimidate their enemies with the prospect of annihilation. In fact the Germans did not use the threat of the atomic bomb in their psychological warfare.

August was the month of treacheries. Hitler and Stalin, the dictators who had sworn eternal enmity to each other, suddenly agreed to a pact of mutual friendship and collaboration, with a dismembered Poland providing the ceremonial feast on which they could both gorge themselves. Stalin, like a sleepwalker, found himself walking through a landscape of treachery which was not very different in appearance from the landscape where he had walked for most of his life. He was accustomed to shadows. This time the shadows were a little darker and they bristled with baited traps, and he fell into them.

The Nazi-Soviet Pact, signed in Moscow on August 23, gave Hitler the excuse he wanted to bring the frontiers of the German Reich up to the frontiers of the Soviet Union, which he regarded as the mortal enemy to be annihilated when the time was ripe. His massed divisions marched into Poland on the morning of September 1. The Second World War had begun.

In Poland the blood ran in the streets; in the west there was a "twilight war," the French and the British holding back as though they believed that in some mysterious way the German armed forces would exhaust themselves on the plains of Poland. This was the time for the French army to attack; instead, the French army gazed placidly across the Rhine and attempted with every means in its power not to provoke or antagonize the enemy.

Neville Chamberlain, the Prime Minister, summoned Churchill back to the Admiralty. Once more, after an interval of nearly a quarter of a century, he was First Lord of the Admiralty with power to order the movements of the Royal Navy in all the oceans of the world. A signal went out: "Winston is back." This gave satisfaction to the sailors who felt they were in good hands. But in the beginning the naval war went badly. Six weeks after war broke out, on the night of 13–14 October, a German U-boat sank the battleship *Royal Oak* as she lay at anchor in Scapa Flow with a loss of 786 officers and men. Merchant ships were being sunk by magnetic mines and by U-boats at an alarming rate. The problem of the magnetic mine was partially solved when an exploded mine fell into British hands and a way was found to render ships nonmagnetic by girdling them with charged electric cables. But the sinkings went on. The new cruiser *Belfast* was mined in the Firth of Forth on November 21 and the battleship *Nelson* was mined while entering Loch Ewe on December 4. Both ships survived to reach dockyards, but they were out of action for many months.

Not until December was there any naval news that gave any pleasure to the English people. The German pocket battleship *Graf Spee* had already sunk nine merchant ships when she was tracked down by three British cruisers—HMS *Exeter, Ajax* and *Achilles.* There was a running battle off the River Plate, and the *Graf Spee,* severely mauled, took refuge in Montevideo. She was permitted to remain in port for seventy-two hours by the authorities, and at the end of this time she could run the gantlet of the British ships or blow herself up—no other alternatives were offered. The three cruisers, hungry as wolves, waited for her, but were cheated of their prey, for the *Graf Spee* was blown up at the orders of her captain just outside Montevideo harbor, and the captain himself committed suicide three days later.

A curious sequel occurred two weeks later when the *Altmark,* which had been the *Graf Spee's* supply ship, was tracked down in a Norwegian fiord and boarded by a landing party from HMS *Cossack* under Churchill's orders. Norwegian authorities had pronounced that the *Altmark* had been inspected, was unarmed and carried no prisoners of war. The British had good reason to believe otherwise. They found the guns and they found 299 merchant seamen battened down in the holds. The sailors from the *Cossack* broke down the doors, shouting: "The Navy's here!" This heartening cry lifted the spirits of the people, who began to believe that the navy was invincible. They learned better a few days later when Hitler ordered the invasion of Denmark and Norway by land, sea and air forces. By employing his forces with the utmost violence and speed he conquered Denmark in a day and most of Norway within ten days. There followed confused naval and air battles on the western shore of Norway, as the British attempted to cling to Bergen, Trondheim, Narvik and Namsos, all of them important ports, and to prevent their use by the enemy; and everywhere they were outmaneuvered. At Narvik 6,000 Germans held at bay 20,000 Allied troops for six weeks. Amid the confusion of the Norwegian campaign, Churchill was as confused as all the rest, and his interventions were sometimes fatal and rarely useful. The Norwegian campaign consisted of a series of blunders. The British had no ski troops, no winter equipment, no experience of fighting in the kind of terrain presented by Norway. When the smoke cleared, Norway was lost, thousands of British troops had perished in the mists and snow, and only one important advantage had been gained: The German navy had received such a pounding that not a single major warship was fit for the sea.

The "twilight war" came to an end with the invasion of Denmark and Norway. The long winter trance ended at the time of the melting of the snows, and men knew, or guessed, that the summer would be bright with blood. In Parliament there was a growing feeling of despair over Neville Chamberlain's leadership. He was old and sick and ineffective; no one could have looked or behaved less like a war leader. On April 4, in an unwise moment, he declared roundly that "Hitler has missed the bus." It was only too evident that Hitler had captured the bus, armed it, filled it with iron men and was directing it to go wherever he wanted it to go. On May 7, 1940, Parliament met in a mood of seething indignation over so many defeats off the Norwegian coasts. The specter of Cromwell dominated the scene, for Leo Amery pointed to Chamberlain and quoted the urgent words of Cromwell to the Long Parliament: "You have sat too long here for any good you have been doing! Depart, I say, and let us have done with you! In the name of God, go!"

The debates continued, Chamberlain clung on to power for a few more hours, but he was visibly failing. Churchill attempted to defend him not so much out of gallantry as in an effort to defend himself. Chamberlain realized that he could continue in office only as the Prime Minister of a coalition government and he soon learned that Labour had no intention of serving under him. It transpired that Labour would serve under Churchill not because they had any love for him—they still remembered how thirty years before he had given orders to the troops to shoot down the miners and fifteen years before he had attempted to throttle the General Strike—but because he alone among the ministers in the government seemed to possess the energy and the fury to conduct a merciless war against Hitler. His errors and sins of omission during the Norwegian campaign were forgotten, or pardoned. He was chosen because he was a fighter who would never give in.

Early in the morning of May 10 Hitler launched a sudden savage attack on Belgium and the Netherlands, and at six o'clock that evening Churchill became Prime Minister. "As I went to bed about 3 A.M., I was conscious of a profound sense of relief," he wrote. "At last I had the authority to give directions over the whole scene. I felt as if I were walking with Destiny, and that all my past life had been but a preparation for this hour and for this trial."

For thirty years he had yearned for such a moment; it had come, and he was ready for it.

Triumph

We have but one aim, and one single irrevocable purpose. We are resolved to destroy Hitler and every vestige of the Nazi regime. From this, nothing will turn us—nothing. We will never parley, we will never negotiate with Hitler or any of his gang. We shall fight him by land, we shall fight him by sea, we shall fight him in the air, until, with God's help, we have rid the earth of his shadow. . . . We shall never surrender.

THE MIRACULOUS YEAR

VERYTHING SEEMED TO happen with the strange logic
of dreams. There came a time during that terrible year when only the
unexpected, the improbable and the unthinkable were real, and all the
rest of human activity seemed suddenly to have been thrown out of
focus. In the landscape of intolerable nightmares and inconceivable
anguish Churchill walked surefootedly. This was not an ordinary war,
the stakes were not ordinary stakes, and he was well aware that there
was nothing ordinary about the nightmares now descending upon
Europe. His studies of earlier wars and of Marlborough's campaigns
were of no use to him now. Only one thing was of use to him—defiance.
The lesson he had learned in the headmaster's study when he was nine
years old served him well at the age of sixty-five.

Three days after he assumed power Churchill announced to a
cheering House of Commons: "I have nothing to offer but blood, toil,
tears and sweat."* The words were received as though they were
patents of nobility or promises of glory; he had found the key to the
hearts of his countrymen. He went on: "You ask what is our aim? I can

* In *The Unknown War* Churchill had previously used the phrase: "Their tears, their sweat,
their blood bedewed the endless plain." He was referring to the battles of eastern Europe in World
War I.

answer in one word: Victory—victory at all costs, victory in spite of all terrors, victory, however long and hard the road may be." At that moment victory was the purest mirage. The Germans had advanced across the frontiers of Belgium, Holland and Luxembourg, and 150 miles of the front was in flames. Churchill had scarcely delivered his speech when news came that the Germans had broken through at Sedan, that the French could no longer resist the tanks and the low-flying Stukas, and needed ten more squadrons of British fighters to reestablish lines of defense. The news came with impeccable authority from Paul Reynaud, the Prime Minister of France, who had simply picked up the telephone and reached Churchill without any difficulty. At half past seven on the morning of the next day, May 15, Reynaud picked up the telephone again and said in English: "We have been defeated. We are beaten. We have lost the battle." He acknowledged defeat three times because Churchill thought he was mad, or incompetent, or both, when he heard it for the first time. It was unthinkable that the French army, believed to be the most powerful in the world, would curl up and die after a few hours of fighting. Churchill, still unbelieving, gave Reynaud a short lecture on the laws of the offensive, which always petered out after the original impulse was expended, but Reynaud refused to listen. "We are defeated; we have lost the battle," he repeated, and Churchill promised to fly to Paris the same day to see the situation for himself. It was the first of five flights to France made in the course of a single month. These were desperate and dangerous ventures which could only be defended by the appalling gravity of the events; and with each visit to France the news became more somber, more hopeless and more ludicrous. Churchill was to learn that France was being ruled by men who were totally incompetent when they were not traitors.

He reached Paris in the late afternoon, meeting Reynaud and General Maurice Gamelin at the Quai d'Orsay. Gamelin was the Commander in Chief of the French Army, proud, ambitious, without any particular distinction. He shrugged his shoulders. "Inferiority of numbers, inferiority of equipment, inferiority of method," he explained, and could have added: "Inferiority of leadership," if it were not so obvious. Black smoke rose in the gardens of the Quai d'Orsay, as the archivists trundled out the archives and made bonfires out of them. "Where are the strategic reserves?" Churchill asked. "There are none," Gamelin replied. The shrugging of his shoulders was like a nervous tic. The weight of defeat seemed to fall lightly on him. For Churchill such weights were to be lifted off one's shoulders and hurled out of sight. What could be done to stave off defeat? They replied that they wanted ten British squadrons of fighter planes. That left only twenty-five squadrons for the defense of England, the absolute minimum of squadrons necessary to keep the Luftwaffe from dominating the English skies. Churchill offered it readily. It was the first of many wild gambles. In the following months Churchill would gamble even more strenuously, more dangerously and more successfully.

May was the month when all illusions perished. Churchill flew back to England with a sense of foreboding, which would have been even more terrifying if he had known the full extent of French incompetence and treachery. The British Expeditionary Force had already been encircled by German armored forces in Flanders. On May 20, in one of the deep galleries carved into the cliffs of Dover, Admiral Bertram Ramsay presided over a small group of officers and debated what could be done to rescue the embattled BEF, which was being driven into the sea. He was a man of fifty-seven, crusty, intractable, with his own way of doing things. The navy had retired him early because he had never got on with his superior officers, but he knew the Straits of Dover well and he could be depended upon in emergencies. When the conference came to an end, he had reached the conclusion that it might be possible to rescue 10,000 men every twenty-four hours. Two days later Churchill made his second visit to Paris to learn that the French, although still determined upon defeat, were making the gestures of a reviving corpse. Gamelin had gone, replaced by General Maxime Weygand, who had been the Chief of Staff to Marshal Foch. Marshal Pétain, the hero of Verdun, was in the Cabinet. Reynaud was sixty-two, Weygand was seventy-three, and Pétain was eighty-four. Weygand gave the impression of being the youngest and spoke hopefully of breaking the encircling German lines. Churchill was impressed, but if he had known more about Weygand he would have been considerably less impressed. Weygand was the archreactionary who had long ago announced that it would be better for France to live under the Germans than under a Socialist government. He was to become the resolute architect of France's defeat.

The British held Calais, while the main body of the BEF streamed back on Dunkirk. Churchill warned the House of Commons to expect hard tidings, by which he meant the total annihilation of the British army in France. Reynaud was calling for more and more fighter planes; Churchill was willing to throw them into the battle but desisted under pressure from Air Chief Marshal Hugh Dowding. On May 28 the Belgian army capitulated, and on the following day the first trickle of British soldiers was taken off the sands of Dunkirk. During the next five days Admiral Ramsay, from his command post in the cliffs of Dover, arranged the evacuation of all that was left of the BEF by throwing every available ship into the Straits. The *Gracie Fields*, the *Mary Jane*, the *Folkestone Belle*, and hundreds more, paddle boats and coastal steamers, sea-going yachts and ancient destroyers and all the flotsam of the sea came to the rescue of the soldiers waiting in long thin lines on the sandy shore. His earlier estimate that he might be able to pull 10,000 men a day off the coast of France proved ludicrously wrong. All together 338,226 troops, both British and French, were saved. While the evacuation was still going on, Churchill paid his third and last visit to Paris. Paul Reynaud had appointed himself Minister of War and accordingly he welcomed Churchill in the War Ministry in the Rue Saint-Dominique. It appeared that Reynaud knew nothing or very little about the evacuation at Dunkirk, or indeed about anything that was happening in France. Pétain said little; he seemed to be serenely aware of the advantages of surrender; and his serenity at such a time took Churchill's breath away. "Better that the last of us should fall fighting than to linger on as slaves," Churchill said, but there was no response. When he returned to London, Churchill discovered that the British were celebrating the evacuation from Dunkirk as though it were a victory. One newspaper carried the headline: BLOODY MARVELLOUS. Whatever it was, it was not a victory, and he hastened to remind his countrymen that they had suffered a catastrophic defeat and that Hitler would inevitably attempt to invade the British Isles. He said in the House of Commons:

> We are told that Herr Hitler has a plan for invading the British Isles. This has often been thought of before. When Napoleon lay at Boulogne for a year with his flat-bottomed boats and his Grand Army, he was told by someone, "There are bitter weeds in England." There are certainly a great many more of them since the British Expeditionary Force returned.

The BEF had returned without its weapons, and as he spoke Britain was virtually defenseless and France was seeking a formula for surrender. Nevertheless he was justified in making the proudest of his boasts and the happiest of his prophecies:

The British Empire and the French Republic, linked together in their cause and in their need, will defend to the death their native soil, aiding each other like good comrades to the utmost of their strength. . . . We shall go on to the end, we shall fight in France, we shall fight on the seas and oceans, we shall fight with growing confidence and growing strength in the air, we shall defend our Island, whatever the cost may be, we shall fight on the beaches, we shall fight on the landing grounds, we shall fight in the fields and in the streets, we shall fight in the hills. We shall never surrender, and even if, which I do not for a moment believe, this Island or a large part of it were subjugated and starving, then our Empire beyond the seas, armed and guarded by the British Fleet, would carry on the struggle, until, in God's good time, the New World, with all its power and might, steps forth to the rescue and the liberation of the old.

As Churchill saw it, France, Britain and America were indissolubly linked together. This was true and at the same time quite untrue and totally implausible, for France was visibly crumbling and America was a spectator who could do no more than send ships, airplanes, munitions and good wishes. The New World was not yet ready to rescue the old. Yet Churchill was entirely justified in linking the three countries together, imagining them to be equally determined to fight Hitler to the death. Imaginatively he was right, but the day-to-day facts were otherwise.

He spoke in the House of Commons on June 4. On the following day the Germans unleashed the second major offensive which would take them to Paris and beyond. The French army was being torn to ribbons. Weygand was right: There was no possibility now of smashing through the advancing wall of German armor. Yet his dispositions and erratic commands, his contempt for his own troops and his curious inability to think offensively, were of immense service to the Germans. On June 11 Churchill hurried back to France. The government was installed temporarily at Briare, southeast of Orleans. Churchill attempted to inspire them with confidence, but failed again. They met in an old chateau where the only telephone was in the lavatory and it was necessary to ring up the village postmistress to make a connection. Italy had declared war against Britain and France on the previous day and some British bombers on an airfield near Marseilles were preparing to bomb Turin and Milan. Churchill learned to his dismay that at the orders of the French authorities the runways at the airfield near Marseilles were being crowded with farmcarts and automobiles to prevent the bombers from taking off. He fumed and was told there had been an error. There was no error. The French wanted to avoid fighting against Mussolini. Churchill's last visit to the French government took place on June 15, the day after the fall of Paris. He found the government in Tours. It was more defeatist than ever, more intolerant, more pro-German than he could ever have expected. Churchill offered union between France and Britain. Every Frenchman would possess British citizenship, every Briton would possess French citizenship. They would be a country united, making common cause together. It was not Churchill's idea—the original conception came from the fruitful mind of Sir Robert Vansittart, the Permanent Under Secretary for Foreign Affairs—but he grasped it eagerly. Paul Reynaud liked the idea, but was outvoted in the Cabinet, where Pétain had already acquired a strange domination. Nor was Reynaud as forceful as he might have been if he had not acquired a mistress, the Countess Hélène de Portes, who was even more hysterically defeatist than Weygand. Pétain commented on the Anglo-French Union: "What is the use of being tied to a corpse?" The corpse was alive, without weapons, but very formidable.

Soon the weapons began to arrive from the United States and Canada—enough rifles and antitank guns to equip perhaps a quarter of the army and the Home Guard—and when the French government finally capitulated, the British people heaved a sigh of relief. Now they were fighting alone. David gloried in his slingshot. Goliath loomed on the horizon, held at bay by twenty-two miles of water, his image seeming unreal in the sea mists. They did not know and could not guess what Hitler had in store for them: total slavery, all able-bodied men to be transported to the Baltic, the women to be given to the German soldiers. "Whatever you may do," Churchill declared to the French ministers, "we shall fight on forever and ever and ever." But that was said in broad daylight. In the darkness of the night and in nightmares there came other thoughts: Hitler, too, was capable of "the original and sinister touch," and Churchill spent many hours discussing with his advisers the possible stratagems with which the Germans might conquer Britain in a night. "Wars are not won by heroic militias," he wrote later; they are won sometimes by sudden, overwhelming shocks; and the bravest may die at the hands of men moving stealthily in the darkness.

Nevertheless there were allies—General de Gaulle, the Free French, the Canadians, the 20,000 Poles who escaped from France, the Dutch, the Norwegians and the Belgians who slipped across the narrow seas to join the British. President Roosevelt had rejected the advice of the

American ambassador, Joseph Kennedy, who thought it was the better part of wisdom to abandon Britain to her fate. He was doing whatever could be done within the bounds of the Constitution to send armaments to a country desperately in need of them. "If we go down," Churchill wrote to the President, "Hitler has a good chance of conquering the world." He had more than a good chance; it was almost a certainty. At that moment Hitler was making plans for transforming Berlin into a monumental capital of the world, with his own palace larger than the Basilica of St. Peter. The grandiose plans proliferated; the army, navy and air force were poised for the attack; all that was needed was that a small island off the northwestern coast of Europe should capitulate.

Sudden, terrible decisions had to be made, sometimes on the spur of the moment. The French fleet had not sailed to British ports, as Churchill had demanded. Clearly, if it fell into German hands, it would give the enemy an overwhelming advantage. There were many alternative plans discussed at Cabinet meetings. If the French, for various reasons, refused to join their navy to the Royal Navy, they could at least remove their ships from the reach of the Germans by sailing them to the United States or the West Indies, or they could scuttle them, or they could remove important parts of their guns and discharge their fuel oil, thus rendering them inoperative. The French fleet stationed off Alexandria made itself inoperative, but the fleet off Oran had to be blown out of the water by British ships. All this happened in the weeks immediately following the capitulation. Churchill, to his astonishment, found himself making war on his recent allies.

This was the time when Britain was weakest and deliriously content, before the full realization of the enemy's strength and criminality had sunk into the minds of the people. Churchill's speeches were food and drink to them. When he was young, he had written that oratory gave a man the power of a great king, and now he used this power to the uttermost. His speeches were exuberant and exhilarating; sometimes they were exhausting. He borrowed unashamedly: Shakespeare for the battle cries, Gibbon for the undulating arguments. While his voice was not especially appealing, for he still lisped and the broad vowels were too robust for the weak consonants, it carried immediate conviction. Every pause, every change of pace, every grace note were carefully calculated. All his speeches were fully orchestrated.

He would spend almost a whole day dictating a speech while pacing up and down his room, then sitting down at his desk to revise it, and finally breaking it up into paragraphs, sentences and phrases until he had achieved the desired effect. He was the most impatient and inconsiderate of men, but he was endlessly patient and considerate of words. Lord Moran, his confidant and doctor, who came to know him better than anyone else, said: "Without that feeling for words he would have made little enough of life. For in judgment, in skill in administration, in knowledge of human nature, he does not at all excel."

During the war Churchill made five speeches in secret session in the House of Commons. These speeches all dealt with disasters or approaching disasters, and he felt that the Members of Parliament should know the full facts before they were communicated to the public. On June 20, 1940, he spoke about the fall of France and the impending invasion and bombing raids on Britain. He had no time to prepare a fully orchestrated speech with the proper documentation, and he therefore read from hurriedly prepared notes. These notes survive. They show us the bone structure of the speech before it was fleshed out, the poetry before it became prose. He was talking about the danger of night bombing:

> We have had a couple of nights of bombing,
>   evidently much worse than that.
> Folly underrate gravity of attack impending.
> But if 100 or 150 bombers employed
>   entitled to remark:
>   Not very cleverly employed.
> Hardly paid expenses.
> Learn to get used to it.
>   Eels get used to skinning.
> Steady continuous bombing,
>   probably rising to great intensity
>   occasionally,
>   must be regular condition of our life.
> The utmost importance preserve morale of
>   people,
>   especially in the night work of factories.
> A test of our nerve against theirs.

Here we can observe Churchill's mind at work as he confronts each new thought. He begins with a solemn warning which is followed with a joke (*Hardly paid expenses*) and then with another warning (Learn to get used to it), Which is capped by an even better joke (*Eels get used to skinning*). He is determined to have some fun at the expense of the

Germans. The mood changes swiftly. One moment he is soaring, the next moment he is descending into "the intimate and conversational tone," which according to Harold Nicolson was among his greatest contributions to English oratory. He liked to descend from the language of Gibbon or Shakespeare into the language of the street. Irony, low humor, banter were all useful weapons. At all costs it was necessary to make clear that bombing had come to stay. Hence "Learn to get used to it," "Steady continuous bombing," and "must be regular condition of our life." Later he would say in his most disarming fashion: "The people should be accustomed to treat air raids as a matter of ordinary routine. Everybody should learn to take air raids and air raid alarms as if they were no more than thunderstorms."

As for the invasion of England by the Wehrmacht, there was one simple overriding consideration: the enemy must be struck down as soon as he makes a landing. Among the nine pages of typewritten notes for Churchill's speech there can be found this succinct account of the fate reserved for the enemy:

> ... essence of defence of Britain
> is to attack the landed enemy at once,
> leap at his throat
> and keep the grip until the life is out of him.

For Churchill it was not enough to resist the enemy: the lion must leap at the enemy's throat and choke him to death. Ferocity and defiance were the watchwords. If Hitler was to be defeated, the English would have to become as ferocious as the Germans.

Gradually, as the summer advanced, Churchill became armored into legend. He seemed larger than life and almost as large as England. He became the embodiment of freedom and defiance, and of England's ancient traditions. "Good old Winny," they shouted after him when he made the V for Victory sign as he clambered through the bombed streets, a cigar clenched jauntily between his teeth. He rejoiced in his popularity, for it helped him to reach out for the one thing he wanted most of all—supreme power. To the very end he would proclaim himself the complete servant of Parliament, but during that summer he became the dictator of England. Nothing quite like it had happened since the days of Cromwell.

The legend fed on his defiant speeches, his courage, his resemblance to John Bull, the heavyset prototype of the aroused Englishman. The camera also helped to feed the legend by showing him in close-up with a look of bulldog ferocity, and his commanding appearance on the front pages of the newspapers was a comforting reminder that a competent captain was at the helm. He had a mobile face which could register many different kinds of ferocity. He was uncorruptible and unshakeable, and one glance at the face told you that he would never give in. In photographs he looked tall and strongly muscled, absolutely determined, a man who never gave way to doubts and never brooded upon the consequences of his acts. In fact he was very short, under five feet six inches, and he was physically quite flabby, having lost the habit of exercise. He seemed to have powerful shoulders, but this too was an accident provided by the camera; he had the rounded shoulders of a scholar who spends his days at the writing table. He was not quite as self-assured as he appeared to be. He had many doubts and brooded long and often about the consequences of his acts.

Surprisingly the newspaper and movie photographs failed to do justice to the real man. He was far more complex and mercurial, far more tyrannical and bloodthirsty, far more sentimental and affectionate, and far more self-serving, than anyone would have guessed from the pictures of him. He made no secret of the fact that he enjoyed the powers of a dictator; indeed, he relished them and did what all dictators do when they come into power. He enlarged his powers to the uttermost until on all important matters, even on those matters in which he was ignorant, he was the sole judge, the sole authority. "I did not suffer from any desire to be relieved of my responsibilities," he said later. "All I wanted was compliance with my wishes after reasonable discussion." He permitted very little discussion.

George Mallaby, a civil servant who worked in the Cabinet Office, was surprised to discover that the familiar Churchill of the newspaper photographs had very little resemblance to the real Churchill. He had expected to see someone "rough and rugged like Cromwell or proud and remote like the younger Pitt." Instead he found a man who looked unexpectedly vulnerable:

> He was short, delicate looking, pink and white, round-faced, had wispy hair, frail artistic hands. He stumped along rather than walked, but when he sat, he sat heavily, broodingly, like a man six feet tall and twenty stone, monolithic in his chair. Then when the discussions began, that childlike face became the reflection of the man—the set bulldog look, the sulky look of a pouting child, the angry violent look of an animal at bay, the

tearful look of a compassionate woman and the sudden spontaneous smiling look of a boy. The moods changed rapidly.

That, of course, was part of the trouble: the moods changed with such disconcerting rapidity that a great deal of effort had to be expended by his staff to control them. Some small thing would make him fly off the handle, while for the moment great issues remained unresolved. To deal with him was like dealing with a demanding, high-strung woman. His moods were his weapons. He was outrageously self-indulgent and opinionated, and consciously employed his moods for his own purposes. He could assume an expression of corrosive anger with the greatest of ease, thus resolving a problem, for no one dared to confront him in his rages. Throughout the day he was steadily consuming alcohol, and this too contributed to his moodiness. He drank continuously, but slowly, rarely overreaching the mark he had set for himself. It was a mark considerably higher than most men can contemplate with equanimity.

Nevertheless he worked powerfully to make Britain strong, concentrating his energies on only those things which were essential for the trial of strength that lay ahead, buoyed up by the certainty that the Royal Navy with its immense superiority of sea power in the narrow seas could effectively destroy any German invasion force. From his desk a stream of orders was issued, all labeled with a scarlet tag reading ACTION THIS DAY. The production of bombers and the dispositions of the navy especially interested him, but he was also concerned with the sight-seeing buses which were still plying for hire along the Brighton seafront—why were they not being used for more necessary affairs? Why not send the 20,000 people who had been interned for the duration of the war to Newfoundland or the island of St. Helena? Why was a highly trained Canadian division being sent to Iceland, when it could obviously be thrown into the battle against the invasion forces? Why were not smoke machines being manufactured in order to hide factories from the air? Radar, proximity fuses and every kind of mechanical device fascinated him, and the flow of minutes across his desk showed that there was nothing too small for his attention. But the overriding consideration was to ensure that Britain would quickly be in a position to destroy the invaders. The Germans must be made to "choke in their own blood." He saw, quite accurately, that the first stage of the invasion would be an air war over England. He wrote to General Jan Christiaan Smuts on June 9: "I see only one sure way through now—to wit, that Hitler should attack this country, and in so doing break his air weapon."

Hitler did precisely that. "Operation Sea Lion," the invasion of Britain, could take place only if the Luftwaffe had mastery of the air over the British Isles. Therefore wave after wave of airplanes must be sent over to destroy the Royal Air Force, and only when they were defeated could the German navy ferry the Wehrmacht across the Channel. The barges were being assembled in the invasion ports; the German soldiers were being trained in street fighting; the landing sites had been selected; all that remained was to shoot a few hundred airplanes out of the sky. On a bright summer morning Hitler and Goering gazed across the Channel at the white cliffs of Dover, and it may have seemed to them that Britain was already within their grasp.

The plan was to destroy the Royal Air Force within four weeks beginning on August 10, the most shattering blows taking place in the first four days. For the remaining days of the month there would be merely a mopping-up campaign to ensure that no British airplanes were left in the sky. Meanwhile the invasion routes were to be planted with a protective hedge of mines and the Wehrmacht under cover of the German navy would simply walk ashore from the barges. The date of the invasion was set for mid-September and if the timetable were carried out all of southern England would be in German hands by the end of the month. The victory march through London would take place early in October.

Such was the plan, which very nearly succeeded, for in spite of the prodigious efforts of the factory workers to produce more and more Hurricanes and Spitfires, the British did not have enough airplanes to counter the enemy air offensive. The Germans had 1,900 bombers and 1,100 fighter planes, while the British had 350 bombers and 700 fighter planes. In bombers the British were outnumbered six to one. It was against these frightful odds that the British awaited with outward calm the fury of the German attack, which had the code name of "Eagle."

The Battle of Britain, which lasted for more than a month, was one of the world's most decisive battles. For the first two weeks the British held their own, for they lost nearly 200 fighters while the enemy lost twice as many. But in the two weeks beginning August 24 the scales began to tilt dangerously in favor of the Germans, who lost 338 fighters to British losses of 200. The Germans could afford these losses; the British could not. In the following week the British lost 67, the Germans 102. All together in the period from August 10 to September 14 the losses were: Germans, 846, British 460. These simple mathematics of profit and loss showed that the Germans were very far from being masters of the air and that they were approaching the limit of their reserves. So were the British, but since most of their planes fell on their own territory the Germans were in no position to learn the exact number of their losses. Both sides made extraordinary claims. Official British figures claimed that 1,620 German fighters had been destroyed in that five-week period, considerably more than the total number of fighters available to the German Air Force. Nevertheless the British had won the battle because they had denied the mastery of the air to the Germans, and as a result the barges were not filled with the soldiers of the Wehrmacht, the German navy did not escort the barges to England, and Hitler did not enjoy a victory procession through London.

On September 15, a week after the invasion alert code-named "Cromwell" had been announced, Churchill drove over from Chequers to Number 11 Fighter Group Headquarters at Uxbridge. It was a day of mingled cloud and sunshine, and he could expect heavy German attacks. The headquarters controlled twenty-five squadrons covering most of southeast England and the defenses of London. In command was Air Vice Marshal Keith Park, on whose decisions during those decisive five weeks the fate of Britain depended. An abrupt but kindly man, he had spent the morning at his command post fifty feet below the ground directing the British squadrons as they fought off some of the heaviest waves of German airplanes which had ever reached England, and Churchill's arrival that afternoon, accompanied by his wife, threatened to be an unwelcome distraction. Churchill had never visited these headquarters before; he was in a loquacious mood; he wanted to know all about the huge map of England where the presence of the British and German airplanes was indicated by counters and about the blackboard where each fighter squadron's degree of preparedness and activity were marked with electric lights: standing by, ready, available, in the air, in sight of the enemy, in action. The last was indicated by a red bulb. Churchill kept on talking. Air Vice Marshal Keith Park could not shut up the Prime Minister, but he could do the next best thing. To the man who was answering Churchill's incessant questions he said: "If you go on chattering like this, I shall have to replace you with someone less talkative." Churchill went on talking. The tension was mounting. The red lights were coming up in increasing numbers. All the airplanes of all the squadrons were in the air or being refueled. Finally Churchill asked the Air Vice Marshal the same question he had asked of Gamelin: "What other reserves have we?" He was told: "There are none," and then he realized that the Royal Air Force had reached the limits of its resources and unless a miracle happened the Germans would have mastery of the skies over England. And the miracle did happen—the Germans, too, had reached the end of their resources. Sixty of their planes were shot down that day. Jubilantly the British announced that 183 had been shot down and that Fighter Command had lost 26, from which the pilots of 13 had been saved. Churchill returned to Chequers so exhausted by the excitement that he fell asleep for four hours. He did not know that the turning point had come. Two days later, fearful of the loss of so many airplanes and perhaps half believing the British claims, Hitler called off "Operation Sea Lion" until further notice.

The worst was over and Britain settled down to the long miserable winter of the Blitz. It would continue until almost the very end of the war, but since it was designed to terrorize the people into submission and the people refused to be terrorized, it was wholly ineffective. Churchill promised vengeance and the time came when a thousand bombers flew over Berlin, and this too was ineffective. The Germans dug themselves in; they continued to make machines of war on an increasing scale, and they were not terrorized.

The Blitz was air warfare in its most savage form. There were nights when half of London slept underground and the other half escaped to the suburbs. Churchill was strangely exhilarated by heavy bombing raids and could not be prevented from sitting on the roof to watch the raiders coming over and marveling at the fires raging over the city. "London," he wrote, "was like some huge prehistorical animal, capable of enduring terrible injuries, mangled and bleeding from many wounds, and yet preserving its life and movement." One day before the Blitz he met Julian Huxley, the director of the London Zoo, and was told that in the event of air raids it would be necessary to shoot most of the animals. Churchill was alarmed. He had great sympathy for animals and did not think they deserved to be shot. "Imagine a great air raid over this great city of ours," he exclaimed. "Squadrons of enemy planes dropping their bombs on London, houses smashed into ruins, fires breaking out everywhere—corpses lying in the smoking ashes—and lions and tigers roaming the desolation in search of the corpses, and you're going to shoot them! What a pity!" One day, during the Blitz, Churchill went out to see for himself the effects of some heavy bombing in South London. His car was recognized, and out of nowhere a thousand people gathered to cheer him. A whole street of workmen's dwellings had been reduced to rubble and people were still picking themselves out of the ruins. He was overcome with emotion and began to weep, and an old

woman said: "You see, he really cares. He's crying." She did not know
that he wept easily. He would have wept if he had seen a dead bird and
more loudly if it was a dead tiger.

He lacked any real feeling for other people's sufferings, but that too
was an advantage in war. He could be coldly impersonal, dismissing
good generals because he thought he had detected some personal
weakness which in fact did not exist. And he could accept the consequences of his own blunders more easily because he was not concerned with the people who were killed. In September he ordered an
attack on the French fleet at Dakar. It failed miserably because the
British and Free French forces were not properly coordinated. Prime
Minister Robert Menzies of Australia gently rebuked him for not using
overwhelming forces for the attack. Churchill replied:

> I cannot accept the reproach of making "a half-hearted attack." I hope
> that you had not sustained the impression from these last five months of
> struggle which has excited the admiration of the whole world that we
> were "a half-hearted Government" and that I am half-hearted in the
> endeavours it is my duty to make. I thought, indeed, that from the way
> my name was used in the election that quite a good opinion was enter-
> tained in Australia of these efforts.

That was his mean side: the flailing of anger at an imagined slight,
written late at night when his spirits were low and he had drunk too
much to preserve a sense of justice. But such moods were infrequent.
He was buoyed up by victories, and defeats emboldened him to more
daring exploits. He rejoiced in "the inward excitement which comes
from the prolonged balancing of terrible things." Unfortunately few
others were permitted to do the balancing. When Italy, having invaded
Egypt in September without doing any extensive damage, decided
during the following month to invade Greece, Churchill regarded it as
a point of honor to go to the help of the embattled Greeks and ordered
troops sent to Greece from Egypt. General Archibald Wavell replied
that he needed all the troops in Egypt to throw back the Italians.
Churchill insisted. "Loss of Athens far greater injury than Kenya and
Khartoum," he telegraphed inexplicably, for no one had suggested that
Kenya and the Sudan were in danger. Troops were sent to Greece, to
face the Germans who came on the heels of the Italians, and all were
lost. Sir Alan Brooke, the Chief of the Imperial General Staff, wrote
wearily in his diary: "Why will politicians never learn the simple

principle of concentration of force at the vital point and the avoidance of dispersal of effort?"

Churchill's insistence on sending troops to Greece produced a disaster of the first magnitude, for which he alone was responsible. When General Wavell's forces struck back at the Italians in the Western Desert and advanced five hundred miles to the west, capturing 130,000 prisoners and a vast treasure of military supplies, the order to send an expeditionary force to Greece had the effect of preventing Britain from maintaining a firm control of the Central Mediterranean, and soon enough the Italians, heavily reinforced with German troops, would hurl the British back to the frontiers of Egypt. The desert victory was followed by a desert rout. But as the year ended there were many victories to report. Crete was in British hands; the Italians were in full flight across North Africa; the Italian fleet had been crippled by torpedo-carrying aircraft from the carrier *Illustrious,* and in a single night the balance of sea power in the Mediterranean had been transformed. At the end of the year Churchill wrote to Marshal Pétain in Vichy, saying that Britain was now on the offensive and the time had come for Vichy France to join forces with its natural allies. There was no answer to the message. The senile general still believed he was the savior of France.

Churchill's love affair with France survived the French defeats and his difficulties with General de Gaulle, whose emblem was the cross of Lorraine. "The heaviest cross I have to bear is the cross of Lorraine," Churchill said in an unguarded moment. But it was not true, and he would have been the first to admit it. Two months earlier, speaking in French, he addressed Frenchmen in one of the most moving of his radio speeches delivered amid the rumble of antiaircraft fire and the crashing of bombs. It was a long, reasoned speech calling upon them to keep their spirits high and to remember their heroes, and at the end he said:

> Goodnight then: sleep to gather strength for the morning. For the morning will come. Brightly will it shine on the brave and true, kindly upon all those who suffer for the cause, glorious upon the tombs of heroes. Thus will shine the dawn. *Vive la France!* Long live also the forward march of the common people in all the lands towards their just and true inheritance, and towards the broader and fuller age.

But with the coming of the New Year the forward march of the common people began to falter, and so did Churchill's direction of the war. The Royal Navy, reinforced by fifty overage destroyers from America, could barely hold its own against the U-boats attacking the convoys on which Britain's life depended. General Erwin Rommel, splendidly equipped with armor, stiffened the gentle Italians and drove the British back to Egypt, leaving behind the British outpost at Tobruk, which was besieged but held out. "We seem to have had rather bad luck," Churchill telegraphed to Wavell. It was one of the many understatements delivered that year. Wavell demanded more tanks for the Desert Army; so did Churchill. Brooke, still fearing invasion, protested vigorously. This time Churchill was right and the tanks were sent out in time to prevent Rommel from conquering Egypt. In May Crete was lost to German paratroop forces: for the first time an island had been successfully invaded by air. In the battle three British cruisers and eight destroyers were sunk and 2,000 sailors of the Royal Navy were lost. Crete was another disaster.

Yugoslavia was invaded by the Germans; the Balkans became a German province; and Hitler's daring and resilience was only equalled by the daring and resilience of Churchill. The war was taking on a strange character, as though two giants were locked in mortal combat. They were both tenacious, ruthless, brilliantly intelligent and capable of taking astonishing risks, and they ordered the affairs of the war without taking too much advice from their generals. Churchill described Hitler as "that bad man," "this evil man, this monstrous abortion of hatred and defeat," "this wicked man, the repository and embodiment of many forms of soul-destroying hate, this monstrous product of former wrongs and shame." Hitler described Churchill as "an undisciplined swine who is drunk eight hours out of twenty-four." But these were words. They both knew they were engaged in a war to the death and derived strength from desperation. Like Hitler, Churchill drew strength from mythologies. The vision of the British Empire, radiant above all former and existing empires, powerfully affected Churchill's mind. The myth in its simplest form demanded the presence of a heroic commander of the hosts who would single-handedly lead his warriors to victory, and he saw himself as the chosen leader, the new Beowulf confronting the new Grendel. In this stark fashion he conducted a war, in which there was no room for subtleties.

Yet, surprisingly, Churchill knew very little about Hitler, and had never studied him in depth. He had glanced cursorily at *Mein Kampf*, but it had left no abiding impression on him. He had watched Hitler's rise to power with a strange sense of admiration mingled with foreboding. Yet, while the war was being fought, Churchill had no very clear image of Hitler, who became in his eyes an abstraction of pure evil, totally merciless and totally destructive. Instinctively Churchill realized that there was no limit to Hitler's ambitions and that he was perfectly prepared to wage wars of extermination and annihilation. He must be fought relentlessly, impersonally, cold-bloodedly, without ever for a moment permitting him to gain an advantage.

Since the war was being fought against incarnate evil, there was no necessity to attempt psychological warfare on Hitler. His weaknesses were not explored; obvious propaganda tactics were not used; and no really serious effort was made to plant in the minds of the German people the idea that Hitler was fighting a senseless war for his own personal aggrandizement without any thought of the sufferings that would eventually ensue for the German people. British propaganda efforts were primitive. Hitler, studying British propaganda in World War I, had built up his whole theory of propaganda on his observations of British successes. Churchill had little use for propaganda in World War II. The giants, fighting their mythological war, have other things to do than to throw propaganda leaflets at one another.

For Hitler, too, this was a mythological war: a war of vast spaces, explosive victories and blinding cataclysms. His aim was the conquest of the world and the establishment of the thousand-year-old Reich as the decisive power in the world. Like Churchill, he saw the war as an apocalypse.

It is not surprising that they saw themselves fighting the same kind of war, for they had more in common than is generally supposed. Their training and their purposes were oddly similar. I have sketched here a portrait which applies equally to Churchill and Hitler:

> In his childhood he was close to his mother; his father died when he was young. As a schoolboy he was rebellious and unhappy, and was bad at his lessons. He enjoyed playing at soldiers. Later he read omnivorously, acquiring an education through his reading. He took to painting, acquiring more than ordinary skill. As a soldier he showed extraordinary courage. As a politician he dominated crowds by his spell-binding oratory, which he regarded as his greatest and most formidable asset. He was not however a natural orator, but had studied the subject minutely and scientifically. For long periods he was driven into the political wilderness and at such times suffered fits of acute mental depression and was close to suicide.

He had very little feeling for the sufferings of others. He feared physical pain and was a hypochondriac, visiting his doctor frequently. He wept over the deaths of his favorite animals but rarely wept over the deaths of friends.

He had a passion for seeing films, especially those which celebrated the heroic deeds of his countrymen, but he would sit contentedly through almost any film. He read deeply in history and had little patience for philosophy.

He became the most powerful man in his country and its acknowledged leader in wartime, spending the greater part of his effort in directing the war. He was a bad judge of character and sometimes surrounded himself with incompetents. Fascinated by weaponry, he regarded himself as a brilliant strategist and tactician, often overriding his generals. He was responsible for serious military defeats, but just as often he was more discerning than his military advisers.

His temper was authoritarian; he took wild and improbable risks; he regarded himself as one of "the chosen ones" who walk hand in hand with destiny. He felt that without consulting the people he possessed an instinctive knowledge of their feelings and desires. He acquired a fortune from his writings and was thus able to claim a personal independence. To the end he remained an imperialist, who spoke of an empire that would last for a thousand years, and he lived long enough to see his empire crumbling in ruins.

But if there were surprising similarities between Churchill and Hitler, there were also essential differences of nerve and character. Churchill was most resilient in defeat, while Hitler, long accustomed to victories, found defeat unendurable and unmanageable and was incapable of commanding rearguard actions with success. Churchill's mind was open; he learned from his failures; and on occasion he was capable of acts of charity and generosity. Hitler's mind was a closed circle; he learned nothing from his failures; and he was totally incapable of any real generosity. He was a nihilist, without any respect for existing religions and traditions, or any understanding of them; his religion was self-worship and tradition was whatever he accomplished, for he saw himself as the founder of a new world order. Churchill was the heir of the humanist tradition which derived from the ancient Jews, the Greeks, the Romans, Christianity and the Italian Renaissance, while Hitler believed the humanist tradition was meaningless and absurd, ripe for destruction.

Churchill liked to think of himself as a bulldog, who hung on at all costs, never letting go. Hitler thought of himself as a wolf prowling in the dark, making sudden forays into enemy territory, giving no mercy, slaughtering for the joy of slaughtering. The bulldog and the wolf were at each other's throats.

For just over a year Britain fought alone against Hitler, and inevitably the war took on the character of the opposing chieftains. Britain entered her brief heroic age, and Churchill was justified when he spoke about the Elizabethan spirit of his countrymen. The slogans told the story. "Go to it." "Londoners can take it." "Give us the tools and we will do the job." "Never was so much owed by so many to so few." Most of the slogans were invented by Churchill, but they accurately reflected the spirit of the people. Not since the time of Cromwell had one man so profoundly dominated the British people or acted so dictatorially, but there was a saving grace. His powers, vast as they were, derived from Parliament, which remained in session. He was called upon to answer for all his deeds and misdeeds, and thus there arose a continuous conversation between him and the people. In this way he maintained the dignity of his role and was able to extract the last ounce of energy from a people who had previously distrusted him.

THE CENTERS OF POWER

IN WARTIME ENGLAND there were three nerve centers from which commands poured out in an unceasing flow. One was 10 Downing Street, another was called the Annexe, and the third was Chequers, a large Elizabethan country house, where Churchill usually spent his weekends.

The plain black door with the lion-headed knocker at 10 Downing Street is more familiar than the inside of the house, which is much larger and handsomer than anyone would guess from looking at the unpretentious exterior. This house has been the official residence of the Prime Minister since the time of Sir Robert Walpole, whose portrait hangs in the book-lined Cabinet Room. Here Churchill presided at Cabinet meetings, sitting halfway down the table, with a curious array of writing implements in front of him—pens, pencils, blotters, a paper punch, tags for joining papers together, a bottle of glue and red labels reading: ACTION THIS DAY. A large clock stood on the mantelpiece under the portrait of Walpole, and sometimes there were flowers in a vase. The Cabinet Room has a pleasant view looking over a garden to Horse Guards Parade. The windows face north and west, and therefore very little direct sunlight enters the room, which is a rather plain and simple room, about the size of a middle-class drawing room. For more than two hundred years the prime ministers of England had worked and ruled from this room.

The Annexe, known also as "The Hole in the Ground," was very different. Here at Storey's Gate overlooking St. James's Park, and five minutes' walk from 10 Downing Street, there was a low building which was merely the visible evidence of a vast underground network of rooms, corridors and tunnels stretching across six acres and reaching down one hundred and fifty feet below street level. Originally this maze of underground rooms was a repository for old documents and records belonging to the Office of Works. It was now shielded with reinforced concrete and provided with armored telephone cables and a powerful ventilation system. Above ground a set of rooms accommodated the prime minister and his immediate staff, while thirty-five feet below ground, reached by a spiral staircase, was the Cabinet War Room which was provided with a large table covered in black baize and some uncomfortable tubular metal chairs upholstered in green leather. This room was about forty feet square. Thick wooden pillars and crossbeams, painted bright red, supported the ceiling and gave it something of the appearance of a ship's wardroom.

The Cabinet War Room was even more unpretentious than the Cabinet Room at 10 Downing Street. It had a curiously unfinished and garish appearance, as though the workmen had come in, painted everything in the wrong colors and abruptly departed. There were black, green, red and white telephones. There was a fireplace which had been installed for no reason that anyone could understand, for there were no flues and no chimney. It was purely decorative. Churchill, with his back to the fireplace, would automatically toss cigar ends over his shoulder in the vague hope that they would land somewhere near the fireplace. Since there was some danger that the Cabinet War Room might be set on fire with a cigar butt, someone placed a bright-red fire bucket in the fireplace. The smell of cigar smoke hung heavily over the room.

Churchill always sat at the head of the table in a homely wooden chair with rounded arms and a plump cushion. In front of him were four glass inkwells, two red and two black, and an ornamental dagger used for slitting open envelopes. From time to time he announced that this dagger was the chosen instrument to be used when at last Hitler was brought before him. On a strip of cardboard someone had written some words once spoken by Queen Victoria: "Please understand there is no pessimism in this house and we are not interested in the possibilities of defeat; they do not exist," and this card was propped up in front of him.

Outside the Cabinet War Room a wooden signpost showed the weather above ground for the benefit of the five hundred people working in the Annexe. Some of them remained in the Annexe for weeks on end without ever emerging. Four painted cards could be slipped into a wooden slot. They read: COLD, SUNNY, FINE, WINDY. The last had nothing to do with the wind. It meant that a full-scale air raid was taking place.

The Annexe resembled a film set built for an improbable and not very amusing film produced on a low budget. There was something about the place that denied credibility. The props were the wrong props, the colors were the wrong colors, the doors were in the wrong places and there were too many of them. A visitor to the brick-walled canteen fifty feet below ground might come upon Churchill and the Chief of the Imperial General Staff dining off a tray underneath an enormous fly-spotted photograph of a royal house party at Balmoral during the reign of King Edward VII. One could tell that the house party had taken place in summer, because the ladies standing demurely in the front row were wearing white summer dresses. There were also some bad prints of the English countryside hanging on the wall. No doubt these decorations had been provided by the Office of Works, which was not notable for the exercise of imagination.

In the corridors hung storm lanterns with government issue candles to be used if the electric light system broke down. Brown snakelike pipes wandered down all the corridors, and there could be heard a faint throbbing and whistling sounds as hollow steel balls inside the pipes, propelled by compressed air, traveled at thirty miles an hour to distant receiving posts. The hollow balls conveyed messages from one government department to another. Churchill delighted in his pneumatic post office, which conveyed messages with extraordinary speed. It was by this same principle that money was conveyed to the cashier's desk in millinery stores.

Churchill delighted, too, in all the intricate workings of Storey's Gate. He marveled at the vast tunnelings which extended under St. James's Park, under Whitehall and down to the Houses of Parliament. He vowed that if the German army landed in Britain and London lay in ruins above him, he would continue to fight on from this command post, where he felt entirely secure and where all the necessary instruments for directing a war were present in abundance. But all this was make-believe. After the war, when there was time to make a careful survey of the installations at Storey's Gate, it was learned that the Office of Works had shown itself to be criminally negligent in its calculations. The reinforced concrete shield directly above the Cabinet War Room would have crumpled like paper under a direct hit and even a near-miss would have destroyed the building and all its occupants. What had seemed to be so strong, so impregnable, so powerful, was in fact no more than a frail doll's house. If Churchill had met his Cabinet and given out his orders in a roped-off enclosure in St. James's Park, with a nearby trench to jump into in the event of an air raid, he would have been much safer.

The third nerve center was an Elizabethan mansion some forty miles north of London in the heart of Buckinghamshire. This mansion had been given to the nation as a suitable weekend retreat for prime ministers and their families, and Churchill saw no reason why he should not follow in wartime the usual custom of prime ministers in peacetime. Chartwell had been closed for the duration of the war. He liked to get away from 10 Downing Street and the Annexe, and Chequers, the mansion in Buckinghamshire, suited him admirably. He usually drove to Chequers on Friday evenings in time for a late dinner. Sometimes a policeman rode ahead on a motorcycle to clear the traffic, but if there was no policeman available he used a heavy railway bell which was permanently installed in his automobile and could be operated by the chauffeur with a foot pedal. "Ring the bell! Ring the bell!" Churchill shouted to the chauffeur through the speaking tube whenever he was in a hurry and there was too much traffic on the road. Sometimes, tired out by the exertions of the week, he would lean back with a black bandage over his eyes, sleeping. At such times, when the chauffeur rang the bell, which clanged with the intensity of a shrill steam whistle, Churchill would be instantly awake, shouting: "Dammit, stop ringing that bell! Do you want us to get arrested for bad behavior?"

If the Annexe was a strange makeshift place for running a war, Chequers was even stranger. It was very beautiful, and very old. Lord Lee of Fareham, who bequeathed it to the nation, had acquired a magnificent collection of paintings by Rubens, Van Dyck, Turner and Constable, and all these were included in his gift. He also collected objects of historical interest. Under a glass case could be seen the ruby ring of Elizabeth I, and under another glass case lay the gloves worn by Oliver Cromwell. There were huge four-poster beds, creaking staircases, doors that did not close properly and lavatories that did not work well. The mullioned windows let only a little light in. Ornate tapestries hung from the walls and wonderfully thick carpets were strewn over the larger rooms. Although there were nineteen beds, there was not enough room for all the secretaries and guests, who were sometimes forced to double up or sleep on the floor. There were only two telephones.

It was generally believed that Churchill spent his weekends at Chequers in order to enjoy the country air. But in fact he scarcely ever left the mansion and derived very little benefit from the gardens or the surrounding beechwoods. If the day was especially sunny, or if he was particularly disturbed, he might be induced to take a turn round the garden and examine an ancient sundial in the sunken rose garden. The inscription read:

> *Ye Houres do fly*
> *Full Soone we die*
> *In age Secure*
> *Ye House and Ye Hills*
> *Alone Endure*

There were some observers, and these not the least intelligent, who thought the sundial and its inscription were perhaps not much older than the Victorian era. The mansion, too, although outwardly Tudor, was filled with Victorian gimcrackery.

Churchill developed a great fondness for Chequers, and here he unbent to the extent that it was possible for him to unbend. At 10 Downing Street he wore the conventional business suit with the blue polka-dot bow tie. At the Annexe he wore his blue-gray siren suit which could be thrown on quickly with the help of a zip-fastener. This he called his "boiler suit"; his secretaries called it his "rompers."° At Chequers he liked to appear in an extraordinary mandarin dressing

---

°The boiler suit had many other names including "Teddy Bear." In its earliest form it was made of wool, in air force blue, and followed the lines of the army battle dress. The zip-fastener reached from the neck to the waist. Churchill wore it during air raids, when he was working at night and at late Cabinet meetings, but rarely wore it in public, where he preferred to be seen in his black coat and waistcoat and pinstripe trousers with the gold watch chain and polka-dot bow tie. After the war he took to wearing more flamboyant versions of the boiler suit in blue velvet, made by the best tailors.

None of Churchill's explanations of the boiler suit are quite convincing. It made him appear even rounder and plumper than he really was, and more comical. Like the famous gold, red and green dressing gown with coiling dragons, it appears to have been invented for dramatic effect rather than for any utilitarian purpose, and evidently answered some deep-seated need.

gown, padded like a quilt, and embroidered with red and green dragons. He also wore bedroom slippers which were elaborately embroidered and bore his initials WSC in thick strands of red silk. He resembled a Chinese emperor even to the soft gestures and oracular phrases, and no one could have guessed what an English workman would have thought if he had seen Churchill in this strange disguise. In this uniform, padding heavily about the room, a cigar in his mouth, he cajoled and convinced his military to carry out his orders or bombarded them with questions until late at night.

Chequers gave him an illusion of freedom, and he was therefore more demanding and even more cantankerous than in Downing Street or in the Annexe. Also, he drank more heavily. As usual he worked on his papers for a large part of the morning while still in bed, continually smoking the cigars that threatened to set fire to the bedsheets, rose for lunch, worked, napped, worked, saw a film, worked again. Some, like Sir John Dill, the Chief of the Imperial General Staff, thought him hopelessly disorganized and undisciplined, and could never quite accustom themselves to this extraordinary man who wore the silk gown of a Chinese emperor. Others, more realistically, excused the foibles and marveled at the underlying order and discipline of his mind.

It was at Chequers that he received the news of Hitler's invasion of Russia. For many months he had been warning Stalin that the invasion was imminent, but to no avail. Wherever Hitler prepared a trap for Stalin, the Russian dictator obediently stepped into it. Now, as the summer solstice approached, and more and more information about German troop movements became available, Churchill became convinced that the invasion could be no longer delayed. In the warm dusk after dinner on the evening of Saturday, June 21, 1941, Churchill was walking on the croquet lawn at Chequers with his new private secretary Jock Colville. There had been much talk at dinner about the coming invasion of Russia, and now Colville turned to Churchill and asked him whether as the archenemy of Bolshevism he did not have some reservations about going to Russia's assistance.

"Not at all," Churchill replied quickly. "I have only one purpose, the destruction of Hitler, and my life is much simplified thereby. If Hitler invaded Hell I would at least make a favorable reference to the Devil in the House of Commons."

He went to bed and was asleep when at four o'clock in the morning, the news came that Hitler had attacked Russia. Churchill had given orders that he must not be awakened under any conditions except in the event of a German invasion of England. Until eight o'clock in the morning Colville kept the news to himself. When he went in to see Churchill, he was told: "Tell the BBC I will broadcast at nine tonight."

Churchill spent most of the day writing the long speech which was not completely finished until twenty minutes before he went on the air. He met some of his advisers, telephoned some members of the War Cabinet, and heard from Sir John Dill about the loss of hundreds of Soviet airplanes on the ground and the tremendous thrust of the German army. He especially wanted the advice of two men: Sir Stafford Cripps, the British ambassador to Moscow who had flown back to England only a few days before, and Lord Beaverbrook, the Minister of Supply. Cripps was thin, ascetic, steel-hard. Beaverbrook was small, wizened, tempestuous. Cripps was a Socialist who lived by his abstract principles, while Beaverbrook was a millionaire, hot-blooded, more imperialist than Churchill himself, and possessing no principles at all. Churchill asked Cripps whether the Russians would be able to defend themselves. "No," Cripps answered sadly. "The Germans will go through Russia like a hot knife through butter." This was an opinion shared by most of the generals and especially by Sir John Dill. They believed that Russia was doomed, and it was only a question of time before the Russian army would disintegrate under the hammer blows of the Wehrmacht. Churchill heard Cripps out and then turned to Beaverbrook, a Calvinist who had made his first million before he was thirty and might be expected to have little sympathy for Communist Russia. Beaverbrook declared that everything possible should be done to support the Russians with their enormous manpower and their vast potential in production. Churchill agreed; and whether he agreed or not, he was confronted with one overwhelming fact—Russia was in the war. His broadcast that evening would therefore be an affirmation of an alliance suddenly brought about by Hitler's determination to conquer and annihilate the Russian state. He said: "We have but one aim, and one single, irrevocable purpose. We are resolved to destroy Hitler and every vestige of the Nazi regime. From this, nothing will turn us—nothing. We will never parley, we will never negotiate with Hitler or any of his gang. We shall fight him by land, we shall fight him by sea, we shall fight him in the air, until, with God's help, we have rid the earth of his shadow and liberated its people from his yoke. Any man or state who fights on against Nazism will have our aide. Any man or state who marches with Hitler is our foe. . . ."

Much of this was a repetition of previous speeches. What was new

was the clear offer of aid to the Soviet Union. This meant that Britain
was prepared, although she was herself in danger, to share guns, tanks,
airplanes and other warlike material with Russia to the limit of her
capacity. This was the message he wanted to convey to the Russian
people.

The speech was a very long one, and as so often when he was
speaking most publicly, he introduced themes and arguments that were
intensely personal. He had been the archenemy of the Russian Communist state, having hoped to strangle it at birth. Now, by a strange
turn of fate, he offered himself as Russia's champion. How had this
come about? Clearly as a result of the German attack, but there was
also another reason. He found himself attempting to visualize the vast,
huddled masses of the Russian people who had been oppressed for so
long and who now perhaps, as a result of the war, might achieve some
kind of freedom. He wrote dithyrambically, pulling out all the stops,
composing a choral ode which was printed as prose but deserves to be
printed as verse:

> I see the Russian soldiers standing on the threshold
>   of their native land, guarding the fields which
>   their fathers have tilled from time immemorial.
> I see them guarding their homes where mothers and wives
>   pray—ah yes, for there are times when all pray—
>   for the safety of their loved ones, the return of
>   the bread-winner, of their champion, of their
>   protector.
> I see the ten thousand villages of Russia, where the
>   means of existence was wrung so hardly from the
>   soil, but where there are still primordial human
>   joys, where maidens laugh and children play.
> I see advancing on all this in hideous onslaught the
>   Nazi war machine, with its clanking, heel-clicking,
>   dandified Prussian officers, its crafty expert
>   agents fresh from the cowing and tying-down of a
>   dozen countries.
> I see also the dulled, drilled, docile, brutish masses of
>   the Hun soldiery plodding on like a swarm of crawl-
>   ing locusts.
> I see the German bombers and fighters in the sky, still
>   smarting from many a British whipping, delighted to
>   find what they believe is an easier and safer prey.

Behind all this glare, behind all this storm, I see that
small group of villainous men who plan, organize
and launch this cataract of horrors upon mankind. . . .

So he wrote on that warm summer day in an Elizabethan mansion his
choral ode in praise of Russia. It was neither good prose nor good verse,
but it was effective oratory. There was a rhyme scheme (pray, play,
prey) and some useful assonances. But what was chiefly remarkable was
a kindliness and tenderness toward the Russians, compared with "the
dulled, drilled, docile, brutish masses of the Hun soldiery." In this way
he exorcised the ghosts of the past.

There is some doubt whether Stalin ever read this speech, and nearly
a month passed before Stalin sent the first of a long series of somewhat
contemptuous messages to Churchill. Stalin immediately demanded
the opening of two new fronts, one in northern France and the other in
the Arctic, by which he meant northern Norway. His considered
opinion was that the Arctic front could be opened by British naval and
air operations, and that the opening of the front in northern France
"would be popular with the British Army, as well as with the population of Southern England." Churchill quickly realized that Stalin, who
had recently shown a remarkable lack of understanding of the German
mind, was equally ignorant of the English mind. He would have to be
taught, and very quickly. In his dispatches and later in his conversations
with Stalin, Churchill did his best to convey a more temperate world
view, which had little in common with the feverish world view of a
remorseless dictatorship.

While the German armies knifed their way into Russia, Churchill
was immersed in a vast number of problems connected with the defense
of Britain, the Middle East and the Far East, and it was gradually
becoming apparent that Japan was preparing to strike south and there
was imminent danger of an explosion in the Far East. He felt certain
that the United States would be drawn into a Pacific war, and it was
chiefly to discuss this coming war that he decided to make the long,
dangerous journey across the Atlantic to meet the President of the
United States. There were many other urgent matters to discuss,
including a declaration of common principles which later came to be
known as the Atlantic Charter. The meeting, it was decided, should
take place on August 9, 1941, in Placentia Bay in Newfoundland, and
Churchill chose as his means of transport the battleship *Prince of
Wales*, the latest battleship to be placed in service in the Royal Navy.

The *Prince of Wales* sailed from Scapa Flow into a storm, which pleased her captain, who knew that submarines operate inefficiently in high seas. The foul weather in the Atlantic forced the captain to choose between retaining a destroyer escort, in which case he would have to slacken speed, and journeying alone at the greatest possible speed. The choice was dictated by necessity; greater speed meant greater safety. Churchill was understandably elated by the thought that the *Prince of Wales* was alone in mid-Atlantic, steaming at full speed, under the protection of her enormously powerful guns.

For a few days Churchill enjoyed his enforced leisure. He read novels, attended films, played backgammon with Harry Hopkins, who was Roosevelt's ambassador-at-large and was now returning to America after visiting Stalin in the Kremlin, and paced the deck, wearing a double-breasted blue jacket, blue trousers and a yachting cap. Churchill wept at the showing of the film *Lady Hamilton,* although he had already seen it at least seven times, and was quietly attentive during a showing of an American comedy called *The Devil and Miss Jones.* He was continually visiting the Map Room which showed the dispositions of all the ships and submarines, friends and enemies, known to be in the Atlantic Ocean. Allied merchant ships were represented by red pins, British warships by gray pins, and German submarines by sinister black coffin-shaped pins. Here and there you could see clusters of sixty or seventy red pins escorted by a pathetically small number of gray pins, while to the north and south of them lurked packs of coffin-shaped pins. The Battle of the Atlantic could be followed in breathtaking detail thanks to an extraordinary device called Asdic, an anti-submarine detector invented by British scientists, but now known to the Germans because the secret had been betrayed to them by French naval officers. The map was brilliantly lit, and the dance of the slow-moving pins seemed to be taking place on a stage; the history of the world depended upon how many red pins reached the harbors of England. When a German submarine was sunk, a coffin-shaped pin was tossed unceremoniously into a tray. When an Allied merchant ship was sunk, a red pin was tossed just as unceremoniously away. When someone asked whether a certain U-boat had been sunk, Churchill said: "Only British submarines are sunk—German U-boats are *destroyed!*"

As it happened, this was an exceptionally good week for the sinking of U-boats, and Churchill was in a buoyant mood when the *Prince of Wales* entered Canadian waters. The storm abated, and soon the battleship was gliding through the white fog blowing off the New-

Graham Sutherland's painting of Churchill, presented to him on his eightieth birthday
Paul Popper

Churchill at Royal Academy banquet, May, 1963
Paul Popper

Churchill at the window of his Hyde Park Gate house
on his ninetieth birthday

foundland Banks, more than ever invisible to the enemy, with an escort of three Canadian destroyers to lead her to a safe anchorage at Placentia Bay. The President had already arrived, and the American ships stood against the skyline like a row of fortresses in steel gray. The battleship *Arkansas* and the cruisers *Tuscaloosa* and *Augusta* led the procession, while a flotilla of destroyers stood guard over them. It was a cold gray morning, the wind had dropped and the blue hills were covered with a light mist. In these sheltered surroundings the meeting between a British battleship and an American fleet in wartime acquired an extraordinary gaiety and solemnity.

There are meetings which are more valuable because they have taken place than for anything said in them. In fact very little of importance was said and no hard decisions were made, and what was discussed could have been discussed at less risk over the transatlantic telephone. But Churchill and Roosevelt were eminently justified in their decision to meet off the coast of Newfoundland, for they were well aware of the necessity of performing symbolic acts to reinforce and give emphasis to positions they had reached; and the very secrecy of the meeting gave it a resonance it would not otherwise have possessed. It was the first of nine meetings between Churchill and Roosevelt.

They were both buoyant and outgoing men whose deliberate self-confidence concealed a multitude of psychological problems. They shared a common love for ships and naval history, for fine books and whiskey and for the patrician way of life. They were great drinkers whose minds worked quickest on the edge of drunkenness. Churchill, half American, had an instinctive understanding of the workings of the American mind, and Roosevelt had read so many of Churchill's books and heard him so often on the telephone that he recognized the good sense so often concealed in Churchillian rhetoric. And since Churchill never forgot that he was outranked by the President, who was the head of state while he was himself merely Prime Minister, and showed a proper deference, relations between them remained cordial to the end.

On the morning of August 9 Churchill presented himself on board the *Augusta* and gave the President a letter from King George VI. The discussions began almost immediately. Both President and Prime Minister were accompanied by brilliant advisers. General George Marshall, Chief of the Army General Staff; General "Hap" Arnold, Chief of the Army Air Staff; Admiral Harold Stark, Chief of Naval Operations; Sumner Welles, Undersecretary of State; Averell Harriman, who played a major part in securing the passage of the

Lend-Lease Act; and Harry Hopkins, who was the President's dedicated alter ego, a man of great physical frailty and fierce moral courage. The Prime Minister's advisers included Sir John Dill, Admiral Sir Dudley Pound, Sir Alexander Cadogan of the Foreign Office, Lord Cherwell, and briefly—for he flew across the Atlantic just in time to take part in the concluding conferences—Lord Beaverbrook. These advisers were well-matched.

On the following day, a Sunday, Roosevelt and his entourage came on board the *Prince of Wales*, accompanied by several hundred American sailors and marines, to attend divine service. The gray clouds had cleared away, and a bright watery sunlight shone on the Union Jack and the Stars and Stripes draped over a pulpit. Churchill had chosen the hymns: "For Those in Peril on the Sea," "Onward Christian Soldiers," and "O God, Our Help in Ages Past." Some days later Churchill spoke of the extraordinary impression made on him by the sight of American and British sailors praying and singing hymns together. "When I looked upon that densely packed congregation of fighting men of the same language, of the same faith, of the same fundamental laws, of the same ideals, and now to a large extent of the same interests, and certainly, in different degrees, facing the same danger, it swept across me that here was the only hope, but also the sure hope, of saving the world from measureless degradation."

For Churchill "the sure hope" was an article of faith, not to be rationally explained. It arose perhaps from his sense of solidarity with the United States, but in his wildest dreams he could scarcely have imagined how the United States would be drawn into the war four months later. "The sure hope," from being an article of faith, became an instrument of policy.

The discussions revealed as many differences as agreements. The Americans condemned the Middle East as "a liability from which the British should withdraw"; refused to be drawn into discussions about strategy in the Pacific; raised the strange specter of a Japanese conquest of Madagascar; and were reluctant to discuss anything east of the Azores and French and Spanish Morocco. But while the Americans and British differed on details, there was general agreement on principles. Out of this general agreement was born the "Joint Declaration of the President and the Prime Minister," which came to be known as The Atlantic Charter.

Although Churchill claimed a full measure of credit for the Atlantic Charter, saying for example that the first draft was "cast in my own words," it does not read like anything he could have written and the first draft was in fact written by Sir Alexander Cadogan of the Foreign Office on Sunday, August 10, not long after the service held on the quarterdeck of the *Prince of Wales*. In its original form it read:

1. Their countries seek no aggrandizement, territorial or other;
2. they desire to see no territorial changes that do not accord with the freely expressed wishes of the peoples concerned;
3. they respect the right of all peoples to choose the form of government under which they will live; . . .
4. they will strive to bring about a fair and equitable distribution of essential produce . . . ;
5. they seek a peace which will not only cast down forever the Nazi tyranny, but by effective international organization will afford to all states and peoples the means of dwelling in security. . . .

The Americans disliked Article 4 because it was too vague, and Roosevelt struck out the words "by effective international organization" in Article 5 because he felt that a new Assembly of the League of Nations was undesirable so long as there did not exist an international police force composed of American and British troops. This article was revised, apparently by Churchill, to read:

After the final destruction of the Nazi tyranny they hope to see established a peace which will afford to all nations the means of dwelling in safety within their own boundaries, and which will afford assurance that all the men in all the lands may live out their lives in freedom from fear.

On January 6, 1941, the President in a speech before Congress had announced the doctrine of the four essential human freedoms—freedom of speech, freedom of worship, freedom from want and freedom from fear. Remembering this, he suggested that the last words of the article should read: ". . . may live out their lives in freedom from fear and want." Churchill agreed.

An article on the freedom of the seas had originally read: "They desire such a peace to establish for all safety on the high seas and oceans." This sounds like Sir Alexander Cadogan at his most wooden. With Churchill's help this was changed to: "Such a peace shall enable all men to traverse the high seas and oceans without hindrance." In this way they hammered out the eight articles of the charter, which could and should have been as inflammatory as the *Declaration of the Rights of Man* of August, 1789, and as memorable. But it was composed carelessly and haphazardly, with the result that it evoked little enthusiasm. Both Churchill and Roosevelt appear to have been a little ashamed of it, for they neither signed nor sealed it, and there was no official copy. It was issued as a press release.

Nevertheless the Atlantic Charter contained a charge of dynamite, which is still capable of exploding. Article 3 "respected" the right of all peoples to choose the form of government under which they will live. "Respected" does not mean "guaranteed" or "insisted upon." It was one of those colorless words which fill the bureaucratic lexicon, and the article, which appeared first in Sir Alexander Cadogan's draft, was not intended to apply to the people in the British, Dutch, Belgian and French colonies. The statement was deliberately vague; to respect a right is not necessarily to do anything about it; but this was not how it was read by the people of India, Burma, Malaya, Indonesia and French Africa, or by the ordinary people of England who first heard about the Atlantic Charter when it was read to them over the radio by Deputy Prime Minister Clement Attlee, who had long ago shown that he detested colonialism in all its forms. Churchill would later remind the House of Commons that "at the Atlantic meeting we had in mind primarily the restoration of the sovereignty, self-government and national life of the States and nations of Europe now under the Nazi yoke," and that they were not thinking about colonies. But the Atlantic Charter spoke of "all peoples." In this way a casual phrase written by a bored Under Secretary acquired a revolutionary connotation.

Although the meeting between the two statesmen produced no immediate practical results and there was little to show for the four days of conferences held at Placentia Bay, there were enduring advantages which could not be easily measured. The President and Churchill took the measure of one another, enjoyed one another, drank together and found themselves in agreement on all important matters. General Marshall took a liking to General Sir John Dill, and so it went all along the line. Trust was established; it could not be measured, but it existed abundantly. Roosevelt learned that Churchill could be stubborn as a mule, but he could also be brilliantly accommodating when it served his purpose. Churchill learned that Roosevelt possessed extraordinary reserves of strength and stamina, and could also be stubborn and brilliantly accommodating. They were men who reached out toward the same kind of solutions, with a flair for drama and adventure, even the adventure of running a war, and they were not afraid of anything.

Early in the morning of August 13 the *Prince of Wales* slid out of Placentia Bay for the homeward journey. Everyone was aware that by this time the Germans knew about the meeting and were sending U-boats in pursuit. What the Germans did not know was that the *Prince of Wales* was not returning directly to England but intended to visit Iceland, escorted by American destroyers equipped with depth charges. As Churchill described it in *The Grand Alliance,* the American destroyers "happened to be going the same way too, so we made a goodly company at sea together." The American fleet in the Atlantic was already on a war footing, while in the Pacific the American fleet was still sleeping.

On the way to Iceland, two days later, the *Prince of Wales* encountered a convoy of seventy-two merchant ships and cargo boats of all kinds bringing supplies of food, munitions and guns to England. The presence of the convoy was first signaled by seventy-two red pins in the Map Room. Churchill observed that only a slight deflection from course would bring the battleship into the convoy, and he had no difficulty urging the captain to veer slightly off course. In the evening, as the sun was setting, the great convoy with its eight small gray corvettes guarding it, came into sight. There they were—tramp ships, tankers, whalers, converted passenger ships, cargo ships of every kind, all of them traveling at eight knots and forming six immense columns spread out over two or three miles—and suddenly the *Prince of Wales* plunged down a lane between the columns at twenty-two knots, while Churchill stood on the bridge, saluting and making the V sign. It was the navy's and Churchill's tribute to the merchant marine. The convoy was the lifeblood of England; and the sudden appearance of the battleship among that motley crowd of cargo boats was a symbolic act of great beauty. Xerxes, gazing down at his ships in the Bay of Salamis, had not seen a greater beauty. Churchill was not content with seeing it once. When they had passed the foremost ships of the convoy, the battleship and her American destroyers described a circle and raced back to do the same thing all over again.

The call at Iceland, too, was a symbolic act. Only a few weeks before American Marines had landed to deny the island to a common enemy. Henceforth all ships in a broad area from the New England coast to Iceland would be under the protection of the American Navy, and Iceland herself became a landing stage for supplies, aircraft and men throughout the war. After the invasion of Denmark, Iceland became virtually an independent state under a Regent. Churchill made a ceremonial call on the Regent, was given a huge bunch of hothouse carnations, and then set off on the *Prince of Wales* for Scapa Flow.

This time there was no escort, but the seas were unusually rough for August and no U-boats appeared. Churchill was in a buoyant mood. He felt that in some mysterious way it had been given to the two leaders of the English-speaking peoples to guide the destiny of the world. In his report on his meeting with President Roosevelt delivered six days later, Churchill said:

> This was a meeting which marks for ever in the pages of history the taking-up by the English-speaking nations amid all this peril, tumult and confusion, of the guidance of the fortunes of the broad, toiling masses in all the continents, and our loyal effort, without any clog of selfish interest, to lead them forward out of the miseries into which they have been plunged back onto the broad high-road of freedom and justice. This is the highest honour and the most glorious opportunity which could ever come to any branch of the human race.

Unfortunately it was never to be quite so simple. The leadership of "the broad, toiling masses in all the continents" did not pass into the hands of Roosevelt and Churchill, or even into the hands of Stalin. There was no central, all-pervasive leader, as in Germany, and perhaps this was for the best. The war against Hitler would continue to be fought spasmodically, blindly, heroically, confusedly. To the end Churchill would dream of clear and simple solutions, but there were none. In the late summer of 1941 the perils, tumults and confusions were greater than they had ever been.

THE MORTAL STORM

When the germans invaded Russia in the early
hours of the morning of June 22, 1941, Stalin was lying asleep in his
sumptuous summer house at Gagra on the Black Sea. When he awoke
and heard the news, he refused to believe it. During the following days
he cut himself off completely from Moscow, refused to answer the
telephone, gave no orders, and abandoned Russia to her fate. It was not
until July 3, eleven days after the invasion, that his faltering voice was
heard over the Moscow radio. He was not yet in Moscow and the
recording had been flown up from Gagra. For three years he had not
publicly addressed the Russian people. He began with the words:
"Comrades! Citizens! Brothers and sisters! Men of our army and navy!
I am addressing you, my friends!" The words were extraordinary, for
never before had he addressed the people with such outward affection.
He told them what they already knew—that they were being attacked
by "fiends and cannibals." He went on to tell them things that were
palpably untrue, saying that the Germans intended to restore Tsarism
and the rule of the landlords. Not until the middle of July, when the
Germans entered Smolensk, did he establish himself in the Kremlin and
take full charge of the Russian war effort.

In August, while Churchill was talking to Roosevelt in Placentia Bay, the German army swung north against Leningrad and south against Odessa, which fell after a heroic two-and-a-half-month siege. The Ukraine was in flames. Hundreds of thousands of prisoners were being rounded up, then left to die of starvation and exposure. The entire populations of villages were being massacred, while towns were reduced to rubble. The suddenness of the invasion, the swiftness of the advance, and Hitler's policy of total annihilation—he planned to level Leningrad by naval bombardment and to create a lake over the ruins of Moscow—took the Russians by surprise. They reeled back over their devastated land, with the knowledge that they were confronted by a tyranny even more terrible than the tyranny of Stalin.

From the beginning Churchill hoped to establish a relationship with Stalin which would be as open and trusting as his relationship with Roosevelt. It was not to be. On rare occasions they came to understand one another; there would be sudden flashes of insight; and then the fog gathered. Distrustful, ungracious and unyielding in his demands, Stalin attempted to use Churchill for his own purposes. The fate of Britain did not concern him in the slightest. Churchill sent over 450 fighter planes to the Russian front, and received only grudging thanks; huge supplies of tanks, guns, ammunition and aluminum sheeting, earmarked for the defense of Britain, were sent to Russia and acknowledged with indifference. Only in one theater of war did they appear to agree without too much acrimony: this was in Persia, which was honeycombed with German agents. Stalin and Churchill agreed to send forces into Persia to take over the lines of communication and to insure that the government would not ally itself with Germany. The German agents were rounded up, the pro-German Shah went into exile in South Africa, Russian and British troops met amicably in Teheran, and vast quantities of supplies poured into Russia from ports on the Persian Gulf.

To Stalin's repeated demands that a second and third front should be opened in France and Norway, Churchill replied that the time was not yet ripe. He promised that in the coming winter there would be such full-scale bombings over Germany that Hitler would have cause to regret his invasions. This was small comfort to Stalin, but Churchill meant what he said. "A terrible winter of bombing lies before Germany," he wrote to Stalin. "No one has yet had what they are going to get." In a directive written in September, he said: "We shall undermine them by propaganda, depress them with the blockade, and, above all, bomb their homelands ceaselessly, ruthlessly, and with ever-increasing weight of bombs." But in fact British propaganda was as ineffective as the blockade, and the bombing of the German homeland had only a marginal effect on the course of the war. Yet he had seen enough of the devastation of England to wish the same on the Germans.

England was still faced by the possibility of invasion; the fighting in Africa had not been resolved; Britain's Far Eastern possessions lay unprotected against a threatened Japanese advance; and there were never enough supplies to satisfy the need. The ultimate decisions on the apportionment of supplies had to be made by Churchill, sometimes on the basis of insufficient evidence and sometimes with tragic results. "I was like a keeper in the Zoo distributing half-rations among magnificent animals," he wrote later. "Luckily they knew I was an old and friendly keeper."

But not everyone regarded him as a friendly keeper. Stalin was full of complaints: tanks, airplanes and artillery were arriving at Archangel improperly packed; he saw no advantage in meeting British military envoys who came to Moscow only to acquire information; and he protested against the prevalent lack of clarity and understanding on war aims and on plans for the postwar organization of peace. Stalin wanted Britain to declare war on Finland and was perturbed because Churchill showed so little enthusiasm for one more declaration of war. Finally, after a long delay, Churchill reluctantly agreed to declare war against the Finns.

Churchill's hope was to win a decisive victory in the Western Desert of Africa and drive Rommel back through Libya and Tripolitania. With the German air force occupied in Russia, he saw the conquest of large areas of North Africa as the one possible successful venture open to him. North Africa would be a stepping stone to Sicily and the complete mastery of the Mediterranean. He had few illusions about the dangers of these enterprises. Hopes based on hopes, and all of them so fragile that they might vanish at a touch. If he was victorious in North Africa against the Italian and German armies, then Italy would be demoralized, Turkey and Spain would be confirmed in their neutrality, French North Africa would be stirred into entering the war, and the United States might be induced to send a force into Northern Ireland at least as great as the force sent into Iceland, with a profoundly deterrent effect on the government of Eire, which Churchill regarded with a deep suspicion. And what if Hitler stabilized his front in Russia and decided to send fifty divisions against England in the spring? To most of these questions there were no answers. For Churchill in the fall of 1941 the most cursed thing about the war was that he was compelled to wait upon events and could not shape them.

When there was good news Churchill fastened on it eagerly and drew from it the lesson that the good outweighed the bad; and he delighted in the ironies of war, as when a Lockheed Hudson aircraft of the Coastal Command attacked a U-boat with depth charges somewhere near Iceland, damaging it so severely on the surface that the U-boat commander hoisted the white flag and surrendered. Aid was summoned; a trawler appeared; the U-boat was towed unceremoniously to Iceland, and after being repaired, added to the Royal Navy. But such things happened rarely. Yet it is notable that when in his reports to Roosevelt or to the Cabinet he described air and sea operations he wrote more vividly than when he described land battles. In his memoirs he complains that the description of land battles loses a sense of drama because they take place over wide spaces and over a long period of time, unlike the battles of the eighteenth century which were decided in a day.

During the First World War, when he was sulking over his own failure to bring the Battle of .Gallipoli to a successful conclusion, he wrote: "I never look beyond a battle. It is a culminating event, and like a brick wall bars all further vision." Now, watching the course of the battles in North Africa where Rommel's Afrika Korps was fighting against the British forces known as the Desert Rats, he restated the familiar axiom: "A battle is a veil through which it is not wise to peer." Nevertheless he was continually peering through the veil, for he was a man devoured with curiosity. What if Alexandria fell? What if the Germans rolled up the entire Near East? What if the Japanese attacked in the Far East? As the war slowly mounted toward an inevitable crescendo, he was accustoming himself to looking through the veil at the ravaged face of disaster.

Victories were followed by crushing defeats. On November 8, 1941, an Italian convoy to North Africa consisting of ten merchant ships escorted by four destroyers and two light cruisers was sighted by a British force of two destroyers and two light cruisers. The Italian cruisers fled, and all the merchant ships and one Italian destroyer were sunk. Churchill was jubilant, but not for long. Four days later the battleship *Ark Royal* was sunk near Gibraltar by a prowling U-boat. Two weeks later the battleship *Barham* was sunk between Crete and Cyrenaica by three torpedoes launched by another U-boat. The

Barham turned turtle, her main magazines blew up, and within three minutes there was only a bubbling, oily patch on the calm seas. On December 18 three "human torpedoes" launched from an Italian submarine off the island of Leros made their way past the protective net guarding Alexandria harbor and attached explosive charges to the battleships *Valiant* and *Queen Elizabeth*. The battleships were crippled and put out of action for many months. On the same day the cruiser *Neptune* sank in a minefield off the North African coast. These were disasters of the first magnitude: the Mediterranean fleet was now no more than a shadow.

In the Far East there were even worse naval disasters. Within an hour on the morning of December 7, 1941, Japanese torpedo bombers at Pearl Harbor sank four American battleships—the *Arizona*, *Oklahoma*, *West Virginia* and *California*—and severely damaged four more, the *Maryland*, *Nevada*, *Pennsylvania* and *Tennessee*. They also sank three destroyers, and three light cruisers were crippled and put out of action. Churchill heard the news of the attack on Pearl Harbor from the BBC news broadcast at nine o'clock in the evening. He was staying at Chequers, and Averell Harriman and John Winant were among his guests. He had not expected it, had not even dared to hope for it; and not knowing the full extent of the damage at Pearl Harbor, he was jubilant. He wrote later: "I do not pretend to have measured accurately the martial might of Japan, but now at this very moment I knew the United States was in the war, up to the neck and in to the death. So we had won after all!"

For him this was the most dazzling moment of all: the moment that determined all the remaining years of the war. He telephoned to President Roosevelt, who said grimly: "It is quite true. They have attacked us in Pearl Harbor. We are in the same boat now." He talked for a while with his two American guests. Then, "being saturated and satiated with emotion and sensation," he wrote in his memoirs, "I went to bed and slept the sleep of the saved and thankful."

On the following day he wrote to the Japanese ambassador in London to declare that a state of war existed between Great Britain and Japan, signing the letter: "I have the honour to be with high consideration, Sir, your obedient servant, Winston S. Churchill." He remarked later that if you are going to kill a man, you might as well be polite to him.

But at this moment the Japanese were doing all the killing. They had bombed Singapore and Hong Kong, and were busily preparing landings in Java and the Philippines. The same airplanes that had bombed the

Chinese quarter of Singapore had flown directly over the Singapore Naval Base where the *Prince of Wales* and the battle cruiser *Repulse* were at anchor, having been sent to Singapore by Churchill against the advice of all his naval advisers who wanted the ships to roam the Indian Ocean and harrass the enemy wherever he appeared. "They had been sent to these waters," wrote Churchill, "to exercise that kind of vague menace which capital ships of the highest quality whose whereabouts is unknown can impose upon all hostile naval calculations." There were a good many things wrong with this statement. First, this was not the reason why they were sent to Singapore. Secondly, the capital ships might be menacing, but they were not vaguely menacing: They were clearly visible as they lay at anchor in the Straits of Johore and the Japanese were well aware that they were there and had known about their coming for many days. Thirdly, Churchill had omitted to mention that the ships were not provided with air cover and had been sent to a region where the Japanese would inevitably possess mastery of the air. Originally it was intended that the aircraft carrier *Indomitable* should accompany the two warships to Singapore, but she had run aground off the coast of Jamaica and was disabled. Churchill sent the *Prince of Wales* and *Repulse* to Singapore in the belief that their presence at the huge naval base would act as a deterrent to Japanese ambitions in the South Seas and because he believed, even at this late date, that heavily armored capital ships were inviolable to air attack. He had not studied the situation in Malaya in any detail. He had badgered his naval staff into sending the ships; he had refused to take their warnings seriously; and he had accepted the prevalent notion that the naval base was a naval fortress equipped with heavy guns, when in fact it had no guns at all and was only a dockyard with the usual graving docks, repair shops, refueling depots and ammunition dumps. A dockyard is not a fortress. There existed a romantic illusion that the Singapore Naval Base was a great bastion protecting the British Empire in the Far East, but it was founded on nothing more than a human desire to believe that such a bastion existed. In much the same way Pearl Harbor was regarded as impregnable.

A series of extraordinary accidents led the *Prince of Wales* and the *Repulse* to their doom. Although the city of Singapore was in a blackout and a general state of alert had been proclaimed, none of the small airfields scattered over the length and breadth of Malaya were alerted and no effort was made to conceal or scatter the airplanes. During the early morning hours of December 7, when Japanese airplanes were dropping bombs on Singapore, they were also dropping bombs on the airplanes lined up on the airfields. Out of 146 airplanes in Malaya, 88 were destroyed or put out of action on the ground, and no British airplanes went up in pursuit of the Japanese airplanes. Thus when the *Prince of Wales* and the *Repulse* slid out of the Straits of Johore late in the afternoon of December 8 with the purpose of destroying a Japanese invasion fleet off Khota Bharu on the northeastern coast of Malaya, no air cover could be provided for them. This was not an insuperable problem, because there were low clouds and heavy rain squalls in the Gulf of Siam. Admiral Sir Tom Phillips, commanding the two capital ships and four destroyers, was a short, peppery man in a fighting mood. He hoped to surprise the invasion fleet, destroy it and then return to the naval base. But during the evening of December 9 the weather cleared, and he became aware that he was being shadowed by Japanese airplanes. He was also being shadowed by Japanese submarines. He turned south.

During that night some buffaloes wandered into a minefield near the shore defenses at Kuantan, a small town 150 miles south of Kota Bharu. The buffaloes were mistaken for a Japanese landing party, machine guns opened fire, the shore defenses went into action and a signal was sent to Singapore, giving notice that a landing was in progress. This signal was sent to Admiral Phillips, but there was no following signal telling him that by 2 A.M. the commander of the shore batteries had gone to bed, having decided that the uproar was caused by buffaloes and there were no Japanese troops anywhere near Kuantan.

Thus it happened that by the purest chance the *Prince of Wales* and the *Repulse*, steaming toward Kuantan to investigate the report of the landing, passed within a few hundred yards of a Japanese submarine shortly before dawn. The submarine, which was almost run down by the ships, fired five torpedoes, and all of them missed. The captain of the submarine radioed the position of the British ships to Saigon, where the Japanese were loading bombs on their airplanes for another punishing attack on Singapore. During the next two or three hours the Japanese exchanged their bombs for torpedoes and prepared to hunt down the British squadron now moving off the coast of Kuantan. A destroyer was sent inshore, and the captain signaled: "All is quiet as a wet Sunday afternoon." The seas were calm, the skies were clear, and Admiral Phillips, still hoping to destroy the enemy, turned north again after hearing a report of a tug pulling some barges which were perhaps laden with Japanese soldiers. But the tug was as illusory as the invasion force at Kuantan, and soon, but too late, he was steaming back to Singapore.

Shortly after eleven o'clock in the morning the first wave of Japanese bombers appeared, and all the antiaircraft guns opened up. Through this intense fire the Japanese pilots flew without changing formation and dropped their torpedoes. All of the torpedoes missed, but a bomb dropped on the *Repulse* destroyed the hangar of her spotter aircraft. Thirty-five minutes later another wave of torpedo-carrying planes appeared. This time they did not miss, and two torpedoes struck the stern of the *Prince of Wales*. More and more Japanese airplanes appeared, and all directed their bombs and torpedoes at the two capital ships, as though it was hardly worth their while to attack the destroyers. At 12:22 P.M. the *Repulse* was struck amidships, and ten minutes later, having received four more direct hits, she turned over and sank. Less than an hour later the *Prince of Wales* joined her below the waves. The survivors, some 2,000 men out of an original complement of 2,800, were picked up by the destroyers and brought in safety to the naval base.

In London the following morning the telephone rang at Churchill's bedside. It was the First Sea Lord. "Prime Minister," he said, "I have to report to you that the *Prince of Wales* and the *Repulse* have both been sunk by the Japanese—we think by aircraft. Tom Phillips is drowned."

Of what happened during the next few moments Churchill wrote: "As I turned over and twisted in bed the full horror of the news sank in upon me. There were no British or American capital ships in the Indian Ocean or the Pacific except the American survivors of Pearl Harbor, who were hastening back to California. Over all this vast expanse of water Japan was supreme, and we everywhere were weak and naked."

Whenever Churchill addressed himself to the subject of the Japanese mentality, which he did infrequently, he found himself at an almost total loss. He knew very little about the Far East. He knew very little about China, had read none of the Chinese classical works, and was totally ignorant of Chinese history. As for the Japanese, they were a mysterious and rather sinister people living in their remote islands off the coast of eastern Asia. The West had first heard about them from Marco Polo about 1300 A.D. The war lord Hideyoshi resolved in 1592 A.D. "to embark in mortal conflict with China and used sea power to invade Korea." By 1638 A.D. they had massacred more than a quarter of a million of their own converts to Christianity, and thereafter the entire country had lived in strict seclusion until in 1853 A.D. Commodore Perry's American squadron paid its unwelcome visit to the Japanese shores. Thus, briefly, Churchill describes the history of Japan in the only paragraph in his works devoted to it. Not all of this information was correct, and all of it could be found in a cheap one-volume encyclopedia. Japan lay outside the field of his interests and he stubbornly refused to learn more about it.

When the war broke out in the Far East, Churchill committed the same errors that Hitler was to commit in the following year. He ordered the British forces in Malaya and Hong Kong to hold fast. He held out to the defenders of Singapore and Hong Kong the glorious prospect of perishing in the ruins of their cities. There must be no retreat under any conditions. In all his cables to his commanders in Malaya he refers to Singapore Fortress, as though the whole island and not only the naval base, was bristling with guns and fortifications in depth, so that one wonders whether he had ever so much as glanced at a map of the island with its mangrove swamps, rice fields, rubber trees and patches of primitive forest. "It had never entered my head," he wrote, "that no circle of detached forts of a permanent character protected the rear of the famous fortress. . . . The possibility of Singapore having no landward defenses no more entered into my mind than that of a battleship being launched without a bottom." When he realized that exhausted British, Indian and Australian troops, outfought in the jungles of Malaya, were reeling back on the "naked island" of Singapore, he continued to be sustained by the vision of a powerful fortress to be built overnight or in a few days with the entire male population employed in constructing defense works. He issued a ten-point series of instructions. Booby traps must be laid in the mangrove swamps. All small boats in the Straits of Johore must be seized and denied to the enemy. The "most rigorous compulsion" must be used to exact the utmost compliance by the workers drafted into the labor force. The whole island must be fought over until every unit and every strong point was destroyed. Finally "the city of Singapore must be converted into a citadel and defended to the death. No surrender can be contemplated."

All this was easier said than done. The generals on the spot, confronted with the imminent loss of Malaya and the fall of the island, attempted to obey his orders, rushed more troops to the battle fronts, and fought on without the slightest hope of victory. General Archibald Wavell, the Commander in Chief in the Far East, signaled to General Percival in command of the troops in Malaya: "You must continue to inflict maximum losses on enemy for as long as possible by house-to-house fighting if necessary. Your action in tying down enemy may have vital influence in other theaters. Fully appreciate your situation but continued action essential." That was on February 14, 1942. On the following day, accompanied by an officer carrying a white flag and another carrying the Union Jack, General Percival drove halfway across the island of Singapore to the village of Bukit Timah in order to surrender to General Yamashita, who had set up his headquarters in the Ford Motor Works. It was about 5:35 P.M. At that moment the British Empire in the Far East came to an end.

Much of the blame for the fall of Singapore lies with Churchill. He had never understood the problem, and never, until it was too late, looked at a map of the island. He had not taken the measure of the adversaries. He had insisted on sending the *Prince of Wales* and the *Repulse* to Singapore, knowing that they lacked adequate air cover. When the Japanese were poised on the Straits of Johore, he compounded all his previous errors by ordering that the island of Singapore should be defended to the last man. He was as obdurate and determined as Hitler proved to be at Stalingrad, with the same consequences—he lost everything. Some 130,000 British, Indian and Australian troops, who could have been employed in other theaters of war, were captured and more than half of them died in prison camps and labor battalions. Where resilience and retreat were demanded, he closed his mind to the intricate maneuvers of withdrawal. He had committed not one error but a whole accumulating series of errors. His ignorance was fatal. °

While the Japanese were marching along the forest trails of Malaya, laying siege to Hong Kong, landing in strength in the Philippines and Java, and pouring into Burma, Churchill remained jubilant. The fact that the United States had been drawn into the war overweighed all other considerations. "I confess that in my mind the whole Japanese menace lay in a sinister twilight, compared with our other needs," he declared. "If, on the other hand, Japanese aggression drew in America, I would be content to have it." Throughout the remaining years of the war he left the conduct of the war in the Far East largely to the Americans. The Japanese menace was something he preferred not to think about.

For a year and a half, ever since the fall of France, Churchill had

---

°On November 18, when the *Prince of Wales* was in Cape Town, General Smuts, after a long talk with the captain of the battleship, telegraphed to Churchill his profound misgivings about the division of the Allied naval strength between Pearl Harbor and Singapore "into two fleets each separately inferior to the Japanese Navy. . . . If the Japanese are nippy, there is here an opening for a first-class disaster." Churchill paid no attention to this warning.

been aware that the war could be won only with the unstinted help of the United States. The uneasy alliance with Russia was as much a liability as an asset. He counted on the manpower and the vast industrial potential of the United States to change dramatically the course of the war. He liked to recall the words uttered by Sir Edward Grey thirty years earlier. "The United States," he said, "is like a gigantic boiler. Once the fire is lighted under it, there is no limit to the power it can generate." Now that the United States was in the war and President Roosevelt was the Commander in Chief of a huge army, navy and air force which would soon be thrown into battle, Churchill regarded himself as the senior partner. He had, after all, fought the enemy longer, and he knew the weaknesses and strengths of the German armed forces better than the President. When someone at a chiefs of staff meeting warned him that there might be some advantage in talking cautiously to the Americans, Churchill with a wicked gleam in his eye answered: "Oh! that is the way we talked to her while we were wooing her; now that she is in the harem, we talk to her quite differently!"

In other ways, too, there was evidence of *hubris*, the overweening pride which is the special bane of rulers. He rode roughshod over all opposition and all advice that countered his own judgment; and for many long months he had come to possess dictatorial power. He was not someone who could be argued with. But if he thought he could always have his own way with the Americans, he was mistaken, and during the following months he was to learn at great cost that he was the junior partner in the enterprise. He was Benjamin to Roosevelt's Joseph.

Almost from the moment when Japan entered the war Churchill decided to press for a meeting with the President. He wanted to discuss grand strategy and to receive assent to his own strategic plans. The President agreed to meet him in Washington, and Churchill accordingly set out from the Clyde on the battleship *Duke of York*, the sister ship to the *Prince of Wales*. It was an odd choice for a conveyance, for the battleship was put out of commission as an effective warship for over a month, there was no longer any need to perform a symbolic act as he had done when he had traveled in the *Prince of Wales* to Placentia Bay, and he could more easily, more safely and with much greater speed have made the journey by airplane by way of Iceland and Newfoundland. He was treating battleships as his own private vehicles. It was a rough journey with gale-force winds and fifty-foot waves, and for eight days he was at sea in the teeth of Atlantic storms. He did not like it. His supplies of white wine gave out. He spent a good part of the time immobilized in his cabin. Coded radio messages could be received, but his own instructions could only be relayed to London when an accompanying cruiser received the messages and rebroadcast them when it was a hundred miles away from the *Duke of York*. Thus for eight days the effective command of British military operations fell into the hands of General Sir Alan Brooke, the Chief of the Imperial General Staff, who had been recently appointed to succeed General Sir John Dill. Brooke was formidably sharp, testy and full of admiration for Churchill, while capable of holding his own in any military arguments, unlike Dill, who crumbled at the first sarcastic blow, the first sharp appeal to rhetoric. Dill's wife had suffered a paralytic stroke and was dying by inches, and he was therefore all the less capable of standing up to Churchill. Now Brooke was in London and Dill was on the *Duke of York*, accompanying Churchill to Washington. With Churchill, too, was a small army of advisers, secretaries and high-ranking officers, including Admiral Sir Dudley Pound, the First Sea Lord, and Air Marshal Sir Charles Portal, Chief of the Air Staff. Also, prowling on the outskirts of every discussion and debate was Lord Beaverbrook, Churchill's closest friend, the one man who never showed any fear of him.

On the afternoon of December 22 the *Duke of York* dropped anchor off Hampton Roads at the mouth of Chesapeake Bay. When the pilot came on board and saw Churchill, he very nearly fainted from astonishment. He had not guessed—no one had guessed—that Churchill would make this difficult journey to Washington in wartime.

In the White House Churchill was installed in a large bedroom on the same floor as the President. The room next to it served as his Map Room, and beyond this was Harry Hopkins's room. The upstairs hall of the White House, previously little used, became the nerve center of the British Empire, with dignitaries and staff officers with red tabs continually hurrying along the passageways with their inevitable red leather dispatch cases. They were always in a hurry. The Americans by contrast were slow-moving and placid: They knew they had time on their side and resembled giants slowly flexing their muscles.

Hitler in a moment of insanity had quite casually declared war on the United States soon after the Japanese attack on Pearl Harbor. He had nothing to gain by this declaration, and everything to lose. His alliance with Japan was one of those mythological alliances that begin with grandiose hopes and end in bewilderment; and he knew as little about

Japan as Churchill. In Churchill's view his declaration of war on the United States in support of his ally Japan was one of those "irrational acts" that were likely to become increasingly common as the war continued. Churchill hoped and prayed for more "irrational acts," and in due course his prayers were answered.

Roosevelt regarded the war with patrician calm, certain of eventual victory. Churchill was rarely calm and much less certain of eventual victory than he was willing to divulge in his public pronouncements, for there were days even in wartime when "black dog" settled on him. In comparison to Roosevelt he showed himself to be nervously excitable and more fearful than he need have been. He saw the individual trees, each bent and twisted by the storm. Roosevelt saw the whole forest grandly surviving all the winds that blew against it.

Churchill had many reasons for visiting Washington at a time when he might have been better occupied in 10 Downing Street. Above all he was fearful that America, grievously injured at Pearl Harbor, would throw the greater part of her power into the war against Japan. He need not have feared. As far back as February, 1941, American and British military staffs had met and agreed that Germany was the predominant member of the Axis powers and therefore the European and Atlantic area would be regarded as the decisive theater. The defeat of Germany was given priority over the defeat of Japan.

On the *Duke of York* Churchill sketched out and prepared a series of position papers which he hoped to present to the President. Inevitably they were buoyant and optimistic. He believed that from Leningrad to the Crimea the Russians would hold fast, that the British army in North Africa would sweep through Libya, and that Hitler was unlikely to force a passage through Spain and risk "guerrilla warfare with the morose, fierce, hungry people of the Iberian Peninsula," just as it was unlikely that he would attempt to take over unoccupied France. He believed that the proper strategy was to win over or conquer all of French North Africa and the French West African ports before any landings in Europe were attempted. He asked that the United States should send three divisions and one armored division to Northern Ireland, saying that they were needed as a powerful deterrent against an attempt at invasion by Germany and forgetting to add that he wanted them also because they would be a powerful deterrent against any overtures to Germany that might be contemplated by the government of the Republic of Ireland. To the end of the war he remained deeply suspicious of Eire.

In another position paper he outlined the campaign of 1943 when the Allies would go over to the offensive. He thought there would be a large number of separate landings in Norway, Denmark, Holland, Belgium, the Atlantic and Channel coasts of France, Italy and perhaps the Balkans. He did not feel that vast numbers of men would be needed for these armies of liberation—forty armored divisions amounting to about 600,000 men would be sufficient with the help of the resistance groups to wrest Europe from the Germans. He had faith in the resistance groups. Later, as they fell more and more under the sway of the Communists, he showed less interest in them. His concept of simultaneous landings along the coasts of Europe was also abandoned, and this was perhaps an error. Western Europe might have been reconquered more easily and with less loss of life if there had been twenty landings by armored divisions slicing across the continent and cutting the German armies to ribbons.

Churchill's position papers occupied a good deal of his time in Washington. He had intended to stay a week but stayed for three weeks, secure in Roosevelt's affections and strangely certain that he was not urgently needed in his own country. He addressed Congress and then went to Ottawa to stay with Lord Athlone, the Governor General of Canada, and to address the Canadian House of Commons. In this speech he described his meeting with the French prime minister at Tours shortly before the defeat of France. He was told that the French generals believed that England would have her neck wrung like a chicken within three weeks. "Some chicken!" Churchill roared, and there was a short burst of applause. "Some neck!" he added, and then there was a prolonged burst of applause. Churchill was a little puzzled that the word "neck" should be thought more important than the word "chicken." It was some time later that he learned that "neck" could also mean "insolence" and this is what they thought he meant.

He returned to Washington for more conversations with Roosevelt and the Chiefs of Staff, and then went off to Pompano Beach in Florida for a five day holiday in the sun. He had thought of returning to England on the *Duke of York*, but pangs of conscience assailed him. He had been away too long. Surely it would be possible to fly home. The *Duke of York* was in Bermuda and he flew there with the intention of boarding the battleship, but conscience again assailed him and he flew back in a Boeing Clipper without incident, and it pleased him to recall that there were moments of grave danger when the airplane nearly flew over the

German shore batteries at Brest. In fact the airplane was never within ninety miles of Brest. He enjoyed danger and sometimes comforted himself with imaginary dangers.

Marianne Moore speaks somewhere of real toadstools in imaginary gardens. Now the real toadstools were flourishing, and no imagination was needed to realize that the Pacific War had begun disastrously for the Allies. Hong Kong had fallen, Singapore was about to fall, while Java and the Philippines were already occupied by the enemy. Churchill's holiday was over.

A FLOOD OF CALAMITY

WHEN THE PRIME MINISTER of a country at war leaves his homeland for five weeks to live in a country which has not yet been physically attacked, there are bound to be recriminations. People asked whether it was necessary for him to stay away for so long; and if for five weeks, why not for five months or five years? Was he indispensable? He was Prime Minister, Minister of Defence, leader of the House of Commons and acting Foreign Minister in the absence of Anthony Eden in Moscow. Was it necessary that he should hold all these offices? There was a general feeling in England that the war had entered a new phase which would be far more difficult and complex than anything that had happened before. Was it necessary that one man should hold all the strings?

Churchill had no doubt whatsoever that he was indispensable, and he came to regard his visit to the United States as a personal triumph because he had established close and lasting relations with President Roosevelt. But they had already been established and nothing of consequence was added except that the President had read and approved of the position papers which Churchill had written so painstakingly and with so much help from his military staff that there are few authentic

Churchillian sentences in any of them. Little had been gained, much had been lost, and the public was growing uneasy.

They would have been even more uneasy if they had known the true state of his health. One day in the White House he had left his bed because of the stifling heat to open a window. The window was stiff, he used a good deal of force, and he was surprised to feel a dull pain over his heart and along his left arm. The next morning he asked the doctor what had happened and was told that it was nothing of any importance, he was overdoing things, and would probably be all right as long as he did not exert himself too much. The doctor was taking an extraordinary risk, for he knew that Churchill had suffered a heart attack. He also knew that Churchill was temperamentally unsuited to playing the role of an invalid and would have crumpled up mentally and physically if he had been told the truth. On the long view it was best to tell him nothing and wait on events.

Such was the decision made by Sir Charles Wilson, Churchill's personal doctor, when faced with the evidence of a coronary insufficiency. The proper course would have been to tell the truth in small doses, so that Churchill would gradually accustom himself to doing less and less work. His arteries were hardening, there was always the danger of another heart attack, and meanwhile his decisions affected the lives of millions of people. When he returned to England, he threw himself into work with the fury of a man who had suddenly discovered a new pleasure hitherto denied to him.

His first task was to allay the uneasiness of the public and of Parliament. He was so certain of his indispensability that he offered to engage in a full-dress debate in the House of Commons, ostensibly to review the war situation but in fact to review the Churchill situation. "The Press was full of suggestions that I should remain Prime Minister and make the speeches but cede the actual control of the war to someone else. I resolved to yield nothing to any quarter, to take the prime and direct responsibility on myself and to demand a vote of confidence from the House of Commons," he wrote later. The Manchester *Guardian* noted that he was waving votes of confidence about and asserting the indivisibility of the government, and this was precisely what he was doing, since he regarded himself as the indivisible government and he was absolutely determined to secure so large a vote of confidence that his enemies would run to shelter.

His weapon was oratory, not logic. The three-day debate which opened on January 27 was dominated by the sheer power of his oratory.

He described the disasters in the Far East at length, promised there would be more to come, acknowledged his own responsibility, and reminded his listeners that he had promised them nothing but "blood, toil, tears, and sweat." In the Far East there had been more blood, toil, tears, and sweat then people could endure. Sometimes he painted the picture even blacker than it was; and by stressing the universal disaster and the absolute necessity that everyone should fall in behind him so that a unified country could confront the dictators, he succeeded in avoiding any serious discussion of the real issue, which was whether he should be entrusted with total power, whether in fact he should be permitted to rule like a dictator. The alternative, never mentioned but clearly understood, was that unless he retained all his powers and offices he would retire to Chartwell and live out the war in silence. He was on the defensive; so was Britain; and as he spoke, he gave the illusion that Britain and Churchill were inseparable. "I am the man that Parliament and the nation have got to blame for the general way in which they are served," he declared, "and I cannot serve them effectively unless, in spite of all that has gone wrong, and that is going to go wrong, I have their trust and faithful aid."

He was performing a masterly exercise of begging the question; neither trust nor faithful aid were in dispute. Emanuel Shinwell found a parallel between Churchill and Pitt the Younger, and quoted Macaulay at considerable length in the hope that Churchill would recognize that there were pitfalls in popularity and power:

It may seem paradoxical to say that the incapacity which Pitt showed in all that related to the conduct of the war is, in some sense, the most decisive proof that he was a man of very extraordinary abilities. Yet this is the simple truth. For assuredly one-tenth part of his errors and disasters would have been fatal to the power and influence of any minister who had not possessed in the highest degree the talents of a parliamentary leader. While his schemes were confounded, while his predictions were falsified, while the coalitions which he had labored to form were falling to pieces, his authority over the House of Commons was constantly becoming more and more absolute. If some great misfortune had spread dismay through the ranks of his majority, that dismay lasted only until he rose from the Treasury Bench, drew up his haughty head, stretched his arm with commanding gesture and poured forth in deep and sonorous tones the lofty language of inexhaustible hope and inflexible resolution. Thus, through a long and calamitous period, every disaster that happened without the walls of Parliament was regularly followed by a triumph within them.

Does my Right Honourable friend [Shinwell asked] recognize himself in that vivid and colorful description?

Churchill was stung, but succeeded in concealing the wound. At all costs he would rule, and rule alone. It was not only that he would not consent to the slightest curtailment of his personal authority and responsibility, but he would insist upon acquiring even more authority and responsibility. He expected a ferocious debate, but it was surprisingly well-mannered. Before entering the chamber he reminded himself of a wise French saying: *"On ne règne sur les âmes que par le calme."* "One rules over souls only by calmness." He was one of those who possess a turbulent and vehement calm.

That calm, and his imperious manner, won the day. Six times altogether he had demanded an overwhelming vote of confidence, and he was not especially surprised when it was given to him by 464 to 1. The solitary holdout was the gaunt, smiling Jimmy Maxton of the Independent Labour Party, who represented Scottish miners and shipyard workers and knew better than most the temper of the working classes. He was like a small boy thumbing his nose at a policeman.

Churchill had promised more disasters, and they came in breathtaking numbers. The flood of calamity drowned East Asia and swept over Libya, while the U-boat menace in the Atlantic threatened to destroy more ships than the Allies could afford to lose. In January, 1942, eighteen merchant ships were sunk by torpedoes in the western North Atlantic. In the following month thirty-four ships were sunk. In those two months 586,000 tons of shipping were lost, and men thought the rate of sinking had reached its maximum, but this was only the beginning. In November of the same year 117 ships were sunk to a total of 700,000 dead-weight tons. Seamen thought they were lucky if they could make two crossings and survive.

On the night of February 11 the battle cruisers *Scharnhorst* and *Gneisenau* and the cruiser *Prinz Eugen* slipped out of the harbor at Brest and made their way to their home ports through the English Channel. It was a daring and resourceful feat, carefully planned. The warships passed through the Straits of Dover in broad daylight, invisible in the light mist. Too late the heavy guns at Dover opened fire and torpedo-carrying airplanes set out in pursuit and were blown out of the sky. More airplanes set out in pursuit; destroyers slipped out of Harwich to harass the warships, and none had any effect. The German ships led a charmed life. But the English public, who regarded the Channel as their own inviolate possession, their first and most powerful line of defense, were angry and disturbed. If these warships could come so close to British shores, and so stealthily, what was to prevent them from making a landing? This matter was so important that Churchill discussed it at length during a secret session held in the House of Commons on April 23, where he declared that the Admiralty had come to the conclusion that the German ships might indeed attempt to escape to their home ports through the English Channel and experts had written a memorandum to this effect ten days earlier. Then why had they been permitted to pass? He gave no answer, apparently concluding that the memorandum explained everything.

He thrived on disasters, and his speech was heavy with them. Singapore, Burma, Java, the Philippines, Libya, the ships sunk at Alexandria, all were explained, or explained away. The Japanese thrust into Southeast Asia had not been expected; it had been assumed that they were preoccupied with the conquest of China, "a weak nation, divided, and traditionally unwarlike." For four and a half years the Japanese had been pouring a million men into China and yet they were still far from a complete victory. Now the Japanese roamed the Pacific and the Indian oceans wherever they pleased.

For the first time the Members of Parliament learned about a fiery holocaust of British ships in the Indian Ocean. The cruisers *Dorsetshire* and *Cornwall* were sunk by torpedo-carrying bombers off Colombo and the aircraft carrier *Hermes* was sunk off Trincomalee, the naval base on the east coast of Ceylon. Two destroyers, the *Vampire* and the *Tenedos*, which rescued the survivors when the *Prince of Wales* and the *Repulse* were sunk off the coast of Malaya, were also sunk near Colombo. Churchill did not mention them in his speech. He took some satisfaction from the fact that Admiral Nagumo's carrier force, which had been ranging unmolested in the Pacific and the Indian oceans for four months, had been severely crippled by British airplane attacks and three of his aircraft carriers had limped back to Japan to be reequipped and refitted. It was very small comfort.

The danger—the very real danger—was that the Japanese would make a landing on the undefended coast of India and there perhaps join hands with a German army pressing down through Persia. The whole of Asia might fall in a few months to the Fascist powers. A sharp thrust at

Chungking, and the armies of Chiang Kai-shek would be thrown back toward the borders of Tibet. A landing in Australia, and the entire Australian continent would be lost to the Allies. Never in history had a conqueror emerged in Asia with such a vast preponderance of power employed so speedily and triumphantly. Never had the prospects of an Allied victory looked gloomier than in the first six months of 1942.

The Allies had to content themselves with small, indecisive and sometimes imaginary victories. Chiang Kai-shek announced that a skirmish at Changsha was a battle which would inevitably change the entire fortunes of the war: he proclaimed that he had stopped the westward advance of Japan. In fact, the Chinese, who had been fighting the Japanese since 1931, had no more fight in them; the front was stabilized, and the military commanders on both sides grew rich on the proceeds of trade, while Chiang Kai-shek's government grew increasingly corrupt. China became more a liability than an asset. Vast quantities of American supplies poured into China, to be hoarded by the Nationalist government for eventual use against the Chinese Communists. Churchill sent a special message to Chiang Kai-shek, announcing that the war against Japan was secondary to the war against Hitler: an impolitic and dangerous message, for the enraged Generalissimo concluded that the United States and Britain could now do his fighting for him. Sir Archibald Clark-Kerr, the British ambassador to Chungking, was transferred to Moscow, and with his departure British influence in China came to an end.

Another small, indecisive and perhaps imaginary victory occurred at the end of April, when Churchill ordered the attack on Díego Suarez, the naval base on the northern tip of Madagascar, then a French colony ruled from Vichy. Díego Suarez was captured without difficulty and played no further part in the war. Nothing was lost, but also nothing was gained. Díego Suarez was one of Churchill's follies.

Where to strike? All through the spring and summer Churchill found himself gazing at a map of the world and attempting to determine the weak points in the enemy's armor. Rangoon, Petsamo, Spitsbergen, French Morocco, all these offered dazzling prospects. Then it occurred to him that an attack on northern Norway offered even more substantial prospects. Stalin had asked for it; it would impress Sweden and Finland; the northern convoys would be protected; an army once established in northern Norway could then make its way southward and "unroll the Nazi map of Europe from the top." Churchill liked the idea so much that he gave it the code name "Operation Jupiter" and insisted against the vehement objections of his military staff that the plan should be worked out in minute detail. Brooke spent long nights with Churchill, continually inventing new arguments against the plan, only to discover that Churchill with his greater powers of invention was quite capable of destroying them with arguments of his own. Brooke thought a fifth of the transports would be blown out of the sea before they reached Norway. Churchill replied firmly: "A military attack is not ruled out simply because a fifth of the soldiers may be shot on the way."

At the beginning of June Churchill was telling himself that the time had come for another visit with Roosevelt. There was no urgent need for the journey, and he appears to have regarded it as one of those rites of passage made necessary by his own changing fortunes, which were now at a low ebb. The war was entering a new and unpredictable phase and something might be gained by a journey to the source of power. He had learned one important lesson: warships should not be used as though they were passenger ships. He would go by air, with only Brooke, his doctor and a small staff in attendance. Before leaving for the United States he wrote a letter to King George VI, asking that in the event of his death Anthony Eden should be appointed his successor.

He traveled by special train to Loch Stranraer in southern Scotland where a Boeing Clipper was waiting for him. Brooke remembered him walking up and down the quay waiting to embark on the motorboat which would take him to the huge seaplane, wearing his boiler suit, a black Homburg hat tipped to one side, and a small gold-mounted Malacca cane in his hand. He was humming: "We're here because we're here, because we're here, because we're here," but he did not really know what he was doing there. "We were both somewhat doubtful why we were going, whether we should get there, what we would achieve while we were there, and whether we should ever get back," Brooke commented. The journey from Stranraer to the Potomac by way of Newfoundland would last twenty-seven hours. Churchill enjoyed the exhausting flight, ate hugely, smoked continuously, and he had just finished a large dinner and was relaxing with a whiskey and soda when the Clipper taxied to its moorings on the Potomac. It was 6 P.M. Washington time and he was immediately whisked away to another large dinner at the British Embassy.

This time there was something more than trivialities and general discussions to show for the journey. The huge American industrial machine was now geared for war and was able to dispense armaments on a gigantic scale, and though there was little to show for it in victories, no one in America doubted that the massive machinery would eventually overwhelm the Fascist powers. The tide had not yet turned, but there was that strange quivering of the sea which shows that the tide will soon be turning and carrying everything before it.

Churchill was in good humor when he flew up to Hyde Park to meet Roosevelt. Both the Americans and the British had achieved some important successes, although they could not be described as victories. On May 30 the Royal Air Force sent its first thousand-bomber raid over Cologne, one of the German cities marked for inevitable destruction. Reports from North Africa were encouraging. At the Battle of Midway early in June Admiral Chester Nimitz, while he had failed to break the full force of Japanese naval air power in the central Pacific, had at least demonstrated that the enemy's prowling aircraft carriers were vulnerable, and by sinking four of Admiral Nagumo's carriers, including his flagship, he had demonstrated American power where the Japanese thought it had been lost for ever.

The talk at Hyde Park was leisurely and optimistic. Roosevelt, using a car with manual controls, drove Churchill over the estate, which was thickly wooded and stood high above the Hudson River. Sometimes, in sheer exuberance, Roosevelt backed the car until it was within a few inches of the cliff edge. Churchill confessed that he had "some thoughtful moments." Once Roosevelt flexed his biceps and invited Churchill to feel them; they were indeed very powerful and Churchill was suitably impressed, but he took care not to discuss war matters for fear that Roosevelt would become engrossed in the conversation and drive into the river.

They were still in good spirits when they both returned to Washington. There, on the morning of June 21, Churchill suffered one of the most traumatic experiences of his life. He had just entered the President's study when a secretary came in with a pink slip of paper. The President read it and handed it silently to Churchill. Typewritten on the pink paper were the words: TOBRUK HAS FALLEN, WITH TWENTY-FIVE THOUSAND MEN TAKEN PRISONER. Churchill seemed to crumple. This was another Singapore, another disaster of the first magnitude, and might have even more disastrous consequences than the loss of Malaya and the East Indies. Rommel was now free to advance on Alexandria and beyond and to link up with the German forces in the Caucasus. What made the news all the more surprising was that Tobruk was, as Singapore was not, a fortress defended by seasoned troops, well-supplied and well-equipped, and under the command of officers believed to be more resourceful than General Percival and his staff. In fact, Tobruk had successfully withstood a siege of thirty-three weeks the year before. Roosevelt said quietly: "What can we do to help?"

"Give us as many Sherman tanks as you can spare," Churchill replied, "and ship them to the Middle East as quickly as possible."

The President summoned General Marshall, who now found himself under the necessity of giving to the British weapons that were sorely needed by the Americans. "If the British need is so great they must have them," he said, adding that they could have one hundred 105 mm self-propelled guns in addition. Three hundred Sherman tanks and one hundred self-propelled guns were sent to the Suez Canal, and when the ship containing the engines for the tanks was sunk off Bermuda the Americans provided another fast ship, filled it with engines, and sent it off to overtake the convoy.

Tobruk was an unmitigated disaster; the sending of the tanks was a triumph. It justified Churchill's visit to America, and his grand strategy. A few days later, when he returned to London and found Parliament up in arms against him—for a noisy minority had lost faith in him and accused him of practicing the same dictatorial methods as Hitler, who had long ago announced that "the Fuehrer is always right"—he was able to show that the grand strategy was soundly conceived, however desperate the present straits, and nothing would be gained by throwing Churchill overboard. Nevertheless the opposition was also justified. Sir John Wardlaw-Milne was responsible for the wording on the Order Paper:

> That this House, while paying tribute to the heroism and endurance of the Armed Forces of the Crown in circumstances of exceptional difficulty, has no confidence in the central direction of the war.

Wardlaw-Milne was not a rabble-rouser; he was a Conservative with a long career in politics and was chairman of the powerful Finance Committee; he had thought very seriously about the problem and had come to the conclusion that Churchill should be deprived of one or other of his offices. What was needed was a strong prime minister and a strong defense minister. It was a sound argument, but the speaker went on to suggest that there should also be a strong Commander in Chief of the armed forces and suggested that the Duke of Gloucester should be appointed to this position. The Duke of Gloucester was the least popular and the least intelligent member of the royal family, and even though Wardlaw-Milne wanted him to become Commander in Chief without administrative duties, it was obvious that he had not thought out the problem, was hesitating, and was merely making confused gestures. Sir Roger Keyes, the hero of the naval attack on Zeebrugge in the First World War, seconded the motion, resplendent in his admiral's uniform, but he kept harping so much on Churchill's undoubted abilities that he spoiled his case. The real issue was to decide whether to relieve Churchill of some of his burdens, but Churchill pretended to see it as an assault on his conduct of the war. He had made terrible mistakes; they were pointed out to him; he accepted full responsibility, and advanced to the attack. It was an unfair contest. He said:

> If today, or at any future time, the House were to exercise its undoubted right, I could walk out with a good conscience and the feeling that I have done my duty according to such light as has been granted to me. There is only one thing I would ask of you in that event. It would be to give my successor the modest powers which would have been denied to me.

That, of course, was to beg the question. It was precisely because his powers were so immodest that he was being called to account. There were perfectly satisfactory arguments for his replacement, or for a diminution of his powers, but they were not made. The rebels were defeated by 475 votes to 25, and Churchill's victory was complete.

So, too, was the victory of the Axis in North Africa. General Erwin Rommel was promoted to Field Marshal and Mussolini took the occasion to fly to North Africa to hold a series of victory processions and parades, riding a white horse, brandishing his fists, and looking forward to the time when Egypt would become part of the Italian empire. But while he was on the way to Africa, the wheel of fortune had already turned, for Rommel had been stopped at El Alamein. The long battle would be fought throughout July, but what Churchill liked to call "the hinge of fate" had already turned and opened up as yet unsuspected possibilities for the Allies.

Throughout July decisions were being made that would have enduring influence on the course of the war. The first decision was to abandon all plans for crossing the Channel until 1943 or 1944. The second was to occupy French North Africa from the west, thus catching Rommel in a vise, and opening up a second front. General Marshall was opposed to the invasion of French North Africa; President Roosevelt approved; and thus ":Torch," formerly "Gymnast" came into operation later in the year. The code name "Torch" had the merit of suggesting a flaming attack, while "Gymnast" suggested a wrestling match.

Churchill liked to keep moving, and now it occurred to him that he could combine a visit to Moscow with a visit to Cairo. He had decided to relieve General Sir Claude Auchinleck, Commander in Chief, Middle East, and to replace him with General Sir Harold Alexander, who would assume complete charge of the fighting forces in the Western Desert. Auchinleck had twice saved the Eighth Army from disaster, but there was a general feeling that he was no match for Rommel. Once he reached Cairo and settled down in the British Embassy, Churchill thought only about Rommel. It was like a chorus. "Rommel, Rommel, Rommel," he shouted, striding up and down the carpet. "What else matters but beating him!" So Auchinleck was dismissed, Alexander took over the command, and Churchill flew on to Moscow for his first meeting with Stalin, who was now in Churchill's eyes "the great Revolutionary Chief and profound Russian statesman and warrior."

The Russians had given him "State Villa No. 7" as his private residence while in Moscow. This was a small palace set in some woods and surrounded by a high palisade. The rooms were royally furnished; every kind of wine and food was available; and the brilliant chandeliers shone down on rich carpets and gleaming furniture. Accustomed to luxury, Churchill was overwhelmed by the fantastic luxury provided by the Soviets. The entrance to the air raid shelter was a short distance away in the woods. One went down an electric elevator, passed through a corridor lined with wooden panelling and colored marble, and entered a suite of ten or eleven luxurious rooms all brilliantly illuminated and provided with candles in heavy silver candelabra in case the electricity failed. The refrigerators in the air raid shelter were piled with food; there were servants' quarters; and every door was guarded by the ever-present secret police.

So, too, in "State Villa No. 7" where the beaming servants in white jackets all carried themselves with the unmistakable distinguishing marks of the secret police. Churchill was provided with a massively handsome aide-de-camp who spoke English well and carried himself like a prince. He was so different from all the other Russians Churchill had met that he came to the conclusion that the aide-de-camp was a Russian prince with an impeccable Tsarist ancestry.

Understandably the meetings with Stalin were stormy. Stalin was determined that Britain and America should open a second front in Europe, and Churchill was just as determined to wait until sufficient forces and supplies were available. Stalin, full of rancor, wondered why a vast army could not cross a small ditch. Was it, he suggested, because they were afraid? Was it that they did not really intend to fight? Fighting, he insisted, was not altogether unpleasant once you have started. He spoke in a low gravelly voice, never looking directly at Churchill, making only occasional slow gestures with his right hand, insolent and terrifying.

Churchill also could be insolent and terrifying. He crashed his fist down on the table to indicate that he had had enough and said he knew as much about fighting as Stalin, had been fighting Hitler when Stalin was sitting on the sidelines, and would tolerate no more insults directed at the British fighting forces. It appears that the translator out of misplaced tact did not translate very accurately, but Stalin was aware of the gist of what was being said. He stood up, sucking at his large bent pipe, and said: "I do not understand what you are saying, but by God, I like your sentiment!"

The ice now thawed, and soon they were able to speak more normally, though still under strain. Churchill made it clear that an invasion of France in 1942 was the purest folly; an invasion by 200,000 men would scarcely draw a single German soldier from the Eastern Front, and all the prospects of an invasion in 1943 would be spoiled. He proceeded to unfold a map of Southern Europe, the Mediterranean and North Africa to explain the operation called "Torch": the difficulties and dangers of the enterprise being minimal, the effect on Hitler likely to be very great, for the soft underbelly of Europe would then present itself to the guns of the Allies poised on the northern shores of Africa. Stalin had apparently heard nothing previously about "Torch." Realizing that the invasion of France was not likely to occur in the near future, he accepted the invasion of Africa with good grace, remarking that it would overawe Spain, bring about fighting between the Germans and French in France, hit Rommel in the back and expose Italy to the whole brunt of the war. Churchill thought Stalin was being remarkably perceptive. But there is no evidence to show that Spain was overawed or that "Torch" produced any fighting between the Germans and

French in France, and there is a good deal of evidence to show that the invasion of Italy was an error of staggering proportions. Nevertheless "Torch" had the merit of clearing Rommel out of Africa, which was the main thing. As they stood comfortably round the large globe in Stalin's office, which was decorated only with this globe and a portrait of Lenin, it seemed that the war had become manageable at last. Stalingrad was still a few months away.

Churchill returned to "State Villa No. 7." The weather was fine, the birds sang, the August heat was bracing, and there came the pleasant smell of the pinewoods surrounding the palatial villa. He examined the air raid shelter ninety feet below ground and walked in the well-kept gardens. The high palisade surrounding the property was painted green, and looked innocuous. At intervals there were slits and the guards outside looked in, to see that order was being preserved. Beyond the palisade were barbed wire entanglements, concrete machine gun posts, guards everywhere. It appeared that "State Villa No. 7" was one of Stalin's many residences and that he was taking no chances. The fortifications were designed to protect the villa from the Russians, not from the Germans.

There were more meetings with Stalin, some more stormy than others. Stalin still wanted a second front in France, and from time to time he would revert savagely to this theme, accusing Churchill of incompetence and worse because he could not ferry an army across the Channel. Churchill concluded quite wrongly that Stalin was merely the conveyor of messages from the Russian High Command, and when he returned to this theme it was because he received orders to do so. "They may have more power than we suppose, and less knowledge," Churchill wrote to the Cabinet from Moscow, thus defending Stalin against the *Stavka*. What was really happening was that Stalin was attempting to wear Churchill down, and he continued to do so even during those long ceremonial dinners with their incessant toasts when most of the guests were half drunk and Churchill himself was three sheets to the wind, garrulous and rosy-cheeked, expanding into a vast conviviality over a nineteen course dinner.

There were moments when Stalin went out of the way to please Churchill. Once when Churchill reminded the dictator that in 1920 he had bent all his efforts toward crushing the Russian Revolution, Stalin smiled and said it was all forgiven now. "All that is in the past," he said, "and the past belongs to God." It was surprising how often Stalin invoked God in his utterances. To please Churchill, Stalin spoke of the Dardanelles campaign, saying that he had information that the Turks and the Germans were about to pull out when the British finally withdrew. This was untrue, but Churchill thought it was kindly meant. And when Churchill asked Stalin why he had taken no account of the messages warning him of an imminent German attack, Stalin answered blandly that he knew very well the war was coming but was hoping for another six months' grace. Churchill sensibly refrained from asking why, in that case, he expected that Britain should feel any gratitude toward a man who had connived with Hitler for the sake of a dubious grace. Stalin's errors were conveniently forgotten; a fair amount of agreement was being reached; and still, from time to time, there came the menacing insults, the sullen rages, the interminable sense of being in an alien and incomprehensible world.

At seven o'clock in the evening of August 15 Churchill went to Stalin's office in the Kremlin to say good-bye. It was to be a brief meeting followed by a long night's rest at the villa and a flight at dawn to Cairo. They talked perfunctorily about the defenses of the Caucasus and the German plan to drive southward to Persia, and when it was time to go, Churchill rose, and Stalin suggested that instead of parting, they should have drinks in his own apartment. So they wandered through the Kremlin corridors until they reached the street, and then it was only a short distance to Stalin's modest house, where they were met by a pretty red-headed girl, Stalin's daughter Svetlana, and an old housekeeper. Stalin suggested they should have dinner together, with Molotov. So they dined, and much later in the evening a suckling pig was brought in. Stalin cleaned out the pig's head and ate what was inside with relish; then he cut off pieces of the pig's cheeks and ate them. At one point Churchill asked Stalin about the years when the Russian farmers were forced into collectives. Was it, Churchill asked, as bad as the war? "Worse. Much worse. It went on for years," Stalin replied. He spoke of the kulaks, the rich farmers, who were exterminated. "Most of them were liquidated by the peasants, who hated them. Ten million of them. But we had to do it to mechanize our agriculture. In the end, production from the land was doubled. What is one generation?" It was the usual escalating argument: first, a few hundred thousand kulaks, then ten million peasants, then a whole generation. Churchill was learning how a dictator's mind works.

He flew to Cairo, visited the troops in the Western Desert, visited

General Montgomery in his caravan by the seashore, bathed in the Mediterranean, and was soon back in England to face the problem that the American and British Chiefs of Staff were at loggerheads over "Torch," the Americans wanting to confine it to attacks on Casablanca and Oran, postponing indefinitely the attack on Algiers. Churchill went into shock and emerged fuming. But the quarrel between the Chiefs of Staff was patched up, and early in September President Roosevelt and Churchill exchanged their most felicitous messages:

5 September 1942. President Roosevelt to Prime Minister: HURRAH!
6 September 1942. Former Naval Person to President Roosevelt: O.K. FULL BLAST.

When, in later years, Churchill looked back on the war and pondered what were the most anxious months, he usually concluded that September and October, 1942, were the worst. They were the months when he feared a German breakthrough into Persia and Egypt, a general collapse in the Middle East and Southern Russia, and a grave political crisis in Britain. Opposition to his conduct of the war was increasing; Sir Stafford Cripps, Lord Trenchard, and many more were saying that he was unfit to govern, that he was too capricious, too arrogant, too self-absorbed to take on "the central direction of the war." They would have been even more alarmed if they had known that Sir Alan Brooke, the tight-lipped Irishman who was Chief of the Imperial General Staff, was writing in his diary that he was becoming increasingly exasperated by Churchill's assumption that he had inherited all the military genius of his great ancestor, the Duke of Marlborough, and could be turned away from his wildest and most dangerous ideas only by superhuman efforts. Churchill was his own idol and becoming increasingly idolatrous. As the war continued and his strength flagged and his effective power lessened, for "the central direction of the war" was falling into the hands of Stalin and Roosevelt, so his self-idolatry was being fanned to white heat and his judgment weakened by self-praise. Churchill had always applauded himself; now the applause became deafening.

By October, 1942, the war had acquired its own momentum and existed independently of the war leaders. If Stalin, Roosevelt and Churchill had died in that month, the war would inevitably have followed the same course, the same objectives would have been pursued, the same dead would lie on the same battlefields. The decisions had been made and for all the remaining years of the war there would be only the working out of a long-drawn tragedy. Act one and act two had been written; act three merely developed the characters and attitudes already engendered and led them to their fatal consummation. At the end of the tragedy most of the heroes and villains would be lying dead on the stage.

Meanwhile the flood of calamities was subsiding; the hard, decisive winter was approaching. The Americans landed at Casablanca on the Atlantic coast of Morocco and the British landed at Algiers and Oran, where the French put up a ferocious but short-lived resistance under the orders of the Vichy government. A few days earlier, during the first week of November, the Eighth Army under General Montgomery punched a hole through General Rommel's armor and poured through it, routing the enemy. Montgomery and Alexander had won the first major land battle of the war, and soon there would be more victories. Tunis was captured in December; the rout of Rommel's forces continued; and although the fighting in Africa continued well into the new year—the last Italians and Germans did not leave African soil until May—the outcome was never in doubt. At a luncheon given in the City of London to celebrate Lord Mayor's Day Churchill mused about the exact point the Allies had reached in the war, and though he spoke hesitantly, refusing to commit himself, there was a certain exactness in his statement that they had reached "not the end, not even the beginning of the end, but, perhaps, the end of the beginning." A little later in the speech he proclaimed his article of faith. "I have not become the King's First Minister," he declared, "in order to preside over the liquidation of the British Empire." On this point he was adamant. It was his tragedy that in his lifetime the British Empire would dissolve like a dream that is faded.

So many successes in North Africa demanded a celebration on African soil, and accordingly arrangements were made for a grand meeting between Stalin, Roosevelt and Churchill at Casablanca. Stalin said he was too busy, and with good reason, for the Battle of Stalingrad was still being fought, but Roosevelt and Churchill met on schedule, to be photographed with General Giraud and a reluctant General de Gaulle, both contenders for the military rule over the Free French; and while Churchill had long ago accustomed himself to the genius of the prickly De Gaulle, Roosevelt at last found some merit in him, saying afterward that he had detected something spiritual in his eyes, an odd comment from a man who was not notable for detecting spirituality. At the Casablanca Conference it was decided that Sicily should be the next target, that Eisenhower should become the Commander in Chief of the Allied Forces in Africa, and that "unconditional surrender" would be demanded of the Germans, the Italians and the Japanese. These two words begat many controversies, and the German generals at the end of the war would complain bitterly that these words hampered their efforts to destroy Hitler, an argument which would have been more convincing if they had made any serious and concerted effort to kill him, for he was often in their power. And when the conference was over, Churchill prevailed on Roosevelt to accompany him to Marrakesh, the delectable city, "the Paris of the Sahara," where in the words of Churchill, who loved the city to distraction, there could be found "the largest and most elaborately organized brothels in the African continent."

Churchill wanted to paint the city walls and the Atlas mountains. A certain Mrs. Taylor had placed her villa at his disposal, and since the house was luxuriously furnished and possessed a good view of the mountains, he was perfectly content to rest in it. To this house, early one morning, the Chief of the Imperial General Staff was summoned by telephone to find Churchill sitting up in bed in a setting that suggested he had been transformed into a Moroccan pasha:

> The room must have been Mrs. Taylor's bedroom and was done up in Moorish style, the ceiling was a marvellous fresco of green, blue and gold. The head of the bed rested in an alcove of Moorish design with a religious light shining on either side; the bed was covered with a light blue silk covering with 6-in. wide lace *entre-deux* and the rest of the room in harmony with the Arabic ceiling. And there in the bed was Winston in his green, red and gold dragon dressing-gown, his hair, or what there is of it, standing on end, the religious lights shining on his cheeks, and a large cigar in his face.

General Sir Alan Brooke was nonplussed by the spectacle of Churchill playing the role of a pasha or a Grand Mughal, and he was even more nonplussed when he learned that Churchill had suddenly and quite capriciously decided to fly off to Cairo that very evening. This decision, like so many of his decisions, had been made on the spur of the moment, apparently with the aim of startling his closest military adviser, who had made plans to spend the day partridge hunting. The partridges were spared, and that evening the two Liberators with Churchill and his large staff flew off to Cairo. When he arrived at the British Embassy in Cairo early the next morning, the ambassador's wife offered him a cup of tea, which he indignantly refused, calling for a glass of white wine. He gulped down the wine and announced proudly: "Ah! that is good, but you know I have already had two whiskies and soda and two cigars this morning." That, too, was part of the problem. He was drinking much more than was good for him and his judgment was often clouded.

No one knew what he hoped to accomplish in Cairo. At one time he had considered paying a visit to the Oasis of Siwa, where Alexander the Great consulted the Oracle of Amon and learned, so it was believed, that he would become emperor of the world. But such a journey by the Prime Minister might raise questions in Parliament and he sensibly refrained. Instead he permitted Alexander and Brooke to make the journey in his place. They were received by the local Arabs with gifts of sweet dates and sweet lemons, saw the ruins of the Oracle, drank highly flavored tea and returned to Cairo the same day. Churchill was celebrating a new coup, for the president of Turkey had at last agreed to meet him and the Cabinet no longer raised objections. While lying in his luxurious bed in Mrs. Taylor's villa he had received cables from the Cabinet urging him to do nothing so foolhardy as to visit Turkey, which was honeycombed with German agents. Now the Cabinet relented, and Churchill flew off to Adana to meet President Ismet Inönü and Field Marshal Fevzi Cakmak and representatives of the Turkish armed forces. Churchill addressed them in flowery French with some English words pronounced in French; later he learned that Inönü and Cakmak were both deaf but understood English if it was spoken loud enough. Brooke learned that Cakmak had no conception of modern war; Churchill learned from the Turkish foreign minister that the whole of Turkey was delighted with his arrival. This was a shock because he had thought the visit was supersecret, and he had only to look outside the train, where the conversations were taking place, to observe how incompetently it was being guarded by a handful of Turkish soldiers. Nothing except goodwill came from his conversations with the Turks, and he flew off again, this time to Cyprus or to Egypt—he was not quite sure where he wanted to go, and finally, when they were already in the air, he settled on Cyprus for no reason that anyone was able to discover.

It was observed that his moods changed abruptly from hour to hour.

He was behaving in a very strained manner, wildly excited one moment, morose the next. Something had gone wrong. He flew back to London, and then it was learned that he was ill. He was suffering from pneumonia. For a week he was out of circulation; for a month he was a shadow of himself. Roosevelt, too, was suffering from pneumonia, while Gandhi, in Poona, had chosen this moment to go on a hunger strike. For a brief while it looked as though the three giants would soon be swept from the scene. Brooke went to visit Churchill on the night of March 1. The color was coming back in his cheeks and he was saying cheerfully of the Turks: "We must start by treating them purry-purry, puss-puss, then later we shall harden." Turkey, it seemed, was an extension of the soft underbelly of Europe which would inevitably fall to the Allies. But the Turks remained obdurately neutral, and Churchill was to learn that the soft underbelly was very hard indeed.

THE SOFT UNDERBELLY

ONE OF CHURCHILL's most dangerous beliefs was that there existed a soft underbelly of Europe. It was his impression, derived from youthful studies of geography, that Europe resembled a large animal, perhaps a bison, whose plunging head was Spain, whose body was made up of France, Germany, Poland, Austria, Hungary, Czechoslovakia, Yugoslavia and Rumania, and whose legs were Italy and Greece. The soft underbelly was to be found between the legs, especially along the Istrian Peninsula near Trieste from which Vienna could be reached by way of the Ljubljana Gap. A linkup with the Russians in the Balkans or in Austria would, he thought, bring the war to a speedy end. The idea haunted him, and he was especially pleased when he learned that General Smuts heartily agreed with him. But the Americans resisted the idea firmly. General Marshall was convinced that the soft underbelly was armorplated. As he expressed it, "the soft underbelly has chrome-plated sides."

Churchill had a habit of relentlessly pursuing his ideas even when they were doomed. He never lost an opportunity to advance the cause of the soft underbelly, deplored American intransigence, and was continually gazing at the map of southeastern Europe where, as he believed, a brave man might find the secret key to the destruction of

Nazi Germany. Greece and the Balkans were continually in his mind, and throughout the war he thought longingly of the day when Turkey would declare herself on the side of the Allies. To the Americans, almost from the beginning, Churchill's strategic concepts involving advances in southeastern Europe seemed curiously unreal, as though some impediment of the mind prevented him from recognizing that the only way to defeat Hitler was by means of an armored attack supported by overwhelming air power on a broad front. They felt that he possessed an incurable predilection for eccentric operations of all kinds. Sudden raids, lures, entrapments, simultaneous guerrilla operations, surprise maneuvers powerfully attracted Churchill. The Americans regarded them as a waste of time and energy. Churchill's concept was to "hit 'em where they ain't." The American concept was to hit them where they are, massively, until there was nothing left of them.

Partly, of course, this arose from a difference of temperament. For Churchill, war was a game of cut and thrust like a duel with rapiers, and there was still some element of gallantry in it. For the Americans, war was a mass of armor advancing against another mass of armor and crushing it into the ground. Roosevelt, who enjoyed listening to Churchill's strategical concepts and saw much merit in them, was placed in a difficult position, for he recognized the virtues of both attitudes and had to adjudicate between them. In the end both got what they wanted. Churchill was permitted to spin out his theories and occasionally to embark on those minor raiding operations which were intended as overtures to larger and deeper raids, while Roosevelt and his military advisers (including Harry Hopkins) held fast to the concept of the massive, broad-fronted, heavily protected attack across the Channel: a wall of steel advancing across northern France into Germany. Churchill complained that such an attack would transform the Channel into a "river of blood." The Americans had no illusions about the amount of blood that would be spilled, but they were determined not to engage in small wars of attrition.

Secretary of War Henry Stimson was one of many who saw that the British and American concepts were poles apart. "The difference between us is a vital difference of faith," he wrote to Roosevelt, comparing the American belief that Germany could be beaten by massive armor combined with overwhelming air power and the British belief in "a series of attritions in northern Italy, in the eastern Mediterranean, in Greece, in the Balkans, in Rumania and other satellite countries." This was what he derisively called "pinprick warfare." "We are pledged quite as openly as Great Britain to the opening of a real second front," he wrote, adding that the only way to do it was to mount the cross-Channel invasion under an American commander, preferably General Marshall, because the British, though rendering lip service to the operation, were still terrified by the memory of Passchendaele in the First World War and of Dunkirk. He was saying that the only chance of success lay in doing it in the American way.

But while the Americans held strongly to the belief that massive armor and overwhelming air power were needed to destroy Germany, they did not always practice their beliefs. The Allies had conquered North Africa, the last remnants of the German and Italian forces had been swept into prison camps, and huge armies were poised for action in the Mediterranean theater. What was to be done with them? The Combined Chiefs of Staff concluded that these armies should be used for an attack on Sicily and on southern Italy. The attack on Sicily had the merit of destroying the German air bases on the island, but the attack on southern Italy had almost no merit at all. At no point did anyone suggest that Italy could be left to stew in its own juices, nor, apparently, did any of the Allied commanders study relief maps of the boot of Italy. The Italian campaign followed neither the American nor the British pattern. No massive, annihilating force was directed against a single objective. The campaign was conceived in error and conducted by incompetent generals at a staggering cost in human lives. Here, if anywhere, Churchill's concept of sudden raids and diversions would have produced remarkable dividends. If the objective of the Allies was a knockout blow on Berlin and the heart of Germany, no one in his senses would imagine that the objective could be reached by marching up and down all the mountains and valleys of Italy from the tropical toe in the south to the snow-covered mountains in the north.

Yet this was precisely what was done with the agreement of Churchill, Roosevelt and the Chiefs of Staff, and with the approval of Stalin.

Unknown to the Allies, Hitler had given up all hope of holding Italy and was preparing to build a blocking wall in the northern mountains. He had no liking for the Italians, and no faith in their powers of resistance. After the fall of Mussolini on July 25, 1943, it became obvious that the Italians had no heart for any further fighting and Italy was lost to Hitler. He would inflict as much damage as possible on the Italians, and perhaps arrest the Pope, the royal family, and the government. He did not envisage a long-drawn-out Italian campaign.

He was preoccupied with the war in Russia and regarded Italy as a minor theater of war.

To his surprise the Allies invaded Italy in force and in places where the German troops were waiting for them. On September 9 American and British forces landed on a wide crescent of beaches at Salerno thirty miles south of Naples. They established a beachhead and began moving across a narrow plain in the direction of the jagged mountains ahead. Field Marshal Albert Kesselring was ready for them and ordered a counterattack which was astonishingly successful. The Allies were almost thrown back into the sea and secured a foothold only after a week of wild slaughter. Hitler abandoned the plan of building a blocking wall in the north.

Churchill, who was staying at Hyde Park at the time of the Salerno landing, was full of foreboding. "Operation Avalanche" had his full blessing, but he had never studied the operation in detail and had very little knowledge of the confused situation in Italy. General Smuts, whose advice he nearly always took seriously even when he did not follow it, had just warned him against attacking in southern Italy. Smuts was all for attacking in northern Italy, thus avoiding a long and costly campaign all along the peninsula. Churchill answered: "We hope presently to open a heavy front across Italy as far north as we can get. Such a front will absorb about twenty divisions from the Mediterranean, and may require reinforcements if selected for counter-attack by the enemy." But there existed no plans for "a heavy front across Italy" in the north. Instead British, American, French and Polish troops were battling every inch of the way against skillful and determined resistance in the south, and were lucky if they advanced half a mile in a day. Throughout the autumn, winter and early spring they continued to fight on a terrain where all the advantages lay with the enemy. The heavily fortified Gustav Line, anchored on Monte Cassino and the surrounding mountain massifs, guarded the approaches to Rome. This was a war of attrition with little coherence or discernible design.

It was as though the Allies had been fatally attracted to fighting the wrong war in the wrong place at the wrong time. Hitler was jubilant, for the Allies were being burned and bled and savaged in country where it was virtually impossible for them to use their armor and where their air power counted for little. General Westphal, who was Kesselring's Chief of Staff, observed that the Allies blundered into the trap prepared for them because they lacked the daring to advance beyond the range of their air cover, but it is rarely air cover that decides the issue of a war.

If they had landed at Civitavecchia, forty miles north of Rome, they would have been able to take Rome in seventy-two hours. Instead it took them nine months. "Operation Avalanche" was misnamed. It should have been called "Operation Slow Trickle."

The blunders of the Combined Chiefs of Staff augured badly for the future conduct of the war. It was not only generalship that was lacking; the politicians, too, seemed to be losing their grip. Roosevelt, depending more and more on General Marshall's advice, was withdrawing slowly from the role of Commander in Chief. On political matters he appeared hesitant and uncertain, without any clear-cut vision concerning the tremendous issues which would inevitably arise as the war drew to a close. Stalin baffled him and he was growing weary of Churchill's importunities; it was easier to leave everything to his own military staff. While Roosevelt was in a kind of stupor, Churchill grew visibly more impatient, more reckless, and the tone of his communications was becoming more strident. Above all he was a political animal. He was profoundly aware of the dangerous situation which would arise when Russian troops poured into Germany, and he was still hoping to establish a presence in southeastern Europe even if it meant knifing into the buttocks rather than the soft underbelly. He felt sure that Turkey could be induced to enter the war, but only on condition that the Allies made a show of force in the Eastern Mediterranean. Rhodes could be conquered; the Greek islands would become stepping stones to Bulgaria and Rumania and a meeting with the Red Army on the Danube. On his own authority he ordered General Sir Henry Maitland Wilson to seize the islands of Cos, Samos and Leros in the Aegean Sea. The Germans sent naval and airborne forces to recover the islands; at Leros the British were able to rescue a thousand troops, but five thousand were killed or captured, while four destroyers and two submarines were destroyed and four cruisers were damaged. In the eyes of the Americans this was just one more of Churchill's eccentric and irrational operations. When he pleaded to renew the engagement with the island of Rhodes as the prize, demanding "modest" supplies of troops, ships and airplanes for the invasion, Eisenhower turned him down abruptly; and thereafter Churchill could be heard grumbling about the ingratitude of the Americans who had taken his best armies and rejected his modest request.

More and more in that unhappy autumn Churchill talked about "my" armies, "my" people, "my" policies, where previously he had been careful to deny ownership. *Hubris* was manifesting itself; it fed on his frustrations and glowed in the light of his fears and apprehensions.

He had reason to be fearful, and not only because he felt that his relationship with Roosevelt was slipping into a strange twilight zone of casual friendship. He was fearful of the secret weapons which were being manufactured by the Germans; the Italian campaign was going badly; the loss of the Dodecanese islands had affected him deeply; and he was unwell—physically and emotionally drained. When the long delayed triangular meeting of the three war leaders took place in Teheran, Churchill was not in good shape, and sometimes he displayed an unexpected flash of bitterness. He was going to attend a meeting which might have incalculable influence upon the history of the world, but it was unlikely that he would have the dominating voice.

He left Plymouth on the *Renown* on the afternoon of November 12 for the long journey to Alexandria. It was arranged that he would meet Roosevelt and Chiang Kai-shek in Cairo, and then fly on to Teheran. There had been some questions raised about whether Cairo was a safe meeting place because it was in reach of German bombers based on Rhodes, and Khartoum had been suggested as an alternative. But with eight squadrons of British aircraft based on Cairo, Churchill felt rightly that the meeting could take place in reasonable safety; and when Roosevelt radioed from the battleship *Iowa* some reservations about the choice of a meeting place, Churchill radioed back: "See St. John, chapter xiv, verses 1 to 4." These verses, taken out of context, wonderfully conveyed his mood, his intentions, and his troubled affection for Roosevelt. They read:

Let not your heart be troubled; ye believe in God, believe also in me.

In my Father's house are many mansions: if it were not so, I would have told you. I go to prepare a place for you.

And if I go and prepare a place for you, I will come again, and receive you unto myself; that where I am, there ye may be also.

And whither I go ye know, and the way ye know.

Churchill was a little perturbed by the thought that he was taking too much upon himself, saying in effect: "I am the way," and committing various sins of blasphemy, but he had rarely delivered a more touching message to Roosevelt who, when he reached Cairo, seemed scarcely aware of Churchill's existence.

Cairo, for Churchill, was purgatory. Roosevelt had spent a great deal of time wrestling with the problem of China and her strange, gaunt Generalissimo. He regarded himself as an expert on Chinese matters and was prepared to sacrifice many hours in an attempt to penetrate the iron mask of China's acknowledged leader. While Roosevelt entertained Chiang Kai-shek, Churchill fumed. The military staffs endlessly discussed amphibian operations in the Bay of Bengal which would somehow help to open up the Burma Road. Churchill had no liking for the project and put himself on record as unalterably opposed to it, for he had little interest in China and did not share the American view that China constituted the fourth Great Power. He met Chiang Kai-shek and was not impressed, and was courteous to Madame Chiang Kai-shek, who had once stormed in anger because Churchill in Washington had not made a special journey to New York to visit her. The Combined Chiefs of Staff were busy with the question of whether there should be a Supreme Commander for all the Allied Operations against Germany from the Mediterranean to the Atlantic. Someone pointed out that Marshal Foch had exercised that position in World War I. Once again Churchill vehemently objected, pointing out that while Foch commanded the Western and Italian fronts, his authority did not extend to fronts in Salonika, Palestine or Mesopotamia. He wanted above all to safeguard his own freedom of action. No doubt all these matters would be decided at Teheran; he was waiting on events, and feeling helpless.

Mena, on the outskirts of Cairo, is very close to the Sphinx and the Great Pyramids. From his headquarters at the Villa Bleu in Mena Churchill rode out to commune with the Sphinx, which he had last visited in 1921 in the company of Lawrence of Arabia. It was very hot, the sand blew in his eyes and he retreated to the air-conditioned villa.

Roosevelt thawed on November 25, Thanksgiving Day, and invited Churchill to the Thanksgiving feast. Two huge turkeys were set upon the table and the President carved them expertly, saying of the Americans and the British: "We are a large family, and more united than ever before. I propose a toast to this unity, and may it long continue." Although there was outward conviviality, unity was already fading. Churchill's daughter Sarah had accompanied him to Cairo as his aide-de-camp and after the dinner she danced with the younger men, while Churchill, not to be left out, danced with General "Pa" Watson, the President's military aide. General Watson had long since retired from the army and knew very little about military affairs; he was in fact the President's boon companion, kindly and jovial, very tall and very fat. The sight of Churchill dancing with Watson on the eve of a conference to decide the future of the world was oddly disturbing.

More disturbing things kept happening at Teheran. No proper security precautions had been taken. Churchill, driving from the airport to the British Legation, was puzzled by the presence of a Persian cavalryman every fifty yards along the road for three miles. As his car drove into the city, he found large crowds four or five deep lining the road. For some reason the police car leading the way moved very slowly, and any bomb-thrower in the crowd would have had no difficulty in reaching his target. Churchill sighed with relief when he at last reached the security of the British Legation defended by a strong cordon of British-Indian troops. Some time later he learned that the crowd had been waiting to greet the Shah of Persia, the young man who had been placed on the throne by Churchill and Stalin when it was discovered that his father was sympathetic to the Germans.

The Russian Embassy and the British Legation were very close together on the outskirts of Teheran while the American Legation was in the center of the city. Stalin, who had reached Teheran one or two days earlier, realized almost at once that it would be altogether safer for the President if he stayed within the large compound of the Russian Embassy. He would not have to make the long journey every day; he would have his own guards and communication facilities; he would have the additional protection of the Soviet guards. A large compound would be set aside for him and he would be treated with all the honors due to a guest. Moreover he would be continually under Russian surveillance, and all of them, the Americans, the British and the Russians, would be close together. Churchill, who assented to the plan and had a high opinion of the importance of the meeting, said that the patch of ground forming the British and Russian embassies had become "the center of the world."

There were many questions to be decided, and some which had already been decided were open to review. Churchill wanted to restate his case for the distribution of available forces—six-tenths to the massive attack on northern France in the summer of 1944, three-tenths to the Italian front, one-tenth to operations in the Eastern Mediterranean in the hope of bringing Turkey into the war. He wanted his tithe, but it was not given to him. Then there was the question of what should be done to Germany to prevent her from rising again and inflicting a new war upon Europe and the world. There was the question of Poland's boundaries after the war, and there was all the Far East to be passed in review. Would Russia agree to join in the war against Japan as soon as Germany was defeated? It was necessary to settle the date of the Normandy landings and arrange for a Russian offensive about the same time. Although three plenary sessions were held, the important matters were not discussed in logical order and some of the most fundamental decisions were arrived at almost casually in private discussions.

Stalin dominated the conference like an emperor among kings. Wherever possible, he spoke briefly, categorically and often rudely. Once when Roosevelt asked him a question while he was perusing a document, he said without looking up: "For God's sake let me finish my work!" When he finally realized that the President had spoken, he showed a trace of embarrassment but offered no apologies. And if on occasion he could be rude to the President he could be much ruder to Churchill. On the whole he showed the President a cautious deference; toward Churchill he demonstrated an intermittent contempt. He enjoyed needling the Prime Minister and was amused to discover that the President rarely came to Churchill's defense.

Although this conference was intended as a summit meeting of three friendly allies, there were many moments when friendship was strained. Churchill had the presentiment that evil was abroad, but he could put no precise name to it. Three men had come together to decide the fate of millions upon millions of men. Was it in their power to act wisely? Long ago in a novel written at the beginning of his career Churchill had spoken of the misuses of power: "There are sins, sins against the commonwealth of mankind, against the phenomenon of life itself, the stigma of which would cling through death, and for which there was pardon only in annihilation." So now, in Teheran, seeing himself as one of the three men on whom the fate of the world depended, he drew back momentarily and said: "I believe man might destroy man and wipe out civilization. Europe would be desolate and I would be held responsible." The words were spoken to his doctor, Lord Moran. He went on: "Stupendous issues are unfolding before our eyes, and we are only specks of dust that have settled in the night on the world. Do you think my strength will last out the war? I fancy sometimes that I am nearly spent."

"Black dog" had settled on him at a time when he could least afford the pleasures of melancholy. But it was more than "black dog." The ghost of Savrola, the young revolutionary with the generous impulses and the knowledge that no man has the right to send others to their deaths, had come to haunt him. The ghost had never been exorcised, and even when he was hardened to the uses of power there would come to him from time to time that ghostly, familiar presence.

At a dinner held in the Soviet Embassy at the conclusion of the secondary plenary conference, Stalin was in high good humor. He had ordered the execution of millions of Russians and was looking forward to the time when he could order the execution of the German officers who had taken part in the invasion of Russia.

STALIN: Some fifty or a hundred thousand German officers must be liquidated. The entire General Staff must go.

CHURCHILL: The British Parliament and public will never tolerate mass executions. Even if in war passion they allowed them to begin, they would turn violently against those responsible after the first butchery had taken place. The Soviets must be under no delusion on this point.

STALIN: Fifty thousand must be shot!

CHURCHILL: I would rather be taken out into the garden here and now and be shot myself rather than sully my own and my country's honor by such infamy.

ROOSEVELT: I have a compromise to propose. Not fifty thousand, but only forty-nine thousand should be shot.

At this point Elliott Roosevelt, the President's son, rose from his place at the end of the table and took it upon himself to announce that he cordially agreed with Marshal Stalin's plan and he was sure the United States Army was also in agreement. Churchill was offended by the young man's effrontery but even more by the strange turn in the conversation, and he abruptly left the table and made his way into the next room which was in semidarkness. Suddenly out of the gloom Stalin and Molotov appeared, grinning broadly, eagerly explaining that they were only playing and that the thought of liquidating the entire German officer class had never entered their minds. Churchill appears to have taken their explanations at face value and resumed his place at the table. Some time later Churchill and Stalin were seen standing with their hands on each other's shoulders, gazing into each other's eyes.

If Churchill's relationship with Stalin was now satisfactory, or at least convivial, his relationship with Roosevelt was already deteriorating. Roosevelt was under the impression that Stalin was "get-at-able." With finesse, with abundant flattery and with simple realism Roosevelt believed that it was possible to reach a perfect understanding with Stalin. As far back as March, 1942, he had written to Churchill: "I know you will not mind my being brutally frank when I tell you that I think I can personally handle Stalin better than either your Foreign Office or my State Department. Stalin hates the guts of all your top people. He thinks he likes me better, and I hope he will continue to do so." The letter had come to Churchill like a blow between the eyes, but he had swallowed his pride. The implications were abundantly—only too abundantly—clear. But as the months passed, it became evident that Roosevelt's belief in his own personal ascendancy over Stalin was increasing rather than diminishing. At Teheran Roosevelt found that he could tell jokes to Stalin, that Stalin would laugh, and that on this level they enjoyed a camaraderie which soared above difference of language and tradition. The best jokes, in Roosevelt's view, were jokes against Churchill.

Roosevelt had never previously set eyes on Stalin and knew very little about him. Churchill, who had met him, was impressed by his intelligence and his cunning, and had no illusions about his cruelty and his long-range plans for the domination of Europe. Roosevelt was under the illusion that Stalin could be reasoned with and that once all his legitimate aspirations were granted to him, he would behave with kindliness and decorum.

Much time was frittered away in pointless discussions. Churchill returned frequently to the island of Rhodes, claiming once again that its capture was imperative and would inevitably bring Turkey into the war. Stalin talked about the dummy tanks and airplanes built in vast numbers to fool the Germans, and how successful they had been, and as he spoke a beaming Churchill began to give shape and substance to one of his more deplorable epigrams: "In war-time Truth is so precious that she should always be attended by a bodyguard of lies." Churchill reports that Stalin and his comrades greatly appreciated this remark. The meeting was coming to an end with the appropriate belly laughter.

These men, so powerful and so aware of their power, seemed sometimes to wear the masks of madmen. Paranoia hovered in the air like an avenging angel as they walked in the Persian garden or sat at gargantuan meals while most of the world was starving. Here is Churchill surrendering to a mood of blissful contentment: "On my right sat the President of the United States, on my left the master of Russia. Together we controlled practically all the naval and three-quarters of all the air forces in the world, and could direct armies of nearly twenty

millions of men, engaged in the most terrible of wars that had yet
occurred in human history." This consciousness of his own power
consoled him for his powerlessness, for the knowledge that he was not
permitted to invade Rhodes or mount any operations in the Eastern
Mediterranean.

Nevertheless he was able to achieve some symbolic victories. Symbolic crumbs were fed to him, and he in turn was able to offer symbolic
crumbs to Stalin. To commemorate the gallant defense of Stalingrad,
King George VI had caused to be made a Sword of Honor of gilded
bronze with a pommel of flawless crystal. This sword, encased in a
scabbard of scarlet and gold, bore along the blade the inscription: "To
the steel-hearted citizens of Stalingrad, a gift from King George VI as a
token of homage of the British people." At the ceremonial presentation
of the sword Churchill solemnly offered it to Stalin, who kissed it and
then handed it to Voroshilov, who promptly dropped it. Roosevelt was
impressed by the ceremony. "It was really very magnificent, moving
and sincere," he said. The scene was recorded by cameramen: the
salutes, the honor guard, the great sword lying on a cushion, Stalin
lifting it to his lips, the long kiss, and then in the blaze of the chandeliers, Stalin handing it gravely to Voroshilov, and at that moment
everything becomes confused as the sword falls to the ground and the
camera attempts to follow its downward path, and we see only startled
faces, people milling about, and soon everyone is gazing at the floor, as
though, hidden among all those well-tailored legs, there lay the body of
an assassinated politician.

Teheran was a strange conference, for many issues which should
have been resolved remained clouded and many decisions which should
have been taken were never made. Roosevelt's plan to carve postwar
Germany into seven separate states was discussed briefly and then
forgotten. Stalin, asked to state his own views on postwar Germany,
merely remarked that he would make his demands known in due
course. He dominated the conference but more by his silences than by
anything he said.

Churchill flew to Cairo for a conference with President Inönü of
Turkey. He learned, as he might have expected, that the Turks were
more fearful of the Russians than of the Germans, and were in no mood
to enter the war. He was already a very sick man when he reached
Tunis on the first leg of his homeward journey and was ordered to bed
by his doctor, who diagnosed a congestion at the base of the left lung.
He was again suffering from pneumonia, but also from exhaustion and

frustration. His heart fibrillated, and there were moments when Lord Moran wondered whether he could possibly survive in his weakened condition. Churchill, too, sometimes pondered his approaching death and concluded that it would be appropriate to die in sight of the ruins of Carthage. But on Christmas Day he revived sufficiently to make a few unsteady steps, wearing his boiler suit and a pair of bedroom slippers embroidered with his initials in gold thread, and to preside over a conference which included General Eisenhower and many members of his own military staff. The conference was devoted largely to the forthcoming descent on Anzio and the need for landing craft. His head was clear; he knew exactly what he wanted; and he was thankful that at last there was the possibility of breaking the long-drawn-out stalemate in Italy. In the evening he appeared at a Christmas party wearing over his boiler suit a black silk dressing gown embroidered with silver dragons, perhaps the least outrageous of his many brilliantly colored mandarin gowns.

Two days later he flew to Marrakesh for a period of convalescence. By the orders of his doctor the airplane was not to fly above 6,000 feet, because it was thought that flying at a higher altitude might damage his already weakened heart. Churchill, who had studied the geography of North Africa, and intensely disliked traveling through clouds where mountains might be lurking, countermanded his doctor's orders and insisted that the pilot should fly well above the mountains. At Marrakesh he was soon back at his old form, working in bed during the morning, then going off for a picnic lunch and spending the afternoon soaking up the sun in the foothills of the Atlas Mountains. Yet his health was still precarious, he complained vigorously of lassitude, and once, attempting to climb up a slope, he found the going so hard that he pretended to be engaged in deep conversation with a goat gazing at him impassively from a nearby ledge. Finally, when it became obvious that the conversation with the goat might continue indefinitely, his two companions unceremoniously hauled him up the slope by letting him lean against an outspread tablecloth which they pulled at the two ends.

As his strength returned he set up his easel and painted Marrakesh, the palms, the snow-covered mountains of the High Atlas. General de Gaulle came to visit him, haughty and peppery, talking as though he were Stalin and Roosevelt combined, his military weakness permitting him to take refuge in rhetoric. Another visitor was T'hami El Glaoui, most rapacious of chieftains, now and for a little while longer the Lord of the Atlas and of Marrakesh. He gave Churchill an exquisitely fashioned Moorish dagger and listened uncomprehendingly to a lecture by Churchill on the progress of the war. He said for politeness' sake that he had known from the beginning that the Allies would win the war. Churchill, who had no need to be polite, answered gravely that the Pasha of Marrakesh came nearer than he probably knew to backing the wrong horse.

On January 14, 1944, Churchill was well enough to fly to Gibraltar. On the next day in the early morning he sailed for England on the battleship *King George V.* He had been away for more than two months, governing by remote control, certain that he was still in the good graces of the Cabinet and the British people, but aware that it might be dangerous to extend his leave of absence much longer. There were advantages in being away from London: none of the petty affairs of Parliament passed across his desk and he could spend his time more profitably dealing with military and international affairs. Outside of England he was his own Minister of Defence and Minister of Foreign Affairs. Returning to England he must learn to become Prime Minister again.

THE AGING CONQUEROR

THE CHURCHILL OF 1940, marvelously defiant and resourceful, walking surefooted on the edge of the abyss, possessing a strange gaiety which he shared with all his countrymen and all the English-speaking peoples, had vanished by 1944. To those who knew him well the new Churchill was like another man altogether, almost a stranger. Every wartime journey took its toll of health and energy, and every conference exhausted him. He was becoming increasingly querulous and tetchy, complained violently about small things, and was even more abrupt and demanding than he had been before. All the familiar symptoms of old age, which had been concealed for so long, now appeared in a magnified form. It was as though he had jumped out of perpetual youth into permanent old age.

"Can't you give me something so that I won't feel so exhausted?" he begged his doctor in Cairo. It appeared that nothing, or very little, could be done, especially since he persisted in drinking vast quantities of champagne and brandy, took little exercise, and worked sixteen hours a day. He was sixty-nine and would soon be entering his eighth decade.

He worked on because there was no alternative, because it was unthinkable to him that he should not be in charge of the direction of the war and he expected to be Prime Minister long after peace was declared. But in Parliament and in the factories there were ominous signs that the worship which he had received ungrudgingly in 1940 and now demanded in 1944 was not being given to him in full measure. He was the leader of the Conservative Party and felt insulted when his party lost by-elections. In March the government was defeated in a vote on the Education Bill, which included an amendment calling for equal pay for men and women under the new education code. One hundred seventeen voted for the amendment and one hundred sixteen against. Churchill was furious and immediately demanded a Vote of Confidence. Who were these insignificant creatures who dared to oppose his will? He threatened to resign unless the amendment was defeated. It was a ludicrous situation and could be explained only by his increasing weariness and lack of understanding of the country's mood. Nevertheless the threat of resignation was successful. Many members of the Labour Party were incensed, but impressed by the threat of resignation, they voted for the government. Churchill's motion was carried by a margin of over four hundred votes.

The landing at Anzio, prepared with so much care and with all the advantages of surprise, was bogging down. What had been intended as a crushing blow against the enemy became a slow bloodletting. German troops from Yugoslavia, southern France and northern Italy were rushed to the front with extraordinary speed, proving that the Germans were capable of adapting themselves efficiently to Allied thrusts wherever they took place. Churchill at Marrakesh had imagined a lightning attack which would bring Allied troops to Rome within a few days, but many months were to pass before they entered Rome. Anzio was another disaster. There remained the great thrust into Normandy, which had the merit of pitting such vast forces against the Germans that it was inconceivable that the Allied armies would ever bog down. This was to be the main thrust, while all the others were regarded as holding operations to assist the Russians. It was a characteristically American conception, brilliantly organized, and although the British Chiefs of Staff were permitted to have some say in it and to take part in it, the essential elements were put together in Washington.

The vastness of the preparations boggled even the imagination of Churchill. An immense naval armada of 4,000 ships and thousands of smaller craft swept across the English Channel on June 6, 1944. The assault force consisted of 176,000 men and 20,000 vehicles, and 11,000 first-line aircraft could be drawn upon. The technical problems of marshaling the ships so that each arrived at the appointed time were surmounted: the overflow of shipping was berthed as far north as the Clyde, the Humber and Belfast. Extraordinary measures were taken to see that the plans remained unknown to the enemy. From May 28 all troops were confined to their barracks and no foreign embassies were allowed to communicate with the outside world. As a result of all these precautions and some deliberate acts of deception by the British secret service, German intelligence never learned about the Allied plans.

Churchill's contributions to the D Day landing were many and various. For many months he had devoted a great deal of time and energy to the construction of floating piers which could be sunk near the shore, thus providing harbor facilities where none had existed before. The intricate details fascinated him and he made a special visit in a motor torpedo boat to the Solent to see all these strangely shaped hulks at their moorings before they were towed across the Channel. With General Smuts and the prime ministers of Canada and Southern Rhodesia he toured the armored and infantry units in the southern counties, and it was observed that he kept Smuts close to his side. Meanwhile he issued orders, sent out streams of directives and inquiries, and rejoiced in his secret knowledge of the invasion plans. But when the large-scale model of the coastline from Bremen to the Spanish frontier was unveiled to him in the Map Room at Storey's Gate in all its papier-mâché magnificence, he could not bear to look at it and said: "Cover it up!" for fear that he might by gazing at it long enough weaken at the sight of so many impregnable cliffs.

Since this was to be the most massive invasion ever mounted against the coast of France, he wanted to go with it. General Eisenhower strongly objected. Churchill pointed out that the general's authority did not extend to giving orders to a Prime Minister. "It is not part of your responsibility, my dear General, to determine the exact composition of any ship's company in His Majesty's fleet," he insisted, hinting that the Former Naval Person could appoint himself to any naval rank he pleased. A disproportionate amount of General Eisenhower's time was spent in efforts to dissuade him. King George VI, who claimed that he had a prior right to accompany the invasion forces because he was the head of all three armed services, also attempted to dissuade him. Churchill was polite, but evasive. He intended to go with or without the approval of the King and only desisted when he received a letter which, though couched in gentle phrases, amounted to a royal command. Churchill felt that he had been cheated. "I thought my view and theme of the war were sufficiently important and authoritative to entitle me to full freedom of judgment as to how I discharged my task in such a personal matter," he wrote later, when he was evidently still smarting. His "view and theme of the war" were, he thought, sacrosanct. Others thought otherwise. He was not permitted to enjoy the fireworks display.

In those days he was by turns jubilant, fearful, melancholy and withdrawn. The crunch was coming, but he was still able to view the horrors statistically. "Do you realize," he remarked to his wife on the eve of the invasion, "that by the time you wake up in the morning twenty thousand men may have been killed."

Within a week of the landing he was in France for the first time since his ill-fated meeting with Marshal Pétain and General Weygand. It was exactly four years to the day since he had left Briare for England, having offered to unite France with Britain and sworn that Britain would go on fighting to the end. He was at Montgomery's headquarters five miles from the invasion beaches when a strange incident occurred. General Smuts, who had accompanied Churchill, kept saying: "There are Germans near us." He was sniffing the air and gazing in the direction of a clump of rhododendrons. He was told that the grounds had been gone through with a fine-tooth comb. "I can't help that. There are Germans near us—I can always tell," Smuts repeated, still gazing at the rhododendrons. Montgomery invited Churchill and Smuts into the mess tent. Nothing happened, and no Germans appeared that day. Two days later two young German parachuters emerged from the dugout they had carved in the roots of a rhododendron bush. They were half starving, drenched to the skin, and frightened for their lives, but they were well-armed. They quietly laid down their arms and surrendered.

By this time Churchill was back in London, having enjoyed a desultory conversation with Montgomery and wondered aloud about the risks he was taking—the front was only three miles away and the line was broken in several places. He had also enjoyed a display of naval bombardment, for the ship taking him back across the Channel was induced to fire a broadside into the woodlands of Normandy. It was wasted ammunition, but Churchill was pleased. "We may have killed a German general," he said delightedly, but it is more likely that they killed a French housewife. Churchill and Roosevelt had agreed that all railroad stations, marshaling yards and strong points in France should be ruthlessly bombed to prevent the Germans from bringing up reinforcements to the Normandy front. The matter was not discussed with General de Gaulle, who was understandably appalled by the killing of so many of his countrymen.

Churchill returned to England just in time to observe the coming of the first V-bombs. He had known for a long time about their existence; British and American bombers had sought out their launching grounds, and there had been received in London sufficient scraps of information for scientists to be able to draw blueprints of these flying bombs, but strangely no effort was made to make them in England and send them against Germany. After the war it was learned that Hitler was terrified that similar weapons would be used against Germany. He assumed that an unexploded bomb would one day fall into English hands; it would immediately be copied; it would be sent against Berlin; and, as he said, "the work of the genius of German scientists will be used to bring death to German cities."

In the early hours of June 13, 1944, exactly a week after D Day, the first flying bombs struck London. On the same day a flying bomb soared off the launching pad at Peenemunde and as the result of a freak accident it fell in Sweden. The fragments found their way into British hands and were reassembled, but even with this information no effort was made to reproduce them. Meanwhile the bombs, which were aimed at London and especially at the heart of the city, proved to be almost as terrible as Hitler predicted they would be. By July 19, 1944, between three and four thousand people had been killed, half a million houses were severely damaged, and fourteen thousand houses had been blown to pieces. Plans were made for evacuating hundreds of thousands of Londoners. Nothing came of these plans. It was thought that the war would soon be over and the damage caused by V-bombs was a small price to pay for victory.

Many science fiction writers had predicted flying bombs, and it is therefore all the more remarkable that the Allies did not produce them. Churchill himself had the distinction of having pondered the possibility of scientists producing both the atom bomb and the flying bomb in a magazine article which he wrote in 1925:

> Might not a bomb no bigger than an orange be found to possess a secret power to destroy a whole block of buildings—nay, to concentrate the force of a thousand tons of cordite and blast a township at a stroke? Could

not explosives even of the existing type be guided automatically in flying machines by wireless or other rays, without a human pilot, in ceaseless procession upon a hostile city, arsenal, camp, or dockyard?

The title of the magazine article was, "Shall We All Commit Suicide?" It began ominously with the words: "The story of the human race is War," and hinted at the great wars of annihilation about to come.

While the flying bombs were falling on London, creating much havoc but without having any effect whatsoever on the course of the war, Churchill's hopes for a thrust at the soft underbelly of Europe revived. Rome fell to the Allies on June 4, two days before D Day; and this triumph, so long awaited, stunned the Germans who began to fall back on the Gothic Line in the north of Italy. For Churchill, who had never abandoned the hope of reaching Vienna by a descent on the Istrian Peninsula and a thrust through the Ljubljana Gap, the fall of Rome and the opening up of northern Italy was like a demonstrable sign from heaven pointing to Central Europe. While it was too late to halt the invasion of southern France, which he regarded as totally useless, there still remained the possibility that armored troops could be spared from Italy to make a bold dash on Vienna. Never had Vienna seemed more alluring to him. The partisans in Yugoslavia were winning battles and the Balkans were aflame. If only, at this last moment, the invasion of southern France could be abandoned! If only a motorized detachment could smash into Austria, meeting the Russians somewhere on the Danube.

Churchill's desire to break into Central Europe with or without the approval of President Roosevelt led him to embark on some strange maneuvers. Early in August he flew to Naples for conversations with Marshal Tito, the hard-bitten, youthful looking leader of the Communist partisans. Tito had been provided with a stiff, ill-fitting Marshal's uniform by the Russians and his gold epaulettes were provided by the Americans. Churchill had ordered supplies and weapons to be parachuted into Yugoslavia and his son Randolph had briefly been attached to Tito's staff. Tito was perfectly prepared to provide troops and a port on the Dalmatian coast for the advance on Vienna, but Churchill's hopes for a democratic Yugoslavia after the war were sadly diminished when it became clear that Tito had no use for the exiled King Peter. In Churchill's view, King Peter, acting as a constitutional monarch, would be a guarantee of democracy in Yugoslavia.

This was not Tito's view. But Churchill was buoyed up by the knowledge that he had found an ally for his projected "slitting of the underbelly."

He enjoyed Naples, visited the Blue Grotto at Capri, rejoicing in the intense blueness of the water in that mysterious cavern, and bathed in the hot springs of Ischia. Then he was off to Corsica by air for a close view of the landing in southern France, against which he had argued so long and so unavailingly. Back in Naples he met the Greek Premier, Papandreou, to make some preliminary decisions on the fate of Greece. He feared that when the Germans withdrew, the armed pro-Communist partisans would come to the fore. Greece lay within the British sphere of interest and he was determined to send another military expedition to Greece to wrest it from the partisans if they gained power, and he suggested that the Greek government in exile, now residing in Cairo, should move to Italy to be closer to the headquarters of the British army. Then he flew to Siena, where Field Marshal Alexander had established his headquarters, and drove to the front until he was as close as he ever came in the Second World War to the enemy, for, having crossed the Metauro River, where the last battle between the ancient Romans and the Carthaginians was fought and Hasdrubal and his elephants were defeated, Churchill found himself in a valley covered with scrub, five hundred yards away from the nearest Germans. There was only casual, desultory fighting and he was in no danger. The experience of being within rifle and machine gun shot of the Germans delighted him and took his mind away from pressing political problems.

The most pressing problem concerned Russia. Stalin had once more demonstrated his total ruthlessness, his absolute devotion to power politics, and his contempt for the Polish people. The Warsaw uprising had taken place at a moment when the Red Army was poised to capture Warsaw. Stalin gave the order for the army to halt. He would do nothing to assist the Poles who fought in the streets of Warsaw and allowed them to be massacred by the Germans, and when the British flew in supplies to the embattled Poles and flew on to airfields behind the Russian lines, he pointed out that he had given no permission for such adventures. Like Hitler, he preferred that the cities of his enemies should be uninhabited and reduced to rubble; and for him the Poles, except for the small coterie of Communist Poles he had appointed to the Lublin government, were all enemies. The massacre in Warsaw was one more sign that Stalin was determined to bring Eastern Europe under his domination. Churchill was now more than ever determined to reach Vienna before the Red Army. He wrote to General Smuts on August 31: "My object now is to keep what we have got in Italy, which should be sufficient since the enemy has withdrawn four of his best divisions. With this I hope to turn and break the Gothic Line, break into the Po valley, and ultimately advance by Trieste and the Ljubljana Gap to Vienna. Even if the war came to an end at an early date I have told Alexander to be ready for a dash with armoured cars."

The vision of the great city gleamed brightly, all the more enticing because she was beyond his grasp. It was such a vision as emperors have dreamed on, and it pleased Churchill to write to Smuts in the imperial manner. The soldiers—French, Italian, Brazilian, Nisei, American and British—would have been somewhat dismayed if they had known how difficult it was going to be to march up the whole of Italy. Must they continue everlastingly to fight in a land where every mountain favored the enemy? If all else failed, Churchill had the extraordinary notion of forcing a passage through the Brenner Pass. Geography was not one of the subjects he had studied strenuously. His plans to force the Brenner Pass were mercifully withheld from his soldiers, who sometimes wondered whether the war might not have been over quicker if not a single Allied soldier had set foot on Italy.

When Churchill set out on the *Queen Mary* in September for another round of conferences with President Roosevelt in Quebec, he could congratulate himself that the German army was retreating in Normandy and northern Italy and that with any reasonable luck German resistance would collapse early in the New Year. Roosevelt was not quite so optimistic. Unlike Churchill he knew his geography and he had a special knowledge of the geography of the Rhine Valley, where he had bicycled in his youth. This, too, was land that favored the defender. Meanwhile Churchill was hoping to come to an agreement on the use of the British fleet in the concluding stages of the war against Japan. Honor demanded that the British should be represented in the Pacific, but it appeared that the Americans preferred to fight alone or with as little help as possible. The matter was brought to the President's attention.

"The offer of the British Fleet has been made," Churchill insisted. "Is it accepted?"

"Yes," replied the President.

There was no further discussion on a British naval presence in the Far East.

In the position papers presented to the President Churchill took care to include a brief reference to an assault on the Ljubljana Gap as a hypothetical possibility, but he was more concerned with what would happen when the Germans abandoned Greece. British secret intelligence in Greece had provided voluminous reports suggesting that the partisans would rise, capture Athens and install a Communist regime obedient to Moscow. The President, and later Stalin, agreed that Churchill should be given a free hand in Greece, with the result that Greece alone of the nations of Eastern Europe escaped total Communist domination.

The Quebec conference was friendly and quite unimportant. All the decisions reached there could just as easily have been discussed on the transatlantic telephone or by mail. The *Queen Mary*, which served as Churchill's passenger ship, could have served more important purposes and the 9,000 miles he traveled during this journey could have been safely reduced to 9,000 yards of travel through the streets of England to listen to the people. Something quite strange, but nevertheless inevitable, was happening. He had been in power so long, he had received so much adulation, he had dealt for such long periods only with those people he sometimes described as "persons of consequence," and now at last the authoritarian temper, always present, was beginning to erupt violently, volcanically, just at the moment when he was losing his nerve. He felt more and more isolated, and therefore more and more on the defensive. He was beginning to realize as the war drew to a close that all the advantages lay with Russia and America, the superpowers, and that British influence was diminishing at a time when British armies were cutting the Germans to ribbons.

In October he flew to Moscow for still another conference with Stalin. "Extraordinary atmosphere of goodwill here," he cabled shortly after his arrival on a cold, numbing day, the wind striking across the airfield as he stood at attention while high-stepping Russian guards marched past. Shivering, he was bundled into a car for the long drive to Molotov's luxurious *dacha* twenty miles beyond Moscow. Anthony Eden, Sir Alan Brooke, General Ismay and other assorted generals were accompanying him, but the real work of the conference would take place in face to face meetings between Churchill and Stalin. Churchill's main purpose was to make a last-ditch effort to preserve some kind of democracy in Eastern Europe and especially to see that Poland would be governed by a coalition representing both the Polish government in exile in London and the Communist-dominated Lublin government and secondly that he would receive a free hand in Greece. He bungled the first and Stalin disdainfully granted the second.

At his first meeting with Stalin he presented himself as an honest broker who had studied the market prices and had come to strike a pleasant bargain. "Don't let us get at cross-purposes in small ways," he suggested. "So far as Britain and Russia are concerned, how would it do for you to have ninety per cent predominance in Rumania, for us to have ninety per cent of the say in Greece, and go fifty-fifty about Yugoslavia?" He wrote on a half-sheet of paper:

Rumania	
Russia	90%
The others	10%
Greece	
Great Britain	90%
(in accord with USA)	
Russia	10%
Yugoslavia	50%–50%
Hungary	50%–50%
Bulgaria	
Russia	75%
The others	25%

This was the scheme, at once merciless, impractical and mischievous, that Churchill presented to Stalin on his own authority, having never previously discussed it with anyone. Stalin glanced at the fatal half-sheet and made a large tick with his blue pencil. There was a long silence. It occurred to Churchill that the paper lying in the middle of the table between them was a somewhat incriminating document. He said: "Might it not be thought rather cynical if it seemed that we had disposed of these issues, so fateful to millions of people, in such an offhand manner?" He suggested it would be better to burn the paper.

"No, you keep it," Stalin replied, and Churchill pocketed it.

Churchill would say later that the fatal document was concerned only with immediate postwar arrangements and all the larger issues would be resolved when the victors sat down at the peace conference. In fact, these were the larger issues, and to the extent that they showed the bent of Churchill's thinking, they offered hostages to Stalin. There was one important omission: Poland. Stalin found no difficulty in arriving at the conclusion that Poland deserved a higher percentage figure—Russia 100 per cent, the others 0 per cent. The conference had started well.

Churchill was evidently troubled by this half-sheet of paper and failed to mention it in his cables to the President and to Harry Hopkins, but discussed it in great detail in a letter to Stalin in which he explained that he looked forward to the time when the kings of Greece and Yugoslavia would be restored to their thrones and open, free elections would take place in the countries of the Balkans without the interference of Communist propaganda. As for the percentage figures, this, too, would depend on the approval of the United States, "which may go away for a long time and then come back again unexpectedly with gigantic strength." These last words contained a threat to Stalin, but they also reflected Churchill's own fears. It was a long, turgid, rambling letter, and Churchill wisely decided that it might be better not to send it to Stalin after all.

The leading members of the Polish government in exile in London were flown to Moscow for a confrontation with the Lublin government, which corresponded to the Polish government in exile in Moscow. They argued, they drew maps, they arrived at no conclusions and were even farther apart at the end of their discussions than when they started.

Surprisingly Churchill wore military uniforms with rows of medals during his two week stay in Moscow. It was a rather odd uniform, being the khaki equivalent of the naval uniform of the Lord Warden of the Cinque Ports. He wore this uniform at a Command Performance at the Bolshoi Theatre given in his honor. Sitting with Stalin in the former royal box, he watched the first act of *Giselle* and listened to the thunderous voices of the Red Army Choir. When the lights came on during the interval Churchill and Stalin were seen smiling and shaking hands repeatedly in their box. Thunderous applause leaped up to them and Churchill later confessed that he became aware of a deep, passionate quality in that applause, which seemed endless. He was hugely enjoying these marks of Stalin's favor. When he left Moscow on October 19, it was another cold cheerless day with a heavy rain falling. Stalin had come to say farewell at the airfield. This, too, was a mark of favor, for he had never previously accompanied any distinguished foreigner to the airfield.

The adulation of the crowd works wonders on politicians. They adore to watch themselves being adored and assume wrongly that adoration is a reward for lives devoted to high principles and virtuous actions. But there is poison in that deafening applause.

On the eve of Armistice Day Churchill flew to Paris to attend the military parade and to give his blessing to the new Provisional Government of France now at last recognized by the Allied powers. Three months had passed since General Leclerc's armored division liberated Paris, and for all those three months General de Gaulle's government had existed in a kind of limbo. Churchill's visit, therefore, provided the seal of legitimacy to a government whose power scarcely extended beyond the chief cities and industrial centers. Churchill flew in to Orly to a tumultuous reception, and the roads from Orly to the center of Paris were lined with flag-waving Parisians roaring out their approval. With General de Gaulle beside him, he beamed, made the V sign, got up and down in the car and wept with joy. The long years of servitude under the Germans were over, and the Parisians saw in Churchill and De Gaulle the symbols of their deliverance.

In Paris Churchill was given the sumptuous apartment in the French Foreign Office which had been previously occupied by Hermann Goering. There were Gobelin tapestries on the walls and the bath was plated with gold. Outside, on the Quai d'Orsay, the crowds waved British and French flags and kept shouting his name.

But the applause of that wintry day was only a small foretaste of the delirious reception he received on the following day when he laid a wreath on the tomb of the Unknown Soldier under the Arc de Triomphe. Then, with De Gaulle, he walked half a mile along the Champs Elysées to the reviewing stand, and once again he bowed and made the V sign and seemed in some strange way to become larger than life as the applause lapped round him; and if the applause in Moscow was passionate, this was even more violent and more exhausting, as though a huge wall of affection was being created around him and was threatening to fall on him. Never before had he received such applause and he was trembling with excitement when he reached the reviewing stand.

Ironies abounded. The French army, which had collapsed at Sedan and fallen back on Paris in a rout, was now marching past him as though there had never been a whisper of defeat. General de Gaulle, whose abrupt and demanding manner had often made life so difficult for him, was now his ally. Within less than a year Churchill would be asking sadly whether his friend Eisenhower might not be able to provide him with a house in the south of France where he could paint. But now on the reviewing stand, with the crowds on the Champs Elysées shouting his name, he was at the height of his fame.

A French army was fighting in the mountainous Vosges frontier and Churchill thought it proper that he should pay tribute to General de Lattre de Tassigny at his headquarters in Besançon. By the time they reached the town the general had moved closer to the front, the snow was falling, the roads were nearly impassable, and though he found De Lattre's headquarters and reviewed some of his troops, and listened as they sang to him, he was so worn out by the excitement of the previous days that he seemed a remote and forbidding presence, querulous and ill-humored. Nevertheless he spent ten hours in the bitterly cold weather among the French troops and his naval aide wondered whether he could avoid another bout of pneumonia. He would be seventy in a few days and was showing his age.

One of the subjects he discussed with General de Gaulle was the danger of a Communist uprising in France. The *maquisards* had kept their arms and were determined not to surrender them, and some, perhaps half of all those who had fought in the resistance, were under Communist domination. De Gaulle insisted that he had the power and the will to prevent the overthrow of his government. When Churchill flew back to England he found that the Communist partisans in Greece were attempting a *putsch*, using the arms left behind by the retreating Germans. They had also acquired stores of dynamite which they were employing skillfully to capture large areas of Athens. British troops had been landed in Athens to maintain order, but there was no effective government. Churchill, remembering the famous half-sheet of paper on which he had scribbled *Greece: Great Britain 90%—Russia 10%*, was dismayed by the possibility that the percentages were being reversed. On December 5 he sent a cable in code to General Scobie commanding the British troops in Athens, ordering him to use extreme measures to put down the uprising of the ELAS, the military arm of the Greek Communist Party. He wrote:

> Do not hesitate to fire at any armed male in Athens who assails the British authority or Greek authority with which we are working. It would be well of course if your commands were reinforced by the authority of some Greek Government. Do not however hesitate to act as if you were in a conquered city where a local rebellion is in progress.
>
> With regard to E.L.A.S. bands approaching from the outside, you should surely be able with your armour to give some of these a lesson

which will make others unlikely to try. You may count on my support in all reasonable and sensible action taken on this basis. You have to hold and dominate Athens. It would be a great thing for you to succeed in this without bloodshed if possible, but also with bloodshed if necessary.

Churchill had written more bloodthirsty messages than this, but never one so chilling in its repetitions. He was saying everything four or five times over, as though he was hoping to establish his domination over Athens by words alone, by the repeated exercise of an act of will. His temper was authoritarian, and he was aware that in the absence of a working Greek government, the only effective authority in Athens was his own.

As he was writing this dispatch late at night, there echoed through his mind the words of Arthur Balfour, Secretary of State for Ireland in the eighties of the last century. The usually mild and sweet-tempered author of a treatise called *A Defence of Philosophic Doubt* had sent an open telegram to the British military authorities in Ireland, reading: "Don't hesitate to shoot." Balfour's orders were carried out, and Parliament was in an uproar. He had sent an open telegram so that no one should be under any illusion that he meant anything but what he said. Churchill, sending his extraordinary message in code, was under the illusion that only General Scobie and his superior officer, General Maitland Wilson, would see it, and that Parliament would never hear about it.

The telegram was sent through Rome and for some mysterious reason copies of all military telegrams found their way to the American Embassy. It appears that an enterprising clerk in the embassy copied the telegram and sent it to an American columnist who published it on the eleventh. This bombshell had not yet fallen when Churchill found himself hotly defending his policy toward Greece in the House of Commons. He said:

Democracy is not based on violence and terrorism, but on reason, on fair play, on freedom, on respecting the rights of other people. Democracy is no harlot, to be picked up in the street by a man with a tommy gun. I trust the people, the mass of the people, in almost any country, but I like to make sure it is the people and not a gang of bandits who think that by violence they can overturn constituted authority.

The problem, of course, was that there existed no constituted authority in Athens and Churchill's argument was based on a nonexistent premise. The real argument was expediency and Churchill's manifest desire to save Greece from Stalin. The publication of the telegram in the United States stirred up a deep-seated distrust of Churchill's imperialist aims, but Churchill, with the support of President Roosevelt, felt sure he could weather the storm. But as the weeks passed, the fighting in Athens became fiercer and soon General Scobie was in command of only a small section of Athens, the airport at Kalamaki near Piraeus, and parts of Piraeus itself. The road between Piraeus and Athens was under enemy fire and could only be traveled by armored car.

Churchill decided to act at seven o'clock in the evening of Christmas Eve. At one o'clock in the morning of Christmas Day he flew off from Northolt accompanied by Anthony Eden, his doctor and his secretaries. His airplane was a Skymaster, the first to reach England, a present from the American government, with a flying range of 4,500 miles. On the afternoon of the same day the Skymaster landed at Kalamaki. It was a stormy day, the wind blowing from the sea, with piled-up snow and masses of tumbleweed flying across the field, and the airplane shook in its moorings. The wind howled, and above the wind came the sound of cannon fire. The question was where to find a warm and comfortable resting place. Since the British Embassy in Athens was under siege, it was decided that Churchill should be taken on board the cruiser, HMS *Ajax,* flagship of the Eastern Mediterranean Fleet, which had fought in the Battle of the River Plate at the beginning of the war. An armored car took him along the coastal road to a jetty, and so by motor launch to the *Ajax.* On the airplane it was decided to invite two of the Greek leaders to a conference on the cruiser. They were George Papandreou, the Prime Minister of the Greek government in exile who had recently reached Athens, and Archbishop Damaskinos, a man of imposing presence and great sanctity, who was regarded by many as a potential regent in these troubled times. Churchill had asked what the Archbishop was like and someone told him: "He is a crafty mediaeval priest." "Splendid!" replied Churchill. "Just the man we are looking for!" But Damaskinos was neither crafty nor medieval; he was intelligent, direct, uncompromising. George Papandreou was a demagogue who airily promised all things to all people and rarely came to conclusions. All this became clear to Churchill, who soon decided that Archbishop Damaskinos was the wiser man with the greater following.

The meeting with Damaskinos very nearly failed to take place, for as the Archbishop stepped on board the cruiser, wearing a black stovepipe hat and a voluminous black gown with a gold Byzantine eagle at his breast, he encountered a group of sailors celebrating Christmas in fancy dress made up to resemble clowns, Chinese, Red Indians, Negroes, Charlie Chaplins and Tahitian girls in grass skirts. The sailors, seeing the Archbishop who was well over six feet tall, with dark beard and beetling brows, assumed he was a Greek Father Christmas and danced round him, howling with laughter. Damaskinos was not amused by the Saturnalia and attempted to leave the ship. When the proper apologies were made, he settled down to business.

Churchill's aim was to bring about a truce and to establish a provisional government. This could be done only by bringing Damaskinos together with the ELAS, and on the following day, in the Greek Foreign Office, in the presence of the American ambassador, the French minister and a Russian military representative, together with assorted British generals, he accomplished his purpose. It was an eerie meeting in a shuttered room lit by hurricane lamps, because the electricity had been cut off. Everyone was shivering, Churchill wore a heavy greatcoat and a rug over his knees, Damaskinos sat very quiet and upright, and the ELAS representatives, who took up their places near the door, looked as though they had just come from the mountains and would soon return. Churchill said: "We came here because we were invited by all parties in Greece. We cannot leave until we have brought this matter to a conclusion. We want nothing from Greece, not an inch of her territory. We must, of course, ask acceptance of General Scobie's terms." He had not been invited by all parties to Greece and General Scobie's terms were Churchill's terms. But what Churchill said was less important than the fact that he was sitting down with them at the table. The ELAS leaders took notes, whispered among themselves and agreed to discuss the truce and the setting up of a provisional government. Churchill then left them, taking care to shake hands with everyone. On the way back to the cruiser in the armored car Churchill remarked that the Communists could not be as bad as they had been painted because they shook his hand vigorously.

A shaky truce and a shaky provisional government were born and Churchill flew back to England in good spirits, congratulating himself that he, and he alone, had brought peace to Greece. In fact the same results would have been achieved if he had sent to Athens his Foreign Secretary, Anthony Eden, who sat beside Churchill throughout their many meetings with the Greek leaders. Eden complained bitterly: "I do wish he would let me do my own job." He was waved aside. He was a spear-carrier, and Churchill insisted on occupying the center of the stage.

Churchill's authoritarian manner, the violence of his telegrams, his sudden decision to board an airplane and spend Christmas in Athens with all the attendant dangers of the journey, all these sprang not from strength but from an awareness that power was slipping from his hands. The war was in its final phase and the major decisions were being made by generals in the field. He needed to dominate events, to show that he was still capable of acting decisively. Soon he would fly to Yalta for another meeting with Stalin and Roosevelt, whose powers were so much greater than his own.

THE FLAMES OF
THE APOCALYPSE

CHURCHILL'S HEADQUARTERS AT Yalta was the former
Vorontsov Palace, which stood in a pleasant park surrounded by
cypress and olive trees. Built in 1837 at a cost of 3 million rubles, the
palace resembled an ancient British fortress with round castellated
towers and ivy-covered walls, to which there had been added as an
afterthought the domed splendors of the Taj Mahal. Directly facing the
Black Sea stood the high, pointed gateway covered with mosaics. The
steps leading up to the palace were guarded by stone lions. Altogether
there were six lions—two couchant, two rising and two standing. The
Vorontsov family was closely allied with the Romanov dynasty, and
everything about the palace suggested a feverish magnificence.

In the years before the fall of the Romanov dynasty the Vorontsovs
lived in the greatest luxury, and accordingly the palace contained
several banqueting halls and reception rooms, but for some
unexplained reason there were very few bathrooms. Churchill was
provided with a three-room suite overlooking the Black Sea with a
breathtaking view of the craggy coastline. He had his own bathroom,
but the rest of the delegation, which consisted of the Foreign Secretary,
the three Chiefs of Staff, two field marshals, assorted high-ranking
officers together with their secretaries and servants, had to share a

single bathroom among them. This was not due to any malignance on the part of Stalin. It was simply not possible in wartime to install temporary bathrooms in the palace. The whole region had recently been occupied by the Germans, and it was something of a miracle that the palace was still standing. Churchill confessed himself very pleased with the arrangements made for him, and in fact the Vorontsov Palace was more sumptuous than the great white Livadia Palace, all marble and gleaming limestone, built by Tsar Nicholas II in 1910, which was occupied by President Roosevelt, or the Koreis Palace, which once belonged to Prince Yusupov, where Stalin set up his headquarters. All these palaces looked out on the Black Sea and were close to one another. In this unlikely setting, in the balmy springlike weather of a Crimean winter, the fate of Europe and perhaps the world was to be decided.

The three men who presided over the Yalta Conference had all recently celebrated their birthdays. Churchill was seventy, Stalin was sixty-five, and Roosevelt was sixty-two. Churchill, the oldest, was to live longest, and Roosevelt, the youngest, had only a few more weeks to live. Roosevelt indeed already bore the marks of death, being pale and drawn and curiously remote, sometimes staring into the distance with his mouth hanging open. He had suffered an attack of heart failure some months earlier, but for long periods remained mentally alert. All three possessed the imperial manner and were capable of discussing the fate of countries and empires as though they were no more than ninepins. From time to time a strange air of levity and irresponsibility could be detected. The conference demanded the utmost efforts of the principals, but they frequently bickered and descended to irrelevancies or talked at cross-purposes.

When President Roosevelt explained to Stalin that in his correspondence with Churchill he used the affectionate term "Uncle Joe," Stalin took umbrage and threatened to leave the conference table. He was not accustomed to being addressed with familiarity by anyone except perhaps his daughter. He was so deeply offended that he stood up and made the gesture of turning toward the door. Churchill mollified him with a toast, saying that the eyes of the world were watching the conference which, if successful, would bring peace for a hundred years. Only the three Great Powers who had shed so much blood and fought so many battles could maintain the peace.

Stalin sat down; the conference was resumed; the three Great Powers abandoned themselves to high-minded irrelevancies. Churchill, full of foreboding, spoke on behalf of the Polish government in exile in London and of the French right to have a place in the control commission which would supervise the affairs of Germany. Poland and France were minor powers and were likely to be steamrollered by the major powers. Stalin thought it a waste of time to discuss the minor powers, but Churchill defended them vigorously. "The eagle should permit the small birds to sing and care not wherefore they sang," he declared. The doctrine of permissiveness was not one that commended itself to Stalin, who preferred his small birds in cages. Unwisely Churchill spoke up for the freedom of oppressed nations, thus laying himself open to the obvious retort that there were many oppressed nations in the British Empire. There were better arguments at hand, but the best of them went by default. The history of the Yalta Conference was a history of missed opportunities, with Stalin too arrogant to think out his problems afresh, Roosevelt too weary to understand what was happening, and Churchill too deeply aware of the waning strength of Britain compared with the two continental giants who were providing the main sinews of the war.

The code name of the Yalta Conference was "Argonaut." This was a strange choice, for the voyage of the Argonauts involved false oracles, ghosts, dismembered bodies, fire-breathing bulls and the armed men who sprang out of the earth sown with dragons' teeth. There was nothing peaceful and little that was hopeful in this voyage in search of the Golden Fleece.

For Stalin the Golden Fleece was almost in sight. He demanded $20 billion as reparations from Germany, as though there had never been a history of reparations after World War I. Germany, devastated and despoiled, her industries at a standstill and her people starving, was an unlikely prospect for so much treasure. Churchill thought the demand was unrealistic, and said so. Stalin insisted. Accordingly there was written into the records that the sum of $20 billion of reparations was to be given to the Soviet Union. The subject of the dismemberment of Germany was raised and then abandoned, and no one inquired how a dismembered Germany could pay any reparations at all. Roosevelt, urged by his Treasury Department to abandon the whole question of reparations and by his State Department to go along with the Russians, sided with the Russians. At all costs he was determined to satisfy the legitimate interests of Russia, forgetting that other countries also had legitimate interests, including the right to exist. Churchill's attitude was well expressed when he said that the superpowers had a moral responsibility to exercise their power with moderation and great respect for the rights of smaller nations. Stalin insisted that the superpowers had the right to dictate to the small nations. The question of the continued existence of Latvia, Estonia and Lithuania was not raised. These states were already lost. The question of how many other states would be swallowed up by Russia was also left unresolved.

At the military meetings Air Marshal Sergey Khudyakov wondered aloud why the British forces in the Mediterranean had not attempted to strike through the Ljubljana Gap to Graz, thus helping the Soviet drive on Vienna. The ghost of Churchill's original plan to invade the soft underbelly of Europe emerged for a moment and then quietly departed. Sir Alan Brooke pointed out that the western Allies were concentrating on delivering a deathblow in western Germany. General Antonov asked whether the German troops retreating by sea from Norway could be captured or destroyed by Allied naval forces and was told that the sea lanes were too heavily mined for any such action. A more difficult subject was liaison between the Soviet high command and the American-British high command. As Allied military observers had long suspected, the Russian high command was in permanent session in caverns under the Kremlin. Everything was centralized, all orders were issued from the Kremlin, and the general in the field merely executed his orders and directed operations, whereupon the shock troops sent to assist him were withdrawn. The last thing the Russians wanted was the presence of an Allied military liaison group attached to the Supreme Headquarters, the *Stavka*. Coordination between the Russians and the western Allies remained loose until the end of the war, when it was abruptly terminated.

The impasse was never surmounted, and there was scarcely a single matter on which the three leaders were in agreement. Sometimes they seemed to agree, and they would announce among themselves that they were in full agreement. Thus they agreed that Germany should be dismembered, but disagreed on the meaning of the word "dismember." They agreed that France should have a zone of occupation in defeated Germany, but Stalin agreed with reluctance and was prepared to sabotage the French zone at the first opportunity. They agreed that a free and democratic Poland should rise out of the ashes of the war, but could come to no conclusions about the meaning of "free" and "democratic." Stalin offered inconsequential compromises about frontiers and about the nature of Poland's postwar government. Whatever happened, he was determined to have a submissive, Communist-

dominated Poland on his borders. The western powers would have
France on their side, he would have Poland; and when the west talked
about "democratic" France, he reminded them that no Frenchmen had
ever elected General de Gaulle to office. As for Greece, there seemed to
be considerable doubt about whether it was a true democracy.
Churchill improvised on the theme of a free and democratic Greece,
but remained unconvincing. Stalin saw his opportunity and
pronounced judgment on Rumania, Bulgaria and Hungary, which
would enter the Russian sphere of interest. It was all very polite. He
was saying: "You can have France, Italy and Greece, and I will have the
Baltic States, five or six countries of eastern Europe and half of Germany."

The western powers capitulated. Churchill sometimes capitulated
for quite private and personal reasons. He did not think highly of the
Poles, saying: "I do not care much for Poles myself." The truth was that
he had met very few Poles and knew almost nothing about their history
and culture and was totally indifferent to their music, preferring Gilbert and Sullivan. He had a high regard for some Polish airmen who had
fought in the Battle of Britain but was determined not to let this
interfere with his judgment on the future of the Polish nation. The final
agreements on Poland were, he said, "the best I could get." If this was
the best, it was almost indistinguishable from the worst, for he capitulated all along the line.

The question of the United Nations, the supranational body which
would keep the world's peace, was discussed in the same way and
doomed to ineffectiveness from the beginning. It was generally agreed
that the superpowers should possess a veto: the smaller states must
submit to them. The smaller states had an unchallengeable right to
utter opinions, but it was questionable whether they had the right to
make decisions; and if for example all the world's smaller states combined to denounce the Soviet Union, Great Britain or the United States,
it was proper that the denunciation should remain available to historians, but it was a matter of indifference to the superpowers. All that
mattered was that the decisions should be made in agreement with the
superpowers.

But who were the superpowers? France? Chiang Kai-shek's China?
And what about the self-governing dominions of Britain? How many
would have seats in the General Assembly? Why should the Soviet
Union be limited to only one seat? Should not White Russia, the
Ukraine and perhaps Lithuania each have a seat? Stalin accepted the

elevation of France to a superpower with indifference, and he had more faith in Chiang Kai-shek's China than in the China of Mao Tse-tung. President Roosevelt was prepared to promote the Soviet Union as America's junior partner in Asia; no doubt China would become an economic dependency and Japan would be occupied by American troops, and the Soviet Union would receive her proper share of Manchuria and Korea. Churchill growled that Hong Kong would remain within the Commonwealth of Nations and so would all the other British dependencies. The Titans were carving up the earth; they did not consult the people, for they were a law unto themselves. Harry Hopkins described Yalta as "the dawn of the new day we had all been praying for and talking about for so many years." It was not dawn. Blind men were groping at midnight, saying to the darkness: "This is mine."

Churchill declared that he would not consent to the United Nations "thrusting their fumbling fingers into the British Empire." Stalin forbade anyone from touching Eastern Europe. Roosevelt had taken possession of China and Japan.

They parted amicably, as befitted Titans. Churchill went off to visit the battlefield of Balaklava where, ninety years before, the Light Brigade charged into the mouths of the Russian guns. He reviewed two hundred officers and soldiers of the NKVD, the dreaded secret police—a slow task, for he paused long enough to look each man in the eye. Then he left Russian soil for the last time and flew to Greece with an escort of six fighter planes, pleased by the drama of arriving unexpectedly in a country now at peace which only seven weeks before, at Christmastime, had been seething with civil war. Here there were no Roosevelts and Stalins to keep him preoccupied with the larger problems of world peace. Here he was the hero who walked alone, greeted on all sides with applause and reverence, for at Christmas the city had been a shambles and now it was at peace, although there were Communist guerrillas in the hills. He was close to weeping when he addressed a crowd of 50,000 people in Constitution Square. "Let there be unity, let there be resolute comradeship!" he cried. "Greece for ever! Greece for all!"

While at Yalta, he had been flabbergasted to learn that President Roosevelt planned to hold conferences with King Farouk, Emperor Haile Selassie and King Ibn Saud on the *Quincy*, anchored in Great Bitter Lake. Churchill suspected a dark plot against the British Empire and asked Harry Hopkins what the President was up to. Hopkins did not know and suggested that it was "a lot of horseplay." Roosevelt received the potentates in grand style on the foredeck, wearing a huge black cloak. He was a monarch receiving other monarchs in audience, exchanging gifts, engaging in polite conversation. Churchill caught up with Roosevelt in Alexandria for a brief meeting. They had lunch together and then bade farewell. The President looked frail and ill, his life already flickering out. They never saw each other again.

Now it was Churchill's turn to hold conferences with the potentates. The meeting with Ibn Saud was oddly one-sided, for while the Arabian King came with splendid gifts—jeweled swords, damask robes, pearl necklaces, jewels and diamonds scattered negligently among the robes—Churchill's presents consisted of a few bottles of perfume bought in the streets of Cairo at the last minute. This showed perhaps how little Churchill knew or cared to know about the Arab mind. He saved himself from total disaster by promising Ibn Saud an armored Rolls-Royce as a present from His Majesty's Government and in due course the promise was fulfilled.

The strange encounter between the plump and rosy Churchill and the dark king with the profile of a desert eagle resounded with historical ambiguities. They had been enemies and were now friends. Ibn Saud, who began life as a guerrilla chieftain, had fought the Hashemite dynasty and thrown them out of Arabia. Churchill had thereupon placed two members of this dynasty, Abdullah and Feisal, on the thrones of Trans-Jordan and Iraq—thrones especially created for the purpose of satisfying the Hashemite pretensions. Ibn Saud bore no rancor. The royal cupbearer offered Churchill a glass of water from the sacred well of Zamzam in Mecca, and Churchill later remembered that it was the most delicious water he had ever drunk. In the eyes of the King this gift of water was of far greater significance than jeweled baubles and damask robes. The water was a gift beyond price.

Churchill flew back to London to find the war coming to an end, the Allies still divided about the future of Germany, uncertain of their future relations to each other. Already there was the feeling that victory might crumble like Dead Sea fruit. In the House of Commons Churchill was questioned about the Yalta agreements concerning Poland, which was now overrun by the Red Army. The Members of Parliament remembered that Britain had gone to war because Hitler had invaded Poland, and they had not forgotten that Stalin invaded Poland at the same time. Now Stalin was on the march and there was the uneasy feeling that all of Europe up to the Pyrenees and perhaps beyond would come under the rule of his merciless *apparatchiks* once Hitler was destroyed.

It was the twilight hour, the armies poised for their last battles, the fortresses crumbling. Hitler's Ardennes offensive had failed; the Germans still had a toehold west of the Rhine; the lost legions were scattering in the rubble for a last-ditch fight. Churchill flew to Eisenhower's headquarters for lunch, and a surprised General Omar Bradley heard him talking about the rocket weapons which would soon supplant all piloted airplanes. Britain would become "one vast bazooka aimed at the aggressors who threaten Europe." He went on: "There may come a day when we shall walk into a Cabinet room, break a glass over a switch, dial to the nation to be bombed, and press a button to declare war." It was a very odd remark, and while it seemed to show that he knew very little about the development of the atom bomb, it revealed a chilling foreknowledge of how future wars would begin. Men break the glass in police boxes to summon an ambulance or to announce a murder or a robbery. Here the glass was being broken to dial long-range massacre.

Churchill went to General Montgomery's headquarters at Venlo to watch the crossing of the Rhine by the Ninth American Army and the Second English Army. Near Ginsbeck, in the early-dawn light, he watched one of the greatest armadas the world has ever seen as it roared above his head. Some 3,000 aircraft and gliders escorted by 900 fighters raced eastward, and in addition there were 2,000 more fighter planes forming a defensive screen to the east. The sky was black with airplanes and the earth lay in a smoky haze. A German barrage attempted to scratch the airplanes from the sky. Puffs of black smoke arose. An airplane exploded in fire and smoke, another simply disintegrated and vanished into the haze. Meanwhile the airplanes continued to pour across the sky, and when they returned after dropping their loads of parachutists, Churchill saw the open doors and dangling parachute strings.

The generals had no illusions about Churchill's passionate desire for a grandstand view of the battle. He was a nuisance; he usually stayed too long, talked too much and gave too much advice. The British generals, who were appointed by him and existed at his pleasure, were at his mercy. Therefore they welcomed him with open arms and prayed that he would be summoned urgently to London. Sir Alan Brooke, who was accompanying him, noted in his diary: "Winston then became a

little troublesome and wanted to go messing about on the Rhine crossings and we had some difficulty in keeping him back." This cryptic note
referred to an incident on one of the bridges at Wesel. This was a big
iron-girder railroad bridge, broken in the middle but providing good
perches in the twisted ironwork. What especially delighted Churchill
was to watch the huge fountains of spray when the German shells fell in
the river. The shells were coming closer, one falling very close to the
bridge, and at this moment General Simpson, the American general in
command of this sector, insisted that the Prime Minister should leave at
once. Churchill refused. He was watching the waterworks and enjoying
himself. He threw his arms round the nearest girder, clung to it, and
assumed an expression of fierce tenacity, resembling an angry child who
has been told it is time to put his toys away. Finally he permitted
himself to be escorted off the bridge.

When he returned to London, there came news of more dissensions
among the Allies: Churchill's half-hearted encouragement of the Polish
government in exile in London, his hopes that at least the new Polish
government would include representatives of all classes of society,
strained his relations with the President, who was growing weary of
East European problems. In a long series of messages to the President
Churchill emphasized the dangers of a Soviet takeover. He hoped the
Americans and the British could get together to prevent it. "Our
friendship is the rock on which I build for the future of the world, so
long as I am one of the builders," he wrote the President in one of the
most quietly grandiloquent passages that ever came from his pen.
Roosevelt sent Judge Samuel Rosenman, one of his speech writers, and
the millionaire Bernard Baruch, a close friend of Churchill's since the
First World War, to discuss all these matters in London. And when
Stalin took offense at the secret negotiations being conducted in Switzerland for the surrender of the German armies in Italy, claiming
wrongly that there was an Anglo-American plot to turn the German
army round and send it fighting against the Russians, Roosevelt at last
saw the light. "I cannot avoid a feeling of bitter resentment toward
your informers, whoever they are, for such vile misrepresentations of
my actions or those of my trusted subordinates," Roosevelt wrote on
April 5, 1945, for the first time expressing his outrage and anger against
Stalin. A week later, on the afternoon of April 12, he died at Warm
Springs, Georgia, of a massive cerebral hemorrhage.

April was the cruelest month for the leaders of nations. On April 28
Mussolini was executed by partisans while attempting to escape into

Switzerland, and his body was brought to Milan for a ritualistic hanging upside down outside a garage. On the last day of the month Hitler shot himself in the mouth in his bunker under the Chancellery in Berlin. Three men who had dominated the world's stage for many years vanished from the scene in less than twenty days. The war in Europe, which had brought so much agony and cost the lives of more than 40,000,000 people, was over at last.

Over but not quite over, for the wounds were still bleeding and the killings continued. In the territories occupied by the Red Army the secret police and the *apparatchiks* resorted to torture and murder to force the populations to accept the authority of Stalin. In many different subterranean ways the war continued, but it was another war, which had already been going on for a long time: Stalin against the world.

Churchill's first impulse when he heard of Roosevelt's death was to fly over to attend the funeral. President Truman added his own pressing invitation, saying he hoped to have two or three days' talk with Churchill afterward. But at that moment the war still had many days to run and the prospect of being outside of England when the guns were finally silenced was not one that commended itself to Churchill when he had time to think about it. He was heartbroken, but he had other things to attend to. In the course of his long association with Roosevelt, which began with their first exchange of messages in September, 1939, they had met nine times, spending a total of one hundred twenty days together, and they had exchanged over one thousand seven hundred messages, some of them of great length. In his tribute to the President in the House of Commons Churchill spoke of "the beatings of that generous heart which was always stirred to anger and to action by spectacles of aggression and oppression by the strong against the weak."

Roosevelt's successor, Harry Truman, was a man of sober judgment, quiet and unassuming, with no pretensions to imperial grandeur. He could be hard-hitting when provoked and he was well aware of the naked powers of the Presidency. Churchill, who had never met him, was somewhat fearful that the new President might be lacking in the knowledge of international affairs, especially in the knowledge of how to deal with Stalin. He need not have been fearful. Truman was blunt, forceful, without illusions. Within a day of assuming the Presidency he had taken the measure of Stalin.

The war against Hitler ended decisively at the moment when Hitler raised his 7.65 Walther pistol to his mouth on the afternoon of April 30, but the official end of the war came at midnight on May 8, after all the ceremonies of capitulation were completed. Jubilation spread across London, the lights came on, the Union Jack was being waved everywhere by a population made delirious by peace; and although the church bells pealed and Churchill was cheered as his country's savior and spoke from a balcony in Whitehall, saying: "This is *your* victory. In all our long history we have never seen a greater day than this!" Churchill himself was weighed down by the knowledge that victory might be barren and peace elusive.

He spoke somberly over the radio to his countrymen, warning them of the totalitarian and police governments which might soon be installed in Europe and the many other dangers that confronted an exhausted, impoverished and triumphant Britain. "I should be unworthy of your confidence and generosity," he said, "if I did not cry: Forward, unflinching, unswerving, indomitable, till the whole task is done and the whole world is safe and clean!"

His government had been in office for more than five years and it was time to hold new elections. The coalition government was dissolved, a caretaker government came into existence, and new elections were set for the first week in June. Confidently—too confidently—Churchill expected to receive an overwhelming mandate from the people. Just as confidently he hoped to sweep the Labour Party into the gutter where he felt it belonged. The violence and virulence of his speeches against the Labour Party came as a shock. Obsessed by the thought of the political police in Eastern Europe, he imagined that the Labour Party would employ the same weapons as Stalin. "I declare to you, from the bottom of my heart, that no socialist system can be established without a political police," he said on the eve of the elections. If the Labour leaders tried to carry out a fully socialist program, "they would have to fall back on some kind of Gestapo, no doubt very humanely directed in the first instance." This long rambling speech, which came to be known as the "Gestapo speech," did him far more harm than good. Overnight the beloved war leader had transformed himself into a political hack.

It was a strange transformation which could be explained only by a kind of desperation. He told Lord Moran: "I am worried about this damned election. I have no message for them now."

The polling day was fixed for July 5, but the results of the election would not be announced for three weeks to enable the votes of servicemen overseas to be counted. Since the Potsdam Conference—the final meeting between the leaders of the Allied powers—was scheduled to begin in mid-July, Churchill was aware that he might be out of office before the conference came to an end. He had dominated the people for five years, his decisions had reached down into all their lives, and now through the mystery of the ballot box they were about to declare their verdict on his stewardship. He seems to have had a presentiment that he would be defeated.

On July 7, two days after the election, he flew to Bordeaux and then motored to the Chateau de Bordaberry near the Spanish frontier. Here he gave himself to painting, swimming and sunbathing. He spent the mornings in bed, the afternoons in the open air, the evenings in desultory conversations with his family. The thought of the elections oppressed him; there was no escape from it. Once, during a visit to St.-Jean-de-Luz, the people lined the streets, cheering him. He turned to his doctor and said: "I believe I could go to any country in the world and be received with cheers from humble folk." It was heady wine and he was still drinking it in long drafts. What disturbed him was that the humble folk of England had not been cheering him recently, or at least not with the ardor demanded by great statesmen and politicians.

From Bordeaux Churchill flew to Berlin for the Potsdam Conference, which had been given the code name "Terminal." The Russians had decided that the conference should take place in the vast Cecilienhof Palace, which had been erected in mock-Tudor style for Crown Prince Wilhelm and named after the Crown Princess Cecilie. It was completed and dedicated in 1917, thus demonstrating the truth that monarchs erect their largest buildings when the monarchy is on the verge of extinction. There were 176 rooms in the palace, and the one where the conference was held, with its wood paneling and Elizabethan windows, was hurriedly furnished with three enormous wooden armchairs, like thrones, upholstered in scarlet plush and with carved cherubs on the chair backs. Twelve smaller chairs were provided for the accompanying ministers, advisers and translators. For some reason Stalin chose to wear a white summer uniform with gold epaulettes, Churchill wore the light, gray-blue air force uniform made especially for officers in the tropics, and Truman wore a business suit. Churchill lodged in nearby Babelsberg at 23 Ringstrasse in a house that had once belonged to Dr. Hjalmar Schacht, the Nazi finance minister. Babelsberg was a film colony and the Cecilienhof Palace resembled a film set with its pirouetting Elizabethan chimneys and half-timber façades.

Stalin had suffered a minor heart attack and came a day late, thus giving Churchill and Truman time to observe the ruins of Berlin. Churchill wandered over the Chancellery where Hitler's study was a shambles, his marble-topped writing table upside down, the floors littered with Iron Crosses and ribbons, the air thick with the dust of destruction. He was on his way down to Hitler's bunker when his daughter Mary laughed and said: "Don't go down the mine, Daddy," and he barked at her: "Mind your bloody business." He was in a grim mood, for he was coming at long last to the wolf's lair to see the place where the wolf had died. But the ruins of Berlin made little impression on him, and he remembered that some Germans greeted him warmly and only one shook his head disapprovingly. Later he sipped whiskey on the lawn of the lakeside villa, gazing gloomily at the lake where, it was said, the Russians had thrown some German soldiers too badly wounded to walk.

He was in the Russian sector of Berlin. Indeed, all of Berlin at this time was occupied by the Russians, and all the conferences between the war leaders had taken place on Russian soil. Even at Teheran Stalin remained technically on Russian soil, for he remained within the high walls of the Soviet Embassy. The advantages therefore lay entirely with Stalin, the host.

The conference, which lasted from July 17 to August 2, was the longest, the most inconclusive, the most fateful of all the conferences. Stalin was the master strategist, playing on the weaknesses of the Allies, determined against all opposition to secure the greatest advantage. The arguments grew bitter, especially when they touched on the Polish question. When President Truman suggested that the Soviet-controlled governments of Rumania and Bulgaria be reorganized, according to the agreement made at Yalta that all the Eastern European nations should be governed by freely elected officials, Stalin pretended to be ignorant of any previous agreement and asked why the Fascist general Franco was permitted to remain in power with the support of the Americans and the British. Such arguments proliferated. Stalin had answers for everything. He would cheerfully make promises and just as cheerfully break them.

Stalin's main purpose was to acquire reparations, booty, massive supplies of grain, coal, iron. He wanted a third of the German navy. Churchill replied that these ships were terrible weapons of war and it would be better to sink them. "Let us divide the Fleet," Stalin replied. "Mr. Churchill may sink his share if it pleases him."

By cajoling, by pleading, by insisting, Stalin got nearly everything he wanted. Hungary? He mentioned the word tentatively and asked Churchill what his intentions were toward Hungary. Churchill answered that this was a matter which should be raised among the foreign ministers; he had not studied it; others would decide the issue. This was exactly what Stalin wanted to know, and Hungary was dropped in the bag. There were many other subjects that a weary Churchill had not studied sufficiently or thought of very little importance. He had not done his homework, and the consequences were sometimes disastrous.

During the afternoon of July 17 Henry Stimson, the seventy-seven-year-old Secretary of War, came to 23 Ringstrasse with a strange message, which read: "Babies satisfactorily born." The "babies" were not babies, they were not born, and there was nothing particularly satisfactory about the beginning of the atomic age. Churchill, who knew in a general way about the making of the atomic bomb, had not been told the date of the experiment in the New Mexican desert and in the excitement of the closing stages of the war in Europe he had forgotten all about it. "The atomic bomb is a reality," Stimson said, but he could provide no more details. On the following morning a more complete account of the explosion of the atomic bomb reached Potsdam by courier airplane and Churchill was given a full and graphic account of the events at the Alamogordo testing ground.

For a man who had spent his life pursuing greatness, the invention of this bomb with its unimaginably great powers of destruction came as a godsend. Here at last was an object worthy of admiration. Japan could be defeated without the need of landing hundreds of thousands of troops, fighting yard by yard across the inhospitable hills and valleys of the islands. Instead there was the vision—"fair and bright it seemed" —of putting an end to the war "in one or two violent shocks." Perhaps only Churchill could have conceived of an atomic explosion as "fair and bright." Sir Alan Brooke, in his diary, has an extraordinary picture of Churchill in the full tide of enthusiasm for the bomb, happy as a child eager to play with a new toy. "He was already seeing himself capable of eliminating all the Russian centers of industry and population without taking into account any of the connected problems, such as delivery of the bomb, production of bombs, possibility of Russians also possessing such bombs, etc. He had at once painted a wonderful picture of himself as the sole possessor of these bombs and capable of dumping them where he wished, thus all-powerful and capable of dictating to Stalin!"

The fantasies of powerful men are fantasies of power, and Churchill, debating with himself over a whiskey and soda in a lakeside garden about which of his enemies he proposed to annihilate if the atomic bomb came into his possession, would be a subject for high comedy if it were not so dreadfully and desperately tragic. In an hour or two he would be having dinner alone with Stalin, appealing to the Russian dictator on behalf of the Poles, and asking sharp questions about the British mission in Bucharest, which was under Russian guard and unable to observe what the Russians were doing in other parts of the city. Stalin angered him, but it was necessary to behave with democratic decorum. But the bomb, so fair and bright, hovered in the air, the most desirable of visions. It demanded to be used, and Churchill was already thinking of using it against his ally.

The twin goddesses of Irony and Annihilation hovered over the Potsdam conference where the gilded cherubs peered from behind the shoulders of the celebrants. The mysteries of power were being exhaustively examined, for these three men possessed at their fingertips more destructive power than had ever been accumulated by three men before. Churchill said it was necessary to guarantee the religious freedom of Catholics in Poland, and Stalin slowly stroked his gray mustache before replying: "How many divisions has the Pope got?" That was one aspect of power. Churchill was exulting in the power of the bomb to annihilate Stalin, his friend and enemy, and rejoicing like Hitler in his power to reduce Moscow and Leningrad to rubble. That was another aspect of power. Truman, who had never expected or hoped to be President, was the possessor and the prime mover of the bombs that would fall on Hiroshima and Nagasaki. Power, ultimate power, assumed the form of a mushroom-shaped cloud with a seething core of radioactive flames.

Just as monarchs build their most extravagant buildings when they are about to go down to defeat, so Churchill enjoyed his most extravagant fantasies of power just at the moment when he was about to be thrown out of office.

Meanwhile the tragic comedy was pursued to its ironic conclusion. On July 24, a week after news of the Alamogordo explosion reached Potsdam, at around 7:30 P.M., at the end of a long day of conferences, President Truman rose from the table and sauntered over to Stalin. He had no intention of telling Stalin exactly what had happened on the New Mexico testing ground, but after long discussion with his advisers he thought he should at least prepare him for the day when the bomb would be exploded over Japan. So Truman mentioned casually that the

Americans possessed a new bomb of unusual destructive force. Stalin seemed unimpressed and said he hoped good use would be made of it. Churchill, standing about five yards away, watched in fascination while Truman took Stalin by the arm and briefly conveyed the news. Stalin's face, reported Churchill, "remained gay and genial and the talk between these two potentates soon came to an end. As we were waiting for our cars I found myself near Truman. 'How did it go?' I asked. 'He never asked a question,' he replied."

At that moment the twin goddesses of Irony and Annihilation smiled briefly at one another, for Stalin had known about the bomb for nearly a year and was already building a prototype.

That night Churchill had a prophetic nightmare. He dreamed he was dead and gazing at his dead body under a white sheet in an empty room. He knew it was his own body because he recognized the feet projecting from under the sheet. "Perhaps this is the end," he told his doctor, and so it was.

In the afternoon he flew back to London to prepare for the electoral returns. The Conservative Party was so overwhelmingly rejected by the electorate that he had no alternative but to offer his resignation to the King and to issue a guarded message of gratitude to the British people for the many expressions of kindness they had shown to their servant. But he was never their servant; he had mastered them too long; and they threw him out because he had taken all the power to himself, leaving none to others, and they were weary of him.

The Withered Garland

I have achieved a great deal to
achieve nothing in the end.

THE ANCIENT OF DAYS

Something in Churchill died on July 26, 1945; the stuffing went out of him. He had achieved great eminence under the wildest and most improbable circumstances, for no one could ever have imagined that an obscure Austrian corporal would one day hold the world by the throat and that Churchill would be one of those chosen to cut off the strangler's hand. The war in its horror exceeded all imaginable fantasies, and both Hitler and Churchill had something fantastical about them, as though they had emerged out of dreams and nightmares. Now Hitler was dead, and less than three months later Churchill was dismissed from office. It was as though the people of the world wanted to get back as soon as possible to the familiar, workaday world where fantastic creatures no longer played a role in history.

Throughout his political life power had been Churchill's obsession, his food, his motive force, his *raison d'être*. Without it he could scarcely breathe. Now power had been taken from him and handed over to the quiet, dull, efficient Clement Attlee, who had never made a memorable speech or commanded armies. It was absurd; it was unforgivable; and Churchill raged against the ingratitude of the British people.

There had of course been some warnings that his popularity was not quite so great as he imagined it to be. He had suggested that he might

visit a British canteen in Berlin, and had done so. The commanding
officer had previously ordered the men to cheer their distinguished
guest. Instead, they raised only a faint apology of a cheer and there
were some catcalls. Churchill was offended. He liked to be cheered, and
was put out if the cheering lacked the requisite strength. "Have I," he
asked innocently, "done anything wrong?" He was told that he had
done nothing wrong: it was simply that the vast majority of the soldiers
belonged to the Labour Party and they wanted the Labour government
in power. Churchill stalked out of the canteen white as a ghost.

Now, out of office, he was confronted by the fact that his life had
become meaningless, without direction or purpose. There were no
great themes to be orchestrated, no great decisions to be taken, no
messages to be sent to heads of state. "The election," he declared
angrily, "is one of the greatest disasters that has smitten us in our long
and chequered history." What he meant was that his fall from power
was a disaster of incalculable proportions—to himself. He was stunned
and shocked by the size of the Labour majority. He said: "It is a strange
feeling, all power gone. I had made all my plans. I feel I could have
dealt with things better than anyone else. This is Labour's opportunity
to bring in socialism, and they will take it. They will go very far."

The thought that Labour would inevitably go too far and that the
British people would inevitably summon him back to office to redress
the wrongs inflicted upon them buoyed him up, but not for long. He
calculated that Labour would govern England for a full four-year term,
and by that time he might be too old to fight. Meanwhile how would he
occupy himself during those long slow years?

The King offered him any honors he cared to name: a dukedom, an
earldom, a new title specially created for him, and he rejected all
except the Order of Merit. What greater honor was there than to be
called Winston Churchill? Cities all over the Empire clamored for the
privilege of offering him the ceremonial gold keys which entitled him
to be called "a freeman of the city." He rejected these offers. The kings
and queens of Norway, Denmark and Holland invited him to their
courts, and they too were rejected. He denounced everyone who would
attempt to honor him. "I refuse," he said, "to be exhibited like a prize
bull whose chief attraction is its past prowess."

Because his furniture was being removed from 10 Downing Street he
lived for a few days in a sixth-floor penthouse apartment at Claridge's
Hotel, the most sumptuous and expensive in London. There was a
balcony outside the apartment with an eighty-foot drop to the ground.

Heights had always troubled him and he carefully avoided the balcony, saying: "I don't like sleeping near a precipice like that. I've no desire to quit the world, but thoughts, desperate thoughts come into the head."

"Black dog," the constant companion who could be kept at bay only when he was in full enjoyment of power, came bounding up to him. He slept badly; his stomach troubled him; small things irritated him. He was taking sleeping pills regularly. He kept waking up at four o'clock in the morning to wonder what he had done wrong and how he could have prevented his fall from grace, and then he would take another sleeping pill. Fabulous sums of money were being offered to him for his articles and memoirs—*Life* had offered him £20,000 for four short articles amounting altogether to 20,000 words—and he was wondering why he should make the effort, since most of the money would vanish in income tax. Like many very rich men he was wondering whether he had enough money to live on.

People spoke of his unflagging zest for life, but it was flagging now. There were childish outbursts of petulance, sudden tirades against former friends, explosions of helpless anger. From South Africa General Smuts cabled his congratulations to Clement Attlee for his "brilliant victory." General Smuts had been Churchill's friend for half a century: this was an act of gross disloyalty. "Brilliant victory?" Churchill shouted. "Why brilliant? It wasn't brilliant at all!" General Smuts was properly punished. He had sent two separate messages to Churchill congratulating him on his great accomplishments and commiserating with him on his fall from power. The messages were left unanswered.

Churchill in the first flush of defeat was an unpleasant spectacle. He felt that the English had betrayed him and had scarcely deserved him. "I don't mind if I never see England again," he told Lord Moran. "Ah, Charles, blessings become curses. You kept me alive and now—" Had he been kept alive by his remarkable doctor only so that he could preside over his own downfall? There were tears of fury and exasperation in his eyes. The truth was that rejection by the voters had brought on a nervous breakdown and the wound would take a long time to heal.

To recuperate he flew to Italy with his doctor and his daughter Sarah, leaving his wife behind to prepare the new house he had bought at 28 Hyde Park Gate, a secluded dead-end street in Kensington, which would be his London home for the rest of his life. Field Marshal Alexander invited him to stay in his large villa, La Rosa, on Lake Como. He was strangely apathetic when he arrived at the villa. Gradually, as the days passed, he began to thaw out. For six days no mail reached him—no letters, no telegrams, no newspapers. During all those six days not a single piece of news reached the man who had always been hungry for news, and he seemed not to care. Thirty years earlier, after the disaster of Gallipoli, he had taken up painting as a means to quiet nerves stretched to the breaking point. Now with his paint box he went in search of a painting.

He was ferried across the lake in a motorboat and decided to paint a yellow kiosk, shaded by willows, on the lakeshore. The weather was still summery, the crickets chirped and there was a cool breeze. He enjoyed painting the willows and their reflections in the lake, and he managed the kiosk well, giving it solidity and a shadowy grace. The lake is dappled with gold and flashes of emerald green, and it is a pleasant enough painting except that the willows appear to have no roots and will crash into the lake if anyone so much as raises a whisper. Churchill pronounced that he had never painted so well. He would spend the rest of his life painting, and be damned to politics! "I'm damned glad now to be out of it!" he said with more force than conviction. The newspapers which had been held up at Naples finally arrived; they bored him; he threatened never to read a newspaper again; and soon "black dog" settled on him again, and once more he was wondering what he had done wrong. His failures? Perhaps the return to the Gold Standard, but that was long ago. A visitor arrived with the gifts he wanted above all others, a handful of brushes and nearly a hundred tubes of paint. Squeezing the tubes, he was happy again.

One day when a swarm of flies entered the palatial villa, he decided to make war on them. Everyone was ordered to destroy as many flies as possible by swatting them with napkins. When the assault was over, all the dead flies were lined up on the table to be counted. There were thirty of them, and he was well pleased.

Peasants came with offerings of flowers, there were picnics, he continued to paint, and time stood still. Time had not always stood still, and he pondered the matter deeply. One evening, when they were gazing across the darkened lake and listening to the goat bells, Churchill turned to young Captain John Ogier, the aide-de-camp thoughtfully provided by Field Marshal Alexander, and said: "Out of a life of long and varied experience, the most valuable piece of advice I could hand on to you is to know how to command the moment to remain."

"That," said Captain Ogier, "is what I am trying to do."

The advice was well-meant and couched in the appropriate rhetorical manner. Unhappily it was totally useless. Time was eating away at him and abjectly refused to remain.

He was by turns truculent and downcast when he returned to England, and there was little fight in him. Occasionally, as leader of the Conservative Party, he made speeches in Parliament against the policies of the Labour Party, reserving his choicest barbs for the Prime Minister, Clement Attlee, whom he thoroughly despised. In private he would say: "I'll tear their bleeding entrails out of them!" But the barbs were strangely ineffective, Attlee maintained his quiet good humor, and Churchill found himself wondering whether he was losing his customary fire.

He was still fretting about his powerlessness to command events when there came to him a heaven-sent opportunity to make himself heard and he seized it eagerly. The invitation to speak came from an obscure town in Midwestern America with a population of about 7,000 people. In normal times he would have asked his secretary to write a polite letter of regret, but these were not normal times. He decided to speak in the heart of America about "The Sinews of Peace."

Although he was in a chastened mood, there remained one subject on which he was determined to be heard—the intransigence of Stalin. On this subject he was an authority, and his belief that the world should be warned against the growing might of the Soviet Union led him to make the most famous of his postwar speeches, which he delivered when receiving an honorary degree at Westminster College in Fulton, Missouri, on March 5, 1946. He was introduced by President Truman. The speech provoked an outcry and seemed to be deliberately provocative; and when he spoke of "the iron curtain," people half-imagined he had himself rung down the curtain. But in fact the speech was notable for its moderation. His message was the overwhelming need for an understanding between East and West. He said:

> From Stettin in the Baltic to Trieste in the Adriatic, an iron curtain has descended across the Continent. Behind that line lie all the capitals of the ancient states of Central and Eastern Europe. Warsaw, Berlin, Prague, Vienna, Budapest, Belgrade, Bucharest and Sofia, all these famous cities and the populations around them lie in what I must call the Soviet sphere, and are all subject in one form or another, not only to Soviet influence but to a very high and, in many cases, increasing measure of control from Moscow. Athens alone—Greece with its immortal glories—is

free to decide its future in an election under British, American and French observation. The Russian-dominated Polish government has been encouraged to make enormous and wrongful inroads upon Germany, and mass expulsions of millions of Germans on a scale grievous and undreamed-of are now taking place. The Communist parties which were very small in these Eastern States of Europe have been raised to pre-eminence and power far beyond their numbers, and are seeking everywhere to obtain totalitarian control. Police governments are prevailing in nearly every case. . . .

In great numbers of countries, far from the Russian frontiers and throughout the world, Communist fifth columns are established and work in complete unity and absolute obedience to the directions they receive from the Communist centre. Except in the British Commonwealth and in the United States, where Communism is in its infancy, the Communist parties or fifth columns constitute a growing challenge and peril to Christian civilisation. These are sombre facts for anyone to have to recite on the morrow of a victory gained by so much splendid comradeship in arms and in the cause of freedom and democracy; and we should be most unwise not to face them squarely while time remains. . . .

From what I have seen of our Russian friends and allies during the war, I am convinced there is nothing they admire so much as strength, and there is nothing for which they have less respect than weakness, especially military weakness. . . .

Last time I saw it all coming and cried aloud to my own fellow-countrymen and to the world, but no one paid any attention. Up to the year 1933 or even 1935, Germany might have been saved from the awful fate which has overtaken her and we might have all been spared the miseries Hitler let loose upon mankind. There never was a war in all history easier to prevent by timely action than the one which has just desolated such great areas of the globe. It could have been prevented in my belief without the firing of a single shot, and Germany might be powerful, prosperous and honoured today; but no one would listen and one by one we were all sucked into the awful whirlpool. We surely must not let that happen again. This can only be achieved by reaching now, in 1946, a good understanding on all points with Russia. . . .

This was the last rumbling growl of the aging lion. There would be more speeches, more warnings, more utterances, but never again would he speak so memorably. The words "iron curtain"* entered deep into

*The idea of the "iron curtain" had been born ten months earlier in a telegram from Churchill to President Truman on May 12, 1945. "An iron curtain is drawn down upon their front. We do not know what is going on behind. There seems little doubt that the whole of the regions east of the line Lubeck-Trieste-Corfu will soon be completely in their hands." On June 4, 1945, in another

people's consciousness. The shuddering clang of the curtain coming down echoed across the world, and it was generally forgotten that Churchill had been hoping above all for "a good understanding on all points with Russia."

He returned to the half-obscurity of Chartwell Manor, his farms, his racing stable, his painting, and his books. That was the year in which he first seriously engaged in farming, buying 500 acres to the south of the estate, hoping to derive a profit from the land and placing his son-in-law, Christopher Soames, in charge of the farmland. He was painting vigorously and preparing himself for the great, lumbering six-volume history of World War II which was to absorb much of his energy during the following years. *The Second World War,* financially the most successful of all his books—he received $1,000,000 for the syndication rights alone—was not quite the great work everyone had hoped it would be. As usual he employed armies of researchers and scholars and technical experts to study the vast accumulation of documents assembled at Chartwell. They attacked these forests of documents like mechanical cutting machines; one row of trees was felled, then another and another, until by the end of the sixth volume there was nothing left to be said about the entire course of the war. Inevitably there was logrolling. Churchill's view of the war suffered from the profound conviction that he was at the heart and center of it. He is unfair and contemptuous of many of his subordinates, and he glosses lightly over his own errors. Much of the story is told in terms of his own documents and the minutes labeled FOR ACTION TODAY. His letters to Roosevelt and Stalin are quoted at formidable length, but we are not always given their replies.

A photograph taken about the time when he was writing *The Gathering Storm,* the first of the six volumes on the Second World War, shows him out hunting with the Old Surrey and Burstow Hunt, wearing an impeccable hunting costume, square black hat on his head, riding crop in his hand, and there is about that heavy, solemn face something of the look of the conqueror, indrawn, conscious of his own glory, like

---

telegram to President Truman, he wrote of his profound misgivings over the retreat of the American army to the occupation line, "thus bringing Soviet power into the heart of Western Europe and the descent of an iron curtain between us and everything to the eastward." At Potsdam Churchill confronted Stalin with the "iron fence" which surrounded Soviet-occupied territories. "All fairy tales," Stalin commented. But it was not a fairy tale, and the history of Europe for generations will depend upon the fortunes of this fence.

Although Churchill's Fulton speech was one of the most important he ever delivered, President Truman scarcely mentions it in his memoirs.

the Duke of Marlborough as depicted on the tapestries at Blenheim. So in his history of the war we are continually made aware of the conqueror—the condescending glance, the consciousness of the power pouring out of his five-sworded hands. He dominates the stage, and all the rest of the players except Stalin and Roosevelt are mere spear-carriers. This is bad enough, but the prose is so florid, so flaccid, that we rarely see the events he describes in clear focus. During the war he had struck off memorable phrases by the dozen. They soared like colored rockets to illuminate the darkness. There was urgency in the phrasing and a sense of the immediate grandeur of the occasion. But when he wrote after the war, all these are lacking. Here, for example, he sums up his conclusions at the end of the second volume of his history, which he called *Their Finest Hour:*

> We may, I am sure, rate this tremendous year as the most splendid, as it was the most deadly, year in our long English and British history. It was a great, quaintly organized England that had destroyed the Spanish Armada. A strong flame of conviction and resolve carried us through the twenty-five years' conflict which William III and Marlborough waged against Louis XIV. There was a famous period with Chatham. There was the long struggle against Napoleon in which our survival was secured through the domination of the seas by the British Navy under the classic leadership of Nelson and his associates. A million Britons died in the First World War. But nothing surpasses 1940. By the end of that year this small Island, with its devoted Commonwealth, Dominions and attachments under every sky, had proved itself capable of bearing the whole impact and weight of world destiny. The citadel of the Commonwealth and the Empire could not be stormed. Alone, but upborne by every generous heart-beat of mankind, we had defied the tyrant in the hour of his triumph.

A schoolboy could have written this passage, and done it better. There is no sharpness in the vision: only a blur of triumph. The heavy syrup flows, the centuries pass, Marlborough and Nelson assume their proper places in English history, and England, in December, 1940, achieves its finest hour in prose that falls so far short of the occasion that it would have been better if it had never been written.

Churchill at his worst is scarcely credible, so ponderous, so pontifical, so self-indulgent that he might be an elderly archbishop gone to seed. He enjoyed words, the heavier and larger the better. He liked to roll them on his tongue, like rich spicy food. He liked especially to channel them into strange and exotic courses, so that they would fall on the listener's ear with an effect of mounting surprise. It was necessary that the listener should be a little bemused and bewildered by his incantations and that there should be a final thrust to the heart of the matter. But in his summing up of 1940 there is only exaggerated rhetoric and waffling.

When he wrote at his best, he gave the effect of hammering metal into shape. He gave new colors to words and saw that they moved in proper order toward an inevitable end. But in the *Second World War* there are fewer memorable passages than in *The World Crisis*. Churchill throws all the documents into the *Second World War*, and there comes at last the suspicion that even when he was writing these directives and memoranda he was thinking about how they would appear in a majestic six-volume history of the war.

General Smuts complained bitterly that this was not the history Churchill should have written. Churchill had glossed over the failures, the treacheries, the compromises; he had painted himself throughout as the heroic leader surrounded by lesser men and as the man who had shaped the war and dominated it; and it had not always happened as he said it happened. When Sir Alan Brooke, now Lord Alanbrooke, published his *Diaries*, Churchill was furious. Brooke claimed that Churchill's military advisers deserved some credit for the long-range planning of the war. In fact Brooke himself had been responsible for most of the major decisions and had prevented Churchill from committing his most dangerous follies. He was a good judge of character; Churchill was not. He was quiet, reticent, self-contained; Churchill was noisy, bombastic, self-explosive. Lord Moran asked Churchill once whether Brooke had not done a pretty good job. "He has a flair for the business," Churchill grunted, but that was all he would concede. He regarded Brooke simply as one of his servants.

Churchill enjoyed writing the *Second World War*. He had a well-trained staff of ghost writers and research assistants, but he revised so much and so often that these books bear his own unmistakable stamp. They served their purpose, they kept him busy, they blunted the wounds of defeat, and his efforts were well paid.

The first volume *The Gathering Storm* was published in 1948; the second volume, *Their Finest Hour*, came out in 1949; then came *The Grand Alliance* in 1950, *The Hinge of Fate* in 1951, and *Closing the Ring* in 1952. Thus the first five volumes came out at the rate of one a year. The delay in the publication of the sixth volume was apparently caused by the fact that in October, 1951, after he had completed *Closing the Ring,* he became Prime Minister again. At the elections the Socialists received 48.77% of the votes, the Conservatives 47.98%, and the Liberals, once the dominant party, 2.55%. While the Socialists had won more votes, the Conservatives had won more seats. With this narrow margin he was able to rule for the next four years.

Happily it was a period when he was not called upon to make any important decisions. Except in Korea the world was enjoying an uneasy peace. He was deaf, he suffered from sciatica, his memory was going, he had only a brief span of attention and he was seventy-seven years old, but he could still go through all the motions of ruling, and the familiar rasping voice was still resonant, though he spoke more slowly now. Almost the first task he gave himself was to arrange a visit to America. Even when he had lost touch with English audiences, he felt close to American audiences: these visits to America had the nature of journeys to the sources of his strength. They revivified him, gave him new ideas, brought him into contact with people like Bernard Baruch, a financier for whom he had nothing but admiration, and he was always stimulated by an invitation to speak to the Congress. President Truman had left the Presidency to General Eisenhower.

Churchill's relations with Truman were tart and friendly; they had liked one another at Potsdam but with reservations. Churchill had enjoyed high office for thirty-four years, Truman had been President for only a few weeks. Now, meeting again for the first time since Potsdam, Churchill went out of his way to make amends for those unspoken reservations. He confessed that he had not thought very highly of Truman's statesmanship but had learned better. The years had shaped and molded Truman into a statesman of extraordinary accomplishment and they could now speak on equal terms. But Churchill could still be prickly.

One evening at the White House it occurred to Churchill that both he and Truman would have to answer at the Judgment Seat for letting loose the atomic bomb. Since Churchill's responsibility was minimal, he was evidently treading on dangerous ground. General Marshall, Averell Harriman, Robert Lovett, General Omar Bradley and Dean Acheson were present, together with some members of Churchill's personal staff. Before the President could answer, Robert Lovett, who was the Secretary of Defense, said quickly: "Are you sure, Prime Minister, that you and the President will undergo your interrogations in the same place?"

"I do not think God will condemn me without a hearing," Churchill replied.

"True," said Lovett, "but to begin with not in the Supreme Court, and possibly in quite a different jurisdiction."

"I admit this possibility," Churchill said, "but I insist that wherever the hearing might take place it will be conducted according to the principles of the English common law."

Churchill's original question had been deftly parried; the atomic bombs had vanished; and now Dean Acheson, the Secretary of State, interrupted to suggest that it was hardly flattering to the Creator's imagination to suppose that His justice was limited to the common law practiced "on a tiny island on a small star in one of His lesser universes." Churchill was enjoying his champagne, and in no mood to disagree. He suggested he should be judged by his peers, and Acheson and Lovett impaneled a jury. Alexander the Great, Julius Caesar, Socrates, Aristotle, Voltaire, Cromwell and George Washington were summoned from the shades, but suddenly Churchill grew alarmed. "You'll not put me in any black hole!" he cried, and suddenly President Truman intervened. Too many ghosts were abroad, and the white flames of paranoia were beginning to glow with an unearthly light. Dean Acheson, who tells the story, remarked: "We had taken liberties enough." So they had, and the evening ended less soberly with President Truman playing the piano.

Soon after Churchill's return from America King George VI died in his sleep. The quiet death of this quiet man profoundly affected Churchill, who had known the King more intimately than anyone outside the royal family. They had often dined together alone, waiting on each other at the table. The King had suffered from cancer; a lung was removed; and it was thought that he was well on the way to recovery when he died unexpectedly. Churchill, grief-stricken, sent a wreath with an inscription in his own handwriting which said only: "For Valour."

With the King's death the new Elizabethan Age began, for the Princess Elizabeth became Queen. Churchill, dazzled by the young Queen's beauty and her obvious competence to deal with affairs of state, rejoiced in his many private meetings with her. After his electoral defeat in 1945 he refused all honors from the King. Now, nine years later, he relented sufficiently to receive from the hands of the Queen the insignia of a Knight Companion of the Most Honourable and Noble Order of the Garter, an order of knighthood created in the middle of the fourteenth century. Originally the knights merely wore garters on their arms, but in the course of centuries a uniform of extraordinary splendor had been devised. On solemn occasions the knight wore a spray of white feathers in a velvet cap, a dark-blue mantle adorned with the blue and gold garter, and from a necklace of diamonds and rubies hung the "Gold George," representing St. George and the Dragon. In addition there were ribbons and sashes and tassels galore, so that anyone dressed in his Garter robes resembled an Italian admiral of the fleet in full uniform. Churchill, who adored uniforms, could not resist this gaudiest of uniforms, and with great solemnity he led the knights in procession to St. George's Chapel, Windsor, the traditional gathering place of the Order. In this way the familiar Winston Churchill became the unfamiliar Sir Winston Churchill, K.G.

In the same year he suffered a stroke, which temporarily paralyzed his left arm and leg. He had suffered a previous stroke in the summer of 1949, when he was out of power. Now, in power, he insisted that his infirmity should be kept secret, for he intended to recover in the shortest possible time. His speech was slurred, he walked badly, his eyesight was failing and his small span of attention grew smaller. A bulletin was issued saying that he was overworked and needed a month's complete rest. He was by no means overworked and needed a year's complete rest. But this was not how he saw his condition. He was in his seventy-ninth year and hoped to live as long as Gladstone, who died at eighty-eight. He was under the delusion that he was still essential and that no one else could rule Britain effectively. "There is a feeling that I am the only person who can do anything with Russia," he told his doctor. It occurred to him that he alone among Englishmen was capable of dealing with the Americans. Stalin had just died and a new government had emerged under Georgy Malenkov. In America his prestige was regarded as a wasting asset, and in the Soviet Union he was regarded as a near-Fascist, a reactionary who had joined forces with Russia only because the accidents of war demanded a temporary alliance.

Nevertheless, he continued to rule and later in the year he recovered sufficiently to deliver a fighting speech at the Conservative Party conference. He announced that he had not the least intention of retiring. "If I stay, for the time being, bearing the burden of my age, it is not because of love for power or office," he declared. "I have had an ample share of both. If I stay it is because I have the feeling that I may, through things that have happened, have an influence on what I care about above all else—the heralding of a sure and lasting peace."

But this was to avoid the main issue, which was that he was no longer capable of accurate judgment. He stayed because he could not tolerate being out of power, because it was intolerable that he, who had played the role of world statesman for so long, should be asked to step down just at the moment when he had most to offer the world, because he was terrified of obscurity and old age, and because he was under the impression that President Eisenhower and Premier Malenkov held him in high honor. So perhaps they did, but they were political realists and were not likely to be swayed by his powers of oratory.

More and more as he grew older his moods became violent and unpredictable. He would say strange things about the French—"Five years of ignominy, and they enjoyed every hour of it." He said stranger things about thermonuclear power, alternately exulting in it and deploring the miserable scientists who brought it about. Britain had exploded its first bomb in the Woomera Range in the South Australian desert in October, 1952, during his premiership. Sometimes he spoke as though he believed with an almost religious intensity that it had been given to him, and to him alone, to save the world from thermonuclear war, but time was running out. Once he had a strange dream of traveling in a train through Russia with Molotov and Voroshilov, and they were all engaged in a counterrevolution. In the dream he was provided with some atomic bombs the size of matchboxes. All of Russia, and all the Russians, were wiped out. It was the same dream which he had enjoyed in a waking form while sitting outside his lakeside villa in Berlin on the day after Henry Stimson first told him about the explosion in the New Mexico desert.

On November 30, 1954, in Westminster Hall, there was a ceremony attended by nearly all the Members of Parliament to celebrate his eightieth birthday. They had come together to pay tribute to him and to present him with his portrait by Graham Sutherland, the leading portraitist of his time. The drums beat out the opening bars of Beethoven's Fifth Symphony—three shorts and a long which signify V in the morse code, the V of victory with which the BBC began all its news broadcasts to the subjugated countries of Europe during World War II, and then the Guards Band played Elgar's "Pomp and Circumstance." There were speeches by the Speaker of the House of Commons, by Clement Attlee, and many more, and then Churchill rose to give thanks to the Members of Parliament for their gift. "The portrait is a remarkable example of modern art," he declared mildly. "It certainly combines force and candour."

The truth was that he hated the portrait, which shows him in his old frock coat, pinstriped trousers and polka-dot tie about to rise from the front bench and make some withering retort. It is a powerful portrait, not elegant, but showing him as he was, gnarled and pitted by age, contemptuous of lesser men, seething with a last surge of pugnacity. Here was Churchill stripped of legends, with the blood of American blacksmiths in his veins. He would have preferred to have been painted in his Garter robes, and indeed he had brought the robes to Graham Sutherland's studio in the hope that the artist would paint him in this uniform. The artist, however, was more concerned with the fierce humanity of the man, and so depicted him. "Filthy," Churchill said. "I think it is malignant." But it was none of these. Here at last, powerfully expressed, was the real Churchill beneath his disguises.

In the peroration to his speech in Westminster Hall Churchill showed that he could still speak superbly. He declared: "I have never accepted what many people have kindly said—namely that I inspired the nation. Their will was resolute and remorseless, and as it proved unconquerable. It fell to me to express it, and if I found the right words you must remember that I have always earned my living by my pen and by my tongue. It was the nation and the race dwelling all round the globe that had the lion's heart. I had the luck to be called upon to give the roar."

THE DEATH OF
A GREAT MAN

ON APRIL 5, 1955, Queen Elizabeth II was graciously
pleased to accept the resignation of the Prime Minister and First Lord
of the Treasury, Sir Winston Churchill. The Court Circular mentioned
the matter briefly and went on to less important things. His successor,
Sir Anthony Eden, kissed the Queen's hands and was appointed, though
unworthy, to fill the place of the man who was regarded as the greatest
Englishman of his time and who was now at last permitted to retire
gracefully at the age of eighty.

Inevitably there were quarrels and recriminations. Churchill
thought he was being edged out a little too abruptly, and he would
sometimes cast a baleful eye on his protégé, Eden, imagining plots and
counterplots, while an even more baleful look was reserved for Harold
Macmillan, regarded as the archconspirator. He had hoped to die in
harness; instead he was doomed to live out his life in shadowy retirement. For how long? This, too, was a question that profoundly
interested him. He thought he might live for three years, perhaps four
and a half. "I will die contentedly," he told his doctor. "I have seen all
there is to be seen." But he was more discontented than ever, and above
everything else he hated the loss of power.

Old age works strangely on the minds of once powerful men. His life had been disorderly, but the exercise of power had imposed its own disciplines and restraints. Now that all disciplines and restraints were gone, he became more self-indulgent, more selfish, more demanding and more querulous. He liked to say that he had divested himself of power like a man who removes a heavy cloak and allows it to fall at his feet, but he was continually grabbing at the cloak and trying to put it on again. In the House of Commons he continued to attack his enemies with the old fury. Old age did not temper him; on the contrary it exasperated him.

Death, his own death, fascinated him, and though he pretended there was nothing in the world he wanted more, the truth was there was nothing he wanted less. He had always been a hypochondriac; now he exulted in his pills, his medicines, his interminable conversations with his doctor. He became violently alarmed if his handwriting became shaky. It annoyed him that Lord Moran could not rejuvenate him. To a visiting American he said: "I look forward to dying. Sleep, endless, wonderful sleep—on a purple, velvety cushion. Every so often I will wake up, turn over, and go to sleep again." In medieval times purple, velvety cushions were reserved for royalty.

Nevertheless there were practical matters to be attended to. There was the four-volume work called *A History of the English-Speaking Peoples*, which he had pondered in the early thirties and begun to write early in 1938, virtually completing it before the outbreak of the Second World War. There were revisions to be made, new introductions to the separate volumes had to be written, and he spent some months tinkering with the work. He had already written about half a million words; a few thousand more were now added. The introduction to the first volume, which took the story up to Bosworth Field, included a disclaimer. He wrote that he had no intention of rivaling the works of professional historians. "It aims rather to present a personal view on the processes whereby English-speaking peoples throughout the world have achieved their distinctive position and character. I wrote about things in our past that appear significant to me, and I do so as one not without some experience of historical and violent events in our own time."

Such modest reminders of his place in history were pardonable but unnecessary. Arthur Balfour described *The World Crisis*, Churchill's history of the First World War, as "Winston's brilliant autobiography disguised as a history of the universe." The same could be said of *A History of the English-Speaking Peoples*, which tells us more about

Churchill than about history. There is almost nothing about social affairs or economics, the rise and fall of classes, the advances of technology; nothing about the English poets; less than nothing about the great scientists. The procession of great panoplied figures, kings and their ministers and generals, continues uninterruptedly. He gives the appearance of someone walking down a great picture gallery, pausing at intervals to examine a battle scene or a richly costumed grandee. Marlborough appears in all the panoply of innocence. Cromwell is examined minutely, with mingled affection and horror. William Pitt the Elder, Earl of Chatham, is described lovingly as one who "called into life and action the depressed and languid spirit of England," and whose policy was "a projection on a vast screen of his own aggressive dominating personality." Lincoln is damned with faint praise, and Robert E. Lee emerges as the consummate hero of the American Civil War, while the courage of the South is exalted at the expense of the North, which is depicted as ruthless and mercenary, given over to the vices of industrialism. Churchill especially admired "Stonewall" Jackson. "Black-bearded, pale-faced, with thin, compressed lips, aquiline nose, and dark, piercing eyes, he slouched in his weather-stained uniform, a professor warrior." Lord Randolph Churchill is given his due place in history and depicted as a model of imperialist propriety.

The first two volumes of the book appeared in 1956, the year of Sir Anthony Eden's fiasco at Suez. Eden was not solely responsible for the fiasco. From his exile Churchill advised and encouraged Eden to commit his follies, leaving his protégé to take the blame. Suez was the last of Churchill's imperialist escapades, and one of the most tragic, for it was to color the history of the Near East for generations to come.

Meanwhile he continued to tinker with *A History of the English-Speaking Peoples*, the third volume, *The Age of Revolution*, coming out in 1957, and the last, *The Great Democracies*, in 1958. The book ends abruptly with the Treaty of Vereeniging which brought the Boer War to a close. The war in South Africa is described almost casually. There are no set pieces, no battle scenes. Queen Victoria dies, and history comes to an end.

But what is history? Churchill never quite comes to grips with it in any of his histories. He writes history as though it were concerned solely with great men, great triumphs and great defeats; the people are notably absent; there is no sense of an unfolding drama. Time stands still, while we move from one picture frame to the next. Yet sometimes he still wrote magnificently, with a feeling for the vast and meaningless tragedy of war. Here he describes the fate of his beloved South in the American Civil War:

> By the end of 1863 all illusions had vanished. The South knew they had lost the war, and would be conquered and flattened. It is one of the enduring glories of the American nation that this made no difference to the Confederate resistance. In the North, where success was certain, they could afford to have bitter division. On the beaten side the departure of hope left only the resolve to perish arms in hand. Better the complete destruction of the whole generation and the devastation of their enormous land, better that every farm should be burned, every city bombarded, every fighting man killed, than that history should record that they had yielded. Any man can be trampled down by superior force, and death, in whatever shape it comes, is only death.

Indeed he wrote best about defeats and annihilation, whose shapes he knew well and was beginning to know better as his life drew to a close.

This passage about the Confederacy was among the last things he wrote, for the manuscript written during 1938 and the early part of 1939 was virtually complete except for an account of the American Civil War. It had been partially written and sketched out, but about forty pages still needed to be written. He wrote these words in 1957, and perhaps more than any other of his writings they may be regarded as his testament. The defiance remains, but it is softly muted at the end. His valediction to the world is expressed in a moving paragraph about a people he scarcely knew, for all his American forbears came from New England and he had made only brief visits to the South.

After finishing *The Great Democracies* he wrote no more books. He had neither the energy nor the intellectual curiosity necessary for sustained work. He was resting on his laurels. Lord Moran noted that in his conversations he always liked to talk about people of high consequence, meaning kings, cabinet ministers, aristocrats of impeccable lineage or the very rich. Lesser mortals bored him. In his fantasies he still consorted with great personages. The world he had loved had come almost to an end. The British aristocracy survived, but had lost all meaning, and the British Empire which he thought would endure for a thousand years had perished from the earth. He was a survivor in a colder age.

He thirsted for the sun, and spent his winters whenever possible in the south of France, where he played bezique for eight hours a day, painted sometimes and continued to eat gargantuan meals and drink brandy, whiskey and champagne in copious quantities. He was growing deafer, and like his friend Bernard Baruch he was adept at turning off his hearing aid. When he stayed at Lord Beaverbrook's villa at Cap-d'Ail, he would sometimes wander over to the casino at Monte Carlo. There he would gamble fifty or a hundred pounds at the tables and was extravagantly ill-humored when he lost and jubilant when he won. He was frittering his life away.

Aristotle Onassis, a multimillionaire shipowner with a dubious past, invited him to cruise on his palatial yacht, the *Christina,* and Churchill accepted with alacrity. It was strange company for a great statesman, but Onassis was suitably deferential and had very little to say. Once Greta Garbo came on board the yacht. She, too, had little to say, and they merely gazed at one another. Churchill was not especially attached to Onassis, but enjoyed the service. In 1960 they went on a three-week cruise in the *Christina* to the Caribbean and later in the same year there was another cruise among the Greek islands. He looked terribly old, his shoulders were stooped and he walked with shuffling steps. Often he fell into a lethargy; many hours passed, and all the time he seemed to be engrossed in an old man's dreams, but suddenly he would start out of his dreams and talk at length, usually about something that had disturbed or annoyed him in the Second World War. The current would be turned on at full strength, but only for a short while. Then it would fade away.

In that same year an American visitor, Cyrus Sulzberger, saw him at Chartwell and accompanied him on a slow postprandial walk to feed the golden orfes in the pond near the manor house and to admire the swans and the rose garden. On the way back he saw a tiny bird lying dead on the path. He pointed to it with his walking stick, unable to speak. Then he was led back weeping to the house where he sank heavily in a chair. The death of any bird or animal had always affected him deeply. He wept when his swans were killed by marauding foxes and when his dogs died, and he was inconsolable when a pet parakeet flew out of the door, never to return. Once a badger was killed by his car; he had it skinned and the fur hung in his bedroom, and he would mutter "Poor fellow" whenever he caught sight of it.

Illness and accidents dogged him. In the spring of 1958 he fell ill with pneumonia and pleurisy. In the summer of 1962, when staying at the Hotel de Paris in Monte Carlo, he broke his thigh in a fall while getting out of bed. He was taken to a local hospital and given an anaesthetic. When he woke up and saw that he was in a strange place with unfamiliar faces around him, he roared: "You monsters! You monsters! Leave me alone! Get out of here, all of you!" It was the old defiance, the old wicked gleam in the eyes.

He was dying by inches and hating it. He weighed 210 pounds, but that was because he had a trencherman's appetite; later, he would lose weight, and for the first time since his youth it became possible to discern the shape of his cheekbones. He still read occasionally, but he was likely to drop the novel he was reading after a few pages. His voice, too, was dying. Once it was vibrant and rasping; now it was low and gentle. And there was in his manner the awful gentleness of the dying.

Yet he lived on. He attended the annual dinners given in the Savoy Hotel for the Other Club, which he had founded in 1911 with the Earl of Birkenhead. The guests, or members, were handpicked by Churchill; and the last dinner he attended was presided over by John Profumo, later to become the central figure in one of the few sexual scandals connected with the British government. Churchill was wheeled into the annual dinner of the Royal Academy, looking strangely white and puffy, wearing his medals and the sash of the Order of the Garter. He was given a tumultuous reception, smiled, waved his cane and said nothing. On rare occasions he still attended Parliament, but only for appearance's sake, to bow to the Speaker, to sit there for a few minutes and then to make an unhurried exit.

Churchill made his last appearance in the House of Commons on July 27, 1964, four months short of his ninetieth birthday. He had lost weight, walked unsteadily, and there was the pallor of death on him. Two fellow Members of Parliament helped him into the chamber and supported him when he made the customary bow of recognition to the Speaker. He took his place in the front bench, nodded, smiled, or sat quietly with his head bent forward. He had come to say farewell, and Harold Macmillan said perfectly what many others were attempting to say: "The life of the man whom we are today honoring is unique. The oldest among us can recall nothing to compare with it and the younger ones among you, however long you live, will never see the like again."

But the man had vanished; there was only the shell. He was bored with life, spoke little and seemed in some strange way remote from everything that happened around him. He spent the afternoons sitting by the fire and listening to records. He liked to hear the Brigade of Guards' Massed Bands with the crashing trumpets and the songs sung by Gertrude Lawrence in the stage version of *The King and I*, but most of all he liked to hear recordings of his own speeches. His cigar would go out; he would stop raking the fire with his walking stick; he seemed to be absorbed by the sound of his own voice speaking twenty years ago. But was he absorbed? His eyes were closed, there was no expression on his face and perhaps he was sleeping.

His nursing staff found him unmanageable; he was as obstinate and truculent as ever. He refused to take his medicines. "What's it for?" he would growl, and listen patiently to the cautious explanations of the long-suffering nurse. "How does it work?" More explanations. "Why?" Another explanation. Finally he would accept the medicine as the least of many evils. Sometimes, too, he would permit himself the luxury of casual rudeness, a trait he had inherited from his father. One day he prodded a young nurse who was standing in his way with his walking stick. "Oh, you're getting saucier!" she gasped. He hated familiarity and was infuriated, and so he leaned forward and said: "And you're . . . getting *uglier*!" She had only been a few days in his employment, he disliked new faces, and this was his way of getting even with her.

One day he was especially abusive to Roy Howells, the male nurse who was constantly in attendance. The nurse lost his temper and soon they were shouting at one another. The quarrel was quickly patched up, but Churchill continued to feel hurt. A few moments later, his lower lip jutting out, he said: "You were very rude to me, you know."

"Yes, but you were rude too," the nurse answered.

Churchill considered this reply and found it wanting in a proper respect.

"Yes, but I *am* a great man!" he said blandly.

It was as though in the hollow shell of old age there remained only the sustaining knowledge of his greatness.

He was a man haunted by greatness as other men are haunted by the past, and indeed his idea of greatness was indissolubly linked with the past, and especially with the Duke of Marlborough who confronted him at every turning in the road. All his energies were bent on achieving greatness. In the modern age, and perhaps in all ages, the great man is understood to be the war leader who changes the course of history almost single-handed. Thus Tamerlane, who destroyed whole civilizations and left half of Asia a desert, was accounted great not only because of the terror of his name and the vast destruction he left behind him, but because history was compelled to change its course in the wake of his adventures. Julius Caesar and Augustus Caesar left such deep claw marks on history that we can still shudder at the sharpness of their claws. By this reckoning, too, Hitler was undeniably great, for he also left claw marks which will not be effaced for centuries.

The pith of the argument lies here: through all recorded history the great man is the man who causes the greatest bloodshed. Describing the bandit chieftain Umra Khan in *The Story of the Malakand Field Force*, Churchill wrote: "He was a great man, which on the frontier means that he was a great murderer." But there are no more frontiers and great men are nearly always murderers.

Churchill sent many men to their deaths, and sometimes he was justified. But when he engaged in his more dubious escapades and when they failed, he showed no remorse and it never occurred to him that he was in error. Thousands died because of his madcap schemes in Russia in 1920 and in the Greek islands during the Second World War. Casualty lists never interested him. If he failed, that was simply a fact; the next time he would succeed. It was easier for him to bear the consequences of his failures because he had very little understanding of people. Sir Alan Brooke, the Chief of the Imperial General Staff, who knew him very well, said: "He wasn't interested in people. When they came to see him he did not listen to them. He did all the talking. How could he find out about them?"

"All great men are bad men," wrote Lord Acton. Churchill, as Lord Beaverbrook had observed long before, had the makings of a tyrant in him. Tyrants enjoy their power, both the real power and the trappings of power, and they make no secret of their desire to enjoy these things to the uttermost. They celebrate their claim to greatness with a multitude of titles and uniforms, build astonishing offices, conduct themselves like men who are remote from other men, delight in inflicting wounds, speak with an authentic arrogance, and in the words of Gregory the Great describing the proud, "they walk silently with themselves along the broad spaces of their thought and silently utter their own praises."

Churchill's tyrannical pride led him to speak to ordinary people as a battleship might speak as it looked down at a leaking rowboat in the high seas. He had no use for ordinary people except in the mass. If he had died in 1938 he would have been remembered as a failure like his father, a man who had made too many mischievous mistakes to warrant a lasting claim to fame. He treated his Cabinet as though they were unruly schoolchildren and sometimes treated his generals in the same way. When he was called to lead Great Britain against Hitler, he welcomed the opportunity with open arms, but at the time he had few claims on his countrymen's affection. He was the man of last resort, known for his defiance, the man who would never under any conditions make a separate peace with the enemy. He had a brief flowering, for by the end of the following year he had almost outlived his usefulness. Nevertheless he held on to power with all the strength he possessed, certain that he above all Englishmen was indispensable in the conduct of the war because he alone possessed a knowledge of the workings of the minds of his allies Roosevelt and Stalin. There came a time when he realized that he had not understood them half as well as he had hoped. When he was abruptly removed from power in the elections of 1945, he still regarded himself as indispensable, the one man who could win the peace.

Like all men who achieve great positions, he had an exalted opinion of his own talents. He was a formidable orator, but not a great writer or even a great wit. He was an astute military strategist, but both General Marshall and Sir Alan Brooke wore themselves out to prevent him from embarking on wild schemes that might have ended in total disaster. He liked to think of himself as a servant of the House of Commons, but he was never its servant. Argument was not his forte. He delivered broadsides, which echoed round the walls of the House of Commons and deafened all its members. His worst fault, as it was his greatest virtue, was his recklessness. He was reckless in 1940 when he uttered his defiant "No!" to Hitler. But he was the first to admit that he was not alone in his recklessness. The British people were just as reckless, just as determined to defeat Hitler.

The saddest thing about him was his megalomania, which he shared with so many dictators. When he told his male nurse that he was a great man and therefore beyond the necessity of ordinary politeness, he was asserting a principle which is totally indefensible, even though it was one he had adhered to throughout his life. In 1966, the year after Churchill's death, Achmed Soekarno, the President of Indonesia, was talking about some accusations leveled against him. "I have been accused of megalomania, the sickness of greatness," he declared. "Yes, I am a great man and my power is the biggest, the biggest, the biggest."

So it was, but only because he exerted it against the interests of the people who had elected him to office, believing him to be honest when in fact he was corrupt. The tyrant quickly learns the arts of corruption while boasting of his integrity. Repetition helps. He is not merely "the biggest." The words must be sounded in an echo chamber and are endlessly repeated. Similarly he is not merely the president. Soekarno gave himself twenty titles. He called himself Lifelong President, Supreme Helmsman, Great Leader of the Indonesian Revolution, Supreme Builder, Supreme Fisherman, Supreme Guardian of the Muhammadiyah, Supreme Educator and First Pioneer of Freedom in Africa and Asia. This last title considerably annoyed some of his fellow dictators in Africa and Asia. Few, if any, of the titles corresponded to any reality, and the least accurate of his titles was Lifelong President. In him "the sickness of greatness" could be observed in a pure clinical form. Unhappily this sickness is widespread among men who have achieved power and Churchill was not immune from it.

The sickness of greatness? The trouble, of course, is that there is no cure, and the sick man infects everyone around him not with portions of his greatness but with the sense of their own littleness. He is great because they are small, and he is all the greater when they are reduced to nearly nothing. He is a colossus who strides over a world of pygmies.

Soekarno was an authentic tyrant. He exerted his utmost powers, caused the deaths of many thousands of people, and his fall from power was accompanied by a bloodbath in which perhaps 2,000,000 people were savagely killed. But the authentic tyrant is not far removed from the small gangster or a small local chieftain who makes everyone pay tribute to him. The contemporary historian Dennis Bloodworth found such a chieftain in Laos. His name was Boun Oum, Prince of Champassak and Lord of Southern Laos. He thought nothing of shooting out of hand the driver of any automobile which got in his way or any person who stepped in his shadow. He wore round his fat belly a leather belt with a brass buckle inscribed: GIANT. In this way, at very little expense, he advertised his greatness.

Once Stephen Graham, the English historian, disguised himself as a Russian pilgrim on a pilgrimage to Jerusalem. To an old *moujik* he spoke about the great men of Russia, but the *moujik* could make nothing of his conversation. "What do you mean with all this talk about great men?" he asked. "Don't you know that nothing is great—except the love of God."

One day during the war Lord Moran recited to Churchill the lines of Walter Savage Landor: "There are no fields of amaranth on this side of the grave; there are no voices, O Rhodopè, that are not soon mute, however tuneful; there is no name, with whatever emphasis of passionate love repeated, of which the echo is not faint at last."

Churchill glowered. "I call that pure defeatist stuff," he said contemptuously.

Yet Walter Savage Landor was not being defeatist, he was merely stating matters of fact. Lord Moran in quoting the passage was gently taunting Churchill after one of his interminable monologues, full of his own exploits and triumphs, which made everyone drowsy.

Churchill did not like jokes against himself, although he was capable of joking brilliantly on occasion against his adversaries. He liked to shatter reputations with a phrase. Henry Fielding also liked to make jokes. His novel *The Life of Jonathan Wild the Great* was ostensibly a rollicking story about a famous highwayman who, when about to be hanged, stole a cork screw from a parson's pocket and was still grasping the screw when the horse cart on which he was standing drove away, leaving him hanging. But in the course of the novel it becomes clear that Fielding was also writing an allegory about Sir Robert Walpole, the King's first minister, a peculator who made a fortune in office, and other great statesmen and politicians who abuse their powers. Fielding had his own opinions about greatness. Here he sums up the short and luckless life of his hero:

> Indeed, while GREATNESS consists in power, pride, insolence, and doing mischief to mankind—to speak out—while a GREAT MAN and a great rogue are synonymous terms, so long shall WILD stand unrivalled on the pinnacle of GREATNESS. Nor must we omit here, as the finishing of his character, what indeed ought to be remembered on his tomb or his statue, the conformity above mentioned of his death to his life; and that Jonathan Wild the GREAT, after all his mighty exploits, was, what so few GREAT men can accomplish—hanged by the neck until he was dead.

With imperturbable irony Henry Fielding took the measure of his adversaries—the cutthroats, highwaymen, peculators and prime ministers, who stood in the way of ordinary decent men, and he saw little difference between Jonathan Wild and Sir Robert Walpole except that the Prime Minister was not brought to the scaffold, a fate he richly deserved. Fielding said of Jonathan Wild that "he was entirely free from those low vices of modesty and good nature, which, as he said, implied a total negation of human greatness, and were the only qualities which absolutely rendered a man incapable of making a considerable figure in the world."

Thus greatness becomes a mirage, the receptacle of many myths and ambiguities, the highwayman and the Prime Minister standing elbow to elbow, indistinguishable from one another. There are no measuring rods. Greater than what? We speak of Alexander the Great, Herod the Great, Ivan the Great, Frederick the Great, but of these only Frederick the Great called himself Great in his own lifetime. The first historian who called Herod the Great was evidently an ironist. Greatness trails its cloak, and any small boy at the appropriate moment can splatter it with mud. The world can rarely afford its great men, for they are luxuries best dispensed with. Throughout the world's history there are perhaps fewer than a hundred men who deserve this title, and most of them are to be found among the poets, the artists, the scientists and philosophers. Nevertheless the myth persists, and for centuries to come men will aspire to the "greatness" which is symbolized by Caesar's crown of laurels. "The greatest poison ever known," wrote the poet William Blake, "is Caesar's laurel crown."

At the end of his days Churchill himself doubted whether he was among the elect. He had been listening with his daughter Sarah to the flood of congratulatory messages that came over the radio on one of his birthdays, but they left him unmoved and unhappy. His daughter tried to cheer him up. Had he not accomplished great deeds? Had he not achieved a secure place in history? He answered wearily: "I have achieved a great deal to achieve nothing in the end."

He knew himself well, had long pondered his place in history, and had come to definite conclusions. He had fought well and truly against the greatest tyranny of the age, he had enjoyed high offices of state, appointed viceroys to India and set kings on their thrones in the Middle East, become a towering legend in his lifetime, and what had it amounted to? The British Empire had gone, the detested Socialists had come to power, the Soviets had advanced more deeply in Europe, the world had not learned the lessons of two terrible wars. It was a just verdict on his life, but it was not the only verdict.

In his lifetime he had accomplished more than any Englishman of his generation. but his triumphs had turned to ashes and all around him lay the evidence that most of the things he fought for had been in vain. An aristocrat, he found the aristocracy in disarray. An imperialist, he found the empire in ruins. He had believed that Britain was chosen by destiny to lead the world, and he had watched the leadership pass into the hands of the United States and the Soviet Union. In his last days he had little to be thankful for.

He passed his days in bed or roused himself sufficiently to sit by the fire. During long empty afternoons Sarah sometimes sat beside him. He could no longer maintain a conversation; his thoughts moved fitfully; he gazed at the crackling flames. Sometimes he read the newspapers and let the pages fall one by one from his hands until they were scattered all over the floor. He had been reading about a world he no longer understood. There was no more panoply, no more Empire, no more cakes and ale. From time to time, without looking up, he would say: "What is the time?" Sarah answered, and half an hour later he would ask the same question. "Oh Lor'," he sighed, and resumed his contemplation of the flames.

The face was no longer round and pink; the familiar features were no longer familiar; he looked drawn and withered, deeply lined, inscrutable. The once brilliant and piercing blue eyes were dulled over; he walked with difficulty and was afraid of falling. Old age, the enemy, held him by the throat. Against this enemy he possessed no weapons, not even the weapon of acquiescence. Long ago he had decided that religious faith was meaningless and the hope of an afterlife was a delusion. He had not a scintilla of Christian faith. He would die without benefit of any sacraments, as he had lived.

So the days passed in an eerie silence for the last survivor of the Victorian age. Sometimes he would murmur that he wanted a book and someone would be sent out to the Kensington Public Library to obtain it, and they would read it to him, but no one was sure he was listening. Words, too, were losing their meaning. Once he had marshaled them vigorously, setting them in order like armies, but now they were no more than echoes. On rare occasions he appeared at the window of the Hyde Park Gate house, looking like a ghost.

For a long time he had been waiting to die. His will, signed on October 20, 1961, remained unchanged except for two short codicils. He left a golden cigarette case to the Earl of Birkenhead, the son of his old friend. Grace Hamblin, his wartime secretary, received an annuity of £500, Roy Howells received a legacy of £250, and Kurn, an assistant gardener, received a legacy of £100. His secretary, Anthony Montague Browne, received £5,000, later increased to £10,000. The remainder of the estate was divided into three shares, one to his wife, two to his children. When the will was administered for probate, it was learned that he left a fortune amounting to £304,044.

Life which had dealt so gently with him and showed him mercy at all times was slowly ebbing away. It had not been so merciful to his children. Diana, his eldest daughter, who had been so beautiful and serene in her youth, committed suicide in 1963, and he was too old, too ill, to feel the full force of the shock. Diana had married twice, first to John Bailey, the son of a South African millionaire. She divorced Bailey and then married Duncan Sandys, a rising politician. Sarah, his second daughter, married three times—to Vic Oliver, the entertainer, to Anthony Beauchamp, the photographer, and to Lord Audley. All her husbands were dead and she was now known as Lady Audley. Mary, his youngest daughter, had married Christopher Soames, another rising politician. Randolph, the heir, had married twice, and was now dying of cancer. He had lived so long in his father's shadow that he had become indistinguishable from the shadows.

It was not a happy family, nor was it an unhappy family. They had muddled through, married well and badly, quarreled occasionally, and sometimes felt the heat of the harsh limelight that beat down on their father. They were among the lucky ones who live for long intervals without a death in the immediate family. Diana and Marigold had gone, but the rest remained. Now the old man was about to join his two daughters.

THE SECOND DEATH

THEY REMEMBERED IT as one of those long winters which seem to go on for ever. The trees in Hyde Park turned black and leafless earlier than usual, the frost came early, the cold rain fell, and sometimes through the fog London seemed to wear the aspect of an earlier age when the streets were lit by gas lamps and the hansom cabs rolled over cobbled roads. People walked through the streets collars up, hating the savage winds and the driving rain.

On the eve of Churchill's ninetieth birthday they gathered outside his house in Hyde Park Gate, that small cul-de-sac of a street, to see him appear at the window. During these last years he had always appeared at the window on November 29 to give the victory sign. The people wished him well, they wanted to be sure he was alive, and they wanted his blessing. In India people will stand for days and weeks to receive the darshan of a great man, the mysterious influences that emanate from him. So it was with Churchill, who in his lifetime was called the greatest Englishman who had ever lived. Predictably it was a bitterly cold day and there was a driving rain.

So they huddled in the street, waiting, watching the distinguished visitors who came to the house to pay tribute to him and the postmen who brought messages. They complained good-humoredly about the photographers who had taken the best positions. Old soldiers wore their medals and old women shivered in their shawls. They were waiting for one o'clock, when he would appear in a siren suit, wave to them, listen to their applause, and the singing of "For he's a jolly good fellow." It had become a ritual embedded in tradition, and they knew what was expected of them.

That morning he came to the window a little late, thus adding to their feeling of expectancy. Suddenly the curtain parted, the window was opened and he was standing there, smiling and waving, with his valet on one side and a nurse on the other. He was wearing a bright-green velvet siren suit bought for the occasion and the inevitable polka-dot bow tie. There was a roar of applause and he spread out his arms to greet the crowd surging against the railings. The applause warmed his old bones, and he would have stood there longer if his wife had permitted it. The curtains were closed only to open again at his insistence. Once more they shouted up at him: "Good old Winny!" His lips trembled, tears came to his eyes, and at last he turned away. The darshan was over. His wife leaned out of the window and called out: "Sir Winston would like to come to the window again but he cannot. He heard you all singing and thanks you very much."

This was his last public appearance. He looked surprisingly well for a man of his age, and the photographer who caught the last unhappy moment when his face crumpled in tears was doing him a disservice. On the whole it was a happy occasion; he was enjoying himself; indeed, applause was what he enjoyed most. He went off to enjoy a Dubonnet and a roast beef lunch.

That evening the BBC put on a special program called "Ninety Years On," with a script written by Terence Rattigan, and with Noel Coward acting as master of ceremonies. Churchill liked music-hall songs and so the program was built around the music-hall songs of the eighties and nineties with modern actors impersonating Marie Lloyd, Ella Shields, Dan Leno, Billy Merson and other singers of a heroic age. He also liked some modern songs. Noel Coward sang "Mad Dogs and Englishmen," and Edmund Hockeridge sang "Oh, What a Beautiful Morning!" from *Oklahoma.*

He was in good form on his birthday, read the newspapers in bed, admired the birds of paradise flowers sent to him by the Queen, and examined the mountain of congratulatory telegrams, including one from the Mayor of Pretoria whose proud claim was that Pretoria was the only great city which had kept him a prisoner. Even the German government sent a congratulatory message. All together there were 70,000 cards, letters and telegrams. In addition there were many birthday presents. From Anthony Eden came a first edition of Byron's *Childe Harold's Pilgrimage* and from unknown admirers in Ireland came a basket of potatoes, carrots and tomatoes packed in peat. Cigars, which he smoked avidly, and cigarettes, which he had smoked occasionally in India and then abandoned forever, came in remarkable quantities. Among the presents was a gold cage with a mechanical singing bird. Most of the day he spent in bed, resplendent in a red paisley smoking jacket, a glass of whiskey within reach and a cigar jutting from his mouth. On his enormous birthday cake, which weighed 120 pounds, there were inscribed the words he had written long ago for a French military monument and used later as the moral for his history of the Second World War: "In War: Resolution. In Defeat: Defiance. In Victory: Magnanimity. In Peace: Good Will."

Many visitors came to congratulate him, including the Prime Minister, Harold Wilson. Visitors tired him, he said little, smiled frequently and was glad when they were gone. What he liked doing was sitting by the fire in his drawing room, poking the logs and watching the flames. Every week a press cutting bureau sent him clippings; he usually read them avidly; now they, too, were tossed aside.

He was failing rapidly. After Christmas he rarely spoke, and seemed strangely detached. He caught a chill and seemed to recover from it, but on January 8 he suffered a stroke which left him paralyzed on the left side. On January 15 Lord Moran stood outside the house and announced: "After a cold, Sir Winston has developed a circulatory weakness and there has been a cerebral thrombosis." Three days later the breathing became erratic. There was nothing the doctor could do, and they all knew the end was very near.

He died very quietly, without a murmur, in the presence of most of the members of his immediate family and his secretary, Anthony Montague Browne, at eight o'clock in the morning of January 24, 1965. He died exactly seventy years to the day after the death of his father, Lord Randolph Churchill. It was as though in some strange way he had wanted to share in his father's death.

According to the death certificate signed by Lord Moran, the Right Honourable Winston Leonard Spencer Churchill, K.G., O.M., C.H., Occupation: Statesman, died of congestion of the lungs, cerebral arteriosclerosis, and a cerebral thrombosis, but this was only another way of saying that he had died of old age in his ninety-first year. Over the years he had given much punishment to his resilient body and now at last it had failed him. His daughter Sarah wrote that during his last months he waited "with courtesy and patience" for the end, but this was not quite true. He had more impatience than patience, and his last recorded remark to his son Randolph, who was soon to follow him to the grave, was: "I am bored with it all."

At one time he had thought of being buried at Chartwell, which he loved above all the places on earth. In later years, although his attachment to Chartwell only increased with time, he thought more fondly of the small country churchyard at Bladon in sight of Blenheim Palace, where his mother and father were buried. Accordingly he drew up a set of instructions to be followed at his own funeral, based very largely on the funeral of the Duke of Wellington in 1852. In the preparation of this formidable document, entitled "Operation Hope Not," he was helped by officials of the Royal Household and the Office of Works. Queen Elizabeth suggested that there should be a lying in state at Westminster Hall, an honor usually reserved for kings. By 1959 the document was completed.

According to the plan the funeral service would be held in St. Paul's Cathedral, and the coffin would then be ferried down the Thames to Waterloo Station, and so by train and hearse to Bladon. He asked that the Order of the Garter, lying on a black velvet cushion, should be placed on the flag-draped coffin and that his banner blazoned with the Marlborough coat of arms should be carried in the funeral procession together with the banner of the Lord Warden of the Cinque Marches. In the document he especially asked that the Anglican funeral service should be abbreviated and that "The Battle Hymn of the Republic" should be sung. The pallbearers who would carry the coffin up the steps of the cathedral would be Grenadier Guards, because he counted it as one of his greatest good fortunes that he had served with the Guards in World War I. And the seating in the cathedral, this, too, was arranged long before the event.

The strange document entitled "Operation Hope Not" was far more than a precise summary of the funeral arrangements; it was also a conscious tribute to his own greatness.

The coffin was taken at night to Westminster Hall, where for three days and nights it lay in state, draped in the Union Jack and surmounted by the black cushion with the jeweled Order of the Garter. Four gilt candlesticks stood at the corners of the crimson dais and an enormous gilt crucifix rose high above the coffin. The long line of people waiting to pay their respects to him stretched over Lambeth Bridge. They moved quietly and solemnly, as though dazed with grief, their breath turning white in those raw January days. Altogether some 300,000 people made their way through Westminster Hall.

On the fourth day he was borne on a gun carriage along Whitehall, the Strand and Fleet Street to St. Paul's Cathedral. It was another raw, wintry day with gray scudding clouds, and the people stood twenty deep along the whole length of the procession. A Royal Navy gun crew pulled the gun carriage in slow march through the sanded streets, and the slow beat of the muffled drums and the grating of wheels in the sand were the only sounds heard on that quiet day. Behind the gun carriage walked the male members of the Churchill family, and behind them came the burnished black coach lent by Queen Elizabeth to carry Lady Churchill and her daughters. Queen Elizabeth was already at St. Paul's, breaking the tradition that no monarch should attend the funeral of a commoner. Six monarchs, five presidents, and sixteen prime ministers attended the service in the cathedral, where the huge organ suddenly crashed out with the opening chords of "The Battle Hymn of the Republic." The television lights burned brightly on the blaze of uniforms and on the coffin with the Order of the Garter glinting fiercely on the black cushion. Lady Churchill, deathly pale beneath her veil, stood erect and silent, rarely taking her eyes away from the coffin.

Then it was all over, and Churchill lay in Bladon Churchyard in sight of the tumultuous towers of Blenheim Palace. It is a small country churchyard without any pretensions of grandeur, quiet and remote. It might be any small churchyard in any small village of England. The simple flat tombstone reads: WINSTON LEONARD SPENCER CHURCHILL 1874–1965. Jennie lies beside him, and he lies very close to his father and to Consuelo Vanderbilt, who became the Duchess of Marlborough.

Some years after his death, in Westminster Abbey near the tomb of the Unknown Warrior, a circular stone of gray marble with the inscription REMEMBER WINSTON CHURCHILL was set into the floor. There at last he received his perfect monument. There was no recital of the honors that crowded upon him, no statues, no jeweled orders. There was only the memory of the man who deserved to be remembered, not so much because he had striven all his life for greatness and found it wanting, but because he was defiant at a time when defiance was necessary. The war would have been won if he had never lived, for there was never a time when the British people were prepared to lay their heads on Hitler's chopping block. But sometimes he gave dignity and drama to the worst of wars.

In the end greatness vanishes like the morning mists, and all men, however proud or miserable, are seen to be equal in their dust. We are all passengers on a small planet, and those who think they are leading are often led and those who have been granted power and authority are often no more than sleepwalkers who suddenly awake to find themselves balanced precariously over the abyss. There is a strange inhumanity about all those men who come to believe they have been chosen by Providence to lead others; and if Churchill was among the most tolerable by virtue of his human qualities, he was also irremediably flawed by pride and self-indulgence, by his contempt for people and for every opinion except his own. He was one of those who do not really care about the people they rule, for the people are only the instruments of their glory.

The error lies in human pride: the proud man swelling up and pronouncing himself greater than others, until at last he comes to believe in his own vastness. "I am the biggest, the biggest, the biggest," said Soekarno, and the words echo through the corridors of history like the wailing of ghosts, the voices of innumerable presidents and kings indistinguishable from one another as each claims all the glory for himself. More "great men" will arise and commit the inevitable murders, but few will have the courage to say they have achieved a great deal to accomplish nothing in the end. Ultimately "greatness" is a disease, a blindness to the human condition, a plague inflicted on humanity. "When you come down to it," wrote André Malraux, who had encountered most of the well-known political figures of his time, "there are no great personages." In the end there are no great men, there are only men, and the glory belongs to all mankind.

CHRONOLOGY

1873	August 12	Jennie Jerome meets Lord Randolph Churchill at Cowes.
1874	April 15	Marriage of Jennie Jerome and Lord Churchill at the British Embassy in Paris.
1874	November 30	Birth of Winston Churchill at Blenheim Palace.
1882	November 3	Winston enters St. George's School, Ascot.
1884	Summer	He leaves the school and is taught by the Misses Thomson in Brighton.
1886	March	Suffers a bad attack of pneumonia.
1888	March 15	Takes entrance examination at Harrow.
1888	April 17	Enters Harrow.
1892	December	Leaves Harrow.
1893	January 10	Falls from bridge at Bournemouth.
1893	June 28	Enters Royal Military College, Sandhurst, as cavalry cadet.
1894	December	Passes out of Sandhurst, eighth in class of 150.

1895	January 24	Death of Lord Randolph Churchill.
1895	July 3	Death of Mrs. Everest.
1895	April 1	Gazetted to the Fourth Queen's Own Hussars.
1895	November 30	Observes fighting at Arroyo Blanco during visit to Cuba.
1896	October 3	Arrives in India and settles down in military cantonment at Bangalore. Reads avidly.
1897	September 4	Takes part in fighting in the Mamund Valley on the Indian North-West Frontier.
1897	October 4	Begins to write *The Story of the Malakand Field Force,* the novel *Savrola,* and "The Scaffolding of Rhetoric."
1898	March 14	Publishes *The Story of the Malakand Field Force,* his first book.
1898	September 2	Takes part in charge of Twenty-First Lancers at Omdurman.
1898	December 1	After returning to England, sails for India.
1899	End of April	Returns to London and engages in politics.
1899	Early July	Presents himself as Conservative candidate at by-election in Oldham and is defeated.
1899	October 14	Sails to South Africa as war correspondent of the *Morning Post.*
1899	November 6	Publishes *The River War.*
1899	November 15	Captured by Boers two weeks after arrival in South Africa.
1899	December 13	Escapes from prison in Pretoria.
1900	February 3	Publishes *Savrola.*
1900	May 15	Publishes *London to Ladysmith via Pretoria.*
1900	June 5	Enters captured Pretoria.
1900	July 20	Returns to England.
1900	October 1	Elected Conservative Member of Parliament for Oldham.
1900	October 12	Publishes *Ian Hamilton's March.*

1900	December 16	Gives first public lecture in New York.
1901	February 14	Takes his seat in the House of Commons.
1901	February 18	Makes his maiden speech.
1901	May 13	Attacks the Army Estimates.
1904	May 31	Joins Liberal Party.
1905	December 9	Becomes Under Secretary of State for the Colonies.
1906	January 2	Publishes *Lord Randolph Churchill*.
1907	October	Sets out on official tour of East Africa, returning January, 1908
1908	March	Publishes *My African Journey*.
1908	April 24	Joins Asquith's Cabinet as President of the Board of Trade.
1908	May 23	Elected Member of Parliament for Dundee.
1908	September 12	Marries Clementine Hozier.
1909	July 11	Diana, his first daughter, born.
1909	September 12	Attends maneuvers in Germany.
1910	November 8	Tonypandy incident; two miners killed.
1911	January 3	Battle of Sidney Street.
1911	May 28	Randolph, his only son, born.
1911	July	German gunboat *Panther* anchors off Agadir.
1911	August	Churchill calls out military to put down railroad strike.
1911	August 13	Writes memorandum "Military Aspects of the Continental Problem" for Committee of Imperial Defence.
1911	October 25	Becomes First Lord of the Admiralty.
1914	June 17	Secures parliamentary approval to buy control of Persian oil to supply ships of the Royal Navy.
1914	June 28	Assassination of Archduke Franz Ferdinand at Sarajevo.
1914	August 1	Orders mobilization of the fleet.

1914	August 4	Great Britain declares war on Germany.
1914	August 5	First naval engagement in the war.
1914	October 3–6	Churchill in Antwerp, organizing its defense.
1914	October 7	His second daughter, Sarah, born.
1914	October 30	Recalls Lord Fisher to the Admiralty to serve as First Sea Lord.
1914	November 1	Battle of Coronel; British defeat.
1914	December 8	Battle of the Falkland Islands; British victory.
1915	January 3	With Kitchener, proposes naval and military attack on the Dardanelles.
1915	March 18	British and French combined fleet attack Dardanelles and withdraw.
1915	May 28	Resigns as First Lord; appointed Chancellor of the Duchy of Lancaster.
1915	November 11	Resigns from Cabinet.
1915	November 19	Commands Second Battalion of the Grenadier Guards in France; later commands a battalion of the Sixth Royal Scots Fusiliers.
1916	May 7	Resumes political career in London.
1917	July 16	Becomes Minister of Munitions in Lloyd George's government.
1918	November 11	Armistice signed.
1918	November 15	Third daughter, Marigold, born.
1919	January 15	Becomes Secretary of State for War and Minister of Air.
1919	June 28	Peace Treaty signed at Versailles.
1921	February 15	Becomes Colonial Secretary and employs T. E. Lawrence as his chief adviser on Middle Eastern affairs.
1921	June 29	Death of Lady Randolph Churchill.
1921	August 23	Death of Marigold.
1922	September 15	Fourth daughter, Mary, born.

1922	October	Resigns from Colonial Office.
1922	November	Buys Chartwell Manor near Westerham, Kent.
1923	April 5	Publishes *The World Crisis*, volume 1. (Six volumes 1923–1931.)
1923	May	Contests by-election at West Leicester; defeated.
1924	February	Breaks with Liberal Party; contests Abbey Division of Westminster and is defeated.
1924	October	Contests by-election at Epping and wins.
1924	November 7	Becomes Chancellor of the Exchequer in Stanley Baldwin's government.
1925	April 28	First budget; return to the gold standard.
1926	May 3	General Strike begins.
1926	May 5–13	Churchill edits *The British Gazette*.
1927	January 15	He visits Mussolini.
1930	October	Publishes *My Early Life*.
1931	December 13	Knocked down by taxi on Fifth Avenue.
1932	November	Publishes *Thoughts and Adventures*.
1933	August	Warns against German rearmament.
1933	October	Publishes *Marlborough, His Life and Times*, volume 1. Fourth and last volume published September, 1938.
1935	July	Joins Committee of Imperial Defence.
1935	October	Mussolini invades Abyssinia.
1935	December	Painting holiday in Morocco.
1936	January 20	Death of King George V.
1936	December 11	Abdication of King Edward VIII.
1937	May 12	Coronation of King George VI.
1937	May 28	Churchill warns Ribbentrop.
1937	October	Publishes *Great Contemporaries*.
1938	March 12	Germany invades Austria.
1938	October	Churchill attacks Munich Agreement.

1939	March 14	German troops enter Prague.
1939	April 7	Mussolini invades Albania.
1939	August 15–25	Churchill visits French Rhine front.
1939	September 1	Hitler invades Poland.
1939	September 3	Britain and France declare war on Germany. Churchill joins Chamberlain's government as First Lord of the Admiralty.
1939	December 17	The *Graf Spee* scuttled off Montevideo.
1940	April 9	Germany invades Denmark and Norway.
1940	May 10	Churchill forms coalition government. Germany invades Holland and Belgium.
1940	May 13	In his first speech as Prime Minister Churchill offers the House of Commons nothing but "blood, toil, tears and sweat."
1940	May 15	Churchill asks President Roosevelt for loan of destroyers. Germans cross the Meuse.
1940	May 24	Germans reach Calais.
1940	May 26–June 4	Dunkirk evacuation.
1940	May 28	Belgian Army capitulates.
1940	June 16	On fourth visit to France since becoming Prime Minister, Churchill offers federal union with the French. The offer is rejected.
1940	July 4	Orders bombardment of French fleet at Oran.
1940	August 10–September 15	Battle of Britain.
1941	March 7	Sends British troops to Greece to halt German advance. British are defeated.
1941	May 10	House of Commons bombed
1941	June 22	Broadcasts assurances of help to the Russians invaded by German Army.
1941	August 10	Atlantic meeting with President Roosevelt on board *Prince of Wales*. Atlantic Charter signed two days later.

1941	December 7	Japan attacks Pearl Harbor and Singapore.
1941	December 10	*Prince of Wales* and *Repulse* sunk off Malayan coast.
1941	December 22	Churchill arrives in Washington for Arcadia Conference.
1942	January 27	He receives vote of confidence in the House of Commons: 464 to 1.
1942	February 14	British Army in Singapore surrenders to Japanese.
1942	June 17	Flies to Washington to discuss invasion of North Africa.
1942	July 2	Receives vote of confidence: 475 to 25.
1942	August 2	Flies to Cairo.
1942	August 12	Flies to Moscow for first meeting with Stalin.
1943	January 14–24	Casablanca Conference.
1943	January 30	Flies to Adana for meeting with President Inönü of Turkey.
1943	February 2	German forces surrender at Stalingrad.
1943	May 5	Churchill leaves London for Washington.
1943	May 30	Visits North Africa for consultations with De Gaulle.
1943	September 1	Visits Washington.
1943	September 3	Allied invasion of South Italy.
1943	November 22–26	Cairo Conference.
1943	November 28– December 1	Teheran Conference.
1943	December 11	Flies to Tunis; contracts pneumonia.
1944	January 22	Allied troops land at Anzio.
1944	June 4	Rome captured by Allied troops.
1944	June 6	D Day. Allied invasion of Normandy.
1944	June 10	Churchill visits Normandy beachheads.

1944	June 13–14	First flying bombs land on England.
1944	June 20	Churchill flies to Cherbourg to visit Montgomery's headquarters.
1944	August 11	Flies to Naples for talks with Marshal Tito. Visits Italian front.
1944	August 24	Liberation of Paris.
1944	September 5	Churchill sails for Quebec Conference with President Roosevelt.
1944	October 9	Meets Stalin in Moscow.
1944	November 10	Flies to Paris to meet De Gaulle.
1944	December 5	Orders British troops to intervene in Greece.
1944	December 24	Flies to Athens.
1945	February 4–12	Yalta Conference.
1945	February 16–17	Confers in Cairo and at Fayoum with leaders of Middle Eastern states and King Ibn Saud.
1945	March 25	Crosses Rhine two days after Allied Armies.
1945	April 12	Death of President Roosevelt.
1945	April 28	Mussolini executed by partisans.
1945	April 30	Hitler commits suicide.
1945	May 8	V-E Day. Unconditional surrender of all German armed forces.
1945	May 23	Wartime coalition government broken up. Caretaker government takes over.
1945	June 4	Churchill delivers "Gestapo" speech.
1945	July 16	First explosion of atomic bomb at Alamogordo, New Mexico.
1945	July 17	Churchill arrives at Potsdam for conference with Truman and Stalin.
1945	July 26	Defeated in general election, he resigns premiership.
1945	August 6	Atom bomb dropped on Hiroshima.
1945	August 9	Atom bomb dropped on Nagasaki.

1945	August 14	V-J Day. Japan surrenders.
1946	January 8	Churchill awarded Order of Merit.
1946	March 5	Delivers "Iron Curtain" speech at Fulton, Missouri.
1948	June 21	Publishes *The Gathering Storm*, the first volume of his six-volume history collectively entitled *The Second World War*.
1951	October 26	Becomes Premier.
1952	February 6	Death of King George VI.
1953	June 2	Coronation of Queen Elizabeth II.
1953	December 10	Awarded Nobel Prize for Literature.
1954	June 14	Becomes Knight of the Garter.
1954	November 30	Celebrations for his eightieth birthday at Westminster Hall.
1955	April 5	Resigns from premiership.
1956	April 23	Publishes *History of the English-Speaking Peoples*, volumes I and II.
1956	November 5	British and French troops land in Egypt.
1958	September 12	Celebrates his golden wedding anniversary.
1963	April 9	President Kennedy declares him an honorary citizen of the United States.
1963	October 19	Suicide of Diana Churchill.
1964	July 28	Presented with Vote of Thanks by House of Commons.
1964	November 30	Celebrates his ninetieth birthday.
1965	January 24	Dies in his home at Hyde Park Gate.
1965	January 30	Buried in St. Martin's Churchyard in Bladon.

SELECT BIBLIOGRAPHY

ACHESON, DEAN, *Present at the Creation.* New York, W. W. Norton, 1969.

ARTHUR, SIR GEORGE, *Concerning Winston Spencer Churchill.* New York, H. C. Kinsey, 1941.

ASHLEY, MAURICE, *Churchill as Historian.* New York, Charles Scribner's Sons, 1968.

ASQUITH, CYNTHIA, *Remember and Be Glad.* New York, Charles Scribner's Sons, 1952.

ASTLEY, JOAN BRIGHT, *The Inner Circle.* Boston, Little, Brown, 1971.

ATTLEE, C. R., *As It Happened.* London, Odhams Press, n.d.

BALSAN, CONSUELO VANDERBILT, *The Glitter and the Gold.* New York, Harper and Brothers, 1952.

BARBER, NOEL, *A Sinister Twilight: The Fall of Singapore 1942.* Boston, Houghton Mifflin, 1968.

BARING, MAURICE, *Lost Lectures.* London, Peter Davies, 1932.

———, *The Puppet Show of Memory.* Boston, Little, Brown, 1922.

BARUCH, BERNARD M., *Baruch: The Public Years.* New York, Holt, Rinehart and Winston, 1960.

BEAUFRÉ, ANDRÉ, *1940: The Fall of France.* New York, Alfred A. Knopf, 1967.

BEAVERBROOK, LORD, *Politicians and the War.* London, Oldbourne, 1959.

BERLIN, ISAIAH, *Mr. Churchill in 1940.* Boston, Houghton Mifflin, n.d.

BLOODWORTH, DENNIS, *An Eye for the Dragon.* New York, Farrar, Straus & Giroux, 1970.

BLUNT, WILFRED SCAWEN, *My Diaries*. London, Martin Secker, n.d.

BOCCA, GEOFFREY, *The Adventurous Life of Winston Churchill*. New York, Julian Messner, 1958.

BROAD, LEWIS, *Winston Churchill: The Years of Preparation*. New York, Hawthorn Books, 1958.

——, *Winston Churchill: The Years of Achievement*. New York, Hawthorn Books, 1963.

BRYANT, ARTHUR, *The Turn of the Tide*. New York, Doubleday, 1957.

——, *Triumph in the West*. London, Collins, 1959.

BURNS, JAMES MACGREGOR, *Roosevelt: The Soldier of Freedom*. New York, Harcourt Brace Jovanovich, 1971.

CALDER, ANGUS, *The People's War*. New York, Pantheon, 1969.

CARTER, VIOLET BONHAM, *Winston Churchill: An Intimate Portrait*. New York, Harcourt, Brace and World, 1965.

CHURCHILL, RANDOLPH, *Winston S. Churchill: Youth, 1874–1900*. Boston, Houghton Mifflin, 1966.

——, *Winston S. Churchill: Youth*, Companion Volumes Part I (1874–1896) and Part II (1896–1900). Boston, Houghton Mifflin, 1967.

——, *Winston S. Churchill: The Young Statesman, 1901–1914*. Boston, Houghton Mifflin, 1967.

CHURCHILL, SARAH, *A Thread in the Tapestry*. New York, Dodd, Mead, 1967.

CHURCHILL, WINSTON, *The Aftermath*. New York, Charles Scribner's Sons, 1929.

——, *Amid These Storms*. New York, Charles Scribner's Sons, 1932.

——, *Blood, Sweat and Tears*. New York, G. P. Putnam's Sons, 1941.

——, *The End of the Beginning*. Boston, Little, Brown, 1943.

——, *Frontiers and Wars*. New York, Harcourt, Brace and World, 1962.

——, *Great Contemporaries*. New York, G. P. Putnam's Sons, 1937.

——, *Great War Speeches*. London, Corgi Books, 1965.

——, *A History of the English-Speaking Peoples*. I. *The Birth of Britain*. II. *The New World*. III. *The Age of Revolution*. IV. *The Great Democracies*. New York, Dodd, Mead, 1956–58.

——, *Ian Hamilton's March*. London, Longmans, Green, 1900.

——, *London to Ladysmith via Pretoria*. London, Longmans, Green, 1900.

——, *Lord Randolph Churchill*. London, Odhams Press, 1951.

——, "Man Overboard—an Episode of the Red Sea," *Harmsworth Magazine*, Vol. I (1898–99).

——, *Marlborough, His Life and Times*. New York, Charles Scribner's Sons, 1933–38. 6 vols.

——, *Mr. Broderick's Army*. London, A. L. Humphreys, 1903.

——, *My African Journey*. London, New English Library, 1972.

——, *My Early Life*. London, Collins, 1972.

——, *Painting as a Pastime*. New York, Cornerstone Library, 1966.

————, *The People's Rights*. New York, Taplinger, 1971.

————, *The River War*. New York, Award Books, 1964.

————, *Savrola, A Tale of the Revolution of Laurania*. New York, Random House, 1956.

————, *The Second World War*. I. *The Gathering Storm*. II. *Their Finest Hour*. III. *The Grand Alliance*. IV. *The Hinge of Fate*. V. *Closing the Ring*. VI. *Triumph and Tragedy*. New York, Bantam Books, 1962.

————, *Secret Session Speeches*. London, Cassell and Company, 1946.

————, *The Story of the Malakand Field Force*. London, Thomas Nelson, 1916.

————, *The Unknown War: The Eastern Front*. New York, Charles Scribner's Sons, 1931.

————, *The World Crisis*. New York, Charles Scribner's Sons, 1923–29, 1931. 4 vols.

CLEMENS, DIANE SHAVER, *Yalta*. London, Oxford University Press, 1972.

COOLIDGE, OLIVIA, *Winston Churchill and the Story of Two World Wars*. Boston, Houghton Mifflin, 1960.

COOMBS, DAVID (ed.), *Churchill, His Paintings*. New York, World, 1967.

COOTE, COLIN R. (ed.), *A Churchill Reader*. Boston, Houghton Mifflin, 1954.

CORNWALLIS-WEST, MRS. GEORGE, *The Reminiscences of Lady Randolph Churchill*. New York, The Century Co., 1908.

COWLES, VIRGINIA, *Winston Churchill: The Era and the Man*. New York, Harper and Brothers, 1953.

DANGERFIELD, GEORGE, *The Strange Death of Liberal England*. New York, Capricorn Books, 1935.

DAVIS, RICHARD HARDING, *The Young Winston Churchill*. Austin, Pemberton Press, 1964.

EADE, CHARLES (ed.), *Churchill, by His Contemporaries*. New York, Simon and Schuster, 1954.

FEDDEN, ROBIN, *Churchill and Chartwell*. Oxford, Pergamon Press, 1968.

FIELDING, HENRY, *Jonathan Wild*. (The Life of Mr. Jonathan Wild the Great.) New York, New American Library, 1962.

FISHER, LORD, *Memories*. London, Hodder and Stoughton, 1919.

FISHMAN, JACK, *My Darling Clementine*. New York, David McKay, 1963.

FOOT, MICHAEL, *Aneurin Bevan*. New York, Atheneum, 1963.

GARDINER, A. G., *Pillars of Society*. New York, Dodd, Mead, 1914.

GARDNER, BRIAN, *Churchill in His Time*. London, Methuen, 1968.

The General Strike 1926: The British Gazette and The British Worker. Facsimile edition. Whitstable, David and Charles Reprints, 1971.

GILBERT, MARTIN, *Winston S. Churchill, The Challenge of War 1914–1916*. Continuation of Randolph Churchill's official biography. Boston, Houghton Mifflin, 1971.

————, *Churchill. Great Lives Observed* series. Englewood Cliffs, Prentice-Hall, 1967.

GOUTARD, A., *The Battle of France, 1940*. New York, Ives Washburn, 1959.

GRAEBNER, WALTER, *My Dear Mr. Churchill*. Boston, Houghton Mifflin, 1965.

GREEN, DAVID, *Sarah, Duchess of Marlborough*. New York, Charles Scribner's Sons, 1967.

———, *Sir Winston Churchill at Blenheim Palace*. Oxford, Alden Press, 1959.

GRETTON, PETER, *Winston Churchill and the Royal Navy*. New York, Coward-McCann, 1968.

GUEDALLA, PHILIP, *Mr. Churchill: A Portrait*. London, Hodder and Stoughton, 1945.

HALLE, KAY (ed.), *The Grand Original: Portraits of Randolph Churchill by His Friends*. Boston, Houghton Mifflin, 1971.

HAMILTON, COUNT ANTHONY, *Memoirs of the Count de Gramont*. London, John Lane, 1928.

HANFSTAENGL, ERNST, *Unheard Witness*. Philadelphia, J. B. Lippincott Company, 1957.

HARRIS, FRANK, *My Life and Loves*. New York, Grove Press, 1963.

HARRITY, RICHARD, AND MARTIN, RALPH G., *Churchill, Man of the Century*. New York, Duell, Sloan and Pearce, 1962.

HASSALL, CHRISTOPHER, *A Biography of Edward Marsh*. New York, Harcourt, Brace, 1959.

HORNER, FRANCES, *Time Remembered*. London, William Heinemann, 1933.

HOWELLS, ROY, *Churchill's Last Years*. New York, David McKay, 1965.

HUXLEY, JULIAN, *Memories*. New York, Harper and Row, 1970.

IRVING, DAVID, *The Destruction of Dresden*. New York, Ballantine Books, 1963.

JAMES, ROBERT RHODES, *Churchill: A Study in Failure*. New York, World, 1970. 1970.

JULLIAN, MARCEL, *The Battle of Britain*. New York, Orion Press, 1965.

KENNEDY, SIR JOHN, *The Business of War*. London, Hutchinson, 1957.

KEYNES, GEOFFREY (ed.), *The Letters of Rupert Brooke*. New York, Harcourt, Brace and World, 1968.

KRAUS, RENÉ, *Young Lady Randolph*. New York, G. P. Putnam's Sons, 1943.

———, *Winston Churchill: A Biography*. Philadelphia, J. B. Lippincott, 1940.

KRONENBERGER, LOUIS, *Kings and Desperate Men*. New York, Vintage Books, 1942.

LAVER, JAMES, *Manners and Morals in the Age of Optimism 1848–1914*. New York, Harper and Row, 1966.

LEASOR, JAMES, *The Clock with Four Hands*. New York, Reynal and Company, 1959.

LESLIE, ANITA, *The Remarkable Mr. Jerome*. New York, Henry Holt, 1954.

LESLIE, SHANE, *Long Shadows*. London, John Murray, 1966.

VIEN, JACK, LE AND LORD, JOHN, *Winston Churchill: The Valiant Years*. New York, Bernard Geiss Associates, 1962.

LIDDELL HART, B. H., *History of the Second World War*. New York, G. P. Putnam's Sons, 1970.

——, *The War in Outline 1914–1918*. New York, Random House, 1936.

MARTIN, HUGH, *Battle: The Life Story of Winston S. Churchill*. London, Victor Gollancz, 1941.

MARTIN, RALPH G., *Jennie: The Dramatic Years*. Englewood Cliffs, Prentice-Hall, 1971.

——, *Jennie: The Romantic Years*. New York, New American Library, 1969.

MASON, DAVID, *Churchill*. New York, Ballantine Books, 1972.

MASTERMAN, LUCY, *C. F. G. Masterman*. London, Nicholson and Watson, 1939.

McGOWAN, NORMAN, *My Years with Churchill*. New York, British Book Centre, 1958.

McGURRIN, JAMES, *Bourke Cockran*. New York, Charles Scribner's Sons, 1948.

MENDELSSOHN, PETER DE, *The Age of Churchill: Heritage and Adventure 1874–1911*. New York, Alfred A. Knopf, 1961.

MENZIES, SIR ROBERT, *Afternoon Light*. New York, Coward-McCann, 1967.

MOIR, PHYLLIS, *I Was Winston Churchill's Secretary*. New York, Wilfred Funk, 1941.

MONTGOMERY, FIELD MARSHAL, *The Memoirs*. London, Companion Book Club, 1958.

MOOREHEAD, ALAN, *Winston Churchill in Trial and Triumph*. Boston, Houghton Mifflin, 1955.

MORAN, LORD, *Churchill*. Boston, Houghton Mifflin, 1966.

MORTON, H. V., *Atlantic Meeting*. London, Methuen, 1943.

NEL, ELIZABETH, *Mr. Churchill's Secretary*. New York, Coward-McCann, 1958.

NELSON, JAMES (ed.), *General Eisenhower on the Military Churchill*. New York, W. W. Norton, 1970.

NICOLSON, HAROLD, *Diaries and Letters 1930–1939*. London, Collins, 1966.

——, *Diaries and Letters 1939–1945*. New York, Atheneum, 1967.

——, *Diaries and Letters 1945–1962*. New York, Atheneum, 1968.

PAWLE, GERALD, *The War and Colonel Warden*. New York, Alfred A. Knopf, 1963.

PAYNE, ROBERT, *The Rise and Fall of Stalin*. New York, Simon and Schuster, 1965.

POWELL, E. ALEXANDER, *Fighting in Flanders*. New York, Charles Scribner's Sons, 1914.

ROBERTS, BRIAN, *Churchills in Africa*. New York, Taplinger, 1971.

ROWSE, A. L., *The Early Churchills*. New York, Harper and Brothers, 1956.

——, *The Later Churchills*. Harmondsworth, Penguin Books, 1971.

SASSOON, SIEGFRIED, *Siegfried's Journey 1916–1920*. London, Faber and Faber, 1945.

SHERWOOD, ROBERT E., *Roosevelt and Hopkins*. New York, Grosset and Dunlap, n.d.

SNYDER, LOUIS L., *The War: A Concise History 1939–1945.* New York, Dell, 1964.

SYKES, ADAM, AND SPROAT, IAIN, *The Wit of Sir Winston.* London, Leslie Frewin, 1965.

TAYLOR, A. J. P., AND OTHERS, *Churchill Revised: A Critical Assessment.* New York, Dial Press, 1969.

TAYLOR, ROBERT LEWIS, *Winston Churchill: An Informal Study of Greatness.* Garden City, Doubleday, 1952.

THOMSON, MALCOLM, *The Life and Times of Winston Churchill.* London, Odhams Press, n.d.

TRUMAN, HARRY S., *Memoirs: Years of Decisions.* New York, New American Library, 1965.

———, *Memoirs: Years of Trial and Hope.* New York, New American Library, 1965.

WELLES, SUMNER, *The Time for Decision.* New York, Harper and Brothers, 1944.

WHEELER-BENNETT, JOHN (ed.), *Action This Day: Working with Churchill.* New York, St. Martin's Press, 1969.

WILMOT, CHESTER, *The Struggle for Europe.* London, Collins, 1966.

WOODS, FREDERICK, *Young Winston's Wars.* New York, Viking, 1972.

WOOLF, VIRGINIA, *Roger Fry: A Biography.* New York, Harcourt, Brace, 1940.

YOUNG, KENNETH, *Churchill and Beaverbrook.* London, Eyre & Spottiswoode, 1966.

ACKNOWLEDGMENTS

First of all to my father, Mr. Stephen Payne, Royal Corps of Naval Constructors, who designed and built many of the ships which appear briefly in this book and who kept a cautious eye on Churchill throughout his long career in the Admiralty.

Then to my friend, Mr. Laurence Freundlich, who first suggested that after writing about so many of the real monsters of our time (Lenin, Hitler, Stalin), I should write about someone less monstrous and closer to home.

To Miss Patricia Ellsworth for her help at all times; to Prince and Princess Nikita Romanoff for their eager debates on all subjects under the sun, including Churchill; and to Mrs. Patricia Soliman for many courtesies.

NOTES

References are given in a shortened form. Thus "Balsan" refers to Consuelo Vanderbilt Balsan's book *The Glitter and the Gold,* which appears in the Bibliography. References to Churchill's own books are given without the author's name, and his six-volume work, *The Second World War,* is noted as SWW and the four-volume *History of the English-Speaking Peoples* as ESP. The two volumes of the official biography written by Randolph Churchill are noted as Randolph, I and II.

10 Churchill on top of the wave . . . Beaverbrook, 284.
10 The story of the cricket balls is given in Moran, 793.
11 Of all the talents. . . Randolph, Companion Volume I, Part 2, 816.
12 The story told by Hawtrey is given in Gilbert, *The Challenge,* 475.
13 There is required. . . *World Crisis,* II, 5.
20 John Churchill's great-grandfather. . . Randolph, I, 6.
21 You are a rascal. . . Rowse, *Early,* 118.
21 Miss Churchill lost her seat. . . Hamilton, 201.
24 He had no brightness. . . *Marlborough,* I, 209.
25 The battle was bloody. . . Rowse, *Early,* 342.
26 for fear he would pick. . . Rowse, *Later,* 64.
26 the palace of an auctioneer. . . *Ibid.,* 127.
26 in order to perpetuate. . . Randolph, I, 13.
27 You see, Gronow. . . Rowse, *Early,* 205.
31 Your first duty is. . . Balsan, 57.

32   I have given you all. . . Martin, *Jennie: The Romantic Years,* 270.

33   a red vest of baize. . . Harrity, 24–25.

34   The story of Willcox's marriage to an Iroquois girl is given in Shane Leslie, 19.

37   You have only to look. . . Cornwallis-West, 44.

39   a Frenchman or any other. . . Randolph, I, 18.

44   wonderfully pretty. . . *Ibid.,* 2.

45   held the Crown of England. . . Laver, 83.

47   The only excuse. . . *Lord Randolph Churchill,* 82.

47   She shone for me. . . *My Early Life,* 13.

47   more of the panther. . . *Ibid.,* 12.

47   and with a withering volley. . . *Ibid.,* 9.

48   and was therefore a very great. . . *Ibid.,* 10.

50   Go and worship idols. . . Mendelssohn, 63.

51   I rang. . . Attlee, 10.

51   Your nurse has called. . . Mendelssohn, 43.

52   I know it is all wrong. . . *Ibid.,* 43.

53   Who is in charge. . . SWW, I, 110.

57   Generally of course the boys. . . Woolf, 33.

57   His sojourn at this school. . . Baring, *Puppet Show,* 71.

58   Never give in! Robert Lewis Taylor, 79. The speech was given on October 29, 1941.

60   As far as ability goes. . . Randolph, Companion Volume I, Part 1, 169.

60   At the time of John the Baptist. . . *Ibid.,* 164.

61   I am very sorry. . . *My Early Life,* 26.

61   What I ask. . . Hugh Martin, 21.

62   In Calais port. . . Robert Lewis Taylor, 77.

63   One day I shall be. . . Shane Leslie, 21.

63   My only consolation is. . . Randolph, I, 125.

65   the argument was correct. . . *My Early Life,* 38.

65   Death was swimming in the water. . . *Ibid.,* 37.

65   the dull yellow glare. . . *Ibid.,* 38.

66   slovenly, happy-go-lucky. . . Randolph, I, 188.

66   a shabby, unhappy and futile. . . *Ibid.,* 189.

69   While walking along the Wish Stream. . . *Ibid.,* 212.

70   Weah is the London twain. . . *My Early Life,* 76.

71   Where does the Englishman. . . Davis, 10.

71   were under twenty-one years. . . *Ibid.,* 12.

73   Death came very easily. . . *My Early Life,* 80.

73   She had nursed him. . . *Savrola,* 32–33.

74   There seems to be no such thing. . . Randolph, I, 258.

74   The earth is a generous mother. . . Moran, 576.

75   Fifty horsemen can go. . . *My Early Life,* 86.

76   I sympathize with the rebellion. . . Randolph, Companion Volume I, Part 1, 616.

76   It was a chestnut. . . *My Early Life,* 92.

77   Don't they teach you. . . *Ibid.,* 100.

78   The future is to me... Randolph, I, 278.
79   After all, a man's life... *My Early Life*, 119.
80   We are going to withdraw... *Ibid.*, 146.
80   dropping from ledge to ledge... *Ibid.*
81   the courage and resolution... *Story of Malakand*, 379.
81   of all the talents... Randolph, Companion Volume I, Part 2, 816–18.
83   The orator who wished... *Ibid.*, 821.
84   My first idea... *My Early Life*, 198–99.
86   I want help... *Ibid.*, 289. A somewhat different version of the incident was given later by John Howard, who says that Churchill's first words were: "I am Dr. Bentick. I have fallen off a train and lost my way." See Randolph, Companion Volume I, Part 2, 1125.
87   Wanted/Englishman... Robert Lewis Taylor, 183.
88   He is ambitious... Eade, 46.
89   As by a very remarkable... *Harmsworth Magazine*, Vol. 1 (1898–99), 662.
90   *Then-I-say-boys...* *Ibid.*, 663.
90   He threw up his hands... *Ibid.*, 664.
91   He thought of the future... *Savrola*, 34–35.
92   Ambition was the motive force... *Ibid.*, 32.
92   The foundation of the city... *Ibid.*, 15.
93   The room was lit... *Ibid.*, 30–31.
94   I am more ambitious... Randolph, Companion Volume I, Part 2, 833.
94   Ultimately the dominant race... *Savrola*, 83.
95   We are consequential atoms... *Ibid.*, 86.
95   If I thought that... *Ibid.*
95   His speech—he had made many... *Ibid.*, 64–65.
96   When I look at... *Ibid.*, 107.
97   Why, Mirette, my little niece... *Ibid.*, 111.
97   He is a good tool... *Ibid.*, 109.
98   an unabsorbed residuum... *Ibid.*, 129.
98   The back and left side... *Ibid.*, 216–17.
98   It is not murder... *Ibid.*, 217.
99   There are sins... *Ibid.*, 156.
101   the surf that marks the edge... Title page of *Story of Malakand*.
101   How many?... *Ibid.*, 207.
101   a placid people... *Ibid.*, 149.
101   He had been an ugly man... *Ibid.*, 242.
102   Here by the rock... Woods, 209.
102   De Mentz!... *Ian Hamilton's March*, 231. Still another description of the same incident is given in *London to Ladysmith via Pretoria*, 290. This closely follows the original dispatch.
103   General Kitchener, who never spares himself... Davis, 15.
104   All great movements... *The River War*, 45.
108   I do not believe that... Randolph, II, 7.
109   From what I saw of the war... Broad, *Years of Preparation*, 91.
109   It has been extended... Randolph, II, 9.

109 Judging from your sentiments. . . *My Early Life*, 373.
110 I am very glad. . . Randolph, II, 18–19.
110 A European war cannot. . . Broad, *Years of Preparation*, 101–2.
112 He was often. . . *Lord Randolph Churchill*, 581.
113 Engaging in his brother's quarrels. . . *Ibid.*, 69.
114 He is most tiresome. . . Randolph, II, 222.
115 They have a very strong prejudice. . . *My African Journey*, 50.
115 It is no good trying to lay hold. . . *Ibid.*, 47.
116 Let us be sure that order. . . *Ibid.*, 60.
116 They began to salute each other. . . *Ibid.*, 62.
117 fringed by splendid trees. . . *Ibid.*, 75.
117 They come in such gay atire. . . *Ibid.*, 87.
119 The longer I live. . . Cowles, 125.
119 so obviously ignorant. . . Randolph, II, 243.
120 The bride was pale. . . Blunt, 222.
120 Say what you have to say. . . Sarah Churchill, 31.
122 a little gentle persuasion. . . Mendelssohn, 579.
124 The anarchists who murdered. . . *Amid These Storms*, 68.
125 I was only there to support. . . Randolph, II, 394.
126 one of those wild beasts. . . *Amid These Storms*, 67.
128 This is not a mediaeval. . . Mendelssohn, 617–18.
129 as if the weight of the world. . . Asquith, 189.
129 MILITARY ASPECTS. . . *World Crisis*, I, 58–59.
131 I'm very sorry to hear it. . . Masterman, 208.
132 I am thinking about a *diagram*. . . Carter, 8.
132 On the idle hill of summer. . . *Ibid*, 186.
133 I don't want tea. . . *Ibid.*, 188.
133 Hear, O Israel. . . *World Crisis*, I, 67.
134 He has completely changed. . . Hassall, 175.
135 The tradition of the Navy. . . Broad, *Years of Achievement*, 72, who wrongly describes the incident as taking place during World War II.
137 *April 7, Afternoon.* . . Randolph, II, 604–7.
139 I think I know the English. . . Cowles, 166.
140 The great movement in politics. . . Randolph, II, 629.
140 Cromwell was a great man. . . *Ibid.*, 274.
146 At one o'clock in the afternoon. . . Powell, 181–82.
148 Little pools glimmered. . . Keynes, 623.
149 I can't tell you how much. . . Gilbert, *The Challenge*, 121.
150 He is always unconsciously. . . Gardiner, 57–58, 63.
152 My name is Hall. . . Gretton, 198.
152 Please burn at once. . . *Ibid.*, 198–99.
155 The only place. . . *World Crisis*, II, 87.
155 Please assure the Grand Duke. . . *Ibid.*, 87.
156 I CONSIDER THE ATTACK. . . *Ibid.*, 88.
156 by extended operations. . . *Ibid.*, 91.
157 You are very wrong. . . *Ibid.*, 241.
158 if the English will. . . Liddell Hart, *The War in Outline*, 93.

158   a wall of crystal. . . *World Crisis,* II, 258.
159   We are now in a very difficult. . . *Ibid.,* 358.
159   he had been against the Dardanelles. . . *Ibid.,* 368.
160   I told you so!. . . *Ibid.,* 371.
160   First Sea Lord to see after action. . . *Ibid.,* 373.
160   YOU ARE BENT ON FORCING. . . *Ibid.,* 377.
160   Well, there is one thing. . . *Ibid.,* 391.
161   Mr. Churchill is still his own. . . Cowles, 201.
162   It looks as if poor Winston. . . Gilbert, *The Challenge,* 378.
162   What are you hesitating about. . . *Amid These Storms,* 308.
163   Take Constantinople. . . Gilbert, *The Challenge,* 567.
163   I think I ought to tell you. . . *Amid These Storms,* 101.
164   Gentlemen, I am now your commanding. . . Gilbert, *The Challenge,* 632.
      164   If they knew. . . Robert Lewis Taylor, 287.
165   Much as war attracts me. . . Gilbert, *The Challenge,* 481.
165   Filth and rubbish everywhere. . . *Ibid.,* 579.
165   99 people out of every 100. . . *Ibid.,* 581.
167   Pacing the room. . . Sassoon, 78–79.
167   I will fight in front of Paris. . . *Great Contemporaries,* 273.
167   I have no political system. . . *Ibid.,* 273.
168   *C'est mon grand plaisir.* . . *Amid These Storms,* 177.
170   In the twinkling of an eye. . . *Ibid.,* 213.
176   If you go on like this. . . Sarah Churchill, 24.
177   Writing a long and substantial book. . . SWW, I, 181.
179   Consider these ships. . . *World Crisis,* I, 123–24.
179   Their worst misfortune was. . . *The Aftermath,* 76.
180   Implacable vengeance. . . *Ibid.,* 65.
180   [War] has at last. . . *Ibid.,* 479, 483.
181   Some pot! . . . Hassall, 544.
182   He is so far and away. . . *Ibid.,* 565.
185   The cleverest thing. . . Broad, *Years of Preparation,* 352.
186   Nearly all the newspapers. . . *The British Gazette,* May 5, 1926.
188   Nothing like it has been done before. . . *Ibid.,* May 13, 1926.
189   *The British Gazette* may have had. . . *Ibid.,* May 13, 1926.
189   a great newspaper office. . . Guedalla, 237.
190   I could not help being charmed. . . London *Times,* January 2, 1927.
190   That he is a great man. . . SWW, II, 548.
191   I heard an order. . . *My Early Life,* 151.
193   It is my hope to recall. . . *Marlborough,* I, 8.
195   I lived mainly at Chartwell. . . . SWW, I,72.
196   A great round white face. . . Nicolson, *Diaries 1930–1939,* 38.
197   It is alarming. . . Speech at Winchester House, February 23, 1931.
198   An anxious and bewildered nation. . . *Daily Mail,* October 2, 1931.
198   If the Chinese now suffer. . . Coote, 355.
199   There was one moment. . . Broad, *Years of Preparation,* 25.
200   I understand you are willing. . . Moir, 32.
203   evil and malignant Brahmins. . . James, 237.

203   I remember when I was a child. . . Broad, *Years of Preparation*, 364.
204   a sheep in wolf's clothing. . . Coote, 117.
204   Nothing trivial, I hope. . . Moran, 807.
205   a female lama. . . *Ibid.*, 813.
205   humble primitives who are unable. . . James, 237.
205   Gandhi-ism and all it stands for. . . *Ibid.*, 219.
206   He had succeeded. . . *Great Contemporaries*, 226, 232.
206   There is no likelihood. . . James, 247.
206   They are not looking for. . . *Ibid.*
207   We are as vulnerable. . . *Ibid.*, 255.
207   The tank cannot stand up. . . *Ibid.*, 265.
207   Lindemann could decipher. . . SWW, II, 328.
207   a scientist *manqué*. . . James, 267.
208   It would be dangerous folly. . . *Ibid.*, 285.
211   I do not find people angry. . . Nicolson, *Diaries 1930–1939*, 282.
211   If the King refuses. . . James, 302.
212   You won't be satisfied. . . *Ibid.*, 304.
213   In that case, war is inevitable. . . SWW, I, 200.
213   an air of disillusionment. . . ESP, II, 26.
214   the harsh, terrific. . . ESP, II, 275.
214   One man's will now ruled. . . ESP, II, 302.
215   With all his faults and failures. . . ESP, II, 306.
217   this great country nosing. . . Nicolson, *Diaries 1930–1939*, 321.
218   I have watched this famous. . . Cowles, 308.
220   One pound was demanded. . . SWW, I, 292.
220   All is over. . . *Ibid.*, 293.
221   Supposing (as I do not. . . Nicolson, *Diaries 1930–1939*, 396.
224   You have sat too long. . . SWW, I, 589.
224   As I went to bed. . . *Ibid.*, 596.
227   I have nothing to offer. . . SWW, II, 22.
228   We have been defeated. . . *Ibid.*, 37.
228   Inferiority of numbers. . . *Ibid.*, 43.
230   We are told that. . . *Blood, Sweat and Tears*, 295.
231   The British Empire and the French. . . *Ibid.*, 296–97.
232   Wars are not won. . . SWW, II, 141
233   If we go down. . . *Ibid.*, 344.
234   We have had a couple. . . *Secret Session Speeches*, 10.
235   The people should be accustomed. . . Vien, 76.
235   essence of defence. . . *Secret Session Speeches*, 13.
236   I did not suffer. . . SWW, IV, 78.
236   He was short, delicate. . . Calder, 93.
237   I see only one sure way. . . SWW, II, 126.
239   If you go on chattering. . . Pawle, 64.
240   Imagine a great air raid. . . Huxley, 248.
241   You see, he really cares. . . SWW, II, 298.
241   I cannot accept. . . *Ibid.*, 618.
241   Loss of Athens. . . *Ibid.*, 459.

241 Why will politicians. . . Bryant, *The Turn*, 198.

242 Goodnight then; sleep to gather. . . SWW, II, 437.

243 this wicked man. . . Bocca, 187.

252 Not at all. . . SWW, III, 313.

253 Tell the BBC. . . *Ibid.*, 314.

253 We have but one aim. . . *Ibid.*, 314–15.

254 I see the Russian soldiers. . . *Great War Speeches*, 107.

255 would be popular. . . SWW, III, 324.

256 Only British submarines. . . Morton, 68.

259 Their countries seek no. . . SWW, III, 386.

259 After the final destruction. . . *Ibid.*, 375.

259 Such a peace shall. . . *Ibid.*

261 happened to be going the same way. . . *Great War Speeches*, 127.

262 This was a meeting. . . *Ibid.*, 121.

263 Comrades! Citizens!. . . Payne, 558.

264 A terrible winter of bombing. . . SWW, III, 327.

264 We shall undermine. . . *Ibid.*, 734.

265 I was like a keeper. . . *Ibid.*, 433.

266 I never look beyond. . . Gilbert, *The Challenge*, 509.

266 A battle is a veil. . . SWW, III, 465.

267 I do not pretend to have. . . *Ibid.*, 511.

267 I have the honour to be. . . *Ibid.*, 514.

268 They had been sent. . . *Ibid.*, 518–29.

270 Prime Minister, I have to report. . . *Ibid.*, 522.

270 to embark in mortal conflict. . . *Ibid.*, 487.

271 It had never entered my head. . . SWW, IV, 43–44.

271 the city of Singapore. . . *Ibid.*, 45.

271 You must continue. . . *Ibid.*, 91.

273 The United States is like. . . SWW, III, 512.

273 Oh! that is the way. . . Bryant, *The Turn*, 225.

276 Some chicken!. . . SWW, III, 572.

279 The Press was full of. . . SWW, IV, 54.

280 I am the man. . . Coolidge, 189.

280 It may seem paradoxical. . . Broad, *Years of Achievement*, 183.

284 A military attack. . . Bryant, *The Turn*, 302.

284 We're here because we're here. . . *Ibid.*, 332.

285 TOBRUK HAS FALLEN. . . SWW, IV, 332.

286 What can we do to help. . . *Ibid.*, 333.

286 If the British. . . *Ibid.*

286 That this House. . . *Ibid.*, 341.

287 If today, or at any future. . . *Ibid.*, 353.

288 Rommel, Rommel, Rommel. . . Bryant, *The Turn*, 365.

288 the great Revolutionary Chief. . . SWW, IV, 415.

289 I do not understand. . . Bryant, *The Turn*, 374.

290 They may have more power. . . SWW,IV,427.

290 All that is in the past. . . *Ibid.*, 430.

291 Worse. Much worse. . . Moran, 70.

292 5 September 1942. . . SWW, IV, 471.
293 not the end, not even. . . *The End of the Beginning*, 268.
294 the largest and most elaborately. . . SWW, IV, 603–4.
294 The room must have been. . . Bryant, *The Turn*, 461–62.
295 Ah! that is good. . . *Ibid.*, 464.
296 We must start by treating. . . *Ibid.*, 479.
298 The difference between us. . . *Ibid.*, 573.
300 We hope presently. . . SWW, V, 110–11.
302 See St. John. . . *Ibid.*, 279.
303 We are a large family. . . Burns, 405.
305 For God's sake let me. . . Payne, 591.
305 I believe man might. . . Moran, 151.
306 Some fifty or a hundred. . . Moran, 152; Payne, 592; SWW, V, 319.
307 I know you will not. . . SWW, IV, 174.
307 In war-time Truth. . . SWW, V, 328.
307 On my right sat. . . *Ibid.*, 329.
308 To the steel hearted. . . Payne, 594.
311 Can't you give me. . . Moran, 517.
313 Cover it up. . . Pawle, 303.
313 It is not part. . . *Ibid.*, 303.
314 I thought my view. . . SWW, V, 536.
314 There are Germans near. . . Pawle, 305.
314 We may have killed. . . *Ibid.*, 306.
315 Might not a bomb. . . *Amid These Storms*, 250.
318 My object now. . . SWW, VI, 103.
318 The offer of the British Fleet. . . *Ibid.*, 132.
319 Extraordinary atmosphere. . . *Ibid.*, 198.
320 Don't let us get at. . . *Ibid.*, 197.
320 Rumania/Russia. . . *Ibid.*
320 Might it not be thought. . . *Ibid.*
321 which may go away. . . *Ibid.*, 201.
323 Do not hesitate. . . *Ibid.*, 249.
324 Don't hesitate to shoot. . . *Ibid.*
324 Democracy is not based. . . *Ibid.*, 253.
325 He is a crafty. . . Pawle, 347.
326 We came here. . . Moran, 227.
326 I do wish he would. . . *Ibid.*, 229.
333 the dawn of a new day. . . Sherwood, 870.
333 Let there be unity. . . SWW, VI, 340.
333 a lot of horseplay. . . Sherwood, 871.
335 one vast bazooka. . . Pawle, 371.
335 Winston then became a. . . Bryant, *Triumph*, 434.
336 Our friendship is the rock. . . SWW, VI, 369.
336 I cannot avoid a feeling. . . *Ibid.*, 385.
337 the beatings of that generous. . . *Ibid.*, 405.
338 This is *your* victory. . . Broad, *Years of Achievement*, 457.
338 I should be unworthy. . . SWW, VI, 470.

338   I declare to you. . . Gardner, 297.

338   I am worried. . . Moran, 273.

339   I believe I could. . . *Ibid.*, 275.

341   Babies satisfactorily born. . . SWW, VI, 544.

341   The atomic bomb is a reality. . . *Ibid.*, 544.

341   fair and bright. . . *Ibid.*, 545.

341   He was already seeing himself. . . Bryant, *Triumph*, 478.

343   How did it go? . . . SWW, VI, 573.

343   Perhaps this is the end. . . Moran, 306.

348   It is a strange feeling. . . *Ibid.*, 308.

349   I don't like sleeping. . . *Ibid.*, 309.

349   Brilliant victory? . . . *Ibid.*, 315.

349   I don't mind if I. . . *Ibid.*, 311.

350   I'm damned glad now. . . *Ibid.*, 324.

350   Out of a life. . . Sarah Churchill, 98.

352   An iron curtain is drawn down. . . Moran, 846–47.

353   thus bringing Soviet power. . . Truman, *Years of Decision*, 355.

353   All fairy tales. . . *Ibid.*, 424.

354   We may, I am sure. . . SWW, II, 534.

355   He has a flair. . . Moran, 765.

356   Are you sure. . . Acheson, 716.

358   There is a feeling. . . Moran, 529.

358   I have had an ample. . . Broad, *Years of Achievement*, 567.

360   The portrait is. . . Moran, 655.

360   Filthy, I think it is. . . *Ibid.*, 659.

360   I have never accepted. . . *Ibid.*, 655.

361   I don't mind dying. . . *Ibid.*, 667.

362   I look forward to dying. . . Graebner, 118.

362   It aims rather to present. . . ESP, I, viii.

362   Winston's brilliant autobiography. . . Guedalla, 226.

363   Black-bearded, pale-faced. . . ESP, IV, 171.

364   By the end of. . . ESP, IV, 192.

366   You monsters! . . . Howells, 94.

366   The life of the man. . . *Ibid.*, 168-69.

367   What's it for. . . *Ibid.*, 176.

367   Oh, you're getting saucier. . . *Ibid.*, 177.

367   You were very rude. . . *Ibid.*, 62.

368   He wasn't interested. . . Moran, 746.

368   they walk silently. . . Gregory the Great, *Moralia*, xxiv, 48.

369   I have been accused. . . Bloodworth, 130.

370   There are no fields of. . . Moran, 158.

371   Indeed, while GREATNESS. . . Fielding, 218.

371   he was entirely free from. . . *Ibid.*, 215.

372   I have achieved. . . Sarah Churchill, 17.

373   What is the time. . . *Ibid.*, 19.

376   Sir Winston would like. . . Howells, 184.

377   after a cold. . . *Ibid.*, 201.

INDEX